1820

Manchester University Press

1820

Disorder and stability in the United Kingdom

Malcolm Chase

Manchester University Press

Published by Manchester University Press
Altrincham Street, Manchester M1 7JA, UK
www.manchesteruniversitypress.co.uk

British Library Cataloguing-in-Publication Data is available

Library of Congress Cataloging-in-Publication Data is available

ISBN 978 0 7190 9746 1 *paperback*

First published by Manchester University Press in hardback 2013

This paperback edition first published 2015

Printed by Lightning Source

Contents

Figures

Acknowledgements

The award in 2011 of a Fellowship by the Arts and Humanities Research Council was integral to the completion of this project, as was study leave granted by the School of History at the University of Leeds. I am grateful to both institutions and can only hope the pages that follow vindicate their confidence. If they do then much of the credit will be due to my colleagues at Leeds for their personal support, especially Richard Whiting, as well as to numerous other individuals who have provided advice and/or a good humoured audience when I have been thinking aloud. They include Fabrice Bensimon, Brian Barber, Mike Brennan, Sherwin Chase, Fred Donnelly, Piers Forster, Kevin Linch, Robert Poole and Ed Spiers.

I have accumulated debts at numerous libraries and archives, especially the Brotherton Library of the University of Leeds, one of the UK's finest libraries for historical research. Further afield, acknowledgements are due to the staff of Burnley Central Library (especially Alison Hey), Dublin City Library (Local Studies and Archives), Exeter Central Library (Devon Studies Centre), Newcastle Central Library's Local Studies Section, York Central Library, the Borthwick Institute of Historical Research and Morrell Library (University of York) and York Minster Library. My thanks are also due to staff of the British Library (St Pancras and Colindale), the National Archives at Kew, Devon Record Office, Sheffield Archives, West Yorkshire Archives Service and the National Library of Ireland (Dublin). Also in Dublin I particularly wish to record my thanks to the staff of the National Archives of Ireland, especially Elizabeth McEvoy.

I have had the good fortune to present papers based on this research to seminars at Huddersfield, Leeds, London and Sheffield universities. In addition the York Bibliographical Society, the 2011 and 2012 conferences of the Social History Society and the 2011 'Politics and Performance' conference at Lancaster, all provided further bracing scrutiny and stimulating discussion.

Shirley Chase's enthusiasm for, and critical interest in, this project has never flagged, even when mine did. She has read everything at least once and discussed all of it many times over. To her are due thanks and appreciation beyond the telling of mere words.

Osbaldwick, June 2012

Abbreviations

Add. Mss	Additional Manuscripts
BL	British Library
BCL	Burnley Central Library, Community History Department
CSO	Chief Secretary's Office (NAI)
DRO	Devon Record Office
HC Deb	Hansard House of Commons Debates
HL Deb	Hansard House of Lords Debates
HO	Home Office (TNA)
HP	D. R. Fisher (ed.), *The History of Parliament: The House of Commons, 1820-1832* (Cambridge: Cambridge University Press, 2009)
LC	Lord Chamberlain (TNA)
NCL	Newcastle Central Library, Local Studies
NAI	National Archives of Ireland
PP	*Parliamentary Papers*
SC	Select Committee
SOC	State of the Country Papers Series 1 (1796–1831) (NAI)
TNA	The National Archives, Kew
TS	Treasury Solicitor (TNA)
WYAS	West Yorkshire Archives Service

Throughout the text and notes, unless otherwise indicated, all dates refer to 1820.

Introduction

In 1839 Mary Shelley took an unpublished sonnet, 'England in 1820', by her deceased husband and finally published it as 'England in 1819'.[1] Under a name Shelley never intended, this sonnet has had an enduring influence on how Regency Britain is conceptualised in literary and historical scholarship alike. The year of its eventual publication has a similar epochal status to 1819 because of Chartism, the mass movement for parliamentary (and a raft of other) reform that dominated the early years of Victoria's reign. Indeed the Chartists did much to define the prevailing view of 1819. For them the blackest benchmark of a ruling elite's dereliction was to be found in 'Peterloo', the word a mordantly ironic echo of Waterloo, applied within weeks to the tumultuous dispersal of a political rally at St Peter's Fields, Manchester, on 16 August 1819. Responding to an order from local magistrates, the Manchester Yeomanry charged a peaceful political demonstration, injuring over 700 and killing 18.[2] Peterloo has long defined the years following 1815. As much as the 1832 Reform Act, it was the milestone to which radicals (working and middle class alike) would later refer in asserting the moral bankruptcy of aristocratic government. For Edward Thompson in *The Making of the English Working Class* (a work that has done so much to shape the historiographical landscape of this period), Peterloo 'was without question a formative experience in British social and political history'.[3] More recently James Chandler in *England in 1819* argued eloquently that the literature produced that year was concerned with 'a national operation of self-dating, or redating ... meant to count as a national self-making, or remaking' of history. Chandler suggested that Peterloo transcends time itself, 'an event of indeterminate duration that makes a major transformation in the practices of modern literary and political representation, one understood in its moment to have revolutionary potential'.[4]

One of the contentions of this book is that Peterloo's revolutionary potential has been as much manufactured as it was innate. Both the nature of its potential and, no-less crucially, the means through and by which it was contained, have been misapprehended. Thus the present study focuses on England *in 1820*, or rather and emphatically the United Kingdom in this year, for our understanding of the period has been hobbled by the habitual Anglo-centricity of so much 'British' history. Even the four kingdoms cannot be conceived in isolation for 1820 was a year of European revolution. It was without parallel until 1848 and the actions of the British Government (led by a Prime Minister who had witnessed the storming of the Bastille in 1789), need to be evaluated in that context.

The year 1820 was also a year of political dislocation unparalleled in peace time, but the gravity of the situation has been obscured for four main reasons. First, the dominant historical narrative of the United Kingdom in the early nineteenth century has remained so English-centred that Ireland only begins to intrude upon it in the mid-1840s, and Scotland scarcely at all; but the nature of the challenge confronting the UK Government in 1820 cannot be comprehended from such a perspective. (Wales is similarly marginalised, however it barely troubled the Government in 1820.) Second, as already hinted, Peterloo has over-determined the interpretation of the period. The third reason why events that year are misinterpreted or ignored is that the Government itself actively sought to efface the challenges confronting it. To do otherwise would have jeopardised its very survival in a year that combined a general election, a constitutional crisis, a seemingly irreparable rift with the monarch, and a surge of radicalism both within and beyond Parliament.

The fourth reason why the true significance of events in 1820 has been obscured derives from the late-twentieth century's preoccupation with the Queen Caroline affair. From the early 1980s, increasingly gender-aware scholarship made the second half of 1820 one of the most intensively investigated six months in modern British history. What Thompson dismissed in 1963 as 'humbug' into which 'we need not enquire', Thomas Laqueur in a path-breaking article of 1982 explained was a domestic melodrama, 'a play about marriage, about women, home and family'. For Leonore Davidoff and Catherine Hall, writing in 1987, it was a cradle for the public affirmation of middle class values, and for Tamara Hunt it constituted more explicitly 'the first wide-spread popular expression of the moral standards that have come to be labelled "Victorian"'. Anna Clark has argued that the Caroline affair was a victory for a style of politics independent of male middle-class parliamentarianism. Dror Wahrman reconfigures the affair as an essentially peaceful carnival that consolidated the development of 'public opinion' and the Habermassian public sphere. Most recently (2008) Louise Carter has argued that it constituted a trial of British masculinities.[5] One argument in the present study is not that the Caroline affair was none of these things (indeed it was quite possibly all of them, except for humbug needing no investigation), but that 1820 cannot be understood through a mono-focal lens marked 'Caroline'. The key issues at the heart of 1820 were the viability of aristocratic Tory rule and the feasibility of any alternative.

These issues were played out against the background of one of the deepest economic recessions to afflict the United Kingdom during the nineteenth century. 'Nothing but ruin stares us in the face', the author of a report on Norfolk agriculture wrote in the *Bury & Norwich Post* on 5 January. The previous autumn's harvest had been poor in both quality and quantity. In both rural and urban areas the severity of the winter had led to a surge in unemployment. Even after a thaw in late January the winter weather was still frequently severe, and the last death of the winter from exposure (at Moffat in south-west Scotland) was reported as late as 5 April.[6] The weather, however, was only a fraction of the challenge confronting the United Kingdom in the early months of 1820. A post-war slump afflicted both Britain and Ireland as some 350,000 men returned from the armed services, and as industry and agriculture felt the loss of defence contracts. Wheat prices had been falling since 1817 and general commodities since 1818.[7] While in theory wage earners should have benefitted from these movements, by 1820 average full-employment money wages had dropped almost 14 per cent since 1812. Though 'real wages' increased over the same period, this is a concept that conceals wide seasonal, regional and sectoral disparities. Improvements were unevenly distributed and it is unlikely any were felt during the winter and spring. Under-employment, unemployment and business failures beset the post-war years; and since demobilisation particularly swelled the market for less-skilled labour, it is also likely that wage differentials were becoming more apparent from 1814.[8]

In particular the earnings of that huge section of the industrial labour force based outside factories in home-based domestic manufactures were susceptible to wide variation. For example during 1820 William and Margaret Varley, handloom weavers of Higham (a hamlet now part of Burnley) spent three-quarters of their combined earnings on food for themselves and their two children. Their diet was mainly bread and butter, and oatmeal with skimmed milk, augmented by home-reared salt pork. By a considerable distance a pig purchased in July 1820 (for £1 2s 6d – £1.125) was their largest item of expenditure. At times the Varleys barely made ends meet: their average weekly outlay of 13s 8d (68p) during the first quarter of the year was scraped together from a combined weekly income of between twelve and fifteen shillings (60–75p).[9] Small wonder then that in his forty-seven diary entries for 1820, William remarked about wages as often as the weather, and considerably more than any other topic.[10] At six shillings (60p) a month, rent was the couple's only sizeable non-food expenditure, though rates of one shilling a month paid to the vestry would also have needed finding (this was almost as much as the Varleys spent on oil for lighting). Food luxuries were rare: two-and-a-half pounds of tea over the course of the year, eight ounces of currants each quarter day, and a tub of apples for jam making. On only five occasions during 1820 was meat purchased, the cumulative weight of which was only eighteen pounds. Clearly the pig was crucial to William and Margaret: it provided most of the family's first-class protein and in doing so released funds that would otherwise have been devoted to scratching the barest subsistence. Pig keeping was a commonplace economic strategy in English villages and towns, 'so well known' according to one contemporary 'that there remains but little to be said with regard to them'.[11] In this respect English workers may have faired better than their counterparts in Scotland, where pig keeping appears to have been less prevalent in a diet otherwise very similar to the industrial north: oatmeal, potatoes, milk, cheese and 'not much Butcher Meat', sugar or tea, in the words of a minister of a Kirk near Paisley.[12]

Glasgow had the dubious distinction of some of the worst living conditions in Britain. The decade 1811–21 had seen a 46 per cent population increase in the town, more than a third of whose residents lived in one parish, the Barony. A fifth of these were Irish-born. One measure of the Barony's character was that in its most populous locality, Calton, there was a 1 in 92 ratio of servants to general inhabitants, compared with just 1 in 6 in the socially exclusive Glasgow parish of Ramshorn.[13]

That working people in 1820 lived in conditions that were impoverished by modern standards can be regarded as axiomatic. However, squalor was a norm that extended beyond manual workers. William Lucas, apprenticed by prosperous Quaker parents to a London chemist and druggist at the close of 1819, recorded his horror at enduring food 'as coarse as workhouse diet ... We slept in the attics in dirty beds swarming with bugs, and one of the apprentices had for months to sleep in the shop under the counter'.[14] Accounts of the mistreatment of Georgian apprentices are commonplace, but Lucas's parents had paid a premium of £250 for him to train at one of the capital's most fashionable firms, whose Haymarket premises were frequented by, among others, the Duke of Kent, brother of the King. However, while the kind of conditions Lucas endured may help to explain the frequent participation of apprentices in unrest on the streets, men like him generally accepted such deprivations as the pay off for anticipated prosperity in later life. For manual workers, however, the prospect of upward social and economic mobility was almost invariably chimerical. The ideal lifecycle of apprentice-journeyman-master craftsman had very largely decayed, and the Tudor legislation that required and regulated apprenticeship – long honoured in the breach – had finally been repealed by Parliament in 1814. Yet the institution of apprenticeship retained considerable emotional pull upon the mindset of skilled workers. An estimated 300,000 people (around 2.5 per cent of the total population) had signed petitions against the repeal of statutory apprenticeship in 1813–14.[15] Their failure reinforced a widening sense that Parliament legislated only in the economic interests of its members. At the same time labour, especially skilled labour, was conceptualised as a form of property, the only property that a worker such as William Varley had. 'Labour is the abundant product of this country', declared John Wade in the influential post-war weekly *The Gorgon*, and 'it is by trading in the blood and bones of the journeymen and labourers of England, that our merchants have derived their riches, and the country its glory and importance'.[16]

In April 1819 Wade had given up *The Gorgon* to begin an ambitious part-work, *The Black Book, or, Corruption Unmasked!!!* Upon its completion in February 1820, he dedicated it 'to the Working, the Agricultural, the Commercial, and Manufacturing Classes of the Community'.[17] Both *The Gorgon* and *Black Book* helped supply a burgeoning market for popular reading matter and both reinforced the increasing militancy of the organised trades (not necessarily organised in the form of a trade union, but cohering around a strong mutual commitment to the good of 'the trade'). This in turn informed the dominant popular mood in the industrialising regions of Britain. 'As wealth can only originate in labour', Lancashire cotton weavers argued in June 1820, 'the productive powers of the labouring community are entitled to the protection of the Legislature'.[18]

The decade during which the Prince of Wales ruled as Regent on his ailing father's behalf (he assumed the responsibility in February 1811) had been one of increasing political restiveness. Excluded from office since the fall of 'the ministry of all the talents' in 1807, the Whigs had abandoned any hope that the Regent, their former political patron, would prefer them to their Tory parliamentary opponents. The latter, referred to simply as the Ministry as often as they were designated Tories, were the direct successors of the wartime governments of William Pitt. Their leader, the Earl of Liverpool, had served under Pitt as both Foreign and Home Secretary. In the ministry (1809–12) headed by Spencer Perceval, Lord Liverpool became Secretary for War. When Perceval was assassinated in May 1812, Liverpool earned Whig enmity by immediately being invited by the Regent to form a replacement government. His initial failure to command a majority in the House of Commons led Liverpool to offer his resignation (and rendered him ever after excessively apprehensive about the management of the Commons). The following month, however, Liverpool was confirmed in office: the Whigs were both rejected by the Prince Regent as a potential ministry and found the prospect of a coalition partnership unpalatable. After thirteen years in opposition, many Whig politicians were hungry for office: but this could not be said for their leadership in either House of Parliament, and as a party little held them together beyond their commitment to remove the civil disabilities endured by Roman Catholics. They were far from comfortable with propositions for even moderate parliamentary reform, and still less for radical reform, the popularity of both of which grew in pace from 1806.

Considering the nature of extra-parliamentary politics during the Regency it is easy to see what repelled a party of wealth and privilege (and, we might add, limited ideological substance). The 1813–14 campaign against the repeal of statutory apprenticeship, in many ways remarkable for its measured tone and tactics, was but one of several facets to the popular politics of the Regency years. The best known of them is Luddism, which confounded local authority across the English midlands hosiery and northern textiles districts in 1811–12. Luddite machine-breaking has become part of a collective memory of futile resistance to industrialisation. It should be stressed, therefore, that Luddism was deeply rooted in constitutional endeavour by the trades concerned to extend or restore parliamentary regulation of their particular industries. But as a letter sent in the name of Ned Ludd, 'General of the Army of Redressers', to a West Yorkshire manufacturer in April 1812 stated: 'We will never lay down our Arms [until] The House of Commons passes an Act to put down all Machinery hurtful to Commonality … We petition no more – that won't do – fighting must.'[19]

The popular politics of the Regency years turned on the perception that Parliament neither heeded, nor even cared about, those who perceived themselves part of the 'commonality'. Though Perceval's assassin had been a bankrupt shipbroker (John Bellingham), urged to the task by mental instability rather than a political creed, recent scholarship has shown how thinly sympathetic to the victim popular responses were. Bellingham had obsessively lobbied a wide variety of government offices, culminating in the Home and Foreign Offices, the Prime Minister, Prince Regent and the Privy Council. His every petition had been in vain. After he was hanged, invoking his name became both a figurative assault upon governmental indifference and 'a convenient shorthand', with which to criticise the futility of petitioning.[20] It was within this context of despair that Parliament would ever pay heed to the interests of the unenfranchised that demands for parliamentary reform gathered pace, with Sir Francis Burdett, William Cobbett and Henry Hunt the movement's best-known figures. After the war Hunt became the commanding figure of this movement. We shall see in Chapter 2 that some detail of Hunt's activities in these years is needed to understand events in 1820, though by then Hunt was first on remand and then gaoled.

Hunt's career, however, does not supply the full narrative of post-war radicalism. With the introduction of a protective tariff on corn prices in 1815, a further grievance was added to the radical agenda. The corn laws were met by mass petitioning and rioting in London on a scale not seen since the 1780s. There was a renewed spate of machine-breaking in 1816–17, and an attempted rising on the Derbyshire-Yorkshire border in June. A temporary up-swing in the economy the following summer saw strikes on an unprecedented scale across the Lancashire and north Cheshire cotton district. Although a spinners' dispute dominated the strike wave, power- and hand-loom weavers, dyers, carpenters and joiners, glassworkers, hatters, miners and bricklayers were all involved in disputes at some point between May and September. The strikes attracted the concerted support of the organised trades of London, while Birmingham, Glasgow, Hull, Liverpool and Nottingham all contributed to supportive subscriptions. The 1818 strikes also provide the earliest documented interest in general unionism. No other industrial disputes of the post-war years matched their intensity. The ferocity of the employers' response was also unequalled. After seven weeks the cotton spinners' strike ended with their union in financial tatters and the entire organising committee arrested on conspiracy charges; the weavers fared no better, with three officials prosecuted under the Combination Act. Prison sentences of twelve months or two years were handed down to them the following February.[21] 'Do you think', Cobbett demanded, 'that such an Act would have been passed, if the Journeymen of England *had had a vote at elections?*'[22]

Increasingly, localised grievances converged with broader radical arguments. Meanwhile an administration, in power for thirteen years, was in danger of losing whatever moral authority it might have mustered over those who were excluded from the parliamentary process. 'The people can expect no favour from such men as Castlereagh, Sidmouth, Canning, and Liverpool', argued veteran radical William Fitton, rounding on the Cabinet in a speech supporting the Lancashire spinners in 1818. They were, Fitton continued, 'men of the most diabolical principles, who have robbed you of the fruits of your industry, of your liberty, and independency, and reduced you to abject slavery'.[23] By 1820 there was a sense in which, for many people, their mental map of the United Kingdom (certainly that of England and Scotland) was beginning to shrink. Print, graphic satire, and rapidly evolving networks of communication among the politically excluded, all helped to ensure that this was the first Cabinet in Britain's history to contain several 'household names'. But there was no parallel shrinkage, however, in the challenges faced by government in the post-war search for stability, as the following examination of this critical year makes clear.

Notes

1 J. Donovan *et al* (eds), *The Poems of Shelley: Volume 3, 1819–20* (Harlow: Longman, 2011), p. 190; and see below, Chapter 1.
2 M. Bush, *The Casualties of Peterloo* (Lancaster: Carnegie, 2005), pp. 44–6.
3 E. P. Thompson, *The Making of the English Working Class*, 2nd edn (Harmondsworth: Penguin, 1968), p. 754.
4 J. Chandler, *England in 1819: The Politics of Literary Culture and the Case of Romantic Historicism* (Chicago: University of Chicago Press, 1998), pp. 5, 18.
5 Thompson, *Making*, p. 778; Thomas W. Laqueur, 'The Queen Caroline affair: politics as art in the reign of George IV', *Journal of Modern History*, 54:3 (1982); L. Davidoff and C. Hall, *Family Fortunes: Men and Women of the English Middle Class, 1780–1850*, revised edn (London: Routledge, 2002); T. L. Hunt, 'Morality and monarchy in the Queen Caroline affair', *Albion*, 23:4 (1991), p. 697; A. Clark, 'Queen Caroline and the sexual politics of popular culture in London, 1820', *Representations*, 31 (1990), also *Scandal: The Sexual Politics of the British Constitution* (Princeton: Princeton University Press, 2004), Chapter 8; Dror Wahrman, '"Middle-class" domesticity goes public: gender, class, and politics from Queen Caroline to Queen Victoria', *Journal of British Studies*, 32:4 (1993); L. Carter, 'British masculinities on trial in the Queen Caroline affair of 1820', *Gender & History*, 20:2 (2008); see also C. M. M. Macdonald, 'Abandoned and beastly? The Queen Caroline affair in Scotland', in Y. G. Brown and R. Ferguson (eds), *Twisted Sisters: Women, Crime and Deviance in Scotland since 1400* (East Linton: Tuckwell, 2004).

6 C. J. Fynes Clinton (ed.), *Literary Remains of Henry Fynes Clinton* (London: Longman, 1854), p. 148; *Times,* 5 April.

7 B. R. Mitchell, *British Historical Statistics* (Cambridge: Cambridge University Press, 1998), pp. 719–21, 756.

8 C. Feinstein, 'Pessimism perpetuated: real wages and the standard of living in Britain during and after the industrial revolution', *Journal of Economic History,* 58:3 (1998), p. 653. On the contentious issue of skill differentials at this time see M. J. Daunton, *Progress and Poverty: An Economic and Social History of Britain, 1700–1850* (Oxford: Oxford University Press, 1995), p. 437.

9 BCL, Accounts of William Varley (transcript), pp. 3–13. See also W. Bennett, *History of Burnley, 1650–1850* (Burnley Corporation, 1948), pp. 236, 271, 379–82.

10 BCL, Memorandum Book of William Varley (transcript), pp. 1–8.

11 W. Salisbury, *The Cottager's Agricultural Companion* (1822), quoted by R. Malcolmson and S. Mastoris, *The English Pig: A History* (London: Hambledon, 2001), p. 48.

12 TNA, HO 102/32/34 (Monteith to Sidmouth, 6 January).

13 T. M. Devine and G. Jackson (eds), *Glasgow. Volume 1: Beginnings to 1830* (Manchester: Manchester University Press, 1995), p. 407.

14 G. E. Bryant and G. P. Baker (eds), *A Quaker Journal, being the Diary and Reminiscences of William Lucas of Hitchin* (London: Hutchinson, 1934), vol. 1, p. 44.

15 M. Chase, *Early Trade Unionism: Fraternity, Skill and the Politics of Labour* (Aldershot: Ashgate, 2000), pp. 95–100.

16 *Gorgon,* 12 September 1818; for *Gorgon,* and the concept of property in skill more generally at this time, see Chase, *Early Trade Unionism,* esp. pp. 118–25.

17 J. Wade, *The Black Book, or, Corruption Unmasked!!!* (London: Fairburn, 1820), p. 1; see also Chapter 3 below.

18 Cotton weavers' petition, reported in *Manchester Observer,* 24 June.

19 Reprinted in K. Binfield, *The Writings of the Luddites* (Baltimore: Johns Hopkins University Press, 2004), p. 211.

20 G. Pentland, '"Now the great Man in the Parliament House is dead, we shall have a big Loaf!" Responses to the Assassination of Spencer Perceval', *Journal of British Studies,* 51:2 (April 2012), p. 358; Binfield, *Writings of the Luddites,* p. 230.

21 Robert G. Hall, 'Tyranny, work and politics: the 1818 strike wave in the English cotton district', *International Review of Social History,* 34 (1989); Chase, *Early Trade Unionism,* pp. 103–5.

22 *Cobbett's Weekly Political Register,* 19 December 1818.

23 Quoted by Hall, 'Tyranny, work and politics', p. 442

1   The United Kingdom in 1820

Prologue

On 1 January Joseph Farington rose at 8.20 a.m., feeling 'very unwell'. This may explain why he failed to step outside his home in London's Charlotte Street, as was his custom, to note the temperature. But he recorded in his diary that it was 'a thick discoloured morng and day'. The temperature on rising on New Year's Eve had been minus 3 degrees centigrade in a 'thick frosty haze'. By Wednesday 5 January his thermometer read minus 8: he had last recorded a positive reading on 23 December. A highly regarded landscape artist and Royal Academician, the widowed Farington led a comfortable life sustained by a housekeeper and, we may safely assume, a fire burning in each grate of his home. Even so, when the distinguished sculptor Sir Richard Westmacott called on 2 January, Farington's diary suggests the two men spoke only 'of the coldness of the weather'.[1]

London had the better of the weather. In Dumfries on 2 January thermometers slumped to minus 19 degrees. The lowest reported January temperature in the capital was minus 13 on 14 January, but mid-January temperatures between minus 15 and minus 23 centigrade were reported in a range of locations from Perth, south to Dorset.[2] Detailed aggregated temperature data for central England suggests that the mean monthly temperature for January 1820 – 0.3 degrees below freezing – was considerably lower than both the decadal means for both the first and second decades of the century, and the corresponding figures for 1819 and 1821. There would be no colder January until 1838.[3]

This 'winter of uncommon severity' was a constant thread in the correspondence of the novelist Walter Scott. Countess Cowper wrote to her brother of six weeks' severe frost and recurring snow. 'The frost is intense. The town is empty', commented London diarist Charles Greville as the old year drew to its close.[4] 'The weather very cold, frost and snow', recorded Francis Witts, a Gloucestershire parson, on 3 January, 'the roads very slippery … [our] horse fell in the chaise in the streets of Tetbury'. Scheduled coach services were abandoned along many routes during the first fortnight of 1820. Others ran hours late, even with the traction of additional horses. The Humber estuary was impassable due to drifting ice floes and, inland, the canals and rivers which connected it to the midlands and Yorkshire were frozen, sometimes to a depth of 46 centimetres. The situation was similar at Stockton-on-Tees where the river, though tidal, was frozen until 23 January, and on the Clyde. Ships froze at buoys and jetties on the Thames, while at Deptford booths were erected on the ice, recreating the celebrated ice fairs of centuries past.[5] Snow drifts more than two metres deep were reported in Wiltshire and Dorset, over three metres on the Glasgow road out of Edinburgh, and exceeding 3.6 metres in Gloucestershire.[6] In western Ireland, rural protesters known as Ribbonmen exhibited 'unparalleled audacity' in Galway, 'out every Night in some quarter or other of the County as the hard frost enables them to cross the bogs in every Direction.'[7]

The cold struck hard in even the most well-appointed homes. On 13 January in his Windsor Castle sickbed, George III suddenly 'drew himself up in his bedclothes, and said "Tom's a cold".'[8] Quoting Shakespeare's *King Lear*, knowingly or not, was an instance of eerie prescience, for the octogenarian King had enjoyed pitifully few lucid moments during the past decade. A Hampshire diarist, Peter Hawker, noted 15 January was 'the coldest day in the memory of any person I have met with'. Poole harbour was frozen solid. Hawker's manservant, who had once crewed a whaler, 'said it was quite equal to Greenland'.[9] 'This severe winter has taken away many old people', William Wordsworth noted.[10] Newspapers carried reports of weather-related deaths: a carter found dead, his horse's reins still in his hands on the Great North Road in Yorkshire; farm labourers dead from cold in Devon; two children frozen to death on a Somerset baggage wagon; elderly Londoners discovered dead in homes 'not having clothing, bed, nor fire'.[11] 'Individuals able and willing to work are literally starving', the *Cork Chronicle* reported in an item simply headed 'The Weather – The Poor'.[12] A 'temporary establishment for shelter to the homeless' was set up in some empty London warehouses, while in parishes across Britain subscriptions were raised to alleviate escalating distress 'in consequence of the severity of the season'. At its peak a Birmingham appeal was distributing over 11,000 litres of soup each week.[13]

More prosaically, provincial theatres opened 'to dismal emptiness'.[14] With the prolonged cold came a spate of fires as Britons struggled to keep warm. The most notable casualties were Birmingham's Theatre Royal and Magdalen Hall, Oxford (where the water froze in the pumps of the fire-tenders).[15] In Somerset William Baker, a currier, found that the impact of the frost was so great that 'blackbirds, thrushes, and other small birds would scarcely fly from the banks as I came up to them'; at Bridgewater 'the river [was] filled with ice, the country covered with snow, and the atmosphere dark and heavy'.[16] Hawker noted that 'dead rooks, small birds &c. were lying about in every direction, starved to death' and, more shockingly, how two wildfowlers had 'frozen to death in their punts'.

Of course the weather was not the sole topic of conversation. 'Half the kingdom had colds', recorded one diarist on 27 January, noting that Prince Edward, Duke of Kent, was killed by his.[17] Charles Greville had just met the Prince Regent's son-in-law, Prince Leopold of Saxe-Coburg: 'his pomposity fatigues, and his avarice disgusts.' Farington's first visitor on New Year's Day was a senior employee of Cadell & Williams, Farington's publishers. He told him earnestly that the firm, 'and many other of the principal Booksellers', would stop producing cheap pamphlets. As 1819 had drawn to a close, in response to popular political unrest, Parliament had passed six acts severely curtailing both freedom of assembly and political publishing. Cadell & Williams were fearful of these new legal restrictions on publications. They were 'an injury to trade', he told Farington, expanding for good measure on the unpopularity of Lord Castlereagh, the leader of the House of Commons.[18]

Neither Farington nor Cadell & Williams could remotely be mistaken for political radicals. That the publisher of books such as *The Literary Works of Sir Joshua Reynolds* and Hannah More's *Strictures on the Modern System of Female Education* entertained such views says much about the political mood at the turn of 1819 and of how generalised criticism of the Government had become. 'What a state England is in!' wrote the poet Percy Shelley two days before Christmas in a letter home from Florence to the journalist and critic Leigh Hunt. With it he enclosed a manuscript, probably of his sonnet now known as 'England in 1819'.[19] Written in response to the 'Peterloo' massacre, Shelley's poem is arguably the most widely known literary work of the Regency.

> An old, mad, blind, despised, and dying King;
> Princes, the dregs of their dull race, who flow
> Through public scorn,– mud from a muddy spring;
> Rulers who neither see nor feel nor know,
> But leechlike to their fainting country cling
> Till they drop, blind in blood, without a blow;
> A people starved and stabbed in th'untilled field;
> An army, which liberticide and prey
> Makes as a two-edged sword to all who wield;
> Golden and sanguine laws which tempt and slay;
> Religion Christless, Godless, a book sealed;
> A senate, Time's worst statute, unrepealed,
> Are graves from which a glorious Phantom may
> Burst, to illumine our tempestuous day.

Shelley wrote this in Italy: distance from home as well as poetic temperament influenced the mood of the concluding couplet. After twelve lines of unrelenting gloom the poet dares to hope for change. Yet the vision is tentative, for a phantom lacks all material substance, it is a mirage; and even if the emotions evoked by its appearance produce physical changes, this illumining phantom only *may* emerge. Shelley's sonnet is suffused with deep pessimism as much as with anger.

John Keats' ostensibly apolitical 'Ode to Autumn' similarly reflected the prevailing mood of political powerlessness. The 'season of mists and mellow fruitfulness' it evokes is ambiguous in its portents. Keats thought not of 'the songs of Spring' but of a brooding, stifling autumn wherein the dominant human pose is inertia. The mood is one of oppressiveness as much as fecundity, a mood that any contemporary reader would have caught since the harvest of 1819 was far from bountiful. We shall never know if, as the critic Tom Paulin has argued, the opening line was intended as an allusion to 'the mists and intricacies of the state', a phrase John Milton used in his resolutely republican tract *Eikonoklastes* (1649), or perhaps to Satan, whom Milton characterised as a mist in *Paradise Lost*.[20] But it is difficult to shake off the sensation of brooding uncertainty that accompanies Keats' absorption with autumn, an absorption so intense that the poet almost dare not contemplate what may follow.

Peterloo had changed everything. The casualty figures were shocking enough; but the unequivocal endorsement, by first the Government and then the Prince Regent, of the Manchester magistrates' decision to send in the cavalry, gave the tragedy a black and enduring significance. In 1761 more than fifty had died in Hexham, Northumberland, during the suppression of an anti-militia riot. However, in the popular memory Peterloo was rapidly fixed as an unprecedented example of official violence and of the moral bankruptcy of aristocratic government. Furthermore, no Riot Act had been read at Manchester and the claim that the assembly was illegal was (as trials during 1820 would illustrate) highly contentious.

Many of Shelley's and Keats' contemporaries shared the belief that the immediate future was uncertain and potentially calamitous. In January 1820 the Scottish intellectual Sir James Mackintosh wrote gloomily of 'a complete separation and enmity between the upper and lower ranks, the governors and the governed, the rich and the poor in society'.[21] Lord Holland, a leading member of the Whig opposition in parliament, detected 'a spirit grown up & growing every day throughout the country, against the nature & practice of our Government, & tending I fear to the separation of the Upper & middling classes of Society'.[22] 'The protection afforded to the Perpetrators of the bloody outrage of the 16th of August, clearly manifests a design to subvert the laws by those who are sworn to maintain them; and to establish on the ruins of the English Constitution, a military despotism', one author declared.[23] 'I compare the present time to the French Revolution', shoemaker Allen Davenport told a meeting of London ultra-radicals, adding ominously 'we must arm ourselves as they did'.[24] Politician Robert Ward, offered a ride along Pall Mall in the Duke of Wellington's carriage, recorded with astonishment how Wellington locked all the doors and gave him an impromptu tutorial in defending themselves from attack. '"By leaning back you may fight a window better than a parapet wall." This he accompanied with the appropriate action.'[25] For the poorest, it was almost impossible to see beyond the immediate recession. Lancashire weaver William Varley commenced his 1820 diary with, inevitably, a comment about the severity of the weather, 'the poor weaver is now very hard put to it'. But in the same sentence he commented tartly on the '200 soldiers of Infantry and Cavalry' garrisoned at Burnley: 'these soldiers must be mentained if the poor weaver die in the looms.' February opened with criticisms of the 'unhuman and relentless masters of Burnley … but poor vassal remember that a day will come when these base fiends shall meet their certain doom.'[26]

Neither the winter's acute economic depression nor the memory of Peterloo alone created this mood. Since the 1790s, a radical political tradition distinct from 'the friends of the people', as the Whigs liked to be known, had ebbed and flowed, while domestic politics had grown increasingly truculent since the end of the wars against France and Napoleon. But what is extraordinary about the winter of 1819–20 is the extent to which public opinion had polarised. A future President of the Board of Control for India, John Cam Hobhouse, languished indefinitely in Newgate for contempt of parliamentary privilege. The 'true practical protectors' of MPs, Hobhouse had argued, were 'to be found at the Horse Guards and the Knightsbridge barracks; as long as the House of Commons majorities are backed by the regimental muster roll, so long may those who have got the tax power keep it, and hang those who resist'.[27] Meanwhile a nervous Government kept Parliament sitting right up to 30 December, in order to force through the six acts that so exercised Farington's New Year's Day visitor. 'All must see the propriety of never leaving the subject till finished', Castlereagh had told Government supporters: 'there must, therefore, be no recess, except a couple of days at Christmas, otherwise the meetings would go on with a fresh violence during the interval.'[28]

At least an end to the freezing weather could be expected, and so indeed it came. 'This day a grand and long wish'd for thaw commences', recorded William Varley on 23 January. 'Yesterday, for the first time, after two month's silence, I heard a Robin sing', a Derby diarist noted the following week.[29] Beyond prediction, however, was whether the six acts would have the desired effect, and what reactions they might in turn inflame. The Government entered the New Year anticipating the sternest test of its authority.

Religion and the State: 'a federal and equitable union'

Not all diarists commenced their account of 1820 by detailing the weather as Joseph Farington and William Varley did. Most diaries that posterity thought fit to preserve were spiritual and introspective. Of these the Independent minister John Townsend is a fair example:

JANUARY 1, 1820. I have this day entered upon a new year, and when I reflect upon all the way which the Lord my God has led me these more than forty years in the wilderness, with what humility and self-abasement should I confess my numerous failures in duty, my backslidings, and multiplied imperfections. Yet, while mourning over my sins, what reason is furnished for thankfulness and gratitude to God, for His abundant goodness. The streams of mercy have flowed towards me, in a broader and deeper channel than during any preceding year of my life.[30]

Religion mattered a great deal in 1820. Faith was both highly personalised and highly political. Most Sundays Farington would sit down and 'read prayers &c' to his housekeeper: yet he was not an ostentatious Christian, rarely attended church and as a diarist was never given to spiritual introspection. When at his Surrey country seat, the Prime Minister Lord Liverpool led the household to Kingston parish church each Sunday morning. Then, 'in the afternoon the whole family including the servants, assembled in the great room and Lord Liverpool read the evening prayers at ½ past 5 oClock from the book of *Common Prayer*'.[31] The Book of Common Prayer was the liturgy of Anglicanism, the established or State religion in England, Wales and (albeit increasingly incongruously) Ireland. In Scotland the Church of Scotland similarly enjoyed the status and privileges of establishment. In contrast to the Church of England (but like English dissenting sects) the Scottish Kirk had rejected the authority of bishops at the Reformation. It also adhered to a Calvinist theology, though by the early nineteenth century a large proportion of its clergy espoused 'moderatism', emphasising the moral teachings of Christianity rather than the bleak certainties of Calvin.

Clergymen were figures of substance. Around one in six of all Church of England ministers were magistrates. Their churches were typically a geographical and social focal point in their communities. Nor were absenteeism and the holding of multiple benefices as crippling to the Church's effectiveness as it might at first seem. By the 1820s only 40 per cent of English parishes were in the charge of a resident incumbent, yet consistent pastoral care seems to have been maintained while the Church of England was in the formative stage of a process of renewal (much though contemporary radical, and later general, commentators scorned its complacency).[32] The formation of the National Schools Society in 1811 had (albeit belatedly) focussed the Church's efforts in day school provision; and the Church Buildings Society (established 1817) signalled a new intent to remedy the increasing mismatch between the physical resources of the Church of England and the rapid growth of urban populations. The Government's million-pound grant to the Society, made through the 1818 Church Building Act and backed by the personal authority of the Prime Minister, represented a major investment by the State in the consolidation and furtherance of the establishment.

With status and privilege went responsibility. The parishes of both the Anglican Church and the Scottish Kirk were charged with the relief of poverty. Considerable civil authority was vested in Church of England parishes, extending to all their residents (a point to which we shall return). Similar assumptions underpinned the role envisaged for the Church of Scotland's approximate equivalent to the vestry, Kirk sessions. In rural areas especially these exercised considerable influence in matters of social discipline while, in urban communities, town councils were often enmeshed with the Kirk. Scottish poor law legislation was permissive in character and contributions at services were meant to provide the core of poor-relief funds. Where these were inadequate a rate might be set on the landed proprietors of the parish. However this practice was erratic: the revitalisation of voluntary donation was central to the Glaswegian ministry of the leading Scottish establishment divine of the day, Thomas Chalmers, whose vision of a godly urban society was much admired.[33]

The responsibilities adhering to the Church of Ireland were frequently no more than theoretical. The chronic weakness of its parochial structure, and widespread absenteeism among Ireland's Anglican clergy, meant poor relief was typically but haphazardly dependent upon local philanthropy. Some Ulster towns had reasonably comprehensive municipal mechanisms, and Cork and Dublin had publicly funded workhouses. However even Dublin largely depended on voluntary effort to relieve its poor; paupers receiving relief might be paraded through the streets in grotesque fund-raising processions, organised by the city's recently founded (and perpetually financially embarrassed) mendicity association.[34]

Religion mattered politically in much more than the mundane context of local affairs. State churches, headed by the monarch, enmeshed government in ecclesiastical appointments. This power was an important source of patronage but could also be a significant distraction from the daily affairs of ruling the United Kingdom. Because full enjoyment of civil rights rested upon sacerdotal tests of loyalty to establishment, the status of Protestant dissenters and Roman Catholics in the eye of the law was a recurrent political issue. Maintaining a balance between supporters and opponents of Roman Catholic emancipation had become an important consideration in determining the composition of the Cabinet. The intimate relationship of Church and State went far beyond the material. An especially forceful statement to this effect was made in the spring of 1820 by the Oxford theologian Geoffrey Faussett in the University's Bampton Lectures (a prestigious annual series endowed in 1780 to expound Anglican orthodoxy). Faussett dwelt on 'the criminality of schism', attacking what he saw as 'the unqualified liberality of the times'. Within the Anglican Church itself, he argued, there were many who not merely tolerated but actively consorted with Protestant dissenters. Faussett was referring here to Evangelicalism (a strand of which the anti-slavery campaigner and MP William Wilberforce remains the best-known member). Evangelicals placed primacy on the individual's relation-ship with God, giving to the laity a greater active role in the Church, and downplayed the notion of Anglican supremacy in favour of a communion of all believers that embraced Protestant dissenters and Anglicans alike. For Faussett and others like him this was schismatic: it undermined Anglicanism's unique

claim (Roman Catholicism excepted) to 'an apostolical Episcopacy' along with
the authority of its 'divinely instituted priesthood' and liturgy. Extempore prayer
and the relaxation of legislation that admitted dissenters to political office were,
Faussett argued, alike symptomatic of a corrosive

> modern liberality … the idea that sincerity is all in all; that, provided we are secure
> of our 'integrity before God', and conscientiously embrace religion under the form
> that best accords with our views, it matters not whether we be of this or that
> communion, or whether we be of any communion at all.[35]

The phrase 'integrity before God' was a quotation from Benjamin Hoadly, an
early eighteenth-century bishop who had argued for a broader and more
generous (latitudinarian) Church. In the process Hoadly had attacked those who
remained loyal to the Jacobite monarchy, overthrown at the Revolution of 1688
and ultimately displaced by the Hanoverian royal house in 1714. Significantly
perhaps, Faussett's grandfather and great-grandfather had been Jacobite sympathisers.[36] The last Jacobite Rising was only seventy-five years away and although
Jacobitism had dwindled into vestigial romanticism, such attachments demonstrate how an almost tribal sense of loyalty could endure, even in England. On
the wider political stage it was certainly tribal loyalties that sustained the Whigs
during their long period in political opposition (from 1807), while the 'third
party' at Westminster was universally known as the Grenvillites, after the
extended Buckinghamshire family that largely supplied its members.

Not all Anglicans would have agreed with Faussett. His theology was
steeped in the values of Oxford University: the perspective from Cambridge was
decidedly more latitudinarian.[37] But latitudinarianism had lost much of the intellectual vigour and support that it had exhibited in the eighteenth century, while
'High Anglicanism' was strengthening. The latter dominated an Anglican Church
which was itself quietly undergoing a process of renewal and reform.[38] The
central premise of the 1820 Bampton Lectures commanded wide assent. As we
have seen, Lord Liverpool used the Book of Common Prayer when leading
family prayers, rather than improvising (as, for example, Wilberforce did); and
leaders of the Methodist Church went out of their way to emphasise to the
Government their 'affectionate regard for the ecclesiastical establishment', that
they held 'without exception all her Doctrines, venerating her authority, & using
her religious Services', and that many Methodists were 'regular attendants and
communicants at the established church'.[39] Faussett's concluding lecture was a
passionate defence of 'the alliance of Church and State' which, he argued, was 'a
model of a federal and equitable union'.[40] His arguments mattered because they
concerned the authority of the Crown and the 'King's Ministers' who governed
on the monarch's behalf. The claims of the United Kingdom Government
ultimately rested neither on the consent of the people nor on the precedents of
history: they rested on divine authority. This view prevailed even in Scotland.
Thomas Chalmers set out both in print and through practical example that

nothing but the revival of the established church 'will ever bring us back again to a sound and wholesome state of the body politic'.[41]

Chalmers was writing to William Wilberforce, whom he counted among his closest friends, illustrating that churchmen outside of the tradition espoused by Faussett still believed in a divine injunction to civil obedience. This explains the zeal with which the Government pursued works of religious as well as political controversy: indeed the six acts barely drew a distinction between them. Blasphemy undermined both Church and State: many dissenters, and certainly most Methodists, approved of the Government's Blasphemous and Seditious Libels Act, the sixth of the repressive measures passed in December 1819:

> Pamphlets and printed Papers containing observations upon public Events and Occurrences, tending to excite Hatred and Contempt of the Government and Constitution of these realms as by Law established, and also vilifying our Holy Religion, have lately been published in great Numbers, and at very small Prices; and it is expedient that the same should be restrained.

The Act then proscribed newspapers and other periodicals commenting on news 'or upon any matter in Church or State' unless they retailed for at least sixpence, exclusive of the penny tax already imposed on them. (There were also taxes on paper and advertisements and a tax of three shillings on pamphlets.) Prosecution for seditious or blasphemous content had long been possible: the significance of this new measure was that it targeted cheap political literature purely on the grounds that it was accessible to a mass readership.[42]

Old corruption?

The year 1819 had seen a surge in publishing activities linked to widening politicisation. Claims for parliamentary reform derived much of their force from a broader critique of the corruption and venality of government. Initially this had been spearheaded by successive editions of *The Extraordinary Red Book, Containing a List of all Places, Pensions, and Sinecures* (first published in 1810). However in 1819 it was transformed into a genuinely populist assault by *The Black Book, or, Corruption Unmasked!!!* which appeared in cheap fortnightly instalments from June 1819. 'The object of this Work is, to trace the corruptions and influence of Government through all their ramifications', declared its front wrapper: besides being expensive, the *Red Book* ignored the Church of England and aristocracy 'who form the basis of the present order of things' while lacking 'illustration and comment, which in such subjects, are indispensable, to render them either useful or intelligible'.[43] Illustration and comment were increasingly the hallmarks of popular political publications, especially those by London radical William Hone and the engraver George Cruikshank. Hone had first come to prominence in 1817 when he was tried and acquitted for blasphemy in

" Great offices will have

Great talents."

This is THE MAN—all shaven and shorn,

All cover'd with Orders—and all forlorn ;

Figure 1   George IV as Prince of Wales, 'The Dandy of Sixty'

publishing parodies of the Athanasian Creed and Anglican catechism and litany; but it was *The Political House that Jack Built* (1819), enlivened by Cruickshank's satirical woodcuts (see Figure 1), that set a new standard in political publishing. Close on its heels, and deliberately misdated to 'January 15th 1819', followed Cruikshank's depiction of 'Poor John Bull – the Freeborn Englishman – Deprived of his *Seven Senses* By the *Six New Acts*' (see Figure 2), depicting Castlereagh ripping up a copy of *Cobbett's Two-Penny Trash*. The hands of a starving John Bull have been locked in a vice, his ears stopped, eyes covered and mouth padlocked. Magna Charta is skewered by a dagger inscribed 'Manchester Steel'.

A further stream in radical political publishing derived from the enduring influence of Thomas Paine. Here another London publisher, Richard Carlile, was paramount. Principled, passionate and personally reckless, Carlile had blatantly sold Hone's parodies during the latter's eighteen-week imprisonment before his trial. He was then imprisoned himself in October 1819 for six years on charges relating to his new edition of Paine's *Age of Reason*; but Carlile had got under the skin of the political establishment in several other ways. Within days of Peterloo, he had published his own eyewitness account, denouncing the

Figure 2   John Bull deprived of his senses by the six acts

authorities, in *Sherwin's Weekly Political Register* which he conducted. He then relaunched the *Register* as the *Republican*, explicitly proclaiming the political and religious strands of Paine's thought. With the assistance of Jane and Mary-Ann Carlile, his wife and sister, Carlile managed to keep both *Republican* and his publishing and bookselling business afloat during his imprisonment. The tide of blasphemous publishing may have slowed but it was never stopped. Joseph Mayett, a farm labourer and Baptist, lived in Quainton, Buckinghamshire, a village of only 900 souls isolated from all main roads. But 'this winter I fell into Company with some men in my Journeys to and from my work that were of a Deistical principle', wrote Mayett. 'These men had got several Books that were … against all revealed religion and these men often put them into my hands.' He considered himself 'a sufficient Judge to read them without any danger of being drawn aside', but for a while Mayett wavered, 'in Such a strait that I knew not what to do nor which way to turn'.[44] Thomas Paine, posthumously abetted by the Carliles, struck raw nerves among the disfranchised poor and political elites alike, as the titles of loyalist literature of 1820 reveal.[45]

Polite society could draw some solace from the fate of Tom Paine's bones. Disinterred from their New York grave in September 1819 by two other prominent radical publishers, William Cobbett and William Benbow, they were brought back in triumph to Liverpool by Cobbett in November 1819. He intended to reinter Paine in his native soil beneath a fitting memorial, but Cobbett made little headway with fundraising for the project. He was widely ridiculed by loyalists, while many admirers of Paine felt the project was unseemly. Cobbett's twopenny weekly *Political Register* was one of the first casualties of the six acts, closing on 6 January. Relaunched in a sixpenny format, it appeared erratically until weekly publication was stabilised in April, but by then Cobbett had launched and closed his *Evening Post*, an attempt to break into the mainstream newspaper market, and fought and humiliatingly lost a parliamentary election. Within the month he had been charged with bankruptcy and had to surrender to the rules of the King's Bench Prison, effectively under house arrest in a cheap lodging house adjacent to the gaol. Released in October into a period – as we shall see – of extraordinary political turmoil, Cobbett lost sight of his plans for Paine's bones. Eventually he lost the bones too.[46]

Cobbett's failure to turn what remained of Paine into an object of popular veneration suggests that establishment anxiety surrounding Paine's 'vilifying our Holy Religion' was exaggerated. Yet it is easy to draw such conclusions with hindsight. An incipient cult of Paine appeared to be forming during the winter of 1819–20. As the editor of one of several new editions of Richard Watson's 1795 attack upon *Age of Reason*, hypothesised: 'What, indeed, has not society to dread from those, who may have deeply imbibed the wicked opinions of that and similar books?'[47]

The local state

The cement that held Britain together was not, however, the depth of popular piety alone (and in England the extent of this was dwindling in comparison with Scotland and Wales). The most powerful cohesive forces were pragmatism and social deference. The landed elites of England, Wales and Scotland controlled their regions and local communities largely through a combination of economic power, patronage and a near-monopoly of national political processes. The fulcrum of this arrangement was the office of Lord Lieutenant of the County, an important vector of communication between central government and their region, with responsibilities for the militia, maintaining law and order in any extraordinary circumstances, and for recommending candidates to be appointed Justices of the Peace. The latter were Crown appointments made from the principal landowners of the county. They occupied a pivotal position in society: they could dispense summary justice for minor offences; at divisional (sub-county) Petty Sessions they tried lesser offences and decided which cases should go to higher courts; and they also exercised extensive, informal social leadership. They did so by virtue of their office and the social stratum from which they were drawn: Anglican males who either owned freehold property worth £100 per annum or who were heirs apparent to property worth at least £300. In Hampshire and the Isle of Wight (a not untypical southern county) a population of 283,000 people yielded a mere 900 who were eligible to serve as JPs, less than one fifth of those qualified to vote in parliamentary elections for the county.[48] The maintenance of main roads, bridges, gaols and, increasingly, asylums were the responsibility of each county's magistrates, assembled at Quarter Sessions. Crucially, these Sessions also tried many serious crimes which were not punishable by death: the latter were heard by periodic Assize courts in each county, for the grand juries at which magistrates provided the bulk of the membership. Judges, in their charge to the Grand Jury with which each Assize began, would take the opportunity to summarise new legislation and comment on current issues relating to crime and social order. The charge was also an opportunity to flatter jury members. Assizes were also significant social events, the point in the season when members of the county establishment played (and indeed prayed) together.

The office of magistrate was central to good governance as Liverpool's Cabinet well knew. The Government was profoundly attentive to the voices of local *political* establishments. Sidmouth's and Liverpool's correspondence with leading provincial figures, be they Dukes or postmasters, bishops or curates, was voluminous: but the Ministry took particular care to listen to and flatter the magistracy. What historians have widely seen as the cause almost of this Government's undoing, namely its inflexible support for the actions of the Manchester magistrates at Peterloo, was arguably a key source of its strength. The Ministry knew that day-to-day government rested with and upon magistrates who dispensed justice and, through the Quarter Sessions, undertook significant swathes of the business of local government. The Cabinet risked temporary opprobrium to keep secure a long-established principle of efficient government. Its policy was aptly summarised by George Canning (President of the Board of Control for India), in a letter to William Huskisson, an influential 'backbench' supporter of the Ministry. Stressing 'the difficulty of our position in respect of the Mctr Case, & at the same time the absolute necessity of our maintaining it', Canning argued:

> To let down the Magistrates would be to invite their resignations – & to lose all gratuitous service, in counties liable to disturbances for ever. If the nature of the danger is not now understood, & if, in understanding it, the Country Gent. are not prepared to meet it with the necessary firmness, there is an end to all the functions of government so far as it relates to the internal peace & safety of the Country. It is, to be sure, very provoking that the Magistrs, right as they were in principle, and nearly right in practice, should have spoilt the completeness of their case by half an hour's precipitation. But their defence must therefore, I apprehend, be conducted on general grounds, and the details of the particular transaction merged, as much as possible, in the overwhelming question of the magnitude of the mischief, & the necessity of a remedy.[49]

So profound was the Government's commitment to the defence of the Manchester magistracy that – shortly after Christmas 1819 – it was prepared to face down criticism and secure for the Revd William Hay (the leading magistrate at Peterloo) the living of Rochdale, one of the most lucrative in the country. Sidmouth personally visited the Archbishop of Canterbury at Lambeth Palace to ensure the appointment.[50] Even more significantly, the Ministry risked the delicate balance of political relations in the West Riding, Britain's most populous county, by dismissing Earl Fitzwilliam from the Lord Lieutenancy after he had appeared on the platform of a county meeting that had called for a public enquiry into Peterloo. Historians have commonly supposed Fitzwilliam chaired the meeting, and unequivocally approved the resolutions of censure adopted by it. In fact he did neither: he spoke only to propose a vote of thanks to the chairman, whilst a relatively anodyne draft of the resolutions in his private papers deplored how 'false and absurd theories of Government, inculcated by artful & designing men' deluded the labouring classes. 'The conduct of such men', Fitzwilliam's draft added, deserved 'reprobation and punishment'.[51]

The Lord Lieutenant's discomfort epitomised the dilemma of leading Whigs in 1819–20, as they sought to defend the case for reform without conceding the political authority of the landed establishment. For the Ministry it was a Cabinet-level matter, though Liverpool hesitated about dispensing with Fitzwilliam until Castlereagh gave an assurance that he was confident of being able to defend the decision in the Commons.[52] As Leader of the House much depended on the Foreign Secretary and Castlereagh's position was unequivocal: 'the noble Ld. in lending himself to a Radical mob, and ... joining or countenancing the opposers of all loyalty ... had made it impossible to go on with him – he had therefore been justly dismissed, and he hoped it would be a lesson to great men how they kept bad company'.[53] The Lord Chancellor's assessment of Fitzwilliam was more succinct: 'sheer weakness of mind'. The tone of Sidmouth's letter dismissing the Earl was terse to the point of insolence: 'I have received the Command of the Prince Regent to acquaint your Lordship that his Royal Highness has no further Occasion for your Lordship's Services'.[54] Fortunately it was possible to replace Fitzwilliam with another West Riding magnate of similar wealth and status (Viscount Lascelles, who six months later inherited the Harewood earldom). The importance of being able to make such a replacement was apparent a few weeks later when the Earl of Glasgow was appointed Lord Lieutenant of Ayrshire. This met hostility because he was 'an almost Entire Stranger to the County, with little Property in it'. Lord Aisla (pointedly writing to the Home Office using his ancient Scottish title, the Earl of Cassilis) described the action as 'an indignity offered to every great Landholder in the county'.[55] Of even greater significance in Scotland, however, was the office of sheriff, a central element in local government and the law (justices of the peace were vested with less authority in Scotland) and an appointment that governments took care to confine to politically pliant members of the Scottish social elite.

However remote from the common people sheriffs, lords lieutenant and magistrates might be in terms of social status, the localities they led tended to cohere around shared senses of regional identity, ethnicity, religious affiliation and self-interest. This contrasted sharply with the situation in Ireland. English radicals might still talk of the Norman Yoke, the concept that the aristocracy was an alien imposition, but this rhetoric was little heeded at the local level. The Irish aristocracy, however, was overwhelmingly just such an imposition, alien in terms both of its ethnic and religious identity. Major landowners' monopoly of the main instrument of Irish local government, the grand jury for each county, did nothing to obviate this impression, since the cesses (taxes) these bodies imposed fell upon occupiers, not owners. 'Their influence in the grand juries', wrote Thomas Spring Rice in 1815, meant

> public burdens have augmented in a most formidable progression: the public works have become deteriorated in a similar ratio. The landlord is lowered in the general estimation, by his acquiescence in a corrupt system; the peasant is impoverished and the community is plundered.[56]

The dislocation of Irish government had been increased by the 1800 Act of Union, which permanently dissolved Ireland's Houses of Parliament. Only twenty-eight Irish peers sat in the House of Lords at Westminster, while Ireland's hundred MPs were not especially vocal in the Commons (though they augmented its size to the point that it could be absurdly over-crowded). The consequences of this were exacerbated by British governments' unwillingness 'to regard Ireland as anything but a colony', whereas 'the Scottish landed elite was accepted as equivalent to that of England and effectively controlled the local communities'.[57] English political and cultural primacy was therefore powerfully hedged: in Scotland by the extent to which indigenous Scottish institutions and elites had continued to conduct the country's affairs after the Union of 1707, and in Ireland by fundamental incompatibilities between colonists and colonised. Welsh sense of linguistic and historical identity also helped maintain a separate sense of nationhood, though it has been argued that any 'idea of Wales as a "nation" on a par with Scotland and Ireland' was conspicuously absent. Welsh MPs 'had no conception of Wales as a "nation" with specific grievances requiring separate legislative attention' and devoted themselves to representing not their country but their constituencies precisely as did their English counterparts.[58]

The debate around reforming the Court of Great Sessions (the Welsh equivalent of the English Assizes) that emerged in 1820 provides only a partial exception to this generalisation. When Wales was subjected to English law in the sixteenth century the Court of Great Sessions was established to hear both civil and criminal cases. Great Sessions were held over six days in each county twice a year. The view had become widespread that the Court was inferior to the English central courts in terms of efficiency and the abilities of the lawyers who practised there. 'Almost every person of property I have spoken to on the subject thinks with me, that the judicature in Wales should be placed on the same footing as in Great Britain', Lord Kensington told a parliamentary Select Committee on the Welsh judiciary in June 1820 (cheerfully oblivious of Scotland's independent judicial system). 'The general feeling of persons of fortune and education', a Welsh barrister told the committee, is 'very much against the existing system'.[59]

However, concerns expressed in 1820 that what remained of a distinctively Welsh judicial system should be consolidated, offer an early glimpse of nascent national sentiment in Wales. Awareness of the distinctiveness of the Great Sessions coincided with a surge of scholarly interest in the remarkable legal code established by the tenth-century Welsh King Hywel Dda.[60] Idealists argued that 'Wales as well as Scotland [should] have some institutions of her own, to distinguish her sons, by calling forth their talent and genius, and embodying whatever may give dignity to the descendents of the primordial Britons'.[61] Yet of the nine judges who presided in the Court of Great Sessions in Wales in 1820, eight were English and the ninth Irish. Indeed, of the 230 judges across the Court's whole history (1542–1830) only thirty had ever been born in Wales.[62] The paucity of native Welsh judges reflected both the lack of professional opportunities in the country and the linguistic context. English was the language of the law. Although courts in Wales readily accommodated witnesses who did not speak English, the thrust of education belittled Welsh as a language. The Welsh school pupil was 'menaced out of a use of his own language'.[63] Paradoxically, sharing a language with England may actually have facilitated the continuation of distinctive Scottish institutions.

An influential argument in recent years has been that Britishness was formed out of the prosecution of the 'second hundred years war' against France, especially the revolutionary and Napoleonic wars. Yet is far from clear that the sense of Britishness endured during the peace that followed. Even excluding Ireland, it is preferable to think in terms of a United Kingdom that was 'a multi-national state, not just an amalgam of many identities'.[64] Not only did the vestige of a distinctively Welsh legal system survive in Wales, in Scotland the legal system, like its established church, was fully distinct and independent of English intervention. Another powerful vector of a sense of Scottish uniqueness was the extent of the nation's military service in the cause of the British monarchy, but always in distinctively Scottish regiments. Even professional people seldom saw themselves as primarily Britons. Neither English nor Scots 'used the terms "Britain" or "Britons" as anything other than a geographical marker'. Britons residing in France (around 12,500 of them by 1831, the largest group of foreign nationals there) were uniformly labelled *Anglais* by the French press and authorities. *Les Anglais* included Welsh ironworkers, Scottish cotton spinners and linen operatives from both Scotland and Ulster.[65]

But powerful economic forces increasingly differentiated England, along with western central Scotland, from its neighbours. It was increasingly an urban, if not exactly urbane, society. Eighteenth-century urban growth had contributed to the erasure of regional differences (arguably, nineteenth-century growth would accentuate them). Even Cornwall, a travel writer of 1817 opined, was no longer 'terra incognita'. While 'the degree of reserve before strangers, which is so peculiarly in some instances unpleasantly the characteristic of Englishmen, is very discernible among all ranks in Cornwall … The gentry, in general, are polite and well-informed, the trading members of the community are industrious and obliging'.[66] Towering over all was London, the aggregate population of whose various components comfortably exceeded one and a half million. The United Kingdom's next largest cities, Glasgow, Edinburgh and Liverpool, were each less than a tenth of the capital's size. All four cities were maritime in their orientation, and ports figured significantly among the other most populous cities, with Bristol, Plymouth, Newcastle, Portsmouth, Hull, Aberdeen and Belfast among the twenty largest. But significant too were inland manufacturing centres (Manchester, Birmingham, Sheffield, Leeds, Nottingham, Paisley and Stoke). Only the presence of Norwich among the twenty largest cities evoked the earlier pre-eminence of East Anglia in the British economy; the spa and resort town of Bath (at 44,000 a similarly sized community to Aberdeen and larger than Nottingham) was a special case, though even here textile manufacture was significant with around a thousand employed in the city's largest mill.[67] By contrast, the largest Welsh community, Merthyr Tydfil, mustered a population of barely 19,000.

Urbanisation, however, is not to be measured in demographic behemoths alone. The previous two decades had seen the number of English communities with a population of 2,500 or more leap from 253 to 352.[68] Everywhere the population was growing, though in mostly rural counties the rate of this increase was diminishing. Socially, the leitmotif of English social history in the years leading up to 1820 was one of prodigious population increase. In retrospect, the half decade before 1820 was the point in England at which the gross reproduction rate reached its highest-ever peak; ever after, the secular trend in this key demographic variable has been downward.[69] It would be spurious to claim that specific events around 1820 initiated this trend. But in early industrial society the regulation of fertility rested heavily with women and on their capacity to assert a right to control the frequency of sexual intercourse. Towards the end of 1820 women mobilised autonomously and in large numbers to support Queen Caroline. Many contemporaries saw this as a novel and disturbing assumption of independence on the part of women; retrospectively, it can be seen as of a piece with the shift towards closer female control of reproduction.

While shifts in women's control of reproduction were as yet unfathomable, a social change that was readily visible in England and Wales in 1820 was a rapid evolution in the purpose and personnel of local government. The stimuli for this were several: the often diminishing authority of traditional landed elites in urban and populous rural communities; the challenge of applying a system of parochial government devised in the sixteenth century for a completely different set of social and economic circumstances; coping with the post-1815 economic recession and the social dislocation wrought by it; and the increasing assertiveness of 'the middling sort' in social discourse and affairs. Barely a quarter of English towns were incorporated boroughs (and many of these were nominal bodies, making little practical impact on their often decaying communities).[70] But it is boroughs that tend to dominate histories at the expense of the far-greater number of less-glamorous bodies involved in local government.

Urban government particularly was delivered through an often complex matrix of overlapping and sometimes competing bodies. Leeds well illustrates this even though it had an active corporation. Few aspects of local government in 'the principal seat of the woollen manufacture in England' rested exclusively with the corporation of twelve aldermen and common council of twenty-four. Responsibilities were distributed across the corporation, the vestry, the court leet (a medieval survival) and an improvement commission established by a parliamentary act of 1755. Such commissions were an increasingly frequent method of circumventing the vested interests and limited powers of local corporations, or of bringing an element of corporate governance to communities where hitherto there had been none. The extent to which the control of commission, corporation and vestry in Leeds lay entirely within 'a little knot of wealthy Tory Churchmen', all of them 'friends and relations of the Mayor [and] Aldermen', has arguably been exaggerated.[71] However, by 1820 increasing dissension was apparent in Leeds politics, as Whig reformers made a concerted move to have their voices heard. Critics of newspaper proprietor Edward Baines, who led the Leeds reformers, pilloried him as 'his Majesty of the Workhouse', and sought to associate municipal reform with ultra-radicalism.[72] At least the process of election to the Leeds commission made this possible: at nearby Bradford the improvement commission was constituted purely by co-option.[73]

Under its Improvement Act, the Leeds vestry was empowered to elect fourteen commissioners who, with the Mayor, Recorder and borough magistrates could levy a rate for lighting and improving the pavements. The size of this commission varied over time, during which it also acquired responsibility for water supply, nuisance removal, prosecuting encroachment onto the highways and the Leeds courthouse and prison. The commission also enjoyed powers similar to those of a turnpike trust over the main roads of Leeds.[74] A separate act of 1815 established a police force and a night watch. Leeds was unusual at this time in having a designated police force (for daytime duty as opposed to simply a night watch): Bath, Birmingham, London, Macclesfield, Manchester and Cheltenham are the only other communities known to have done so.[75] Most localities still relied on the erratic services of unpaid parish constables, supplemented in larger towns by a night watch if powers had been obtained from Parliament to establish one.

Since it acted as an electoral college for several other bodies, elections to the Leeds vestry, by the principal ratepayers of the town, were keenly contested. Seven of the eight churchwardens were chosen by annual election. They also formed a powerful tranche on a separate poor law board, which also comprised overseers appointed by the magistrates and trustees nominated by the vestry.[76] The vestry also appointed a highway surveyor who doubled as the collector of the rates. In addition it chose the 'Commissioners of Lamps', for 'a large portion' of Leeds' streets; 'many of the shops and some of the manufactories' had basked in gaslight since 1818. Finally the vestry also elected half of the town's street commissioners, another quasi-autonomous body whose annual accounts the vestry had the right to audit.[77]

Leeds also provides a good example of the contentious survival of feudal elements: a resident of the manor of Leeds who bought grain in bulk was obliged to have it ground by the occupiers of the King's Mills, who levied one thirty-second part of all malt, and one sixteenth of wheat, as their fee.[78] A manorial court leet with a jury drawn from resident householders, inspected weights and measures and prosecuted traders whose equipment was short of the proper standard. The court also prosecuted encroachments on the rights of the Manor. In Manchester, which had no incorporated authority whatsoever, the court leet appointed officials to undertake these roles along with two constables and the boroughreeve. These were the town's most influential citizens and *ex officio* members of a separately constituted police commission, though the latter, with several hundred members (650 were sworn in on one occasion) was independent minded and 'almost democratic in character'.[79] Birmingham was similarly governed by a combination of manorial court, street commissioners and highway boards.

Leeds is a striking example of a historiographical penumbra. Innumerable corporate bodies had been set up under local acts of parliament in the eighteenth century: around a thousand turnpike trusts; more than a hundred boards of guardians for the poor; and commissions for improvement, paving or drainage in around 300 towns.[80] 'In Scotland, where there were fewer improvement acts, clubs and societies sought to direct and invigorate municipal action.'[81] Local acts, procured at a pace determined solely by local preferences, advanced standards of public life piecemeal and unevenly. Thus the Hastings Streets Act of 1820 required each householder in the Sussex port to sweep the pavement outside his home, collecting the detritus ready for collection by a public scavenger; but a not dissimilar requirement had been made of Coventry's householders as far back as 1419, while the eighteenth century had seen a steady advance of commissioners with local powers of this nature.[82] Cheltenham, Hastings and Worthing obtained regulatory control over hackney carriages in 1820. Worthing's local act also consolidated provision for a fire service funded from the rates and provided for the public funding of groyns on the beach to arrest coastal erosion.[83] By contrast in Gloucester initial attempts to provide street lighting were blocked by a parish whose residents deemed it a dangerous experiment with an untried technology.[84] By 1820 York's 1763 Improvement Act was widely deemed 'inefficient' (and it did not authorise gas lighting) but 'the grossest ignorance … loudly applauded by the mob' resulted in attempts to secure a new paving, lighting and cleansing act being stymied until 1825.[85] Overall, however, the years 1818–28 represented the peak of adoption of gas light in English towns, with more than fifty adopting gas illumination in this period. Ten did so in 1820 alone.[86]

Although the requirements of the oft-deplored Test and Corporation Acts (which excluded non-Anglicans from public offices, such as election to incorporated boroughs) were relaxed by annual indemnity legislation, the extent to which the latter was taken up is far from clear.[87] Membership of improvement and other commissions, however, involved no doctrinal tests – though it was unlikely that an improvement commission, where there was also a corporation, would not include significant representation from the latter; nor were all commissions elected.[88] As should already be clear, there was also a wide variety of other corporate bodies (with various elective franchises all similarly free of religious qualifications) overseeing roads, drainage, poor relief and aspects of local government. In addition, perhaps as many as 500 manorial courts were still extant across England, actively responsible for drainage, roads, hedges, fencing, and occasionally (as at Leeds) market regulation.[89]

However the basic unit of local government, ubiquitous because they covered the whole of England and Wales, overlapping the jurisdictions of all incorporated boroughs and commissions, were the vestries. Leeds' was unusually busy, but not atypical of the central role a vestry would often play in local life. Conceptually and constitutionally vestries were linked to Anglican parish churches; but they potentially comprised all the rate payers (male and female) of a parish, irrespective of religious affiliation, who cared to attend. In theory, declared the Poet Laureate Robert Southey, 'every parish being in itself a little commonwealth, it … might be almost as well ordered as a private family'. However, he opined, 'the diseased growth of parishes frustrated the political as well as the religious purposes of our old parochial system'.[90] Vestries were potentially very open, and therefore contentious, bodies. One commentator deemed bull-rings, prize-fighters' parlours and 'a French Chamber sitting' decorous compared with the quarterly finance meetings of the Manchester vestry.[91]

The inconsistency with which vestries approached their responsibilities was increasingly contentious since they were particularly charged with administration of poor relief. In the rural south especially, they might set paupers to work at wage levels agreed with local employers, which tended to depress wages across the parish as a result. Most vestries pursued robust policies to exclude outside labour (for fear that in times of hardship such workers would become a drain on the rates). 'Even if it was not the predominant employer in the parish', a recent study comments, 'in many if not most areas of the south of England the vestry had by the 1820s become the de facto regulating authority for rural labour'.[92] Control of relief potentially also placed a powerful tool for social policing in the hands of a tightly organised vestry, especially where discretionary relief was concerned. For example, in the New Forest (Hampshire) parish of Fawley, William Butler applied for two shirts in January 1820: 'he being a very old man the Vestry allows them', noted the clerk. However, the previous year another applicant, on requesting a pair of shoes, was met with a flat refusal: 'not granted, keeps a dog.'[93] Other core responsibilities were for the highways and for policing, through a surveyor and parish constable, both officers of the parish. During the eighteenth century vestries had also acquired responsibilities for maintaining parish fire engines, inspecting slaughter houses and suppressing gin shops.[94] Various strategies were devised to increase administrative efficiency and place vestry governance more firmly in the hands of local oligarchies. Especially in the north-east self-perpetuating 'four and twenties' (vestigially linked to the tenure of particular pieces of land) appropriated much vestry business. Leeds had excluded the poorest ratepayers from participating in elections to its vestry. Some London parishes had placed executive responsibilities in the hands of a socially 'select' vestry as early as the sixteenth century. St George's, Hanover Square, was one of the most successful of these.[95]

This takes us to the heart of the rapid evolution in the purpose and personnel of local government around the year 1820. It was a resident of St George's, Hanover Square, who took the chair of a House of Commons select committee established to investigate poor law relief in 1817. A Hampshire landowner and MP for Christchurch, William Sturges Bourne, was 'a comfortable supporter of the Liverpool administration'. He was awarded a salaried commissionership at the Board of Control the following year, and it was then that he embarked on 'the most ambitious attempt to reform the poor laws undertaken between 1601 and 1834'.[96] His two acts (1818 and 1819) sought both to render poor relief more efficient and its management more socially exclusive. The first, which was compulsory, awarded multiple votes to those with the heaviest-rated properties (an additional vote for each £25 of rateable value over £50, up to a maximum of six votes). This was the first time that plural voting upon a property basis within a single electorate was introduced.[97] The second act permitted these lop-sided electorates, on a two-thirds majority, to devolve poor law responsibilities to a standing committee of between five and twenty 'substantial householders'. This act was also the first step towards professionalising the administration of poor relief, by permitting the appointment of assistant overseers, facilitating the detailed investigation of claimants' circumstances and day-to-day management of parish poor relief activities. Around 2,000 assistant overseers had been appointed by 1822.[98]

One seasoned Essex lawyer described the years from 1820 as the 'Select Vestry Period'.[99] The term swiftly passed into common parlance as vestries rushed to apply these new powers. Although no central listing of parishes adopting the Sturges Bourne Acts was compiled, the rate at which this enabling legislation was taken up was impressive. Around a fifth of all Oxfordshire parishes adopted it, for example.[100] Nationally there were 2,006 parishes operating Select Vestries by March 1822; by 1827 there were 2,868.[101] Widespread adoption of the Sturges Bourne Acts is also reflected in the paucity of new local acts conferring poor law powers (hitherto the only medium for reform available) during the years 1818–24.[102] At the end of the decade, a parliamentary committee gathered extensive evidence revealing that the 1818–19 legislation had been particularly taken up in populous parishes. Prior to 1820, for example, Liverpool's vestry had managed affairs 'very badly'; by 1821 a saving of 30 per cent had been achieved on outdoor relief, rising to 56 per cent the year after. Significant, though smaller, economies were also achieved at the workhouse. Salford achieved a 45 per cent saving. In London in 1819–20 attendance at vestry meetings at St Matthew's, Bethnal Green was estimated by the clerk at between 1,500 and 2,000, with reading the Riot Act necessary to disperse one meeting, held inside the church in April 1820. Implementing a select vestry, on which only the hundred wealthiest ratepayers were eligible to serve, reduced popular interest in parish politics and attendance at Bethnal Green's full vestry (now meeting only annually) fell to around 600. At St Mary's, Lambeth, rates fell from 4s 10d in 1819–20 to 4s 6d in 1820–21, and to 2s 11d by 1822.

The introduction of a select vestry did not merely signal fiscal prudence. The 1819 act required 'Select Vestries to take into consideration the conduct of the persons to be relieved'.[104] In Burwash, Sussex, a select vestry was established in 1819 and immediately sought to promote a moral reformation among the poor of the parish. Those it deemed to have become unemployed by their own misconduct were denied parish employment. An allowance was withheld from a father 'in consequence of his Sons behaviour in the Street'. There were attempts to cut by a shilling the weekly doles of those who 'follow smoaking,' and a consistent policy from the vestry's inception denied payments to dog-owning claimants. The parish constables were instructed to check licensed premises for pauper drinkers and then, in April 1820, printed lists of 'Paupers receiving relief' were given to each publican for 'conspicuous' display.[105] The same month also saw a riotous assault on the poor law overseer by four men denied dole; prison sentences of between two and twelve months were handed down to them at the next Assize. In all, thirteen cases from Burwash were brought to the Assizes between 1819 and 1822, a 'stark contrast to the absence of any Burwash cases sent to the Assizes between 1806 and 1818'.[106]

In retrospect, parish government in the 1820s was on the brink of a rapid demise.[107] But contemporaries saw in these late Regency reforms both the prospect of reversing the spiralling cost of poor relief and a welcome reinvigoration of the local political status quo. And so it proved: across England and Wales expenditure that had reached £7.3 million in the year ending 25 March 1820 was reduced to £6.4 million two years later. Parish officers' commended select vestries as 'very useful', 'essential', 'a great saving', 'a great benefit', 'a considerable benefit', an 'infinite service'; 'the annual expenditure has been greatly reduced in consequence'.[108] 'By clothing the parishioners with authority,' a Welsh magistrate wrote, select vestries had arrested 'the progress of an evil, which is making rapid strides to overwhelm the resources of the country'. 'Sloth and idleness, the handmaids of vice become his welcome guests', unless the vestry can restrict the relief the pauper receives.[109] Where adopted, the Sturges Bourne legislation systematised parish government and it did so exclusively in the interests of the elite. These were enclosure acts, but the space they enclosed was not land but sites for open discussion and the expression of dissent. 'A Parish or Township is a kind of republic', wrote a West Yorkshire enthusiast for select vestries: 'its common business, as far as it is conducted by majorities, is conducted as the business of a republic often is; without system, without consistency; and, therefore, without the best effect.'[110]

Ireland

The refinement of vestry government was not, however, operative in Ireland; nor did an effective ecclesiastical establishment work in tandem there with civil authority. Whereas the story of local government in Britain is essentially one of central government reposing its trust in traditional institutions to adjust to new conditions – haphazardly and unevenly but adjusting nonetheless – the story in the second most populous nation of the United Kingdom is a narrative of central government distrust and intervention (often military) in a system with limited capacity for effective self-government. The problems of governing Ireland, without using military force to an extent that would have been anathema in Britain, constitute a vivid counterfactual argument. It illustrates how much strength the State drew, first from the English and Scottish established churches; and second from the voluntarist ethic that underpinned local government in Britain, along with a capacity for innovation and accommodation. Neither of these was at all apparent in Ireland. First, around four-fifths of Ireland's 6.8 million population were the incongruous Roman Catholic subjects of a staunchly Protestant monarchy, entirely unconnected to the established Church of Ireland except as tithe payers, and largely ignored (but occasionally hassled) by a government whose authority derived from a distant parliament. They could vote in elections to the latter (if they otherwise met the requisite qualifications) but they could not be members of it. From such public offices as were legally open to them, they were almost habitually excluded. 'For the Catholic middle classes, the refusal to grant full political rights left a legacy of distrust and resent-ment against the Union'.[111] Outside the principal cities there were few institu-tions anyway that might have secured the active participation of the middling sort, whatever their faith. As we have seen, even if parochial vestries functioned, there was no poor law to administer. Philanthropic effort sought to fill the gap. However, even where it was effective, it did not bind those who gave charity to the State.

Economic backwardness compounded these problems and increased the tendency for Britons to perceive Ireland as something 'other' and, almost alien. Subsistence farming was not necessarily impoverished farming, but the weak marketisation of Irish agriculture and the exclusion of the greater part of her rural population from the benefits of such markets as did exist, meant that the pursuit of subsistence was more unremitting and precarious than in Britain. Peat was the chief fuel of the rural Irish poor and unusually wet seasons in 1816–17 had prevented cutting and drying it in adequate quantities for the winters that followed. As a result by 1820 large tracts of Ireland were denuded of hedges and trees. Potatoes constituted 'the principal or only food of the poor in most parts of the country'. Here again 1816–17 had been disastrous: casual labour, even if available, was paid as little as six or even four pence a day – this at a time when even inferior potatoes might sell for ten pence a stone (6.35 kg, a quantity barely sufficient to support a small family for a day). Ireland was no stranger to general distress, but the previous scarcity of 1800–01 had been partly alleviated by the impact on wage rates of military enlistment, and while both periods were racked by epidemic fever, the typhus which afflicted Ireland in 1816–19 was the most severe since 1741. While deaths from the disease (the lowest estimate of which was 65,000) had been contained by an often impressive communal response, at least 1.5 million (a quarter of the population) had been afflicted by the fever, along with its sometimes debilitating consequences in the medium term.[112]

By 1820 the fever was behind Ireland: the Central Committee of Health, belatedly established by the Government in November 1818 had been stood down in December 1819. However, in rural societies the expression of politicised discontent is most likely in the period *after* a subsistence crisis, not during it. Francis Barker and John Cheyne, the Dublin physicians upon whose research the above summary draws, commented that 'the equanimity and forbearance of the poor were in general conspicuous … Violence or riots occurred but in a few instances, and only when scarcity and want of employment were at their greatest height'.[113] Writing in 1821, Barker and Cheyne already knew that equanimity and forbearance were not the hallmarks of the post-fever years.

While the extent of Ireland's economic backwardness before the tragic Famine of the 1840s is open to exaggeration, no Irish region, not even proto-industrial Ulster or the south-eastern arable belt, had prospered since 1815. 'The wars benefited Ireland as an economy specializing in agriculture, but they also brought a vast increase in taxation and indebtedness.' More so than in Britain, the scale of government borrowing also stifled investment in domestic economic activities.[114] So the 1816–19 fever epidemic had exacerbated an already serious post-war slump. This had hit Irish commercial farmers severely because of the sector's heavy reliance on victualling contracts for the armed services. The situation was further complicated by a shift from tenanting to lease holding in the later eighteenth century which brought with it an increase in sub-letting. At the base of the pyramid of sub-divided holdings were the plots held by rural labourers. Those who were bound to a farmer generally held between half and one acre free of rent in return for labour. Few day labourers, especially in the post-war period, could survive on paid employment, and therefore rented potato grounds, a practice known as conacre and notorious for the inflated rents demanded. This system was under acute pressure in 1820, especially in Ireland's western province Connacht and the adjoining part of the Irish midlands (where many cattle were raised for the Dublin and English markets) because of the growing prevalence of pastoral farming.

Another index of Ireland's 'otherness' was that, unlike the rest of the UK where population censuses were conducted in 1801 and 1811, the first Irish census was not held until 1821. (More pressing issues were at stake in 1801, and an attempted census in 1811–12 had had to be abandoned.)[115] In addition many quotidian features of Irish administration had yet to be assimilated to Britain, including Customs and Excise, currency, the management of Crown lands and the post office and taxation mechanisms.[116] While taxation had largely been harmonised in 1817, Irish coastal shipping was only finally relieved of tariffs, and thus placed on the same footing as the rest of the UK, in 1821 (the year Ireland's protective tariffs on British cotton textiles and haberdashery were also removed).[117] Military organisation was similarly bifurcated, the office of the Commander in Chief of the Army being limited primarily to officers' commissions, promotions, resignations and retirement terms. Under the supervision of the War Office, a separate command structure was maintained for Ireland, sustained by separate Irish defence estimates. This made the disposition of troops in Ireland a potentially contentious matter if security considerations required that they be augmented at short notice. Though the British Government could and did send emergency reinforcements, commissariat business was haphazard. March 1820 yielded an especially stark example of this when Dublin Castle needed 5,000 greatcoats for a military establishment much swollen to defeat the Ribbon insurgency. The expenditure not being covered in previously agreed estimates, an urgent request was sent to the Home Office, also asking that the coats be shipped direct from London rather than Liverpool which would have required a lengthy wagon journey first. After a conspicuous silence and a further request, the Home Office responded that 'it appears the necessary directions have been given for providing 5000 Great Coats'. Yet six months later they had still not been sent as the Castle and Home Office continued to dispute whose budget should bear the cost.[118]

When Britons thought of Ireland as a distinct, almost colonial entity, it was perceptions of Connacht and south-west Munster that above all shaped their outlook. Mainly Protestant Ulster, sophisticated Dublin and its Leinster hinterland, and the southern coastal cities of Wexford, Waterford and Cork at least had a veneer of familiarity. What lay beyond often did not. In 1824 Thomas Crofton Croker, a Cork-born clerk in London's Admiralty Office, published observations based on tours he had made between 1812 and 1822 through Munster. 'It is an extraordinary fact', he wrote that Ireland should be 'comparatively a *terra incognita* to the English … in political feeling, in language, in manners, and almost every particular which stamps a national character, the two Islands differ essentially'.[119]

Robert Peel (Chief Secretary for Ireland, 1812–18) told Lord Liverpool, *apropos* of Tipperary: 'You can have no idea of the moral depravation of the lower orders in that county. In their fidelity towards each other they are unexampled, as they are in their sanguinary disposition and fearlessness of the consequences.' 'In truth', Liverpool replied, 'Ireland is a political phenomenon – not influenced by the same principles as appear to affect mankind in other countries'.[120] It was plausibly claimed that British officials knew more of Africa or Siberia than they did of Ireland.[121] George Canning, one of the most prominent offspring of Irish parents in public life, and who described himself as an 'Irishman born in London', had yet to visit Ireland (he would do so for the first and last time in 1824).[122] The Duke of Wellington, born there in 1769, left it in 1794 never to return, except for a few months in 1807–08 during a reluctant spell as Chief Secretary.[123] An air of uncertainty, even suspicion, hung over even Irishmen of unimpeachable loyalty and integrity: discussing who should become the next leader of the Anglican Church in Ireland, George IV flatly told Liverpool, 'I cannot reconcile myself to have the Primacy of Ireland filled by an Irishman'. This position Liverpool happily upheld, despite representations from Dublin Castle.[124]

It is scarcely surprising, then, that Peel concluded that 'an honest despotic Government would be by far the fittest Government for Ireland'.[125] His policy as Chief Secretary had been framed by a robust defence of the Irish political establishment, which meant Protestantism, coupled with extensive measures to energise Ireland's magistrates. Peel declared they were 'supine from timidity'. While ascribing Ireland's regular episodes of agrarian unrest to 'sheer wickedness', Peel believed them to be 'encouraged by the apathy of one set of magistrates and the half connivance of another'.[126] In 1820, the *Dublin Evening Post* said much the same, while the Archbishop of Tuam deplored the 'want of Magistrates ready and willing, and discreet' to use military assistance intelligently. 'The best and most conscientious and humane Magistrates' were clergymen, he continued, 'forced into the Commission of the Peace by the want of active resident Gentlemen'. And Charles Grant, Peel's successor, rounded on the 'too general abandonment, by the magistrates of Ireland, of their proper functions, and the consequent destruction of the mutual relations of dependence and support between them and the people'. The want of justices of the peace, 'capable and willing as in England to discharge with correctness all the high duties entrusted to them', was lamentable, Grant noted.[127]

Peel's response had been to establish an Irish constabulary through the medium of the 1814 Peace Proclamation Act. This measure, it has been observed, was almost waved through by MPs, 'who would have reacted very differently had a police force organised along unambiguously military lines been proposed for any other part of the United Kingdom'.[128] The intrusion on civil liberty was tempered by the fact that the force was established for temporary periods only and solely in those districts that required it. Thus 'Peelers' made their appearance only when a district was 'proclaimed' by Dublin Castle under the Act. They worked closely with military detachments in their districts and answered directly to the Castle rather than any local or county authority. Constables, almost invariably recruited from army veterans, improvised uniforms from whatever they had retained from their service or was available locally.[129] The force lacked a permanent establishment of any kind while local elites, though they might crave the additional security that proclamation brought, were also wary of its stigma. Proclamations were therefore typically delayed and once made there was a further delay while personnel were recruited: four Galway baronies were proclaimed, for example, on 21 December 1819 but it was a full month before Peelers were deployed.[130] When they were, the peace proclamation force powerfully supplemented 'the wretched system which professes to protect the country', the traditional baronial constables whom Grant believed did 'more harm than good'.[131] Constables for groups of neighbouring parishes (baronries) had been established under an act of 1787, but their duties were ill-defined, as sometimes were the barony boundaries themselves. A third of the costs of the Peelers had to be borne locally, 'which galls the resident gentry', Grant noted unsympathetically. 'The two great grants' of England, the Chief Secretary opined, were 'a good clergy, & a good magistracy'.[132]

Unable to do much about the clergy, the Government had begun reinforcing traditional justices of the peace with stipendiary magistrates (unknown in Britain outside London at this time). In addition in 1807 it placed on the statute book an Insurrection Act. The Act's application, which required explicit parliamentary approval and was restricted to specified regions, imposed a curfew, suspended trial by jury, and made both the unauthorised swearing of oaths and possession of arms punishable by transportation. The Home Secretary was reputed to be wistful for '*local* measures of severity and power, such as there were in Ireland', for use in Britain.[133] However, in practice the Government was wary of applying the Insurrection Act, less because of any tenderness towards Irish liberties but rather due to a fear that invoking it would be seen as a sign of weakness. Between 1818 and 1822 the Insurrection Act was therefore not invoked, despite extensive pleading ('all the Irish Gentry are for it'), including formal petitions in 1820 from both the Galway and Roscommon Grand Juries.[134]

Much governmental authority depended – or was felt to depend – on the politics of gesture. One of the primary functions of the Lord Lieutenant of Ireland, a genuinely vice-regal position very different in character from the British county lord lieutenancies, was to provide a decorative focal point for the Irish political nation in the absence of a native parliament. Dublin Castle maintained a voluminous correspondence with local dignitaries great and small, to whose letters it replied with prompt and studied politeness.

In an age with limited appetite for intervention in economic and social affairs, there was a widespread belief that Ireland's problems in any case lay too deep for legislative intervention. 'Parliament can do little', observed the *Dublin*

Evening Post, a paper sympathetic to Dublin Castle but frequently frustrated at what it saw as British failure to comprehend Ireland's predicaments:

> They cannot go to war with the Landed Interest and the Church. But even a discussion on the State of the Nation – the opinion of ministers fully and unequivocally expressed and embodied in Resolutions, would create a force, and would be attended with an effect on the Landlords of Ireland.[135]

How enduring such an effect might be was a moot point: privately Dublin Castle was sceptical as to how far the Protestant ascendancy could be persuaded to conduct itself in the interests of the Irish nation as a whole. The situation would be all-too obviously illustrated in 1820 by events in Connacht and the adjacent counties of Munster. This was one of the most distinct economic regions of Ireland, where structural shifts in the rural economy were inclining growing numbers of landowners and their larger tenants both to switch to pastoral farming, which limited the demand for labour, and increasingly to regard renting land to the rural poor as a purely commercial transaction, rather than as a social obligation or a return for labour service. Rents for the potato grounds 'which the poor people take on, or starve' were 'at a price which no man can pay, or earned by labour, at a rate no man can subsist', thought the Lord Lieutenant, Earl Talbot. 'Can it be wondered at,' he asked the Home Secretary, 'that a people so circumstanced, should be ready instruments of every wicked scheme for the disturbance of the public peace?'[136] Although the disturbances and economic crisis of 1820 did eventually subside, Lord Lieutenant and Chief Secretary alike expressed frustration at the political incapacity of government to intervene in the Irish economy: 'while it can & must inflict merited punishment on the criminals whom misery and oppression have driven into guilt', Grant observed to Sidmouth, Government 'cannot touch those whose conduct has really produced these calamities'.[137]

Just how serious these calamities were becomes apparent if we turn to the immediate challenges confronting Lord Liverpool's Ministry in the early weeks of 1820.

Notes

1 K. Cave (ed.), *The Diary of Joseph Farington* (London: Yale University Press, 1984), vol. 15, p. 5444; vol. 16, pp. 5446–7.

2 *Courier*, 6 and 15 January; *Hampshire Telegraph*, 24 January; *Evans and Ruffy's Farmers' Journal*, 7 February. Temperatures have been converted from the original Fahrenheit readings.

3 D. E. Parker, T. P. Legg, and C. K. Folland, 'A new daily central England temperature series, 1772–1991', *International Journal of Climatology*, 12 (1992); Met Office Hadley Centre Central England Temperature (HadCET) databases, http://www.metoffice.gov.uk/hadobs/hadcet/index.html, accessed 28 April 2011. Mean temperatures for the first and second decades of the century were 1.9 and 2.4 degrees respectively; mean January temperatures were 4.4 degrees (1819) and 3.6 (1821).

4 J. G. Lockhart (ed.), *Memoirs of the Life of Sir Walter Scott*, 2nd edn (Edinburgh: Cadell, 1839), vol. 6, pp. 183–5; Emily to Frederick Lamb, 22 January, reprinted in T. Lever (ed.), *The Letters of Lady Palmerston, Selected and Edited from the Originals at Broadlands and Elsewhere* (Edinburgh: Murray, 1957), p. 25; L. Strachey and R. Fulford (ed.), *The Greville Memoirs, 1814–1860: Volume 1, January 1814–July 1830* (London: Macmillan, 1938), p. 85.

5 D. Verey (ed.), *The Diary of a Cotswold Parson: Reverend F. E. Witts, 1783–1854* (Stroud: Sutton, 1978), p. 20; J. Brewster, *Parochial History and Antiquities of Stockton-upon-Tees*, 2nd edn (Stockton: Jennett, 1829), p. 279; *Dublin Evening Post*, 18 January; *Caledonian Mercury*, 8 January; *Hampshire Telegraph*, 24 July.

6 *Morning Chronicle*, 3 January; *Caledonian Mercury*, 20 and 22 January.

7 NAI, SOC 1/2171/13 and 16 (15 and 20 January).

8 *The Diary of Henry Hobhouse, 1820–1827*, ed. by A. Aspinall (London: Home & Van Thal, 1947), p. 1.

9 *Greville Memoirs*, p. 85; *Diary of a Cotswold Parson*, p. 20; P. Hawker, *The Diary of Colonel Peter Hawker* (London: Longmans, 1893), vol. 1, p. 257.

10 Letter to Lord Lonsdale, 23 February, reprinted in *The Letters of William and Dorothy Wordsworth … The Middle Years, Part II: 1812–1820*, arr. and ed. by E. de Selincourt, rev. and ed. by M. Moorman and A. G. Hill (Oxford: Oxford University Press, 1970).

11 *Morning Post*, 6 and 12 January; *Ipswich Journal*, 15 January; *The Times*, 4 January.

12 Quoted in *Dublin Evening Post*, 18 January.

13 TNA, HO 44/3/133; *The Committee Appointed to Manage a Subscription Raised for the Purpose of Affording Nightly Shelter for the Houseless* (London: Crew, 1820); *Durham Chronicle*, 22 January and 5 February; J. Bowen, *A Brief Memoir of the Life and Character of William Baker* (Taunton: May, 1854), pp. 65–6.

14 James Tate, letter 10 January, quoted in S. Rosenfeld, *The Georgian Theatre of Richmond, Yorkshire, and its Circuit* (London: Society for Theatre Research, 1984), p. 76,

15 *The Times*, 10 and 11 January.

16 Bowen, *Brief Memoir*, pp. 64–5, 65–6.

17 L. J. Jennings (ed.), *The Croker Papers: The Correspondence and Diaries of the Late Right Honourable John Wilson Croker … 1809 to 1830* (London: Murray, 1884), vol. 1, p. 156.

18 *Diary of Joseph Farington*, p. 5446.

19 F. L. Jones (ed.), *The Letters of Percy Bysshe Shelley, Volume 2: Shelley in Italy* (Oxford: Oxford University Press, 1964), p. 166.

20 T. Paulin, *The Secret Life of Poems: A Poetry Primer* (London: Faber, 2008), p. 81.

21 Sir James Mackintosh to Lord John Russell, 12 January, quoted in R. Russell (ed.), *Early Correspondence of Lord John Russell, 1805–40* (London: Unwin, 1913), vol. 1, p. 210.

22 Holland Papers, BL, Add. Mss 51609, fol. 12, letter to Robert Adair, 8 March.

23 Anonymous preface to a new edition of W. Jones, *An Inquiry into the Legal Means of Suppressing Riots, with a Constitutional Plan of Future Defence*, first published 1780 (London: Fairburn, [1819]), p. iv.

24 TNA, HO 42/197 (18 Oct 1819).

25 E. Phipps (ed.), *Memoirs of the Political and Literary Life of Robert Plumer Ward, Esq.* (Edinburgh: Murray, 1850), vol. 2, p. 31.

26 BCL, transcript of William Varley, 'Memorandum Book for 1820', pp. 1, 2.

27 J. C. Hobhouse, *A Trifling Mistake in Lord Erskine's Recent Preface* (London: Stodart, 1819), p. 50. The author was committed on 14 December 1819 and only released when Parliament was dissolved on 29 February 1820.

28 Ward, *Memoirs*, pp. 28–9.

29 *A Brief Memoir of the Life of John Gisborne* (London, Whitaker, 1852), p. 144; Varley, 'Memorandum Book', p. 1.
30 *Memoirs of the Rev. John Townsend* (London: Courthope, 1827), p. 121.
31 William Collins, quoted in *Diary of Joseph Farington*, p. 5463, entry for 11 February.
32 J. Walsh and S. Taylor, 'Introduction: the Church and Anglicanism in the "long" eighteenth century', in J. Walsh, C. Haydon and S. Taylor (eds), *The Church of England, c. 1689–c. 1833: From Toleration to Tractarianism* (Cambridge: Cambridge University Press, 1993), pp. 7–9, 19–20 and 28.
33 S. J. Brown, *Thomas Chalmers and the Godly Commonwealth in Scotland* (Oxford: Oxford University Press, 1982), pp 93–151; C. G. Brown, *Religion and Society in Scotland since 1707* (Edinburgh: Edinburgh University Press, 1997), pp. 95–101.
34 R. Mitchison, 'Permissive poor laws: the Irish and Scottish systems considered together', in S. J. Connolly, R. A. Houston and R. J. Morris (eds), *Conflict, Identity and Development: Ireland and Scotland, 1600–1939* (Preston: Carnegie, 1995), pp. 161–71; P. Gray, *The Making of the Irish Poor Law, 1815–43* (Manchester: Manchester University Press, 2009), pp. 9–13, 18–19.
35 G. Faussett, *The Claims of the Established Church to Exclusive Attachment and Support, and the Dangers which Menace her from Schism and Indifference, Considered* (Oxford: Oxford University Press, 1820), quotations from pp. 19–20, 37–8. The lectures were published at the beginning of November, as we shall see a particularly fraught period for monarchical and governmental authority: *The Times*, 7 November.
36 W. W. Wroth, 'Faussett, Thomas Godfrey Godfrey- (1829–1877)', rev. S. B. Black, *Oxford Dictionary of National Biography* (Oxford: Oxford University Press, 2004); online edn, Jan 2011 [http://0-www.oxforddnb.com.wam.leeds.ac.uk/view/article/9215] and Nigel Ramsay, 'Faussett, Bryan (1720–1776)', *Oxford Dictionary of National Biography* (Oxford: Oxford University Press, 2004); online edn, Jan 2011 [http://0-www.oxforddnb.com.wam.leeds.ac.uk/view/article/9214], both accessed 29 Jan 2012.
37 P. Searby, *A History of the University of Cambridge, Volume III: 1750–1850* (Cambridge: Cambridge University Press, 1997), pp. 277, 288.
38 For which see Walsh, Haydon and Taylor (eds), *The Church of England*.
39 BL, Add. Mss 38286 fol. 263–4 (Thomas Kaye to Liverpool, 25 July); TNA, HO 44/2/105 (Robert Clarke to Sidmouth, 4 June).
40 Faussett, *Claims of the Established Church*, pp. 295–379 (quotations from pp. 298 and 338).
41 Letter to Wilberforce, 18 April, quoted in W. Hanna, *Memoirs of the Life and Writings of Thomas Chalmers* (Edinburgh: Sutherland & Knox, 1850), vol. 2, p.263.
42 60 George III c. 9 (30 December 1819); C. D. Collet, *History of the Taxes on Knowledge: Their Origin and Repeal* (London: Unwin, 1899), vol. 1, pp. 16–23.
43 *The Black Book, Hitherto Mis-named 'The Red Book'*, part 1 [12 June 1819], front cover. Cf. Commoner, *The Extraordinary Red Book, Containing a List of All Places, Pensions, and Sinecures … the Expenditure of the Civil List up to 1818* (London: Johnston, 1819). P. Harling, *The Waning of Old Corruption: The Politics of Economical Reform in Britain, 1779–1846* (Oxford: Oxford University Press, 1996), pp. 143–50 critiques the claims of the *Black Book*, finding them 'exaggerated and misleading' (p. 147). Accurate though that may be, the potency of Wade's polemic seemed unassailable and the Ministry's piecemeal reforms were no answer to it. As Harling himself points out (p. 149): 'It was easy for radicals to ignore Tory ministers' ability to accept and even sponsor piecemeal economical reform so long as the Tories refused to touch the political monopoly that ostensibly made possible *all* of the myriad forms of "tax-eating".'

44 A. Kussmaul (ed.), *The Autobiography of Joseph Mayett of Quainton* (Aylesbury: Buckinghamshire Record Society, 1986), pp. 70–1.

45 For example *The Blind Guide; or, Thomas Paine Ignorant of the Bible* (London: Christian Knowledge Society, [1820]); T. Broughton, *The Age of Christian Reason: Being a Refutation of the Theological and Political Principles of Thomas Paine, M. Volney, and the Whole Class of Political Naturalists* (London: Rivington, 1820); 'A clergyman, late of Oxford', *Radicals and True Patriots Compared; or, Living Evidence, from New York, of Paine's Character and Last Hours Contrasted with those of the Patriotic Duke of Kent and the Late Great and Good King George the Third* (London: Hatchard, 1820).

46 G. Spater, *William Cobbett: The Poor Man's Friend* (Cambridge: Cambridge University Press, 1982) vol. 2, p. 398; P. A. Pickering, 'A "grand ossification": William Cobbett and the commemoration of Tom Paine', in P. A. Pickering and A. Tyrell, *Contested Sites: Commemoration and Popular Politics in Nineteenth-century Britain* (Aldershot: Ashgate, 2004), pp. 57–80.

47 F. Wrangham, *An Apology for the Bible, Abridged from Bishop Watson's Answer to Second Part of Paine's Age of Reason* (London: n.p., 1820), p. 7.

48 Possibly rather fewer than 900 as this is the figure for 1851 (when the population exceeded 400,000): R. Foster, *The Politics of County Power: Wellington and the Hampshire Gentlemen, 1820–52* (London: Harvester, 1990), pp. 27, 131.

49 Huskisson Papers BL, Add. Mss 38741 fol 315, Canning to Huskisson, 14 August [*sic* – an error for October] 1819.

50 DRO, 152M/C/1820/OZ (Sidmouth to Bathurst, 2 July 1820).

51 Sheffield Archives, Wentworth Woodhouse Muniments, F/52/58; B. Barber, 'William Wrightson, the Yorkshire Whigs and the York "Peterloo" protest meeting of 1819', *Yorkshire Archaeological Journal*, 83 (2011).

52 Letter to Sidmouth, 14 October 1819, reprinted in Historical Manuscripts Commission, *Report on the Manuscripts of Earl Bathurst, Preserved at Cirencester Park* (London: HMSO, 1923), pp. 479–80.

53 Ward, *Memoirs*, p. 34, quoting Wellington's summary of Castlereagh's comments in Cabinet, 23 October 1819.

54 Letter to his brother 29 September 1819, quoted in H. Twiss, *The Public and Private Life of Lord Chancellor Eldon* (London: Murray, 1844), vol. 2, p. 345; TNA, HO 43/29/146 (31 October 1819).

55 DRO, 152M/C/1820/OH/19 (30 December 1819).

56 T. Rice, *An Inquiry into the Effect of Irish Grand Jury Laws* (London: Murray, 1815), pp. 19-20. See also V. Crossman, 'Peculation and partiality: local government in nineteenth-century Ireland', in R. Swift and C. Kinealy (eds), *Politics and Power in Victorian Ireland* (Dublin: Four Courts Press, 2006), pp. 133–5.

57 Mitchison, 'Permissive poor laws', p. 170.

58 M. Cragoe, 'Welsh electioneering and the purpose of parliament: "From Radicalism to Nationalism" Reconsidered', in D. Dean and C. Jones (eds), *Parliament and Locality, 1660–1939* (Edinburgh: Edinburgh University Press, 1998), p. 115.

59 *PP* 1820 (273) SC Administration of Justice in Wales, pp. 6 and 23.

60 See for example *Cambro-Briton, and General Celtic Repository*, 2 (February–June 1821), pp. 247–56, 295–304, 342–9, 393–9, 439–45.

61 *Cambro-Briton*, 2 (June 1821), p. 456.

62 W. R. Williams, *The History of the Great Sessions in Wales, 1542–1830* (Brecknock: the author, 1899), pp. 18–19, 54, 68, 117–18, 150, 187.

63 *Cambro-Briton*, 1 (June 1820), p. 76.

64 L. Brockliss and D. Eastwood, 'Introduction', in L. Brockliss and D. Eastwood (eds),

A Union of Multiple Identities: the British Isles, c. 1750–c. 1850 (Manchester: Manchester University Press, 1997), p. 3.

65 L. Brockliss, 'The professions and national identity' in Brockliss and Eastwood (eds), *A Union of Multiple Identities*, p. 23; F. Bensimon, 'British workers in France, 1815–1848', *Past & Present*, 213 (November 2011), pp. 150–1.

66 J. Heard, *Gazetteer of the County of Cornwall* (1817), quoted in J. Palmer (ed.), *Truro in the Age of Reform, 1815–1837* (Truro: n.p., 1999), p. 4.

67 B. R. Mitchell and P. Deane, *Abstract of British Historical Statistics* (Cambridge: Cambridge University Press, 1962), pp. 24–6. For Bath see R. S. Neale, *Bath: A Social History, 1680–1850* (London: Routledge, 1981).

68 R. Sweet, *The English Town, 1680–1840: Government, Society and Culture* (Harlow: Longman, 1999), p. 10.

69 H. Cook, *The Long Sexual Revolution: English Women, Sex, and Contraception, 1800–1975* (Oxford: Oxford University Press, 2004), p. 14; E. A. Wrigley and R. S. Schofield, *The Population History of England, 1541–1871* (Cambridge: Cambridge University Press, 1989), p. 234.

70 Sweet, *English Town*, p. 33.

71 S. Webb and B. Webb, *The Manor and the Borough (English Local Government from the Revolution to the Municipal Corporations Act, Volume 2)* (London: Longman, 1908), pp. 421–2.

72 [William Atkinson], *Letters to Lord Viscount Milton; to which is added a Sermon to Electors and Men in Office* (Bradford: Inkersley, 1821), p. 5.

73 S. Webb and B. Webb, *Statutory Authorities for Special Purposes (English Local Government from the Revolution to the Municipal Corporations Act, Volume 4)* (London: Longman, 1922), p. 244.

74 Webb and Webb, *Statutory Authorities*, p. 161.

75 J. Wardell, *The Municipal History of the Borough of Leeds, in the County Of York: From the Earliest Period to the Election of the First Mayor under the Provisions of the Municipal Corporation Act* (London: Longman, 1846), pp. 89–92; Sweet, *English Town*, p. 47; Webb and Webb, *Statutory Authorities*, p. 257; G. Hart, *A History of Cheltenham* (Leicester: Leicester University Press, 1965), pp. 274–6.

76 D. Fraser (ed.), *A History of Modern Leeds* (Manchester: Manchester University Press, 1980), p. 274.

77 E. Baines, *History, Directory & Gazetteer of the County of York* (Leeds: Baines, 1822), vol. 1, pp. 15, 22; S. Webb and B. Webb, *The Parish and the County (English Local Government from the Revolution to the Municipal Corporations Act, Volume 1)* (London: Longman, 1906), pp. 94–8.

78 Baines, *History*, pp. 13, 15.

79 A. Redford, *The History of Local Government in Manchester. Volume 1: Manor and Township* (London: Longman, 1939), p. 204; S. D. Simon, *A Century of City Government: Manchester, 1838–1938* (London: Allen & Unwin), pp. 38–41.

80 Some light is thrown on this penumbra by J. Innes, 'The local acts of a national parliament: parliament's role in sanctioning local action in eighteenth-century Britain', *Parliamentary History*, 17:1 (1990); B. Keith-Lucas, *The Unreformed Local Government System* (London: Croom Helm, 1980), pp. 108–36; and Sweet, *English Town*, pp. 44–56.

81 P. Clark, 'Small towns, 1700–1840', in P. Clark (ed.), *The Cambridge Urban History of Britain: Volume II, 1540–1840* (Cambridge: Cambridge University Press, 2000), p. 770.

82 Webb and Webb, *Statutory Authorities*, pp. 327, 330.

83 F. H. Spencer, *Municipal Origins: An Account of English Private Bill Legislation Relating to Local Government, 1740–1835* (London: Constable, 1911), pp. 267–8, 275, 277.

84 B. Keith-Lucas, *The Unreformed Local Government System* (London: Croom Helm, 1980), p. 109.

85 *Memoirs of Samuel Tuke, Volume 1* (London: n.p., 1860), p. 308.

86 Sweet, *English Town*, p. 46; *A Collection of the Public General Statutes, Passed in the First Year of the Reign of His Majesty King George IV* (London: Eyre & Straton, 1820), pp. x–xv. The other towns were Bolton, Bury St Edmunds, Derby, Peterhead, Shrewsbury, Stockton-on-Tees and Wolverhampton.

87 T. W. Davis, 'Introduction', *Committees for Repeal of the Test and Corporation Acts: Minutes 1786–90 and 1827–8* (London: London Record Society, 1978), pp. vii–viii. That the Indemnity Acts were unsatisfactory is made clear by N. C. Hunt, *Two Early Political Associations* (Oxford: Oxford University Press, 1961), pp. 122–7.

88 Sweet, *English Town*, pp. 48, 52; Spencer, *Municipal Origins*, pp. 143, 145.

89 Brodie Waddell, 'A village parliament? The manor court in England, 1550–1850', paper presented at the Social History Society conference, Manchester, April 2011.

90 'New Churches', *Quarterly Review*, 23 (1820), p. 564.

91 Quoted in Redford, *History of Local Government in Manchester*, p. 257.

92 P. D. Jones, 'Swing, Speenhamland and rural social relations: the moral economy of the English crowd in the nineteenth century', *Social History*, 32:3 (2007), p. 279.

93 Fawley vestry minutes quoted by P. D. Jones, '"I cannot keep my place without being deascent": pauper letters, parish clothing and pragmatism in the south of England, 1750–1830', *Rural History*, 20:1 (2009), p. 33.

94 Sweet, *English Town*, p. 30.

95 Webb and Webb, *Statutory Authorities*, p. 377; Sweet, *English Town*, pp. 31, 33, 36.

96 D. Eastwood, 'Bourne, William Sturges (1769–1845)', *Oxford Dictionary of National Biography* (Oxford: Oxford University Press, 2004) [http://0-www.oxforddnb.com.wam.leeds.ac.uk/view/article/3012], accessed 17 Oct 2010.

97 Spencer, *Municipal Origins*, p. 136.

98 *HC Deb*, 10 July 1822 (vol. 7, col. 1577); D. Eastwood, *Government and Community in the English Provinces, 1700–1870* (Basingstoke: Macmillan, 1997), pp. 42–9, 131.

99 Quoted by R. A. E. Wells, 'Historical trajectories: English social welfare systems, rural riots, popular politics, agrarian trade unions, and allotment provision, 1793–1896', *Southern History*, 25 (2003), p. 92.

100 David Eastwood, *Governing Rural England: Tradition and Transformation in Local Government, 1780–1840* (Oxford: Oxford University Press, 1994), p. 175.

101 *PP* 1822 (556), SC Poor Rate Returns, p. 5; *HC Deb*, 17 April 1828 (vol. 16, col. 1526). See also R. A. E. Wells, 'Poor law reform in the rural south-east: the impact of the Sturges Bourne Acts, 1815–35', *Southern History*, 23 (2001).

102 Spencer, in 'The Local Poor Law Acts', *Municipal Origins*, pp. 281–308, lists none.

103 *PP* 1830 (215), SC Select and Other Vestries, pp. 9, 13, 50, 107–8, 126; A. D. Harvey, 'Parish politics: London vestries, 1780–1830 (part 2)', *Local Historian*, 40:1 (February 2010), p. 30.

104 *PP* 1822 (556), SC Poor Rate Returns, pp. 8–9.

105 R. A. E. Wells, 'Social conflict and protest in the English countryside in the early nineteenth century: a rejoinder', *Journal of Peasant Studies*, 8:4 (1981), pp. 519–20. See also R. A. E. Wells, 'Crime and protest in a country parish', in R. A. E. Wells and J. Rule, *Crime, Protest and Popular Politics in Southern England, 1740–1850* (London: Hambledon, 1997), p. 178.

106 Wells, 'Crime and protest in a country parish', pp. 202, 215.

107 'Rapid demise' is Eastwood's phrase, *Governing Rural England*, p. 181. See also the Webbs, *The Parish and the County*, pp. 147–72.

108 *PP* 1823 (570), SC Poor Rate Returns, pp. 9, 15–19.

109 *A Letter Addressed to the Hon. John Frederick Campbell, M.P. on the Poor Laws and the Practical Effect to be Produced by the Act of 59 Geo. III c. 12 Commonly Called the Select Vestry Act. By a magistrate of the county of Pembroke* (London: Longman, 1821), pp. 1, 3–4, 23–4, 49.

110 H. Roberson, *The Select Vestry or Parish Committee* (London: Hatchard, 1818), p. 17. Roberson, incumbent of Liversedge had earlier engineered the creation of a vestry anticipating Sturges Bourne's. For criticism of select vestries for closing down popular participation in parish affairs see *The Times*, 13 April and 7 May 1818; *Gorgon*, 6 June 1818.

111 D. Ó Corráin and T. O'Riordan, *Ireland, 1815–1870: Emancipation, Famine and Religion* (Dublin: Four Courts, 2011), pp. 20, 159–60.

112 F. Barker and J. Cheyne, *An Account of the Rise, Progress, and Decline of the Fever Lately Epidemical in Ireland: Together with Communications from Physicians in the Provinces, and Various Official Documents* (London: Baldwin, 1821), vol. 1, pp. 33–6, 94, 144–6.

113 *Ibid.*, p. 40.

114 C. Ó Gráda, *Ireland: A New Economic History 1780–1939* (Oxford: Oxford University Press, 1994), p. 46.

115 *Ibid.*, p. 5.

116 P. Jupp, 'Government, parliament and politics in Ireland, 1801–41', in J. Hoppitt (ed.), *Parliaments, Nations and Identities in Britain and Ireland, 1660–1850* (Manchester: Manchester University Press, 2003), p. 148.

117 *Collection of the Public General Statutes*, pp. 117-19; Ó Gráda, *Ireland: A New Economic History*, p. 44.

118 TNA, HO 100/198/229–30 (8 March); HO 122/13, fols 2–3 (Hobhouse to Gregory, 1 April; HO 100/199/125 and 198 (16 August and 16 September).

119 T. C. Croker, *Researches in the South of Ireland* (London: Murray, 1824), pp. 1–2, 4.

120 N. Gash, *Mr Secretary Peel: The Life of Sir Robert Peel to 1830* (London: Longman, 1961), p. 176.

121 K. T. Hoppen, 'An incorporating union? British politicians and Ireland 1800–30', *English Historical Review*, 123 (2008), p. 344.

122 H. W. V. Temperley, *Life of Canning* (London: Finch, 1905), p. 16.

123 N. Gash, 'Wellesley, Arthur, first duke of Wellington (1769–1852)', *Oxford Dictionary of National Biography* (Oxford: Oxford University Press, 2004); online edn, Jan 2011 [http://0-www.oxforddnb.com.wam.leeds.ac.uk/view/article/29001], accessed 18 June 2011.

124 Letter (16 May 1822), quoted by C. D. Yonge, *The Life and Administration of Robert Banks, Second Earl of Liverpool* (London: Macmillan, 1868), vol. 3, p. 10; TNA, HO 100/198/86 (Grant to Sidmouth, 27 January).

125 Letter to Gregory, 15 March 1816, reprinted in C. S. Parker (ed.), *Sir Robert Peel from his Private Correspondence* (London: Murray, 1891), vol. 1, p. 215.

126 Peel to Darby, Oct. 7, 1813, TNA, HO 100/173; Peel to Desart, Feb. 10, 1814, Peel Papers, BL, Add. Mss 40285, quoted in G. Broeker, 'Robert Peel and the Peace Preservation Force', *Journal of Modern History*, 33:4 (1961), p. 365.

127 *Dublin Evening Post*, 25 January, 18 February; NAI, SOC 2171/1/28 (letter to Dublin Castle, 29 January); *HC Deb*, 28 June (vol. 2, col. 100).

128 K. T. Hoppen, 'Nationalist mobilisation and governmental attitudes: geography, politics and nineteenth-century Ireland', in Brockliss and Eastwood (eds), *A Union of Multiple Identities*, p. 170.

129 R. H. Curtis, *The History of the Royal Irish Constabulary* (Dublin: McGlashen, 1871), pp. 5–7.

130 NAI, SOC 1/2188/1, list of proclaimed districts.

131 TNA, HO 100/199/230 (28 September).

132 TNA, HO 100/199/230 (28 September). See also HO 100/198 fols 241 (13 March), 314 (1 April), 327 (8 April).

133 Ward, *Memoirs*, p. 26, reporting a conversation of 21 November 1819.

134 TNA, HO 100/198 fols 314 (1 April) and 325 (8 April); NAI, SOC 1/2176/24 (7 March). Talbot dithered but was inclined to invoke the Act, Grant and the Irish Attorney General were opposed, see TNA, HO 100/198/327 (Talbot to Sidmouth, 8 April) and also fol. 162 (20 February).

135 *Dublin Evening Post*, 7 March.

136 TNA, HO 100/198/325 (8 April).

137 TNA, HO 100/199/230 (Grant to Sidmouth, 28 September).

2 Winter's end

Introduction

In Britain, if not Ireland, the challenges confronting the Government at the New Year appeared to be receding. 'The Accounts from the Country are improving', the Home Secretary wrote to a Cabinet colleague on 2 January, 'the loyal are becoming more confident, & the Radicals less so: but we must be constantly on our Guard'.[1] A few weeks before the situation had seemed far grimmer. Though generally commanding a majority in the House of Commons, Liverpool's Ministry had limited debating strength there, while the Whig opposition could muster some strong performers. In an age when parliamentary parties were essentially rolling coalitions, buffered by a large number of independent members, sponsoring contentious legislation carried high risks. Radical reform was not without its parliamentary sympathisers, notably Sir Francis Burdett and Sir Robert Wilson, while the Whigs were inflamed at the dismissal of Earl Fitzwilliam as the West Riding's Lord Lieutenant (see Chapter 1). Castlereagh, no fluent orator himself, therefore carried a considerable burden as Leader of the Commons, quite apart from the pressure of Foreign Office business. The Cabinet was clear that 'an effectual & permanent remedy' was needed for the 'Monstrous Evils' cohering round the Peterloo affair, likewise that 'the root of them is in the Press'. But 'who is prepared to go to that root directly?' asked Canning: 'I doubt much if this H. of C. be so.'[2]

None could predict how receptive the House would be to the stringent anti-radical measures drawn up by the Ministry in the six bills it introduced on 29 November. We have already seen that considerable constraints were laid upon publishing newspapers and other forms of political comment. However, the rest of this legislation was no less controversial. Unauthorised meetings involving more than fifty people were to be banned; military training, even marching without weaponry, was to be banned; assembling in public with flags or banners, or in any kind of military formation, was to be banned; homes could be searched for arms without a warrant; 'every house, room, field, or other place' where lectures or debates occurred, and an admission charge or collection was made, were to be deemed disorderly unless licensed by magistrates for the purpose; conviction upon a second offence of publishing a seditious or blasphemous libel was to be punishable by transportation for seven years, and the time between indictment and trial on such charges was to be speeded up.[3]

Within Westminster two factors worked in the Ministry's favour. First was the support it received from the Grenvillites, eleven members independent of both government and opposition. Their leader Lord Grenville was carefully courted by Liverpool concerning the six bills.[4] On 30 November Grenville reciprocated with a powerful speech, vindicating the actions of the Manchester magistrates. Wellington declared it 'the finest speech he had ever heard' in the Lords, putting 'the Manchester case much higher than it was put by the Government'.[5] Ministers' performance as parliamentarians was to be a near-constant concern of its supporters throughout the year to come, but for the moment the Government was secure, for the second factor working in its favour was Whig unease at being seen to associate too closely with radical reformers. This was one reason why the Whigs purported to be so indignant over the Fitzwilliam affair: it deflected attention away from the ambiguities of their stance concerning radical reform, and onto the alleged impropriety of the treatment of a loyal provincial leader. Their self-proclaimed stance as 'the friends of the people' made it difficult for them explicitly to voice their distaste for radical reformers, but privately Earl Grey, Whig leader in the Lords, was unequivocal about 'the mischievous designs (which cannot be doubted) of the Ultra-Reformists'. Those designs he wrote, in a letter admonishing Sir Robert Wilson for sympathising with radicalism, were

> no less incompatible with the British constitution, than with any system of settled Government ... Look at the Men themselves who lead in this cause. Is there one among them with whom you w^{d} trust yourself in the dark? Can you have any, I will not say any confidence in their opinions and principles, but any doubt of the wickedness of their intentions? Look at the Men, at their characters, at their conduct. What is there more base, & more detestable; more at variance with all tact & decency, as well as all morality, truth & honour[?] ... Depend upon it, if a revolution follows their attempt to work upon the minds of the People, inflamed as they now are by distress, for which your reform can afford a very inadequate remedy, I shall not precede you many months on the Scaffold, for which you will have assisted in building for us both.
>
> My line must therefore be a line of moderation & cautious policy, & of gradual improvement founded on the Whig Principles, which will not allow me to submit to an invasion of popular rights because bad Men have abused them, but will not allow me either to give my countenance or support to them or their proceedings.[6]

Grey himself, however, performed indifferently in the House of Lords during the debates on the six bills. Though regarded as an accomplished parliamentary orator, he seems to have been in poor health at this time. Westminster gossip had Grey taken ill on the long journey home from Westminster to his Northumberland seat on New Year's Eve, 'and his health appears to be impaired'.

Patterns of radicalism

> From and after the 1st day of January, 1820, we cannot conscientiously consider ourselves as bound in equity by any future enactments which may be made by any persons, styling themselves our Representatives, other than those who shall fully, freely, and fairly be chosen, by the voices or votes of the largest proportion of the Members of the State. (Resolution passed at the Smithfield meeting for reform, London, 21 July 1819)[8]

For the moment therefore the critical political challenges confronting Liverpool's Ministry came not from within Parliament but outside it. Some retrospective scrutiny of these challenges is necessary fully to understand the situation in 1820. They took three interlocking forms: spontaneous popular demonstrations; the constitutional movement for parliamentary reform; and revolutionary conspiracy. Throughout the autumn the popular mood had been truculent. At the inauguration of the new Lord Mayor of London in November, for example, mud and bricks were thrown at carriages with unpopular occupants. 'Hunt's coming' was about the least discourteous cry directed at them. The Duke of Wellington (a recent addition to the Cabinet as Master of the Ordinance) was booed, and the Master of the Mint (another Cabinet appointment) told 'you are a damned rogue and ought to be ashamed to show your face among an honest public'. The Duke of York, second in line to the throne, 'was reproached for his 10,000£ a year'.[9]

Boisterousness of this nature could be contained by the authorities, if necessary with military assistance; and, in any case, the severity of the winter diminished much of the menace of politics at street level. From early January, with the six acts at last in place, some respite might reasonably have been expected by the Government from the reform movement. Sentiments such as the resolution (quoted at the head of this section) passed in July at one of 1819's great reform demonstrations, seemed to be largely bluster. The leading speaker on that occasion – as he would have been at the Peterloo meeting had it not been forcibly dispersed – was Henry Hunt. 'Orator' Hunt, as he was popularly known, was a farmer whose conventional origins among the gentry of rural Wiltshire belied his popular charisma and astonishing facility as a platform speaker. Having been remanded on bail, Hunt grew cautious as the trial for his role in Peterloo approached. The fissiparous nature of reform politics also worked to the Government's advantage. A thinly disguised personal rivalry existed between Hunt and Sir Francis Burdett, whom Cobbett described as 'a democrat in words, and an aristocrat in feeling'.[10] London's ultra-radicals did not share Hunt's optimism that the citadel of old corruption might collapse as the 'mass platform'

he had created gathered further support in the wake of Peterloo; but the relation-
ship between them seemed solid and it was these ultras who organised his
triumphal entry into the capital on 13 September 1819. Hunt however was
increasingly able to dictate his terms: this, coupled with his understandable reluctance to be closely associated (as we shall shortly see) with some of the most
extreme radicals in Britain at this time, led to a breach between them.[11] A plan
for simultaneous meetings across the country on 1 November, to petition the
Prince Regent for universal male suffrage, had to be abandoned when Hunt
attacked it in the influential *Manchester Observer*. Behind the proposal was the
intention of calling further meetings a fortnight later which, if the response from
the Regent was the expected negative, were likely to initiate some form of
uprising. This, claimed Hunt, was precisely what the Government desired:

> The infamous authorities of Manchester, under the sanction of a corrupt and cruel
> ministry, were the first to '*cry havoc and let slip the dogs of war!*' … But, my friends, we
> must be patient and persevering, and not suffer ourselves to be driven off our guard;
> these lawless proceedings are means to irritate us into some indiscreet show of resist-
> ance, of which our watchful enemies are anxiously prepared to take immediate
> advantage; well knowing, as they do, that nothing strengthens and consolidates the
> iron *arm* of despotism so much as the premature and unsuccessful attempt to destroy
> it. I am induced to urge this caution, from the knowledge which I have that spies
> and informers are abroad, and sent amongst you.

'There is not a tap-room or pot-house in the metropolis' without informers,
Hunt continued, and he insinuated some seemingly committed radicals were
among them.[12]

Safeguarding the constitutional movement for parliamentary reform from
any suspicion of extremism was a cardinal point of Hunt's political strategy. He
had played a central role in the creation of a popular movement for parliamentary reform that surpassed anything seen in the 1790s. By 1819 his reputation as
a reformer surpassed that of all others in the field. By contrast, despite the
popularity of his journalism, William Cobbett's reputation was as yet uneven. A
Tory until around 1807, he had fled to America in 1817 rather than face the
consequences of the Government's determination to reverse the popularity of
reform: as we have already seen, his career on returning in October 1819 was
beset with difficulties. In seniority Major John Cartwright (b. 1740) was the
outstanding reformer. In the pamphlet *Take Your Choice* (1776) Cartwright had
written the earliest iteration of a programme that would remain at the heart of
the reform movement for three-quarters of a century. But the broader vision of
this octogenarian reformer was essentially one that saw landed gentlemen
fulfilling the leading role in persuading Parliament to reform itself. Aged only
fifty, Sir Francis Burdett had once cut a radical figure, but essentially his was a
patrician posture, more closely attuned with the Whigs than an incipient
democratic movement.

Though only three years younger than Burdett, Hunt was altogether fresher and more forward-looking. The popular political mood, sustained by the burgeoning literature decrying State corruption, needed a sense of momentum if it was to be translated into sustained activism. The vicissitudes of the economy had not diminished, and Parliament had repeatedly showed itself unwilling to contemplate its reform – most recently in Burdett's heavily defeated reform bill of 1818. In print Hunt could be leaden and querulous, but on a public platform he was a commanding figure. His rhetoric blended appeals to the constitution and the memory of glorious past struggles with a compelling sense of a hitherto latent popular will, now transforming itself into something both purposeful and irresistible. The ultimate rhetorical flourish came not from the platform but from Hunt's audiences – massive, disciplined and drawing heavily on traditional repertoires of both festivity and protest. The actions of the authorities at Peterloo were not only an assault upon peaceable protesters but upon the constitutional freedom of political assembly. What to do now that both the Prince Regent and the Government had upheld those actions, while also severely curtailing the scope for mass politics, presented Hunt and his allies with a profound problem. Did Peterloo signal the futility of constitutional agitation? Or more encouragingly might it be a moral propaganda coup that could be used to shape public opinion and shame the establishment into reform? Hunt always adhered to the latter view. However by the end of 1819 there were many who concluded that constitutional agitation had been closed off and revised their political strategy accordingly.

This is vividly illustrated in the industrial region of west Scotland, which reacted as angrily as anywhere in England to what had happened at Peterloo. The first six months of 1819 had seen the growth of union societies, advocating total abstinence from the purchase of tea, tobacco and spirits as a means of forcing Parliament to consider reform, because the Government derived so much of its tax revenue from them. This was the basis from which concerted protests against Peterloo were organised. After a meeting on Meikleriggs Muir (11 September), near the weaving centre of Paisley, there were three days of rioting when special constables seized banners and prisoners from the Glasgow contingent as it marched home through the town. The unrest spread to Glasgow itself and was so serious the Government dispatched naval frigates to Scotland, carrying two extra regiments of infantry.[13] Reformers saw the actions of Paisley's authorities as deliberately confrontational: the capture of flags and banners had been one of the yeomanry's objectives at Peterloo, even though the crowd had followed Hunt's instruction to attend 'armed with no other weapon but that of a self-approving conscience'.[14] At Meikleriggs Muir an official intention to intervene if 'Flags, bearing Inscriptions and Devices of a political and inflammatory nature' were displayed had not materialised. The returning procession was triumphalist, and the authorities acted on a legal argument (much amplified since Peterloo) namely that the quasi-military discipline of reformers on such occasions was in itself meant to intimidate. For radicals, on the other hand, constitutional rights were being denied in actions intended to be confrontational. In a verbal assault on long-entrenched Tory (or Pittite) authority in Scotland, a lead article in the *Black Dwarf* declared:

> The Magistrates of Scotland, by the illegal seizure of some flags borne in procession at Paisley, provoked a tumult, which has induced the Pitt faction in that country, to propose the taking up [of] arms against the principles of reform … It would have been correct, had the reformers entered into an association *to protect* their flags from any set of robbers.[15]

During the closing months of 1819 there was a rapid acceleration of clandestine activity among Scottish radicals, including armed associations, in parallel with increasing participation by loyalists in volunteer military corps (though the latter was greater in Edinburgh and Midlothian than the west where the need for it was now patently greater).[16] Glasgow's outspoken *Spirit of the Union* was one of the first journalistic casualties of the New Year, appearing for the last time on 8 January. Within six weeks its editor had been tried and convicted for vending sedition.[17] Meanwhile, at a secret meeting on 16 December, union societies' delegates agreed to establish a central committee to coordinate their activities.[18] 'I would say we were on the verge of civil war', Walter Scott wrote to a friend on 17 December: 'in Glasgow the Volunteers drill by day and the Radicals by night'.[19] Across Lanarkshire, 1820 began with 'acts of violence and depredation' because of the 'extreme state of poverty and distress', the Duke of Hamilton told Sidmouth.[20]

'I have no doubt that there are persons in Glasgow and the other manufacturing districts of the West of Scotland whose political views are as mischievous as any of those in Lancashire and elsewhere in England', Lord Melville, the Government's Scottish political manager, believed, but he added, 'though it may be proper and necessary to take all due precaution to frustrate their designs … I have no apprehension of any general disturbance'.[21] Others in the Cabinet were less sanguine. As early as mid-November, 'Sidmouth was more afraid of the Scotch mob than the English', according to the Duke of Wellington. As Master of the Ordinance, Wellington proceeded to conduct a detailed review of internal fortifications, especially in Scotland.[22] A full inspection was made of all Clydeside ironworks, on the supposition that the sprawling extent of such premises, and the relative autonomy in which foundrymen routinely worked, meant that cannon might be manufactured clandestinely. No evidence for this was found, but cannon destined for a West Indies merchant ship were prudently moved to the artillery barracks.[23] 'If the rising broke out anywhere, it would be at Glasgow and Paisley', Wellington believed, and 'no one could certainly foretell how soon it might be put down'.[24] By the middle of January the military were moving fast to secure barrack accommodation 'to eliminate the risk of contamination of the soldiers being billeted' (in Paisley a redundant fever hospital was even pressed into use). Though all 550 cavalry in the western district were in barracks, almost a quarter of the 1,350 infantry were not.[25]

Of all the elements within an increasingly militant radical tradition, however, the most disturbing was centred on London. In terms both of their ideological complexion and long history of involvement in revolutionary conspiracy, the admirers of the agrarian revolutionary Thomas Spence stood out. Spence (1750–1814) had developed a critique of the right to private property in land, the product of radical Calvinism (imbibed in Tyneside's Scottish émigré community where he grew up) and voracious reading in seventeenth- and eighteenth-century political thought. His earliest political works had relied upon education and cheap printing as the mechanisms by which fundamental change would be achieved, but on his arrival in London on the eve of the French Revolution, Spence caught the increasing millenarian temper of the times. Time, he argued, conferred no innocence upon private property: those who acquiesced in the privatisation of land denied the rights they relinquished to their posterity; but to deprive anything of the means of living supposed a right to deprive life itself, which was anathema. Any ascendancy over land was thus an ascendancy over people's lives and private landownership lay at the root of all injustice, inequality and economic exploitation.

Spence's longest and most cogent work, *The Restorer of Society to its Natural State* (1801) cited both the American and French revolutions and the British naval mutinies of 1797 as exemplars. He spent the second of his two lengthiest spells in gaol (he was arrested on at least eight occasions) having been convicted of publishing seditious libel in this work. It broke him financially, but from 1801 active revolutionary conspirators in the capital were consistently associated with his name, though his leadership was intellectual rather than practical. The peaks of Spencean activity post-dated his death, having two climaxes, in December 1816 and again in February 1820. On 2 December 1816 the Spenceans organised a massive political rally at Spa Fields, Islington, addressed by Henry Hunt. The latter's involvement, though, was almost incidental for it was the organisers' intention to use the occasion to foment so much violence that London would descend into chaos. This in turn would be the signal for the commencement of a general rising in the country at large.[26]

In this the Spenceans failed but their deeper purpose had been carefully premeditated and communicated to political radicals across England. A number of provincial delegates were present at Spa Fields to secure early news if it proved successful. Among them were John Kay from Royton and Joseph Mitchell from Middleton. Over the previous few days, men had been on the move towards London, 'avowedly for the purpose of attending the Meeting on Spa Fields'.[27] Linked disturbances were reported in Norwich, Nottingham, Sheffield and Towcester. Paupers at Ely, collecting their weekly dole, told the overseer that whether they would ever need him again depended on what happened in London on 2 December. Sheffield was beset by two days of rioting and demonstrations on 3–4 December, 'intended as counterparts of those in London', the West Riding's Lord Lieutenant told the Home Office. They were 'the offspring of a Revolutionary spirit', he added, 'not the consequence of distress'.[29] In Manchester, according to a detailed report sent the following day to the Home Office,

> the Road [was] crowded with Groups of disaffected. About Midnight Delegates from all adjoining Townships began to flock to Manchester ... When the Mail coach drove up they ran towards the Bridgewater from all Sides ... In the course of the Day it had been reported that the Tower in London was taken by the Rioters ... all agree in expressing the fullest determination to have mustered and armed immediately, in case the Disturbance in London had been attended with Success.[30]

The leading Spenceans – Arthur Thistlewood (a former militia officer), Thomas Preston (a disabled shoemaker) and Dr James Watson – were charged with high treason after Spa Fields. Sensationally, Watson's defence successfully discredited the Crown's principal witness as a pimp, perjurer and *agent provocateur*. Watson was acquitted and the others discharged. In the context of organised Spenceanism after its founder's death, there was a clear logic to the events of 2 December 1816: the ideology that the organisers propounded from the platform had a clear agrarian thrust and they needed no *agent provocateur* to galvanise them into action.[31] Tactically, though, failure at Spa Fields was pivotal to a shift in direction among the Spenceans, though not all committed to it. Watson continued to seeking to bridge London and the provinces, and conspirators and constitutionalists. Thomas Evans, a print-colourer, and his son led a more purist Spencean group pledged to educational endeavour alone. They too had extensive provincial support and it was Thomas Evans junior who on 19 February 1820 became editor of the *Manchester Observer*, pledging the paper to adult male suffrage, annual parliaments and the ballot.[32]

It was now clear that mass meetings alone, however large, would never generate the nationwide chaos needed to destabilise government. So those who were impatient with education as a tool to achieve the political millennium turned to covert tactics. It was reported the Spenceans 'cherished some desperate project' for a demonstration in February 1817, a rumour given force both by meetings they held with provincial delegates a few days before, and by a recent tour of the north by Mitchell and a new radical arrival, William Benbow.[33] The demonstration passed peaceably, but from its platform Hunt pointedly distanced himself from the Spenceans with whom, as a constitutionalist reformer focussed on a parliamentary agenda, he obviously differed. The effect was to incline them further to the politics of conspiracy. Assassinating a government minister was one tactic mooted.[34] Preparations were laid to foment a *coup d'état* in September 1817 during Bartholomew Fair, an annual occasion long noted for disorder. Confronted by hastily assembled official precautions, the Spenceans' aborted their plan. Yet this plot was serious enough for Lord Sidmouth to compare it with the 1802 Despard conspiracy, when a retired colonel had raised a force among labourers and disaffected troops in London, apparently intending to act in concert with Irish rebels and the French authorities.[35]

The Government, concerned to protect its intelligence sources, took no action against those involved. It was smarting, not only from the exposure of a plausible *agent provocateur* involved in the previous December's Spa Fields meeting, but also from far more damaging revelations about the contribution of one of its agents to a disastrous attempted rising, centred on the north Derbyshire village of Pentrich in June, the timing – and perhaps the actual occurrence – of which was the agent's responsibility.[36] It was Thistlewood himself who now invoked Despard, suggesting that the mass assassination of the Privy Council should be their objective. Another prominent Spencean, painter and decorator John George, agreed: 'the best signal would be to assassinate some leading characters – that would set all going.'[37] It was the practice of Lord Liverpool's ministers to take turns in hosting dinners for the Cabinet at which the general direction of government business was discussed. It was these dinners that were soon identified as the likely target for precipitate violence.

It was about this time that perhaps the most notorious of all government informers was introduced into the ranks of London ultra-radicalism, George Edwards. Edwards was a modeller whose business in Eton allegedly thrived on the sale of busts of an unpopular headmaster for use in target practice by disaffected pupils. His brother William was a City of London police officer and *bona fide* Spencean and through him Edwards was commissioned to produce a bust of Spence. He then moved to London, into premises recently vacated by Hone and next door to Carlile.[38] Meanwhile the burgeoning politicisation of England's manufacturing districts during 1819 strengthened Spencean resolve.[39] As 16 August 1819 drew near, Edwards told the Home Office that London's conspirators looked 'with great Anxiety to the Manchr. Meeting on Monday, where they expect the Row to begin, and this they look upon as the Signal to begin.'[40]

The Government's determination to support the actions of the magistracy and yeomanry at Peterloo was doubtless stiffened by the knowledge that the security of the capital might have depended upon events in Manchester. For their part Thistlewood, Preston, John George and their associates were galvanised by Peterloo. This was 'the Revolution begun in blood', 'high treason committed against the people'. In the previous chapter we glimpsed Allen Davenport comparing 'the present time to the French Revolution', and concluding 'we must arm ourselves as they did'. Davenport was one of the most cerebral of the Spenceans (and one of Spence's earliest biographers) but even he now advocated action over words: 'war ... has already been declared against us, why then should we hesitate, for my part I am ready now.'[41] In mid-October Thistlewood visited Leicester and Manchester, while others worked the beershops and taprooms of London's poorest districts, particularly targeting Irish labourers. In Lambeth a veteran United Irishman, Dennis Shaw, was reported as mustering fifty to sixty

Irish labourers.[42] An Irish associate of John George's son Robert, 'who had acted in the [1798] Irish Rebellion', boasted of being able to raise 500 men in a few hours, and 5,000 in a few days.[43] At the Soho 'chapel' of Spencean Robert Wedderburn, the son of a Jamaican slave, armed drilling took place after services. This Soho contingent joined others to drill before dawn on Primrose Hill and other locations on the capital's fringes. Thistlewood, now the undisputed leader of the conspiracy, declared that 'he depends more on Wedderburn's division for being armed than all the rest'.[44] Wedderburn brought a new rhetorical flourish to the conspirators: he likened slave masters to cotton masters, and enslaved black people to oppressed Britons: 'Before Six Months were over there would be Slaughter in England for their Liberty.'[45]

This was the immediate context of Henry Hunt's denunciation of simultaneous public meetings and his claim that spies were to be found among the capital's radicals. Thistlewood took the insinuation personally and the rift with Hunt became very public.[46] A London meeting on 1 November was the sole remnant of the proposed simultaneous meetings. William Davidson, another metropolitan radical of Caribbean slave descent, made an incendiary speech calling on all present to arm themselves before attending any demonstrations. However, many provincial reformers hitherto prepared to follow the Londoners' lead were falling away. So the latter fell back on metropolitan resources, agitating trade societies and sending Thistlewood to stir up crowds at the Lord Mayor's inauguration.[47] He was now utterly convinced that clandestine action was necessary. The realisation (following the speech from the throne at the opening of Parliament on 23 November) that large political meetings would shortly be rendered illegal reinforced this argument. Then, Watson, of all the conspiratorial group the one most inclined to persist with constitutional agitation, was arrested and imprisoned for debt (ironically this stemmed from the costs of the metropolitan reception for Hunt after Peterloo). Without Watson's restraining influence, the allure of precipitate violence was hard to resist.

This, however, did not mean that metropolitan conspiracy developed in a vacuum. Despite Hunt's best efforts, contact between Thistlewood's circle and the provinces was considerable. Many provincial activists were impatient with Hunt (and he had always attracted less support in Scotland). There were 'Unions' in Carlisle, Glasgow, Manchester, Nottingham and Yorkshire. Placards alerting the provinces to a London rally on 24 November, to consider the Regent's speech at the opening of Parliament, were sent into the midlands and north. At least one Lancashire delegate was present on the 24th, returning north via Nottingham to report to radicals there.[48] Monday 13 December was fixed for simultaneous meetings, with the intention that these would initiate a rising. Intelligence of this was taken so seriously by the Government that all army leave was cancelled and extensive military patrols mounted, especially in Glasgow.[49] So effective was this precaution that the meetings in their turn were cancelled, though not before two or three hundred men, armed with pikes, had marched from neighbouring villages into the Stirlingshire town of Kilsyth. 'Finding all quiet there, they retreated – & the Troops being all at Glasgow, there was no means of seizing them.'[50] And in Birmingham placards appeared overnight, apparently anticipating news from the north:

> BRITONS arise, and yet be free
> Defend your rights and liberty!
> Boroughmongers long have shar'd the spoil
> The working class shares all the toil;
> Now, or never, strike the blow
> Exert yourself and crush the foe!!![51]

Expectations were so high that London's ultra-radicals met almost nightly into the New Year, expecting news of disturbances in Glasgow or Manchester. Tetlow of Manchester, a linkman between Lancashire and London radicals since the autumn, apparently visited the capital again on 10 January.[52]

There may even have been an element of collusion with Irish conspirators. Two leading London Irishmen, journalist W. E. Andrews and Richard Hayes, a priest, were part of Watson's circle in 1819.[53] When police searched Watson's home in late February, they discovered correspondence with Richard Kearney, of Banagher on the King's County border with Galway. Kearney, the author of a proposal to eliminate the National Debt was reportedly 'very disaffected and desirous of promoting a connection between the Irish Malcontents and the English Radicals', according to the Home Office.[54] Irish rumours also had Thistlewood touring Ireland during the winter of 1819–20, in the company of Henry Hunt. The latter detail was patently false, as Sidmouth stressed to Earl Talbot, Ireland's Lord Lieutenant.[55] Surveying the 'truly deplorable' level of violent unrest in Galway in early February 1820, the *Dublin Evening Post* reported, 'we have been told they have expressed themselves as expecting *some work* in England, about Christmas last – and that they are preparing themselves accordingly to take part'. The same report referred to 'English Pedlars' touring rural Ireland, stirring up discontent with exaggerated claims about the strength of English radicals, 'and by the exhibition of certain pocket handkerchiefs, containing historical pictures of the field of Peterloo'. Early in January Castlereagh received anonymous letters purporting to know that 'the Directory or headman in London' would shortly inspect radicals' state of preparedness in Scotland and Ireland. Sidmouth thought this dubious but an anxious Dublin administration wanted the contact pursued 'as he promises to reveal what we are most anxious and yet unable to know, the Leaders of the present disturbances'.[56]

We know the movements and opinions of these conspirators in such detail because of the intelligence network built up by the Government following its humiliating failure to secure convictions after the December 1816 Spa Fields meeting. An important part of the context of the Government's determination to suppress radicalism during the winter of 1819–20 was its detailed knowledge of London's ultra-radicals and (though less securely) the extent and frequency of their contacts with provincial reformers. This was of course knowledge it was impossible to share outside the Cabinet. Ministers also comprehended that not all the conspirators were psychopaths; some at least among them had a deep intellectual commitment to an ideology with a potentially wide appeal at a time of economic dislocation and when Parliament was frequently portrayed by those excluded from it as the tool of a corrupt, landed aristocracy. This meant that, however accurate the knowledge of London conspirators at the micro-level, the broader pattern of sympathy for them nationally (and the mood of the metropolis generally) were much more difficult to gauge.

Government intelligence sources were also precarious. At their centre were four spies: John Shegog's reports were impressionistic and he was never admitted to the core conspiratorial group. The latter strongly suspected it had been infiltrated and when these suspicions were voiced a key informer, John Harknett, promptly disappeared. Then, on 29 December 1819, Robert George shot (but missed) a third spy who unsurprisingly then also disappeared. This left Sidmouth almost entirely dependent on George Edwards.[57] He was effectively Thistlewood's lieutenant; but how long that relationship might persist could not be predicted. There is no doubt that by the New Year the group around Thistlewood were intent upon assassinating the Cabinet and potentially capable of doing so. With intelligence limited to one informer, there was a strong case for the Government seeking to precipitate a crisis that would lead to a high-profile prosecution of at least the key members of the London revolutionary circle. However, the collapse of the Spa Fields treason proceedings was a stark reminder of the perilous consequences of failure.

Ireland

The anxiety of Dublin Castle, noted above, to discover 'the Leaders of the present disturbances' reflected the precarious state of the peace in the west of Ireland in January 1820.[58] When the Home Secretary wrote that 'Accounts from the Country are improving' on 2 January he added an explicit caveat: 'in Ireland Appearances are far from favourable; & it is unfortunate that the Lord Lieutenant is coming away for a few weeks.'[59] The Countess Talbot had died three days before: a grieving Lord Lieutenant, suddenly widowed with twelve children, asked for indefinite compassionate leave to return to England.[60] Symbolic though the viceroyalty had largely become, Talbot's absence soon discomforted both Dublin and London governments. The role of the Lord Lieutenant and his consort in securing a sometimes nervous loyalism should not be overlooked, and Lady Talbot, 'our lamented VICE QUEEN' as Irish papers described her, had been a popular figure.[61]

The Irish challenge to the United Kingdom's Government in 1820 was entirely different from that which it faced in Britain. There was little commonality between popular opinion in Ireland and Britain. British radical papers had little circulation in Ireland and even Peterloo had limited impact across the Irish Sea. 'It matters not how many of Hunt's addresses are circulated through Ireland', William Gregory, the permanent Under Secretary at Dublin Castle and the senior Irish civil servant, told the Home Office the week after Peterloo. 'The lower orders here have no feelings in common with the same class in England; the national hatred is much too strong to make them rejoice ... whether the people or the government are successful.'[62] Yet at the same time agitation to repeal the Union and restore the Dublin Parliament was scanty; its recent abolition could not be presented as an enforced transition to British rule, dominated as the Dublin institution had been by the Anglo-Irish ascendancy. Even the agitation for Roman Catholic emancipation was quiescent in 1819–20. The last emphatic attempt to secure it at Westminster had been made by Henry Grattan in 1813. Since then the MP for Dublin had made some headway in securing parliamentary sympathy for the measure (his 1819 motion that a committee be formed to examine the issue had been lost by only two votes in a packed Commons). However, Grattan's willingness to concede powers of veto over senior appointments in any restored Roman Catholic Church to the newly created State of the United Kingdom hugely eroded his reputation in the eyes of younger, more militant Irish politicians. When Grattan died, aged 73, in June 1820, his interment in Westminster Abbey was symbolic of his assimilation to the unionist perspective. It was to be a further three years before the rising star of Irish politics, the Dublin lawyer Daniel O'Connell, founded the Catholic Association and in doing so began to redraw the map of Irish politics.[63] Until then, Irish opposition to the Union offered little that fundamentally challenged the Government. Instead the challenge of Ireland was rooted in the micro-politics of some of its poorest communities.

To understand this some contextual history is necessary. The defining division within Ireland at this time was arguably not that between north and south, nor Protestant and Catholic, but rather between east and west. In the west the Irish language prevailed and religion – even Roman Catholicism – at least in its orthodox observance was significantly weaker compared with the Anglicised east.[64] The early nineteenth century had seen an acceleration of the English language and print culture in Ireland. But the more rugged landscapes of Connacht proved less amenable to penetration by British commodity culture or printed media. In 1840, when the first official survey of literacy in Ireland was compiled, it revealed 72 per cent of the population of Connacht could neither read nor write; in Galway and Mayo the proportion was 85 per cent. English observers, and indeed many educated Irish, regarded these people with disdain, but this was a *pre-literate* rather than an *illiterate* society, and its rich oral culture belied the stereotypes of endemic ignorance and deprivation associated with illiteracy.[65]

In the west of Ireland the pace of both agricultural and road improvement was sluggish.[66] A complicating short-term factor, glimpsed in Chapter 1, was the typhus epidemic in 1816–19. A second short-term complication was the agricultural depression of 1819–20. Irish farming had partially recovered from the immediate post-war recession but the respite was temporary and there were sharp falls in meat, dairy and grain prices from the autumn of 1819. Prices at the great livestock fair at Ballinasloe, Galway, in October 1820 were reported as 30 per cent below the previous year's, with perhaps a third of all cattle unsold. Meanwhile a good Irish harvest in 1819 had depressed the prices of grain.[67] In an attack on land owners, the moderate-Catholic *Dublin Evening Post* predicted these price falls were 'destined to teach them a lesson which they can never forget'.[68]

However the west was not economically inert. A gradual shift in letting practice was driving up the rents of conacre, the potato grounds from which landless labourers (with the help of otherwise under-employed wives and children) could derive a reasonable subsistence. In Roscommon, conacre resulted in what the Marquess of Sligo (a leading Ascendancy figure in Connacht) described as 'exorbitant' rents, driving the people to 'despair, famine, & misery of the highest degree'.[69] Even the head of the Roscommon Peace Proclamation force, an ex-army major who fervently believed disturbances were entirely political and sectarian in character, conceded that annual conacre rents, at five to seven guineas ($£5.25–£7.35$) per acre (0.4 hectares), greatly exceeded the average rents in the county which he estimated at thirty shillings ($£1.50$) per acre. 'There are no Manufactories of any description in this part of the Country', he added and seasonal, if not permanent, migration was the lot of many young Connacht men.[70]

Simultaneously, creeping commercialisation of livestock farming was depressing demand for labour and further depleting the acreage available for conacre. These developments were taking place against the background of landowners' reluctance to adjust rent downward to reflect post-war economic conditions. *Pro rata* the size of their plots, small cultivators also needed to set aside a greater proportion of their income for rent than those with larger holdings. Tithes payable to the Church of Ireland were similarly out of a kilter with contemporary prices and also favoured graziers over cultivators, and thus the poorest subsistence farmers suffered disproportionately. The Archbishop of Tuam may have been exaggerating when he claimed 'no Clergyman in Ireland receives even a twentieth part of his Tytheable produce of the land', but any attempt to collect tithe was likely to see a clergyman 'branded Tyrant, Cruel, oppressive &c &c'.[71] According to the Marquess of Sligo, the peasantry 'feel the tythes are very oppressive to them, as they are collected out of the fag end of their money after rent & other taxes have been extorted from them, probably not in the most lenient way'. His uncle, the Kilkenny MP Denis Browne described tithes as simply 'a tax on the industry and labor of Roman Catholick people'.[72]

One of the first letters received by Dublin Castle in 1820 described a rent strike by the tenantry on a 5,000-acre estate on Galway's sea coast, belonging to Laurence Comyn from Galway town. Livestock that Comyn had taken in distraint of rent had been seized back; cattle from his own herd had been maimed, and an arson attack made on his home. Now Comyn complained, 'all the country openly and forcibly' drove their cattle to graze on his land.[73] Relatively low-level disturbances of this nature were almost endemic in the province of Connacht. However the key note of early 1820 was an escalation in agrarian protests associated with a movement called Ribbonism (named for the red or green ribbons its supporters sometimes wore). In the same week that Comyn wrote, Dublin Castle was informed of an attack on the home of a Church of Ireland minister and seizure of his firearms and the murder of a Galway landowner on an open road in broad daylight, while from Roscommon came news of firearms thefts and a pitched battle as peace proclamation police sought to arrest a prisoner at a village wake.[74]

Who then were the Ribbonmen? During the 1820s the term was applied somewhat indiscriminately to the expression of rural grievances through violent protest. What gave these protests the appearance of coordination, the 'Ribbon System' as contemporaries described it, was the swearing of oaths of allegiance, sometimes forcibly administered in the heat of disturbances themselves, along with hints of coordination from the east or north of the country. In the popular imagination the Ribbonmen were the re-embodiment of the rebels of 1798, acting on the orders of captains who were themselves directed by a shadowy central committee, and pledged to the extinction of Protestantism and British authority in Ireland. The reality was more mundane. For example one 'Ribbonman Capt[n] administering oaths' from the Castle Kelly (Aghrane) area of Galway was described as 'a perfectly illiterate peasant & prior to Christmas when He was sworn, in the most abject poverty, having nothing to recommend him as a Leader but a strong and active body & a stout and daring mind'.[75]

Secret associations were a staple feature of the opaque popular politics of rural Ireland. The *Dublin Evening Post* ridiculed the notion that the Ribbon System was linked in some way to English or French revolutionary conspiracies. Were all France and England content, there would still be 'rustic associations, Moll Doyle's Boys, or Paudeen Gar's Men, or Shanavests, or White Boys, or Ribbonmen in Ireland'. Not five of the past sixty years, claimed the paper, had been without violent rural protest.[76] Many, perhaps most, of the disturbances that beset Connacht and the counties of northern Munster were the work of such pre-existing groups. Doubtless, too, many disturbances were spontaneous. Dublin Castle spoke in terms of Ribbon Societies, supposedly directed by agitators from Dublin. But 'society', as applied to voluntary organisations in the modern sense of the word, conveys nothing of the character of the oath-bound, tightly cohesive yet informal nature of protest groupings in a peasant society.

Ribbon oaths seemed 'to differ in almost every district – nay, in every village', reflecting the strongly oral culture of rural Ireland and the fusion of

Ribbonism with local grievances.[77] But there were consistent themes: an oath found on John Crane, a tenant farmer arrested at Loughglinn, Roscommon, on 1 February, swore to 'dethrone Protestant Kings and Princes, burn Churches [and] cut away Hereticks, all but he that is just and upright in the Catholic faith'. Another Roscommon oath, taken from a prisoner on his committal to gaol in April, spoke of sparing 'Neither Person nor Property of the Protestant Hereticks especially those who feed on the Tenth part of our labour'. This oath also spoke of 'endeavouring to free us from ... the Oppressive Force of George's Laws', whereas Crane's oath spoke only of shoes that pinched for want of liberty. Nor had he been sworn to the often cited Ribbonist promise to 'wade knee deep in Protestant Blood'. In fact Crane had apparently not acknowledged the Ribbon system at all, but rather 'Captain Right', in whose name a number of threats were made along the Galway-Roscommon border in early 1820.[78]

The first Ribbonmen had mobilised to confront Protestant violence in Ulster. The earliest use of the expression, in 1811, specifically used it as 'a new term for U[nited] Irishmen'.[79] Continuities with the Defender tradition that had been central to the Irish Rebellion of 1798 seemed – and to some extent still seem – obvious. Yet this perspective only takes us so far in understanding the phenomenon. Historians' interpretations broadly divide between seeing it as 'a series of local levelling conspiracies', and as an organisation blending 'nationalist, religious and class sentiment'. Ribbonism is also presented as urban in its emphasis and sectarian Catholic and nationalistic in its ideology.[80] However, the temptation to 'read back' these characteristics (especially nationalism), which are essentially those of post-Famine Ribbonism, into agrarian unrest in the 1820s should be resisted. As early as 1824, the Inspector of the Irish Constabulary (who had been County Clare's chief stipendiary magistrate in 1820) drew a careful distinction between 'the system against property, and the ribbon system', telling a parliamentary select committee:

> The persons who made the irruption from Galway ... were called ribbon men certainly: but when I say that, I do not think they were the ribbon men ... the ribbon system was more of a political system than the other.[81]

This 'other', to quote the army's commander in Connacht in 1820, was a struggle that 'appeared to be principally between landlord and tenant' and was 'nothing like disaffection' in the religious or anti-Unionist sense.[82] In his study of social conflict in Roscommon before the Famine, Michael Huggins makes a strong case that the so-called Ribbonism of these years is better understood not through the traditional historiographical optics of nationalism and sectarianism, but rather as the forcible expression of customary 'moral economy' in which popular notions of justice conjoined with radicalism in 'an embryonic repertoire of class, rather than national, affiliation'.[83] (Huggins re-enforces the point by preferring the long-established term for Irish agrarian protestors *whiteboys* to *ribbonists*.) This certainly helps make sense of some aspects of Connacht agrarian protest in 1820, for example complaints against the fees levied by Roman Catholic clergy;[84] the admission that protestors 'have attacked the house[s] of both Protestant and Catholic';[85] the occasional threatening notice disavowing 'that our intention is to destroy our country Protestant men ... we abominate such barbarity'.[86]

The use of blanket terms like 'Ribbonmen' and 'Ribbon System' indicated the deep-rooted mindset of Protestant ascendancy, convinced that agrarian protest was simply a pretext 'the sole, and indeed avowed, objective ... to overturn the present Religion and Government and to establish the Popish Religion'.[87] An inability to comprehend the complex blend of religious-based secrecy, peasant social norms and communal solidarity that underpinned the disturbances meant that even a Catholic sympathiser like Charles Grant was apt to seek evidence for 'system', even when well-placed observers frankly doubted that 'political incendiaries' directed disturbances.[88] As we shall see in Chapter 4, the extent of central direction behind those disturbances which were described as Ribbonism in 1820 is very hard to discern.

Violence in the first weeks of 1820 vividly illustrates the problems confronting the Government. The brief survey of Irish policing in Chapter 1 noted how a month's delay followed the proclamation of Galway districts under Peel's 1814 Act on 21 December 1819. Roscommon, also proclaimed in December, experienced similar problems. Seventy houses were broken into between proclamation and 1 February and ninety-four firearms stolen, few of which were recovered. Five more firearms were taken from Galway parishes adjoining Roscommon in the same period.[89] 'Broken into' hardly conveys the menacing character of these incidents. At Drum, in south-east Roscommon, 'a very considerable number' assembled outside the house of a Mr Bell, 'and drew up in two Ranks, armed either with Pikes or Bayonets when a very well spoken man came in and with great civility demanded his arms which he gave out'. Bell however refused to complain to the authorities 'as he said if it was known he did such a thing he would be murdered'.[90] The home of an Anglican minister at Castleblakeney, Galway, was attacked on 11 January 'by a numerous body of Ribbon-men, about 200 in number'. They broke open the back door and compelled his servants to swear a Ribbon oath. Twelve of them, all carrying guns, then forced their way into his bedroom and 'took away two Guns, & a pistol from me'.[91] An estimated 400 Ribbonmen entered Ballyhannon, Roscommon, and allegedly swore the 'whole town ... gentlemen and even magistrates obeying the summons of these miscreants'.[92]

The most daring act perpetrated in early 1820 was an assassination. On 13 January, while riding on a main road through the Galway parish of Moylough, Edward Brown, 'a young gentleman of some property in this county', was shot dead. Apparently he was mistaken for Moylough's clerical magistrate, the Revd O'Rourke. 'The first feeling excited by it was that of undisguised exultation. When it was found not to be the intended victim, there was some regret;

and a new obligation added to their oaths, "that they should pray for the soul of Browne until O'Rourke's should be sent after it".[93] O'Rourke was forced into hiding, first at Castleblakeney with the High Sherriff of Galway. However a crowd of protestors (allegedly 800-strong) surrounded the house and threatened to demolish it. O'Rourke then escaped under military escort to Tuam where he took refuge in the archbishop's palace. Back in Moylough armed sentries were posted at his home: repelling an attack a few days later, they killed several men.[94] When O'Rourke did finally return he needed permanent military protection.

In a furious letter to Dublin Castle Lord Clonbrock, one of the few major landowners still resident in the area, argued the episode demonstrated that 'every possible advantage has been taken of our unprepared situation in the interval between the application [for] the Police, & their arrival'. Despite troops being rushed to the district, a collapse in the morale of local landowners and their larger tenants was all too obvious: 'these ribbon men find partisans wherever they go, & thus fear of them supersedes all dread of civil & military power, which they begin to think, can no longer be exercised against them.'[95] William Gregory told the Home Office that western Ireland's gentry were leaving their homes and fleeing to nearby towns for security. 'Such as remains in the Country are in a state of Siege with their Doors and Windows barricaded.' Major John Wills, the commander of the Peelers in Roscommon, pleaded with Sir Richard St George not to leave his seat for Dublin, since it might give confidence to the rebellious. Armstrong Kelly of Aghrane in Galway believed a general rising was intended, to level first the established church and then 'make all landed proprietors divide fair with the poor'. Dennis Browne of County Mayo concurred, urging Dublin Castle to 'prepare for a general Rebellion after about two months or perhaps less' (this was on 21 January). 'The Farmers are flying or about to fly' to the towns, he also observed. Browne, a leading loyalist in the 1798 Irish Rebellion, militarised Mayo's border with Galway lest history should 'have to record the rebellion of 1820'.[96] The Church of Ireland's Archbishop of Tuam (a yeomanry captain in 1798) rounded on local magistrates, describing them as unwilling, lacking in judgment and 'afraid of responsibility'.[97] In late February he wrote to the Chief Secretary in despair:

> I feel it is my duty to tell you, that now half the Garrison of Ireland would not put down the system which is established here; Nothing short of the insurrection act will do, and if that does not come soon, it will be ineffective and you will be driven to Martial Law.[98]

The Archbishop's call for the Insurrection Act (1796, revised 1807) was part of a campaign for it to be invoked in Galway, led by a meeting of magistrates at Athenry on 11 February, who declared it 'alone able to check the present rapid progress of disaffection'. One magistrate told Dublin Castle that if it would not implement the measure he personally would travel to London to petition the

Crown for it. Calls for the Act also came from Roscommon and from an anonymous 'Loyal Inhabitant of Ireland'.[99]

Unusually for an anonymous correspondent, the latter was taken very seriously. Amidst a familiar jeremiad about Jesuit 'machinations', 'barbarous outrages' and 'imminent rebellion', the letter voiced stringent criticisms of Chief Secretary Grant for 'feeling no concern for the welfare of the Country'. Since he supported Catholic emancipation, Grant's appointment had always been tinged with controversy. But during Lord Lieutenant Talbot's absence in early 1820 additional anxieties arose. In a correspondence carefully kept from the sight of Home Office officials, Sidmouth wrote to Talbot at his seat in Staffordshire. Talbot in turn took the unusual step of consulting William Gregory. 'It would be a false delicacy to deny that Grant has made Enemies amongst the Gentry of Ireland', Gregory conceded. A lack of punctuality in answering correspondence and attending meetings was part of the problem; rather more was Grant's 'uncalled for and unfounded Encomiums on the Catholic Priesthood'. Gregory offered the reassurance, though, that his superior was now 'sensible of the fatal error with which he undertook the Government' of Ireland and no longer believed that 'Protestant Tyranny and Catholic Slavery' caused Irish unrest.[100] Disconcerted nonetheless, Talbot decided to return to Ireland immediately. 'Every person connected with that Country should be at his post', he told Sidmouth.[101] In a political context where symbol and gesture meant so much, this exchange of correspondence is revealing. Grant never did secure the confidence of the Irish gentry; and the authority of Talbot, preoccupied perhaps by his personal predicament, also began to diminish. The exchange also underlines the responsibilities vested in the Castle's permanent Under Secretary, a point often overlooked in the history of nineteenth-century Ireland.

In his reply to Talbot, Gregory also advised of the difficulties posed by invoking the Insurrection Act. The chief of them was political rather than practical or legal, namely the requirement that the matter be fully debated in, and approved by, both Houses of Parliament. An admission by the Ministry that its security policy in Ireland had failed would always be damaging: to make it in the context of an imminent general election was unthinkable. Yet suddenly at the end of January, this was the circumstance in which Liverpool's Ministry had to operate, due to an event that no government, however prescient or powerful could control: the death of the monarch.

The death of George III

Until 1867 the death of the monarch required that a general election be held within six months. As now, Parliament would also be recalled immediately if not sitting at the time of the monarch's death. Parliament was in recess until 15 February but towards the end of January the news from Windsor Castle was sufficiently disquieting for three of the Government's most talented supporters –

John Wilson Croker, William Huskisson and Robert Peel – to cancel a shooting holiday, anticipating that the King would shortly die and Parliament therefore be recalled. On 28 January the Cabinet was informed the King 'could not survive above a day or two'.[102] At 8.35 the following evening George III died.

In his dotage the King had shed the reputation for controversy and political interference acquired over the first five decades of his reign. 'George the Third will be ranked by posterity among the best and wisest Kings that ever sat upon the throne of England', William Wordsworth averred. In death his reputation for simple personal piety elevated him in popular estimation, while 'his domestic duties were filled with eminent fidelity and uniform tenderness'.[103] The sheer length of his reign meant inevitably that its close was regarded as an epoch-defining moment. 'My real recollections begin with 1820', wrote the republican engraver and poet William Linton in 1894. His earliest memory was the tolling of the great bell of St Paul's Cathedral: 'My father spoke: "The old king is dead."' Harriet Arbuthnot, one of the great nineteenth-century diarists, commenced her diary at this point. In living beyond his eighty-first birthday, George III was most unusual. None of his twelve children who reached adulthood survived to a greater age. The first to die, Edward, Duke of Kent, predeceased his father by a week. Yet even the duke's age at death, fifty-two, exceeded average English life expectancy around this time by a decade.[104] Few Britons had been born other than 'beneath the sceptre of George III' and there were fewer still who had not been 'formed and educated since he began to reign' observed *The Times*. 'No human being ever possessed a claim to such an amount of Veneration, Love and Gratitude as the Sovereign whom we have lost', Sidmouth wrote to Talbot.[105]

Sidmouth had previously served George III as Prime Minister (1801–04) and allowance has to be made for momentarily exaggerated piety and the close regard they had had for each other (George once described him as 'the best friend he has in the world').[106] Sidmouth had additional cause to lament the passing of the monarch. Praise lavished on the Prince Regent as he succeeded to the throne was seldom other than formulaic, as numerous sermons on George III's death reveal. In two sprawling discourses, the ultra-loyalist clergyman Thomas le Mesurier could only pray 'give the [late] King thy judgments, O Lord, and thy righteousness unto the King's son'. Yorkshire Presbyterian minister George Young found numerous parallels between the old monarch and King David, but his hope that George IV would 'like Solomon, be a wise and good prince, inheriting his father's virtues, as well his crown', reads like a mechanical afterthought. Another Yorkshire clergyman failed to mention the new King at all. Sidmouth spoke for most of the Government when he observed to Talbot: 'How much better it is to weep over departed excellence in the nearest & dearest of all connections, than to be harassed by living Profligacy.'[107]

The profligacy of which the Home Secretary complained was threefold. Frugality had not been a keynote in the life of the Prince of Wales and the Government anticipated fraught negotiations around the civil list. On his

Brighton 'palace, or pavilion, or Kremlin, or mosque, for it bears all these names and deserves them' he had lavished well over £150,000 by 1820 (gossip at Court put the figure nearer £700,000).[108] Second, the Regent's life, as the editor of the *Black Book* would later observe, 'if not absolutely rakish, had been that of a splendid voluptuary, who freely indulged in every pleasure that money, high station and a fine person could procure'.[109] This lifestyle was taking its toll: at his accession the Privy Council was forced to convene in the King's private apartments as he had a heavy cold; by 31 January this had developed into pleurisy; by 3 February George IV was himself 'very near dying', Wellington confided to General Beresford. Believing he was breathing his last, the King was persuaded by the Archbishop of Canterbury to be reconciled to his estranged brother, the Duke of Sussex.[110]

However, as well as alienated from his brother, George IV was also estranged from his wife, Caroline. Under no circumstances was reconciliation possible there. This constituted the third and most profound of the problems wrought by the new monarch's personal life and now visited on the Government. Forced to marry in April 1795 by his father, as a condition of liquidating his debts, the Prince of Wales loathed his bride. He was reputedly dead drunk at their wedding. The marriage was also virtually bigamous, for in 1785 the Prince had married Maria Fitzherbert, one of a succession of mistresses, in a ceremony without legal foundation because the bride was a Roman Catholic. In January 1796 Princess Caroline gave birth to the couple's only child, Princess Charlotte, soon after which they permanently separated. Spurned, bored and reckless in roughly equal measures, Caroline had then led a life that managed to scandalise even her husband and in 1806 a parliamentary commission was held to investigate whether she had had any adulterous relationships and any child by them. The commission censured her for indecorous behaviour but established no evidence of adultery. Banished from court during the Regency, and effectively banished too from the company of her daughter (to whose marriage in 1813 she was not even invited), Caroline had little incentive to reform. Her behaviour certainly became more eccentric, and quite possibly adulterous.

The implications of this, especially after Princess Charlotte died following the stillbirth of her only child in 1816, were considerable. George III had no legitimate grandchild; there was thus no direct line of succession beyond the Prince Regent who was almost certain to seek a divorce once he had the authority as monarch to do so. Even before regaining his strength during the illness that so nearly killed him within days of his accession, George IV did exactly that. A Government facing incipient rebellion in western Ireland and revolutionary conspiracy in the capital suddenly had to contend with a new challenge from within the very citadel of the State.

Notes

1 DRO, 152M/C/1820/0Z (letter to Bathurst, 2 January).

2 BL, Add. Mss 38741 fol. 315 (Canning to Huskisson, 14 August [*sic*, an error for October] 1819).

3 The most accurate summary of the six acts is that in A. Aspinall and E. A. Smith (eds), *English Historical Documents, Volume XI: 1783–1832* (London: Eyre & Spottiswode, 1959), pp. 335–41.

4 C. D. Yonge (complier), *The Life and Administration of Robert Banks, Second Earl of Liverpool* (Macmillan, 1868), vol. 3, p. 341.

5 E. Phipps (ed.), *Memoirs of the Political and Literary Life of Robert Plumer Ward* (Edinburgh: Murray: 1850), vol. 2, p. 39.

6 BL, Add. Mss 30109 fol. 56 (Grey to Wilson, 24 October 1819).

7 *Diary and Correspondence of Charles Abbot, Lord Colchester, edited by his son Charles, Lord Colchester* (London: Murray, 1861), vol. 3, p. 103, quoting letter from Henry Bankes (MP for Corfe Castle), 31 December 1819; see also p. 117, (Bankes' letter, 15 February).

8 *Morning Chronicle,* 22 July 1819.

9 *Morning Chronicle*, 10 November 1819; Ward, *Memoirs*, p. 37.

10 *Cobbett's Weekly Political Register,* 12 June 1818; see also J. Belchem, *'Orator Hunt': Henry Hunt and English Working-Class Radicalism* (Oxford: Oxford University Press, 1985), pp. 78–84.

11 I. Prothero, *Artisans and Politics in Early Nineteenth-Century London: John Gast and his Times* (Folkestone: Dawson, 1979), pp. 120–1.

12 *Manchester Observer*, 23 October 1819.

13 J. Parkhill, *History of Paisley* (Paisley: Stewart, 1857), pp. 46–9; G. Pentland, *The Spirit of the Union: Popular Politics in Scotland, 1815–20* (London: Pickering & Chatto, 2011), pp. 59–61.

14 *Manchester Observer*, 14 Aug 1819.

15 *Black Dwarf,* 6 August 1819.

16 TNA, HO 102/32/7 (27 December 1819).

17 TNA, HO 102/32/197b (25 February).

18 N. Murray, *The Scottish Hand Loom Weavers, 1790–1850: A Social History* (Edinburgh: John Donald, 1978), pp. 220–1.

19 Letter to John Morritt, 17 December 1819, printed in H. J. C. Grierson (ed.), *The Letters of Sir Walter Scott* (Edinburgh: Constable 1932–7), vol. 6, pp. 57–8.

20 DRO, 152M/C/1820/OH/48 (13 January).

21 National Library of Scotland, MS 1054, fol. 1073, quoted in M. Fry, *The Dundas Despotism* (Edinburgh: Edinburgh University Press, 1992), p. 339.

22 Ward, *Memoirs*, pp. 22–3.

23 TNA, HO 102/32/17 (4 January); HO 33/2/153 (3 April).

24 Ward, *Memoirs*, p. 43.

25 TNA, HO 102/32/80–88, report of Maj.-Genl Sir Thomas Bradford (January). See also HO 102/32 fols 132, 150 and 183 (1, 11 and 18 February).

26 M. Chase, *'The People's Farm': English Radical Agrarianism, 1775–1840* (Oxford: Oxford University Press, 1988), p. 99: the account of Spencean activity that follows is drawn from this book, pp. 99–120; see also Prothero, *Artisans and Politics*, pp. 99–131.

27 TNA, HO 42/156 (1 December 1816).

28 Chase, *People's Farm*, pp. 97–8.

29 TNA, HO 41/156 (7 December 1816); F. K. Donnelly, and J. L. Baxter, 'Sheffield and the revolutionary tradition, 1791–1820', in Sidney Pollard and Colin Holmes, *Essays in the Economic and Social History of South Yorkshire* (Sheffield: South Yorkshire County Council, 1976), pp. 103–6.

30 TNA, HO 40/4/1[2] (Chippendale to Fletcher, 3 December 1816).

31 Chase, *People's Farm*, pp. 98–9.

32 M. Chase, 'Thomas Evans', in J. Bellamy and J. Saville (eds), *Dictionary of Labour Biography* (Basingstoke: Macmillan, 1987), vol. 8, pp. 59–69; *Manchester Observer*, 19 February.

33 TNA, HO 42/158 (29 January and 7 February 1817); Chase, *People's Farm*, p. 101.

34 TNA, HO 40/7[1] fol. 1929, report of J. Shegoe, 30 June 1817.

35 G. Pellew (ed.), *The Life and Correspondence of the Rt Hon H. Addington, First Viscount Sidmouth* (London: Murray, 1847), vol. 3, p. 200.

36 Malcolm Chase, 'Richards, W. J. (1774?–1827)', *Oxford Dictionary of National Biography* (Oxford: Oxford University Press, 2004); online edn, Jan 2008 [http://0-www.oxforddnb.com.wam.leeds.ac.uk/view/article/57111], accessed 6 June 2012.

37 Chase, *People's Farm*, pp. 106-7.

38 R. M. Healey, 'Edwards, George (1787?–1843)', *Oxford Dictionary of National Biography* (Oxford: Oxford University Press, 2004); online edn, Jan 2008 [http://0-www.oxforddnb.com.wam.leeds.ac.uk/view/article/38374], accessed 20 June 2011.

39 TNA, HO 42/189 (report of W-----r, 14 July 1819) [i.e. Windsor, the alias of Edwards].

40 TNA, HO 42/191 (6 August 1819).

41 TNA, TS 11/202 fol. 872; HO 42/195 (29 September 1819); HO 42/197 (18 October 1819).

42 TNA, HO 42/196 (13 October 1819); HO 42/191, n.d; Prothero, *Artisans and Politics*, p. 115.

43 TNA, HO 44/5 fol. 32 (information of Emanuel Francis, 1 March).

44 TNA, HO 42/197 (18 October 1819).

45 TNA, HO 42/195 (18 September 1819).

46 Prothero, *Artisans and Politics*, p. 122. Their correspondence was reprinted in, e.g. *Lancaster Gazette*, 6 November; *Morning Post*, 25 October; *Newcastle Courant*, 30 October.

47 TNA, HO 42/198 (9 November 1819).

48 Prothero, *Artisans and Politics*, pp. 124–5; Belchem, *'Orator Hunt'*, p. 129 believes this radical was probably an informer.

49 TNA, HO 42/200 (correspondence from Major-General Byng, 2–12 December 1819); DRO, 152M/C/1819/OH/123 (8 December 1819).

50 National Library of Scotland, Melville Letters 1817–19, MS 10, fol. 205 (14 December 1819), quoted in Pentland, *Spirit of the Union*, p. 90.

51 TNA, HO 42/201 (14 December 1819).

52 TNA, HO 42/199 (25, 28 December 1819 and 26 January 1820); HO 44/4/3 (10 January 1820); Prothero, *Artisans and Politics*, p. 128.

53 Prothero, *Artisans and Politics*, p. 143.

54 TNA, HO 79/7 (Hobhouse to Grant, 28 February); NAI CSO/LB/419 (28 February); R. Kearney, *A Plan for the Payment of the National Debt, and for the Immediate Reduction of Taxation* (Dublin: Charles, 1816). The author argued for a single paper-based currency issued by a state-owned 'Imperial Bank' covering both countries.

55 TNA, HO 100/198/283 (6 March); *Courier*, 18 January; DRO 152M/C/1820/OH/32 (Sidmouth to Talbot, 23 March).

56 *Dublin Evening Post*, 8 February; NAI, CSO/LB/419, pp. 288–91.

57 Prothero, *Artisans and Politics*, p. 128.

58 NAI, CSO/LB/419, pp. 288–91.

59 DRO, 152M/C/1820/0Z (2 January).

60 DRO, 152M/C/1820/OZ (Sidmouth to Bathurst, 2 January).

61 E.g. *Chute's Western Herald, or Kerry Advertizer*, 10 January and *Freeman's Journal*, 5 January.

62 TNA, HO 100/197 (Gregory to Hobhouse, 22 August 1819).

63 F. O'Ferrall, *Catholic Emancipation: Daniel O'Connell and the Birth of Irish Democracy 1820–1830* (Dublin: Gill and Macmillan, 1985), pp. 1–29.

64 K. T. Hoppen, 'Nationalist mobilisation and governmental attitudes: geography, politics and nineteenth-century Ireland', in L. Brockliss and D. Eastwood (eds), *A Union of Multiple Identities: The British Isles, c. 1750–c. 1850* (Manchester: Manchester University Press, 1997), pp. 163–4, 166.

65 K. A. Miller, *Emigrants and Exiles: Ireland and the Irish Exodus to North America* (Oxford: Oxford University Press, 1985), pp. 70–1.

66 C. Ó Gráda, *Ireland Before and After the Famine: Explorations in Economic History, 1800–1925* (Manchester: Manchester University Press, second edn 1993), pp. 82–7.

67 J. S. Donnelly, Jr, *Captain Rock: The Irish Agrarian Rebellion of 1821–24* (Cork: Collins, 2009), pp. 24–5, 53–6.

68 *Dublin Evening Post*, 5 October 1820.

69 NAI, SOC 1/2175/6 (Sligo, 19 January).

70 NAI, SOC 1/2176/49 (8 June).

71 NAI, SOC 1/2171/47 (9 February).

72 NAI, SOC 1/2175/6 (Sligo, 19 January) and 9 (Browne, 23 January).

73 NAI, SOC 1/2171/2 (13 January).

74 NAI, SOC 1/2171/1 and 2 (both 13 January), SOC 1/2176/1 and 3 (14 and 10 January).

75 NAI, SOC 1/2172/54 and 62 (2 and 11 April).

76 *Dublin Evening Post*, 7 March.

77 *Dublin Evening Post*, 8 February.

78 NAI, SOC 2176/9 (6 February); SOC 2176/37 [April]; SOC 2176/17 (24 February, enclosing Captain Right letters). Further 1820 oaths and catechisms can be found in SOC 2171/ 41 (Galway, 5 February), 2177/3 (Dublin, 15 March) and 2183/3 (County Clare, 26 January).

79 Belfast informer's letter, quoted in T. Garvin, 'Defenders, Ribbonmen and others: underground political networks in pre-Famine Ireland', in C. H. E. Philpin (ed.), *Nationalism and Popular Protest in Ireland* (Cambridge: Cambridge University Press, 1987), 232.

80 Garvin, 'Defenders, Ribbonmen and others', pp. 221–4; M. R. Beames, 'The Ribbon societies: lower-class nationalism in pre-Famine Ireland', in Philpin (ed.), *Nationalism*, pp. 245–63.

81 *PP* 1825 (20) SC State of Ireland, evidence of George Warbuton, p. 137.

82 *PP* 1825 (181) SC State of Ireland, evidence of General C. B. Gerton, p. 221.

83 M. Huggins, *Social Conflict in Pre-Famine Ireland: The Case of County Roscommon* (Dublin: Four Courts Press, 2007), p. 146, see also pp. 93–7, and J. W. Knott, 'Land, kinship and identity: the cultural roots of agrarian agitation in eighteenth- and nineteenth-century Ireland', *Journal of Peasant Studies*, 12:1 (1984).

84 NAI, SOC 2188/10 (protest notice, 27 May). See also *PP* 1825 (181) SC State of Ireland, evidence of A. R. Blake, p. 99; and *PP* 1825 (129) SC State of Ireland, evidence of Oliver Kelly (Roman Catholic Archbishop of Tuam), p. 259: 'They

generally complained of tithes, taxes, grand jury cesses, vestry cesses, the payment of Catholic clergy, the high price of land: all those things together.'

85 NAI, SOC 2176/49 (8 June).

86 NAI, SOC 2188/10 (protest notice, 27 May).

87 NAI, SOC 2176/49 (Wills to Grant, 8 June).

88 NAI, SOC 2188/12 (letter from Lieutenant General Sir Edward Paget, 5 April).

89 NAI, SOC 2188/4 (8 February).

90 NAI, SOC 2176/5 (28 January).

91 NAI, SOC 2171/1 (13 January).

92 NAI, SOC 2175/1 (18 January).

93 *Dublin Evening Post*, 20 January and 8 February; NAI SOC 2171/3 and 16 (13 and 20 January).

94 NAI, SOC 2171/1/18 (Gately to O'Rourke, enclosed in 25 January); SOC 2171/6 (16 January).

95 NAI, SOC 2171/6 (16 January).

96 TNA, HO 100/198 fol. 138–9 (14 February); NAI, SOC 2175/1–2, 8–9 (15, 18, 20–21 January) and 2171/28 (29 January).

97 NAI, SOC 2176/7 (31 January), 2173/7 (17 January); Timothy C. F. Stunt, 'Trench, Power Le Poer (1770–1839)', *Oxford Dictionary of National Biography* (Oxford: Oxford University Press, 2004); online edition [http://0-www.oxforddnb.com.wam.leeds.ac.uk/view/article/27701], accessed 22 June 2011.

98 NAI, SOC 2171/80 (27 February).

99 NAI, SOC 2171/54 and 61 (13 and 17 February); TNA, HO 100/198/162 (20 February); DRO, 152M/C/1820/OI/19 (11 February).

100 This correspondence was kept with Sidmouth's family papers and is now in Devon Records Office: 152M/C/1820/OI/19 ('A Lover of Ireland', 11 February) and 152M/C/1820/OI/20 (Gregory to Talbot, 22 February). See also 152M/C/1820/OI/21 and 22 (letters between Sidmouth and Talbot, 26 and 28 February).

101 TNA, HO 100/198/160 (24 February).

102 L. J. Jennings (ed.), *The Croker Papers: The Correspondence and Diaries of the Late Right Honourable John Wilson Croker … 1809 to 1830* (London: Murray, 1884), vol. 1, p. 156; Ward, *Memoirs*, p. 50.

103 Wordsworth, letter to Lord Lonsdale, 2 February, reprinted in *The Letters of William and Dorothy Wordsworth … The Middle Years, Part II: 1812–1820*, arr. and ed. by E. de Selincourt, rev. and ed. by M. Moorman and A. G. Hill (Oxford: Oxford University Press, 1970), p. 579; More, quoted in A. Stott, *Hannah More: The First Victorian* (Oxford: Oxford University Press, 2003), p. 317.

104 W. J. Linton, *Memories* (London: Lawrence & Bullen, 1895), p. 1; E. A. Wrigley and R. S. Schofield, *The Population History of England, 1541–1871* (Cambridge: Cambridge University Press, 1989), pp. 228–36.

105 *The Times*, 31 January; DRO, 152M/C/1820/OI/8 (3 February).

106 P. Ziegler, *Addington: A Life of Henry Addington, First Viscount Sidmouth* (London: Collins, 1965), pp. 222–3.

107 T. Le Mesurier, *Two Sermons Preached in the Parish Church of Haughton-le-Skerne … on Occasion of the Death of Our Late Beloved Sovereign George the Third* (Durham: Humble, 1820), p. 43; G. Young, *Parallel Between King David and King George: A Sermon Preached in Cliff Lane Chapel, Whitby, February 16, 1820* (Whitby: Clerk, 1820), p. 28; [H. Elsley], *A Discourse on the Demise of His Late Most Excellent Majesty, King George III* (Ripon: Lodge, 1820); DRO, 152M/C/1820/OH/67 (13 February).

108 C. Hibbert, *George IV: Regent and King* (London: Allen Lane, 1973), pp. 125; P. Quennell (ed.), *The Private Letters of Princess Lieven to Prince Metternich, 1820–1826* (London: Murray, 1937), pp. 22, 76.

109 J.Wade, *British History, Chronologically Arranged*, 3rd edn (London: Bohn, 1844), p. 779.

110 *Despatches, Correspondence, and Memoranda of Field Marshal Arthur, Duke of Wellington, K.G., edited by his son* (London: Murray, 1867), vol. 1, p. 98; *Private Letters of Princess Lieven*, p. 15 (letter to Metternich, 16 February).

3 Politics high and low

Communal celebration of significant occasions was one of the invisible ties that bound British society together. In England the parish church was often at the centre of such commemorations. The ringing of lengthy peals of bells was the norm on the accession of the monarch, on his birthday and on 5 November to commemorate the deliverance of King and Parliament from the 1605 Gunpowder Plot. The death of George III and his son's accession were marked across Britain, though they went largely unheralded in Ireland, except in Dublin. Thus on the afternoon of 16 February, as George III was laid to rest in the Chapel of Windsor Castle, Guisborough, a town of some 1,900 souls on the northern edge of the Yorkshire Moors, marked the occasion with a muffled peal of the parish church bells, costing 9s (45 pence, plus ale for the ringers costing 1s 6d [7½ pence]). A princely £6 3s 4½d (£6.17) had been spent for mourning drapery in the parish church, hanging which had cost 1s 6d. The Guisborough bellman was paid 6d (2½ pence) for 'calling shops closing'. All expenditure was met from the churchwardens' accounts, that is from the rates levied primarily for poor relief.[1] Guisborough's piety may usefully be contrasted with the levity at South Cave in the East Riding, as it celebrated George IV's accession two weeks before. According to an affectionate account by the local clergyman, a procession made its way at noon from the Fox and Coney to the Market Cross, headed by a band, a herald, a 'bum bailiff', and 'Bobby Todd, with a Cask of Ale in a Wheelbarrow' bringing up the rear. The herald (a local auctioneer, selected for being 'in the habit of haranguing') having read the proclamation,

> three Huzzas were given and the populace most loyally began to pay their respects to the Ale Barrel ... Nearly five pounds were subscribed and loyalty was kept up at all Public houses until a late hour. The day passed over in harmony and we felt as satisfied with his Majesty as ever people were with a king, excepting some discontented spirits, who were resolved, after having freely sacrificed to Sir John Barleycorn, to have a King of their own making, and whether by Accident or choice

it happened that Mr. Wm, Cressey, attained to that honour, and was chaired and proclaimed with three times three. But sometimes when at the summit of Ambition, we are nearest to misfortune, and so it happened to King Cress, for the multitude, who are never pleased long together, tumbled his Majesty into the Beck, and repeated their cheering.[2]

Across the country, proclaiming the new King constituted the first legal open-air meetings since the six acts came into force. Some were noticeably more solemn than South Cave: at Truro Yeomanry, dragoons, military and naval officers, constables with staves, freemasons, the Mayor, alderman and capital burgesses processed round the town, halting six times for the town clerk to read the proclamation. The Chief Secretary of Ireland, grappling with incipient insurrection, recorded with relief 'the astonishing manner' of the crowded Dublin streets, 'nothing was more striking than the good humour and loyalty of the people'.[3] However, crowds in many English cities responded ambivalently. In Manchester, 'the people shouted "huzza" but in a very feeble manner for it was a wet, uncomfortable day and George IV is not very popular'. The Manchester Yeomanry, assembled in public for the very first time since Peterloo 'received from the people hisses and revilings in abundance'. The procession in Sheffield was 'rather poor … and some hissing. The yeomanry were very unpopular.'[4] At London's Royal Exchange 'the crowds hardly joined in at all with the cry of "God save the King!" according to a Home Office Under Secretary, 'in spite of the example set by the Officers of State and the Judges who waved their hats and shouted most loyally'. Applause was chiefly reserved for a man waving an old shirt from a ladder precariously placed on a nearby roof.[5] Within days one stretch of Chester's medieval city walls was painted with graffiti: 'No George the 4th'; 'No Damned Royal Crown', 'No Damned King', 'A short Reign & a bloady one: Behead him'.[6]

Irreverence and truculence were much in evidence across the country, although Liverpool's ministers inclined to think the popular mood was quietening: the freezing cold combined with the six acts may have made it so. However evidence of continuing and profound disquiet concerning the moral probity of political authority was hardly fugitive. A spate of prosecutions in the early weeks of 1820 had failed to reverse 'the unsparing circulation of blasphemous and seditious works'. Having been remanded in custody for five months, one Exeter bookseller was gaoled for nine more for selling Hone's parody of the Anglican catechism (a work for which the publisher himself, as we saw in Chapter 1, was acquitted of blasphemy). Two Oxford printers, father and son, were gaoled for two and six months for selling *Sherwin's Political Register*. A Bolton bookseller was gaoled for reprinting from *Sherwin's* a contentious *Letter to the soldiers on the state of the country, and showing the means that were used to separate them from the people*. Simply selling Part 12 of the *Black Book* earned a Birmingham vendor a spell in gaol for libelling the Prince Regent. In late February a special commission was established at Westminster Hall to try ten prosecutions for selling Carlile's *Republican* and one for selling *Sherwin's*.[7]

In all some ninety prosecutions for political libel, the majority against humble vendors, were brought in 1819–20. More than half were successful. On top of these (as we saw in Chapter 1) *Cobbett's Weekly Political Register* only just survived in the new circumstances created by the six acts; and the outspoken Glaswegian journal *Spirit of the Union* folded after its second issue of the New Year. However, Carlile persevered doggedly in publishing his *Republican* while instalments of the *Black Book* and the spirited weekly *Black Dwarf* appeared unabated. The *Black Book* had entered the New Year clad in a blaze of advertisements for its publisher Fairburn's *Manchester Massacre: An Authentic History of the Atrocious Proceedings and Magisterial and Yeomanry Butchery at Manchester*, and declaiming that '*Taxation without Representation is* UNCONSTITUTIONAL'. However, as the six acts took effect, the *Black Book* faltered: its normally lively wrappers were suddenly populated with innocuous advertisements for games compendia and publications of 'crim. con.' proceedings (prosecutions brought by aggrieved husbands for criminal conversation, i.e. adultery). But then, on 22 January, an advertisement announced Fairburn's prescient decision to publish in instalments *The Book*, the text of the 1806 'delicate investigation' by Parliament into the conduct of the Princess of Wales. A week later George III died and the Princess was Queen. The *Black Book's* final instalment advertised *An ode to George the Fourth, and Caroline his Wife, now Queen consort of Great Britain* and *The R____L Divorce, or the Sultan and the Sophy*. Inside the author, John Wade, concluded his assault on a government opposed 'to the opinion and interests of the community' and 'the corruption by which the system is supported from the resources by which England might be restored to prosperity and happiness'.[9]

Black Dwarf espoused the same arguments as *Black Book* but did so argumentatively and satirically rather than through the progressive accumulation of largely unadorned evidence that Wade preferred. Though forced to change its format and increase its price from fourpence to sixpence ('according to the new act, which seems to imagine that those who cannot *spare* sixpence ought not to be allowed to read'), *Black Dwarf* persisted with its extraordinary fusion of muscular political analysis and almost surreal satire: 'I find [it] in every hovel', wrote one appalled Ayrshire landowner.[10] The 12 January issue commenced with 'the dedication of the new series to boroughmongers and ministers of the crown!!!' Then came the regular letter 'from the Black Dwarf in London, to the Yellow Bonze at Japan' (built on the ongoing conceit that the Black Dwarf was a visitor to Britain from the orient). Extracts from Bentham and Cobbett and a string of pieces arguing the case for abstaining from excisable commodities followed, and next 'The Ministers only worse copies of bad originals', based on excerpts from a 1793 attack on Pitt. Underlining its extensive circulation, Sunderland reformers contributed a letter setting out plans to boycott produce from farmers who belonged to the local yeomanry. Comedy closed the number. 'Friends Cas and Can, Sagacious Sid and little Van', milked mirth from the duel that Castlereagh and Canning had fought in 1809, from Sidmouth's reputed humourlessness and the perceived Cabinet lightweight Nicholas Vansittart, Chancellor of the Exchequer.[11]

One would expect radical publishers to fight their corner against a governmental system they believed rested on self-interest and incipient tyranny. A more surprising indicator of how much public opinion was inclining away from loyalism was developments in the theatre. Theatres had assumed a new significance since the six acts prohibited open-air assemblies and also restricted indoor meetings. Theatres had always been sites of animated and often boisterous comment upon current affairs – the main reason why the repertoire and character of dramatic entertainment was hedged-round with restrictions. The performance of plays in their entirety was the monopoly of the theatres royal, established under patents issued by the Lord Chamberlain (an officer of the royal household). This laid open the possibility of prosecuting 'illegitimate' theatres that infringed on the monopoly by not confining their presentations to innocuous musical entertainments. Meanwhile dramas produced in the patent theatres had to be submitted to the Lord Chamberlain's examiner of plays for approval. In theory this should have meant that illegitimate theatre was limited to burlesque, pantomime and variety shows, while in return for their monopoly the theatres royal accepted stifling interference in anything that might be construed as political comment. An often quoted instance of the Lord Chamberlain's interference was the prohibition against performing Shakespeare's *King Lear* during the final years of George III's life, lest the depiction of a mad monarch on the stage drew uncomfortable parallels with the present.

There was a paradox in relying upon scrutiny of the written word to police dramatic presentations. Neither production values nor the individualistic nuances that actors brought to their performances were easily scrutinised, and the capacity of audiences to place their own interpretations upon a production was widely attested and beyond reach. An 1832 parliamentary select committee on dramatic literature interviewed many witnesses whose reputations had been forged during the Regency. 'Sentences which have been uttered in old plays have been taken up at the time they were performing, which neither the proprietors nor the actors thought of till the audience caught at them', the committee was told. 'There is a tendency in the audience to force passages never meant by the author into political meanings', the playwright Thomas Morton observed.[12] Proprietors and managers, however, were not the unwitting dupes of excitable audiences. Another witness in 1832, proprietor of London's Royal Coburg Theatre, flatly denied that it would ever benefit any theatre 'to meddle with political matters'. Yet he candidly conceded that the Coburg had been prosecuted for its production of *King Richard the Third* in its 1819–20 season and its manager fined £100.[13]

The Coburg was an 'illegitimate' theatre and its prosecution had been initiated by Drury Lane and Covent Garden theatres royal in defence of their patent monopoly. Their choice was not a random one. When the Coburg opened in 1818 it had taken its name from Prince Leopold of Saxe-Coburg, widowed son-in-law of Princess Caroline. The theatre's *King Richard the Third, or the Battle of Bosworth Field* was a barely disguised adaptation of Shakespeare's *Richard III*, distinguished mainly for the prominence it gave (to quote the playbill) to 'the Assassination of the Prince of Wales and Duke of York'.[14] This was, of course, a reference to the mysterious death of the young Princes in the Tower. Shakespeare places their murder off-stage: the Coburg turned it into a centrepiece, accompanied by frenzied music. 'I suppose it was to drown out their cries', said one who witnessed the production.[15] In the febrile atmosphere of the months following Peterloo, explicitly to present the assassination of even a twelve-year old, fifteenth-century Prince of Wales was daring. However we must be clear that this was not why the Coburg fell foul of the law; and by itself this *King Richard the Third* could not constitute evidence of theatrical complicity in fomenting popular opinion against authority. However, the production was one of several mounted in the six months after Peterloo that opened up ambiguous perspectives upon contemporary politics.

The first of these was Shakespeare's *Julius Caesar*, revived in Manchester in October 1819. The play had been out of favour for some time (its presentation in York the following March was the first there since 1813).[16] Of *Coriolanus*, another Roman play and one where the assassination of the main character concludes the action, there were no productions in 1819 until 29 November when Covent Garden presented the play (for the first time since 1817). The Theatre Royal Drury Lane quickly followed, presenting *Coriolanus* in a double bill with *Jack and the Beanstalk* (a pantomime heavy with radical overtones: one of the most revolutionary periodicals of the war years had been *Giant Killer, or Anti-Landlord*). Other productions of *Coriolanus* during 1820 included Brighton, Bristol, Doncaster, Dublin, Hull, Leeds, Liverpool, Sheffield, Wakefield and York. Of these provincial productions little is known, but the two London presentations hit a extraordinary problem in January 1820 when the Lord Chamberlain apparently banned *Coriolanus* 'until the popular passages, most in favour of liberty, shall have been expunged'.[17]

Something of authority's dilemma concerning *Coriolanus* becomes apparent when one considers George Cruikshank's depiction of George IV in the character of Coriolanus addressing the London plebs, a caricature issued barely a month after his accession. The citizens wear red caps of liberty and carry banners such as 'Burdett and Reform', 'Revolution and Plunder' and 'Liberty of the Press'. Ostensibly this was a sympathetic depiction by Cruikshank of the man who – as regent and monarch – he otherwise pilloried mercilessly as a fat debauchee. However, the very act of depicting the monarch as Coriolanus was hugely ambiguous: the viewer knows Coriolanus is a deeply flawed character whose contempt for liberty in pursuit of his own aggrandisement will soon cost him his life. Cruikshank knew this, of course, and to emphasise the point inserted himself into the picture, clutching a folio labelled 'Caricature'; his collaborator

William Hone stands in front of him, bearing a club labelled 'Man in the Moon' and 'House that Jack Built' – two of the most popular and resolutely radical pamphlets he and Cruickshank ever produced.[18]

Even without Cruikshank's visual prompting, and however loyal the protestations of theatre managers or heavily censored the script, it would surely have been impossible to watch *Coriolanus* unmindful of the ambiguities of its treatment of political power. Nor was *Coriolanus* the only long-established play to be called in for renewed scrutiny by the Lord Chamberlain in 1820. *Brutus* and *Venice Preserved* were accorded the same attention. William Duncombe's *Lucius Junius Brutus* (first produced in 1735) was based on Voltaire's drama of the same name. Brutus, first consul of Rome (not to be confused with Caesar's assassin) leads the Romans in the struggle against the Tarquins. Duncombe, a Whig, peppered his play with encomia to liberty including this invocation to resist arbitrary arrest:

> T'arrest a *Roman* upon bare Surmise,
> Would be to act like that outrageous Tyrant
> Whom we renounce, and take up Arms t'expell.
> Mean while, let us go forth to rouze the Slothful,
> To chear the Weak, to animate the virtuous,
> And terrify the Sons of Violence.[19]

Competing with Duncombe's drama was John Howard Payne's heavily derivative *Brutus, or the fall of Tarquin* (first performed 1818).[20] Payne's reworking accentuated the theme of Roman greatness having been achieved under enlightened rule, a popular concept with British theatregoers. Playbills for its presentation on the Stafford circuit declaimed how Brutus roused 'the People to break their chains of Slavery, and expel the Tarquins; which laid the foundation of Roman greatness and eventually made them MASTERS OF THE WORLD'.[21]

Voltaire supposedly wrote that Brutus was 'the subject, perhaps, of all others, the most fitted for the English stage'. To this the Tory *Quarterly Review* retorted in January 1820: 'it certainly seems to us objectionable in an eminent degree, and for many reasons.'[22] Chief of these was that it was 'too strictly political'. In Shakespeare's English history plays, 'it is not on public revolutions, a discontented people, or rival factions, that he suffers us to dwell', claimed the *Quarterly*; but the Roman plays could not be entirely exempted from that charge, while imitative works such as the *Brutus* dramas decidedly offended. Pointedly, the *Quarterly Review* combined its critique of *Brutus* with a new play, *Evadne* by Richard Lalor Shiel, a Whig barrister increasingly prominent as an agitator for Roman Catholic emancipation. Set in Naples, *Evadne* centred on a King 'of good dispositions, but corrupted by pleasure' and his treacherous courtier Ludovico. The play concludes with Ludovico's assassination at the hands of a high-minded Neapolitan patriot. Despite its popularity in the 1818–19 season, no London house presented *Evadne* in 1820, possibly because of political nervousness. It was however performed in the provinces, notably at Liverpool and on the York circuit, but in early July news of a revolution in the Kingdom of Naples seems to have killed it stone dead.[23]

Venice Preserved (written by Thomas Otway and first staged in 1682) faired a little better. Subject of only a comic travesty at a London private theatre in 1819, Drury Lane's 1820 revival saw it in repertory for over three months. It was also revived in March for the York Theatre Royal and so presumably toured on its Doncaster, Hull, Sheffield and Wakefield circuit. This was yet another drama centring on conspiracy and betrayal. Although the Venetian republic is preserved, the conspirators against it are given some of the best speeches and die noble deaths. *Venice Preserved* had long been a controversial work, especially since the French Revolution. The drama 'feed[s] the flame of lurking sedition', claimed *The Times* and when John Thelwall was tried for treason in 1793, one charge against him was that he had led uproarious applause at Drury Lane for one of the play's most contentious passages:

> We've neither safety, unity, nor peace, for the foundation's lost of common good; justice is lame, as well as blind amongst us; the Laws (corrupted to the ends that make 'em) serve but for instruments of some new tyranny.[24]

Conventionally, accounts of British theatre history contrast the tightly regulated patent theatres with the latitude and irreverence of houses beyond the Lord Chamberlain's control: but drama was a cut-throat business, legitimate and illegitimate theatres alike reflected the popular mood in the material they selected for presentation. And as subsequent events in 1820 would vividly demonstrate (to quote Thomas Morton again), 'a theatre is a place of peculiar excitement … I do not know anything more terrible than an enraged audience'.[25]

Cato Street

'Who will dispute that the Tragedy of Venice Preserved was not prudently suspended, in times of the greatest ferment?' asked the Lord Chamberlain's examiner of plays in 1825.[26] It was to nationwide ferment that conspiratorial groups looked to transform their local initiatives into a potent challenge to authority. We saw in the previous chapter how, by mid-January, the group assembled round Arthur Thistlewood were in regular contact with northern England, also how in both Britain and Ireland rumours circulated that some kind of precipitate action was imminent. On 10 January, with Tetlow from Manchester in attendance, the London conspirators had met at Thomas Preston's home. The logistics of obtaining firearms was among the topics discussed. Preparations now began in earnest. 'Justice is triumphant & your Tyrants are destroyed', a provisional government decree drafted by the group began. 'Every act passed by the Boroughmongering Usurpation shall from & after this date cease to be obeyed as such'. The decree went on to proclaim universal male suffrage to elect a convention in a month's time; soldiers were promised more pay if they joined 'the Ranks of their Country' or a bounty if they handed over their arms and returned to their families. A second decree announced full civil and religious liberty; and an older document (prepared by James Watson in anticipation of the success of one of the Spenceans' earlier conspiracies) was dusted down, specifically addressed to the 'Brave Soldiers', enjoining them to wait on the projected measures of the 'Provisional Committee' to reward them.[27] Supposedly 20,000 copies of these resolutions were to be printed, many to send to Ireland. But unnerved perhaps by the magnitude of what was contemplated and already facing prosecution for blasphemy, Thomas Davison, the radical printer hired for the job, never supplied the order.[28]

At a meeting on 27 January the core conspirators agreed 'that all were ready to sacrifice their lives'. However the death of George III two days later momentarily caused Arthur Thistlewood to hesitate, anticipating that 'we shall see when the Princess arrives [back in Britain] which will be the strongest the Whigs or the Tories, then the Radicals will come in'.[29] With the exception of Thistlewood and George Edwards, all the conspirators were impoverished tradesmen: for example among the core members John George was a decorator and his son Robert recently released from the navy; Richard Tidd and Thomas Preston (who was also disabled) were shoemakers; James Ings, a butcher, had come up from Wiltshire in the hope of making his way in the world; Jamaican-born William Davidson was a cabinetmaker of slave parentage. They had little money with which to augment their makeshift arsenal of pikes, swords, and home-made grenades with firearms. Their plans were increasingly an ill-kept secret. For example Emanuel Francis, a Methodist labourer, attended a night school off the Edgware Road run by an old radical, Thomas Hazard. The schoolroom was also the meeting place for the Marylebone Union, one of the satellite groups prepared, in principle, to be armed ready to respond to any signal from the central conspirators. Francis and other students would linger after class when the Union assembled. One of its members, a bootmaker named Boston (formerly a junior army officer, Francis believed) spoke of having 'much influence with the soldiers' and of a plan to travel to Yorkshire to raise 'an army of Radicals'. The assassination of the Duke of Berry, heir to the French throne in Paris, on 13 February, galvanised Thistlewood: 'there never was a better time to stir in England' he told the Marylebone Union the following week. But the Union's poor preparations to assist in the rising were also discussed, considerable disquiet being expressed that its promises were mainly empty ones.[30] Aware that their secrecy was compromised, and perceiving that the political establishment was itself volatile in the wake of the King's death, the controversies surrounding the new queen and the impending general election, the London conspirators discussed putting their plans into abeyance. 'All [were] of the opinion that the king would never be crown'd ... Preston said a few days would now soon settle it. They agreed not to dispose of their Ammunition, as it would soon be wanted'.[31]

However on Tuesday 22 February their resolve to stage a rising was secured by an announcement in the *New Times* that the Lord President of the Council, Lord Harrowby, was to host a dinner for his Cabinet colleagues the following day. This was the moment for which they had planned since October and all, especially Thistlewood and Edwards, determined to act upon it. Welshman John Brunt, a bootcloser, said, 'I'll be d----d if I don't believe there is a God. I have often prayed that he would bring all these thieves together in order to destroy them. He has answered our prayer.' Shoemaker Robert Adams, a former trooper in the Horse Guards recruited to the conspiracy for his expertise as a swordsman, would later recall that 'he had seen nothing of Edwards from that moment'.[32] That night at the conspirators' headquarters in Holborn, details of how to gain entrance to Harrowby's house and surprise the diners were discussed. A party of around twenty would be sufficient. Adams and John Harrison, a baker, were to execute Castlereagh and Sidmouth, whose heads would subsequently be spiked for public exhibition. 'If there shall be any good men, kill them for keeping bad company', Thistlewood ordered. The murders complete, the cavalry barracks in nearby King Street would be fired, the Honourable Artillery Company's barracks in Grays Inn Road raided and its cannon dragged first to the Mansion House to force its surrender, then to the Bank of England where 'they would take the books, which would enable them to see further into the villainy of the government'.[33]

Throughout that night and the following day, members kept a watch on Harrowby's Grosvenor Square home. A makeshift headquarters was secured in a mews loft in Cato Street, Marylebone, so as to be closer to Grosvenor Square. It was here that those conspirators most intimately involved in the business gathered during Wednesday afternoon. In the absence of any printed addresses, a handful were laboriously written out and signed by James Ings as Secretary: 'your tyrants are destroyed – the friends of liberty are called upon to come forward – the Provisional Government is now sitting.' Drink was sent for. Richard Tidd was the last to arrive, sometime before 7.00 p.m. Anxious that he was not losing his nerve, Thistlewood urged him not to 'give up what you are going to do; if you do, this will be another Despard's business'. This may not have calmed Tidd (who had allegedly been involved in the 1802 conspiracy) but there was no time for second thoughts. As the conspirators were dividing into two parties (the larger to deal with the Cabinet, the smaller with Harrowby's servants) there was a commotion at the bottom of the loft ladder. Two Bow Street policemen clambered through the hatch shouting they had a warrant to arrest everyone present. Candles were hurriedly extinguished. Officer Richard Smithers, first into the room, at once made a move towards Thistlewood. Without flinching Thistlewood ran Smithers through with his sword. In the pandemonium that followed Thistlewood and around a dozen conspirators escaped into the mews below, evading a party of Coldstream guardsmen who (having marched past the tiny street in the dark when they first arrived) now belatedly supported the police. Nine men were arrested in the loft; Thistlewood and several others were taken the following day.[34]

It was indeed 'another Despard's business' and, like it, the Cato Street conspiracy was swiftly shrouded in speculation and confusion. Reading the pathetic narrative of the chief Crown witness Robert Adams (who was among those arrested the next day), it is hard to shake off the conclusion that however murderous the intentions of this group, their optimism was pathetically miscalculated. This is so even without the knowledge that there was never to have been a dinner at Harrowby's house that night, and that the paragraph in the 'Fashionable Mirror' column of the *New Times* was a hoax ultimately traceable to Lord Sidmouth. Told by Edwards of the conspirators' aspirations, Sidmouth had authorised the paragraph to bring to a head a conspiracy that would otherwise have spiralled beyond the view of Home Office surveillance if Edwards was exposed as a spy. The major interpretive issue, both in the months that followed and among historians since, is how far the conspirators acted of their own volition or were the dupes of George Edwards whose activities arguably blurred those of a spy and an *agent provocateur*.

The account already offered in Chapter 2, of how the conspirators' intentions had evolved since the autumn of 1816, should make clear that the conspirators had deep roots in London ultra-radicalism. However afflicted by poverty they may have been, their actions were not a spontaneous consequence of extreme desperation; and however deadly their intentions, they were not psychopaths bent on murder for murder's sake. Furthermore Edwards alone does not constitute a sufficient – or even a necessary – explanation for Cato Street. This becomes clearer if we consider the conspiratorial swell that surrounded the events of Wednesday 23 February. Though the Government possessed extensive information about support for the conspiracy, it chose to prosecute only eleven of those arrested that night or in the days that followed. Its intentions were primarily to secure swift and exemplary verdicts on Thistlewood and those with him when Richard Smithers was killed, and to efface all evidence of Home Office intelligence gathering. So Preston, not at the loft but on his way there after reconnoitring the Honourable Artillery Company barracks, escaped prosecution; so too did John George who was waiting elsewhere ready to head a band of insurgents. It is indicative of extensive tacit support for the conspiracy that both men merged effortlessly back into metropolitan radicalism, in which they would continue to play significant roles well into the Chartist era.[35] And on London's streets during the days after the arrests, public opinion was far from unanimous in condemning the conspiracy. When Bow Street runners arrived at a Dover Street pub to arrest a drinker who had cursed the King saying 'I had as lief [gladly] shoot him as Thistlewood and be d----d to him', they were forcibly prevented by a crowd that defied both the runners and an off-duty soldier who drew his bayonet to assist him.[36]

Who else was involved? Many among the London trades were aware of what was intended. Occupational groups specified as offering significant support to the conspiratorial group in 1819-20 included coachmakers, navvies, tailors, typefounders and shoemakers.[37] Thomas Hiden, a milkman, 'struck with remorse' wrote to Castlereagh on the afternoon of 22 February with an account of what was planned. Soon afterwards a drunk accosted a neighbour of Lord Palmerston in Grosvenor Square: 'Sir Do you know that the Ministers are all to be murdered tonight?'[38] Thomas Dwyer, an Irish bricklayer arrived 'in great agitation' at the Home Office on the afternoon of the 23rd and told all he knew.[39] A violent row in Covent Garden between an old Jacobin china mender and his wife turned (according to a neighbour who informed the Home Office) on her upbraiding him for opening 'his mouth wider than he has any Right' about 'Thistlewood's Com^tee'.[40] Three or four conspirators managed to flee to North America: one, George Sparrow, drank himself to death in Vermont in 1829.[41] Robert Wedderburn, in the vanguard of would-be insurgents the previous autumn, was in gaol following his arrest for blasphemous libel in December. The closure of his Hopkins Street Chapel may account for the apparent non-involvement of his close associate the shoemaker Allen Davenport. However, shoemakers' trade societies across the capital were poised to lend support to Thistlewood in February 1820. Decades later three shoemakers surfaced, independently of each other, all revealing some knowledge of the conspiracy. In 1858 a Cambridge billiards hall manager, John Brown, revealed he had been close to Brunt, Davidson, Ings and Tidd in 1819–20 while working in London as a shoemaker.[42] In 1867 John Johnson, an elderly Essex shoemaker living out his last days residing in the workhouse, confessed 'he was actually on the way to the loft' but, calling at the Good Woman pub for dutch courage, missed everything. He immediately disappeared on the tramp into Kent.[43]

In 1879 a master shoemaker, still insisting on anonymity, published a detailed autobiography relating how he became involved in politics through attending the Spa Fields meetings in 1816–17. He had first met John Brunt when he completed his apprenticeship: in December 1819 they had taken lodgings together. He was not only aware of arms being accumulated at the conspiracy's Holborn headquarters, but was inducted into the 'Radical Union' at the White Lion in Wych Street, one of the satellite centres for the conspiracy. He described the manufacture of bullets by the typefounders who 'were heart and soul in the cause', and how his trade society strongly supported an insurrection. On the brink of the conspiracy he had fled to Uxbridge, where he shortly met another shoemaker, James Bruton, another conspirator who had escaped from the Cato Street loft itself. On the tramp in Northamptonshire in 1828 he met yet another exponent of the 'gentle craft', named Wilson, who admitted to him that he too was complicit in the events of February 1820.[44]

Awareness was also evident among radicals in Scotland that a rising of some kind was to be initiated from the capital in February, along with indications that they were prepared to act locally if it was successful. Major-General Sir Thomas Bradford, commander of the army in Scotland, was adamant that Scottish reformers 'expected something very important to take place' at this time.[45] On the evenings after Cato Street groups hung round the streets of the principal radical centres eager for news. 'When the account of the fate of Thistlewood and his party at last reached' Glasgow and Paisley, radical delegates 'were staggered and confounded'.[46] However, the minister of the Kirk at Houston and Killellan, six miles north-west of Paisley, told Sidmouth that when news of Cato Street reached his village, local radicals remained optimistic: 'Wait a little, and you will hear of a bony [bonnie] hurry yet, in a day or two.'[47] In Glasgow, advance awareness of Cato Street was mainly due to the Leeds reformer Joseph Brayshaw.[48] During 1819 Brayshaw had made a living in northern England and Scotland as a professional orator, also hawking his pamphlet *An Appeal to the People of England, on the Necessity of Parliamentary Reform*.[49] His standing as a reformer beyond his native West Yorkshire was probably boosted by his membership of the Freethinking Christians, a Universalist sect with close links both to Glaswegian and London radicalism and especially to the Spenceans.[50] While in Scotland Brayshaw had energetically helped establish local union societies; he also advocated abstinence from all excisable articles. Peterloo, and the establishment's reaction to it, forced a sea-change in his political outlook. At Leeds on 9 December, facing down more established local leaders, Brayshaw had successfully moved the adoption of an 'inflammatory' resolution recommending arming: 'the tyrants and minions of corruption, he said, were united to impose upon them laws utterly destructive of their liberty, and it was now time for the people to bestir themselves.'[51]

In February 1820, Joseph Brayshaw was delegated by the Leeds Radical Committee to visit north-east England, Glasgow and Carlisle to assess how prepared radicals were at each for – as he himself later put it – 'commencing revolutionary operations'.[52] Brayshaw would later claim he dampened all expectation of a rising, having found Durham and Northumberland unprepared and Glasgow little better: Carlisle 'was the only place, where any preparations of importance existed'. He also blamed Leeds bookseller James Mann for failing to communicate to Thistlewood how under-prepared the midlands were to act in concert with events in London. Mann had been deputed by the Leeds committee to tour the midlands and south on a similar mission to Brayshaw's: 'the Blow is to be struck suddenly; Revolution is the Word.'[53] However information from Carlisle at the time was clear that Brayshaw had both offered to obtain 'any number of pikes' from Sheffield for Carlisle's 'Secret Committee', and 'pressed very strongly upon them to get everything ready and leaders appointed as he did not know how soon it would take place – that he would not be the least surprised if he heard of it tomorrow'. This conversation took place on 20

February.[54] By the time Brayshaw got home news of Cato Street was breaking. He claimed that illness had prevented him meeting anyone in Glasgow. Suspected of being a spy, he was excluded from a delegate meeting at Huddersfield where future strategy was discussed. Supposedly he then went to stay with his shoemaker father in Heslington, an unremarkable village outside York, so that he could attend Hunt's trial.[55] This, however, may have been a ruse, as we shall see in the next chapter.

Perhaps it was bravado that prompted Bolton and Manchester radical leaders, three months later, to boast of knowing 'the Cato Street Conspiracy was a real & not a sham Plot', and to talk of Thistlewood's plans for 'taking' the local barracks.[56] Yet before February was out one of the Home Office's longest-serving Lancashire correspondents, a half-pay officer and colliery manager called George Chippendale, was clear that leaders of the Oldham Union had travelled to Manchester on Friday 24 February, 'apparently expecting to receive news from London'. His assessment of the mood among Oldham radicals mirrored that at Glasgow: 'Suppression of the diabolical attempt has cast a terrible Gloom upon them.'[57] Another report specified that a delegate set out from Lees (a village south-west of Oldham) on Friday morning for the same purpose. The commandant of the Manchester garrison understood that a Paisley delegate attended a meeting in the town, held in 'the greatest secrecy and caution ... in expectation of receiving important news'. The meeting disbanded shortly after the evening post arrived from London with the first news of Cato Street.[58] Also on the 24th a book-hawker making his way to Bolton, alarmed the landlady of a Sowerby Bridge pub with the remark 'if she lived one Week longer she would hear such a Thing as she never heard in her Life'.[59] John Crowther of Huddersfield, 'principal Delegate from the Neighbourhood', left the town for the capital in mid-February. Suspicions were aroused when he failed to return as expected on the 26th. It seems likely he stopped over in Nottingham where a secret meeting was held that day to discuss the exposure of Cato Street, with a London delegate in attendance. Henry Battersby, the leading radical in the Lancashire manufacturing town of Leigh, told a meeting that an event would shortly take place 'that would lead to a restoration of their rights and they might depend on having their rights very soon'. This was 'a <u>very few</u> days before the discovery took place in Cato Street'.[60]

The general commanding the army's Northern District was clear that 'what occurred on the 23^d in London, was expected by the leaders of the discontented in the Country'. The Mayor of Leeds noted 'an expectation here lately among a certain class of the disaffected that some very serious occurrence would take place'.[61] In Halifax 'many vague rumours speak of Expectations lately expressed that something would happen <u>in the very Week</u>'. 'There are many happy days laid up in Store which must come shortly', wrote Joseph Swann of Stockport four days before the plot's exposure: 'The Angel of Freedom appears upon the Wing ... convulsions and signs are all afloat and burst they must with a tremendous crash.' Perhaps this was the chiliasm of despair, but locals subsequently claimed that Swann knew 'of the time the horrid Deeds were fixed to be perpetrated'. In Lichfield, Staffordshire, a Royal Marine pensioner stunned drinkers in the King's Head when he claimed he had been aware of 'Thistlewood's Plan, and I wish Lord Sidmouth had been there'.[62]

Perhaps the most compelling testimony comes from those who, aside from Thistlewood and his closest associates, arguably knew most about the extent of unrest in February 1820. Invited to dine with the Foreign Secretary a few days after Cato Street, the Russian ambassador's wife was astonished to find police on duty in the house and that 'Lord Castlereagh himself had two loaded pistols in the breeches of his pockets. He showed them to me at the table. I was nervous every time he made a movement to offer me anything.'[63] A disused common sewer beneath Westminster, 'well suited to various purposes of Mischief', was filled in.[64] 'It was believed the plot 'would be the Forerunner of General Confusion and Revolution', Sidmouth wrote to Dublin Castle the morning after it was exposed. The following week he sent word to the King, 'it is certain that committees of the Disaffected in Leeds, Manchester, Carlisle and Glasgow expected to hear of a Blow having been struck last Week in London'.[65] 'Some important Event was throughout the North of Engl[d] anticipated to happen in the last week of Feby, tho' perhaps the precise Plot might not be known', he wrote in early March to his principal Halifax correspondent.[66]

Somewhat more speculatively, a retired officer whose Hampshire home bordered the Farnham turnpike road wrote to Sidmouth about the sudden passage past his house, a day or so after Cato Street, of some 200 working men, scattered in groups of three to five. All had come from London and claimed to be on the tramp in search of work. 'All at once the migration ceased' as quickly as it had begun.[67] Other correspondents seriously advanced the argument that the conspirators were in collusion with radical republicans in France. An anonymous letter to the Home Office suggested Bonapartists supported the plot, believing the overthrow of the Government was a necessary prelude to Napoleon's release from St Helena. Charles Ethelston, a Manchester clerical magistrate, had heard rumours that Thistlewood had been to France within the past year, returning 'with his Pocket full of money'.[68] A Briton resident in Lille told the Home Office he had seen Thistlewood and James Watson in Cassel, northern France, in December 1819. Another ex-patriot related how accounts 'of the assassination of the Duke of Wellington' reached Abbeville from Calais and Boulogne on 23 February. (Similar reports had circulated in Abbeville before the assassination of the Duke of Berry, he claimed.) At the very least, the assassination and Cato Street showed Britain and France 'are in train to be ruined by the Liberty of the Press', claimed Lord Sheffield.[69] The weekly *Farmers' Journal* confidently asserted that 'a Frenchman' was among the conspirators who evaded capture. Even official intelligence sources reported the involvement of Frenchmen in the serious disturbances at Easter in the west of Scotland, but this was almost certainly an elaboration of a popular rumour among the disaffected at the time.[70] Only in the summer of 1820 does it become certain there were some links with France. Migrant British workers in Cambrai, Lyons and Rouen established contact with French reformers by June; this in turn initiated correspondence with Lancashire, Yorkshire and Glasgow radicals. James Wilson, the veteran Strathaven democrat who contributed to the exchange, assumed that the principal British contact must have been the Spencean James Watson.[71] This was not so: the English end of the correspondence was in the hands of Lancashire weaver James Lang and Tootall, an ex-soldier and 'violent Radical' from Bolton. Both had been arrested in December 1819 on suspicion of involvement in plans for a general rising but never charged; and both would surface again at the height of unrest in the spring of 1820.[72]

High politics

For a short but frenetic period Cato Street plunged Britain into panic. 'Every shabby and hungry-looking man met on the road was pronounced "a radical"', Harriet Martineau later recalled. At the time Martineau lived in Norwich, where she remembered country gentlemen scouring 'the fields and lanes ... to fight the enemy who never came', and how 'even in the midst of towns, young ladies carried planks and ironing boards, to barricade windows'.[73] 'It is impossible to think, speak or write concerning anything at present, but this horrible Radical conspiracy', Sir Murray Maxwell told the Home Secretary. Sidmouth himself confided in Earl de la Warr that 'the most hardened incredulity appears to be staggered'.[74] Yet Cato Street and its ramifications was only one of three major issues confronting Liverpool's Ministry in February 1820, the others being the royal marriage and an impending general election. George IV's demand that Liverpool secure him a divorce was made, as we saw in the conclusion to the previous chapter, within days of recovering from the pleurisy that nearly killed him after his accession. Though still too unwell to attend to Government business, the King announced that he would dismiss the administration if Liverpool did not consent. This was no sudden nostrum: the demand for a divorce had been extensively aired by the Regent the previous summer.[75] But now his advisor Sir John Leach (the Vice Chancellor and effectively deputy to Lord Chancellor Eldon) had put it into the royal head that 'what the K. looked to was quite reasonable & quite attainable': the Whigs could form a government and were willing to seek the divorce. 'If he could not carry this point', Leach told Eldon, the King 'was determined to go to, and live in Hanover, where of course he could be divorced'.[76]

Liverpool's Cabinet was far from convinced that a royal divorce was either reasonable or attainable. For several days ministers were 'very downhearted', the Russian ambassador's wife noted on 8 February, adding that Castlereagh's 'mood was as sombre as his clothes'.[77] In theory four procedures were available: divorce, trial for treason, impeachment or a parliamentary bill decreeing pains and penalties for the queen's behaviour. Divorce under any circumstances was no light matter in nineteenth-century Britain and exhaustive and very public procedures were needed to secure one. The ruling of an ecclesiastical court in a plaintiff's favour was ordinarily required, but the King's own behaviour ruled out making such an application. Adultery involving the wife of the heir to the throne was, though, extraordinary and an act of treason by both parties. However, the 1806 commission of enquiry, though it censored her behaviour as indecorous, had been unable to establish evidence of adultery by the Princess of Wales. Furthermore, not only did conviction of treason demand a higher standard of proof than other criminal offences (the corroboration of two witnesses to the act), the status of offences committed abroad was a grey legal area. The third procedure, impeachment by Parliament, was too risk-laden a route to take, since it could be initiated only in the House of Commons of which Liverpool's Ministry did not have an easy command. So the only viable procedure was a bill of pains and penalties, which could be initiated in the Lords. This too would require a quasi-judicial trial, with witnesses examined and cross-examined by counsel for the monarch and his wife, and the peers acting as jury. If peers agreed that adultery had been committed they could recommend a divorce: that decision and the evidence justifying it would then have to pass the House of Commons. With the critical processes located in the Lords, and therefore more susceptible to the Ministry's control, Liverpool's Cabinet could – just – contemplate a bill of pains and penalties with equanimity. Even so it was an outcome the Ministry fervently wished to avoid.

So on 10 February Cabinet members agreed a lengthy minute, advising the King why they could not abide by his royal command. Central was their observation that 'in opposition to a measure of divorce, there can be little doubt but that her Royal Highness would offer to state not only matter of recrimination, but every circumstance which she might be disposed or advised to represent as neglect or ill-usage, even from the time of her coming to this country'. 'Most humbly but most earnestly', the minute also stressed 'the effect which the publicity of such proceedings must have upon public morals'. Having thus impressed on the royal mind the potential discomfort to his own situation, the Cabinet then suggested a compromise. The death of his father had brought to an end the financial settlement enjoyed by the princess. A new settlement should be made, 'payable only during her continued residence abroad', which would therefore of course preclude her coronation as queen by his side. In addition, she would not be mentioned specifically in the liturgy of the Church of England. Critically, the Cabinet declared it had 'just reason' for its suggested policy because the previous summer Caroline's legal advisor, the Whig MP Henry Brougham, had intimated 'she would acquiesce in an arrangement founded upon these principles'. Were the Queen to return to Britain it would be in full knowledge that King and Government would initiate divorce proceedings. 'Very different impressions' would prevail among the public if it were Caroline herself, and not the Crown, that thus took the steps that would initiate a parliamentary bill of penalties.[78]

If the Cabinet thought the King would accept this compromise it was mistaken. It had been sufficiently confident to sanction the publication of the new liturgical formulae. As Princess of Wales she had appeared in the liturgy and there was a widespread feeling, shared by the Archbishop of Canterbury, that it was now proper to include 'our gracious Queen Caroline'. However this formula was omitted, balanced by the further omission of any reference to the Duke of York, George's presumptive heir.[79] The King was not to be bought off with liturgical contrivance, however. He fundamentally opposed the whole thrust of the Cabinet's argument both in writing and in person: 'he treated Lord Liverpool very coarsely, and ordered him out of the room', the diarist Charles Greville heard. The King subsequently sent for Liverpool to retrieve the situation, but the Prime Minister 'refused at first to go'.[80] 'The Government is in a very strange & I must acknowledge to your Lordship in a precarious State', the Home Secretary wrote to the Lord Lieutenant of Ireland on Sunday 13 February. The first demonstrations in support of Caroline were taking place outside as he did so. 'When the Various Congregations were leaving their respective places of Worship, fellows <u>with Horns</u> were proclaiming the <u>arrival</u> of the <u>Queen</u> and selling papers to that effect.'[81]

The coincidence of these demonstrations with the arrival of news from Paris of the assassination of the Duke of Berry emboldened the Cabinet. On the 14th they reiterated their advice to the King but, more than that, contrived with Bloomfield, his private secretary, for Castlereagh to have an audience with him. Henry Hobhouse, who as Sidmouth's Under Secretary was well-placed to know some detail of the negotiations, recorded in his diary that the meeting lasted five hours, during which the Foreign Secretary 'went thro' the recriminatory matter likely to be urged against the King, and particularized his connection with his several mistresses from Mrs Fitzherbert onwards. He left the King in a subdued tone of mind.'[82] Three days later Liverpool received a brief letter from the King stating he was after all willing 'for the sake of public decorum and the public interest to make (thus far) this great and painful sacrifice of his personal feelings'.[83] The phrase 'thus far' reinforced his insistence that, should the Queen return to Britain, the case would be reopened. For the moment the Ministry had what it needed most, an end to the immediate uncertainty as to its future.

The general election of 1820

Having persuaded the monarch not to dispense with its services, the Ministry now had to persuade the country likewise. Though Parliament was not dissolved until the 28 February, it was informed on the 17th that it would be as soon as necessary business was completed. In effect the election had begun almost the moment news of George III's death became public on 31 January, when with ill-disguised haste Brougham had been the first to take out newspaper adverts announcing his candidacy for Westmorland. 'Shocking indecency', his constituent William Wordsworth called this, 'unfeelingly timed' and 'seeming to exult … in the King's death'.[84] But everywhere the elaborate courtship of the electorate by aspiring MPs was soon underway. Polling itself began on 6 March and was mostly completed by Easter (Good Friday was the last day of the month).

While the Whigs were clear they would not lose numbers, they equally stood to gain little. A cardinal point of early nineteenth-century electioneering was that it was expensive. A general election having been held in the summer of 1818, there was limited appetite to repeat the exercise so soon except where there was a real chance of unseating an opponent. In any nineteenth-century general election, the proportion of apparently uncontested seats seems astonishing to modern eyes. This was especially so in 1820 when only 93 (24%) of the United Kingdom's 380 constituencies went to the polls.[85] This does not mean that constituencies without polls were completely uncontested. The small proportion of constituencies where polling occurred reflects the *realpolitik* of early nineteenth-century electioneering. At the centre of each parliamentary election was the hustings, where each candidate was formally nominated and seconded, and then addressed the crowd that comprised as many residents of the constituency as cared to attend. In borough seats not totally in the pocket of a wealthy patron this usually meant most of them. A poll was required only when a candidate was defeated by a show of hands at the hustings: many candidates withdrew from the contest at this point, including some who carried the hustings but knew from canvassing the actual electorate that their chances of success were risible. Even candidates without a declared opponent still had to campaign, usually amidst a swirling fog of rumour and counter-rumour. The costs incurred by candidates, even in 'uncontested' seats, could be eye-watering. To be certain of not being forced to a poll, and thus to even greater expense, a determined candidate needed to spend heavily to discourage the entry of opponents into the fray, and again to try to force their withdrawal if this initial outlay failed.

'A contested Election, preceded by a long canvass, affords, during its progress, so much excitement to the worst passions of the human mind, and leaves behind it so many provocations to disunion and ill-will', the anonymous editor of the pollbook for the 1818 general election in York observed.[86] The 1820 contest provided ample testimony to the veracity of this comment. Hustings were seldom decorous but frequently boisterous and even chaotic; they always had to be held even when an election was uncontested. The proceedings in a populous borough often bordered on the carnivalesque. 'Here is a hellish – yes literally hellish bustle', wrote the novelist Walter Scott, an unwilling witness to the Middlesex and Westminster elections from lodgings in Piccadilly: 'My head turns round with it. The whole mob of Middlesex blackguards pass through Piccadilly twice a-day, and almost drives me mad with their noise and vociferation.'[87] Following riots in Sunderland and Bishopwearmouth at meetings called by a County Durham Tory candidate, a senior Home Office civil servant predicted the election would 'be conducted with more than common animosity'.[88] So it proved. When the ministerialist James Stuart-Wortley visited Sheffield to canvass for the Yorkshire county seat, 'many thousands of working people assembled', wrote the local postmaster, 'and insulted him with the most indecent and daring language'.[89] Nor was such language confined to verbal badinage: 'PENSIONER DICK / You're burnt out like a wick … you would vote for old Nick / Or his bottom would lick', ran one County Durham squib.[90]

Robert Peel drove his sister to the Sussex county election centre at Chichester, expressly to see 'the humours of a contested election'. At the hustings she was treated to the sight of William Huskisson, a key ministerialist, receiving rough treatment from 'radicals who would vote for Thistlewood' given the chance, according to the local magnate the Earl of Ashburnham.[91] Ashburnham's concerns reflected a widely held view among Sussex Tory magnates that the 'Rabble of the Town' intimidated voters and discouraged some from even attending.[92] At the hustings for Lincolnshire County, Sir Robert Heron, a popular independent Whig, was cut short by the Sheriff when he began to criticise the six acts. His proposal that the hustings be adjourned and reconvened in a larger venue was dismissed by the Sheriff, whereupon Heron swept from the hall and the two remaining candidates were returned unopposed. Like so many other hustings demonstrations, Heron's gesture was highly theatrical (his candidature was frivolous as he had already been elected the member for Peterborough ten days before).[93] However just because it was theatrical did not mean it was devoid of meaning.

Elections were also the occasion of a prodigious amount of printed ephemera – pamphlets, addresses, resolutions, squibs, satirical cartoons, placards, broadsides. The total of sixty-nine handbills and four tracts generated at Grantham alone were by no means atypical.[94] This being a general election occasioned by the death of the monarch, proceedings began quietly as sitting MPs regretted 'the melancholy event of the demise of our lamented Sovereign', while taking the earliest opportunity of declaring an intention of again offering themselves as candidates.[95] But each candidate's address would be carefully perused. Here especially was a chance not only to state principles but also to flatter both the electorate and non-voters. Thus at Lanarkshire, the Whig candidate Lord Archibald Hamilton (brother of the 10th Duke of Hamilton) sympathised with the victims of current economic distress but praised the 'patience' of the 'labouring class' and predicted that 'the superior nature of education in Scotland' and its 'habitual reverence' for the law, combined with the attentiveness of the higher classes to the needs of working people would ensure the preservation of social harmony. Hamilton also called on his readers to 'enlighten my judgment by expressions of their feelings'. He was elected unopposed.[96]

Candidates had to be reconciled to incurring considerable expenditure conveying supporters to the poll. This was inevitable in county seats, since polling took place at one location only. The Whig candidate for Sussex, backed by the deep pockets of the Devonshire dukedom, was said to have had forty carriages sent down from London to transport his voters.[97] However, since non-residence did not disqualify a voter, even campaigning for a parliamentary borough could incur huge transport costs: at Berwick-upon-Tweed out-voters were bought by boat from London; at Newcastle upon Tyne the Whig contestant advertised 'commodious conveyances' to bring voters thirty-five miles away from Darlington.[98] Once arrived, out-voters might need to be accommodated, and certainly had to be entertained and flattered. The same applied to those who travelled any distance to vote in the larger county constituencies: 'Caesar in the midst of his triumphs would not have been received with greater enthusiasm', wrote a Lewes resident who had made the forty-mile journey to Chichester to vote in the Sussex county election.[99]

Despite the exclusiveness of the parliamentary franchise, the inclusion of the non-franchised in the overall process was emphasised throughout the election, for example through their participation in the hustings rituals and the widespread ceremony of chairing. An election was also an occasion to disburse patronage, often in accordance with what Frank O'Gorman describes as 'long folk memories and a powerful sense of customary morality'. When the Hon. George Rice was elected unopposed for the county of Carmarthenshire, he sought to reward the church bellringers of Llandeilo with three guineas. They sent him a formal remonstrance, however, reminding him,

> that the customary fee due to them in times past, and in their own memory, for such services (and for which they can vouch precedents) is in the following manner. Viz Two guineas when the candidate canvassed the Town and neighbourhood, and Five guineas for ringing on the Election day.[100]

'No book would do justice to the present spectacle. Everything is called to account, women and children too', wrote one bemused foreign spectator, caught up in the Sussex election during a visit to Brighton. She proceeded to describe 'a regular saturnalia. The proud aristocrat shakes the butcher by the hand, gives sweets to his children, bonnets to his wife, and ribbons to the whole family, and so on, down to dead animals – for the butcher is careful to decorate his meat with pink ribbon.'[101] In Northumberland, Tory Charles Brandling spent over £850 in Alnwick alone to secure one of the county's two seats. Brandling's outgoings included 'the usual payment' of £7 10s (£7.50) each to twenty-seven of the town's publicans and five gin shop owners. Even though his opponents withdrew and polling was avoided, thirteen sedan chairmen received a guinea each; musicians accounted for £14 15s 6d (£14.77½) and Alnwick's bellman a guinea (£1.05). Even ostensible spontaneity had to be supported from the candidates' pockets. In many constituencies it was commonplace, when a candidate arrived for the nomination ceremony, for their carriage to be stopped on the outskirts of the town, the horses removed from the traces and the remainder of the journey turned into a tumultuous demonstration as eager supporters replaced the horses. A sum of £16 17s (£16.85) was paid to A. J. Riley, 'for firing guns and procuring men to draw in Mr Brandling', plus ropes and musicians. 'Drink & refreshment for Riley's men' set Brandling back a further £10. It was also customary for successful candidates to be chaired and carried shoulder high round the town after the result was declared. For this Brandling paid an astonishing £102 'for Chair & Cockades &c'.[102] Cockades were however far more elaborate than mere rosettes: for example a rare survival from the 1820 Newcastle borough contest is seven inches in diameter and constructed from three different coloured ribbons.[103]

Customary morality impelled Brandling to pay half a guinea (52½ pence) to each of Alnwick's seven ward constables and the seven special constables sworn in to assist them at the election. Another £4 15s 4d (£4.77) was paid for them all to dine after the contest. Thirteen bailiffs also each received half a guinea, and the County Court clerk and Town Hall cleaner a guinea each, 'the usual fee'. The two successful candidates also paid £132 for a celebratory ball (plus £49 'for fitting up the Town Hall' for the purpose). As a newcomer to the constituency, Brandling also saw fit to spend £282 for a special dinner for his supporters.[104] Meanwhile in Newcastle, the Whig banker Sir Matthew White Ridley spent £1,501 on his canvass, this in a constituency whose two seats the Whigs and Tories tacitly split between them to avoid the expense of a full contest.[105] Further north in the unabashedly venal borough of Berwick-upon-Tweed, Admiral Sir David Milne spent £4,000 to become MP, only to be unseated three months later when it was shown he had bribed voters and engineered the admission of illegal voters to the electoral register. His margin of seventeen votes over the unsuccessful candidate derived from twenty-five newly created freemen votes, all non-residents, most of whom arrived by sea from London on the third day of polling.[106] Even Milne's expenditure, however, paled in comparison with the £30,000 apparently spent by the Whig who topped the poll in County Durham to the south.[107] Fortunately, this MP was John Lambton, later Lord Durham, who once remarked that a man might 'jog on with' £40,000 a year.[108]

As the Berwick contest showed, careful management of non-resident electors could be critical to a successful campaign. At Coventry between 600 and 1,000 of an electorate of some 3,000 were out-voters, mainly from London or Birmingham, but some from as far away as Calais or Cornwall. Voters for the victorious candidates were routinely paid five shillings.[109] At Hull, 'a pit of fathomless corruption … not 200 men out of 3,000 ever vote without the Payment of Two Guineas for their single, and Four for their double Suffrage': this was the opinion of its Whig MP, who resigned on the eve of the 1820 election citing the expense of defending his seat.[110] At York an uncontested by-election in June 1820 cost the Whig grandee Earl Fitzwilliam £2,800. Overall, Fitzwilliam estimated that electioneering in York during 1818–20 'extracted from my purse £25,000'.[111]

None of the contests mentioned above took place in the much-cited rotten or pocket boroughs of the unreformed parliamentary system, constituencies such as the diminutive Cornish fishing communities of Bossiney and St Mawes (11 and 24 voters respectively) or Truro, the principal town of the county where only the corporation's twenty-four members could vote out of a population of some 2,700. When in May 1820 a Whig bill sought to disfranchise another Cornish borough, Grampound, on the grounds that it was grossly corrupt (the proposal was that its two MPs would be allocated to the unrepresented manufacturing town of Leeds), Grampound's mayor and freemen petitioned Parliament pointing out that only twenty-four of the sixty-nine electors had been found guilty of corruption.[112] The Cornish rotten boroughs were especially notorious – singled out, for example, by the artist George Cruikshank in his satirical print of April 1820, *Freedom & Purity of Election*, depicting a landlord evicting tenants who had voted 'according to conscience'.[113] But Cornwall had no monopoly of egregious examples of the unreformed electoral system. There was no record of the burghers (less than seventy) of Bletchingley (Surrey) ever having been troubled to go to a poll, while another Surrey borough, Gatton, nominally had seven electors but the only freeholder, Sir Mark Wood of Gatton Park, owned all the qualifying properties which he let on *weekly* leases.[114]

Borough constituencies might be closely controlled even if not completely in the pocket of a local grandee. For example in Appleby, Westmorland, the right to vote rested on possession of yearly tenures or burgages. The plots themselves were the properties of either the Earl of Lonsdale or the Earl of Thanet. 'Hogsties have been deemed freeholds here', commented the *Whitehaven Gazette*, 'and purchased by the Thanet and Lonsdale families, at a price exceeding all belief'.[115] Irish boroughs were typically tightly controlled, the electorate comprising only the members of corporations which had negligible local government functions and were little more than dining clubs that legalised the return of candidates nominated by local grandees. For example the thirteen burgesses of Bandon Bridge in County Cork were controlled by the Earl of Bandon, many of them being members of his family. The Bandon Corporation served no local governmental functions whatsoever.[116] Similar examples included Armagh, Belfast, Carlow, Dundalk (Co Louth), Ennis (Co Clare), Enniskillen (Co Fermanagh), Sligo and Tralee (Co Kerry).[117]

Frank O'Gorman suggests that 'serious electoral violence was *infrequent*' in the pre-reform period.[118] The relatively high level of violence that prevailed during the 1820 election is therefore perhaps indicative of heightened social tension. The Oxfordshire borough of Banbury was the worst afflicted. Here the right to vote rested in an eighteen-man corporation, effectively controlled by the

Earl of Guilford. A serious riot disrupted the hustings, because Guilford declined 'to give the Customary Beer & Cockades to the Populace'. The election ceremony was therefore completed under a state of siege inside the Town Hall. Cobbles were ripped from the market place, and all the windows broken. When a placatory large barrel of beer was offered, the crowd promptly poured its contents into the gutter. Then they began hacking away at the pillars supporting the Town Hall, which was on the upper floor. It was three hours before those inside dared make an escape. The newly elected MP fled his constituency disguised as a post boy. Meanwhile demonstrators wearing wood shavings in place of the favours they had been denied paraded a mock candidate ('a poor half-witted fellow') round the streets. Rioting continued into the night and Banbury gaol was not big enough to accommodate all those arrested.[119]

Lord Sidmouth was so alarmed by the Banbury riots that he took the unusual step of sending a Bow Street police officer to investigate them.[120] No other violence during the election prompted this level of concern. Regency England was, in any case, considerably more tolerant of casual violence than the present day. Yet there was no shortage of incidents where violence overstepped the bounds of customary boisterousness. At least two led to prominent court cases. At Petersfield, Hampshire, the agent of the MP who had topped the poll was convicted at the ensuing assize of forcibly entering the home of an elector to secure his vote.[121] In County Durham the stoutly Tory rector of Haughton-le-Skerne, Darlington punched a teenager who shouted 'Lambton forever!' outside his church with such force the youth lost a tooth. The Whigs ostentatiously brought a trial for damages, with Brougham acting as counsel for the prosecution: the hapless cleric (a friend of Lord Sidmouth) was ordered to pay ten shillings.[122] There was no reported violence in the Staffordshire borough of Tamworth, the salutary effect, perhaps, of the sitting MP, William Yates Peel, having just served a month in gaol for threatening to horsewhip the author of an 1818 election squib that attacked his father.[123]

Elsewhere, though, those prosecuted for election violence were not members of the political elite. At Chester a mob attacked the carriage of General Grosvenor, one of the city's MPs, and tried to push it into the River Dee with him in it. He escaped, 'covered with blood and bruises' (the coach came off worse).[124] At Hull a successful ministerial candidate was assailed with bricks at the hustings and obliged to abandon his acceptance speech; chairing was also abandoned and his carriage destroyed.[125] Ministerial supporters were forced to abandon canvassing Sunderland for the Durham county seat, and military intervention was needed to rescue them from the house in which they took refuge.[126] At Coventry a crowd opposed to the candidacy of William Cobbett allegedly threatened to kill him. They had surrounded the house where he was staying, broken its windows, shutters and doors, and were streaming up the stairs to attack the bedroom door behind which Cobbett was barricaded, before the Riot Act could be read and police intervened.[127]

In Scottish boroughs parliamentary elections were considerably different to the rest of Britain and Ireland. Edinburgh excepted, the Scottish burghs constituencies brought together four or five burghs to elect a single MP. Each burgh council mandated a delegate and together these then elected the MP, convening in one of the burghs, selected according to a strict rota. The delegate of the host 'returning burgh' had the casting vote in the event of delegates being equally divided.[128] In 1820 the election for the Aberdeen Burghs hinged on the allegiance of Brechin, a linen industry centre. The radical Joseph Hume had been returned in 1818 and his supporters campaigned energetically against the Tory, a London merchant though a native of Brechin. On 10 March some of Hume's supporters rampaged through the town, breaking the windows of councillors rumoured to be pro-Tory. Special constables had to be sworn-in and troops requested from Aberdeen. However crowds wearing Hume's yellow colours continued to roam Brechin's streets, reinforced from Montrose and Arbroath. A Tory petition against Hume's re-election, alleging intimidation and bribery, was unsuccessful.[129] Walter Scott's account of violence in the election for the Elgin Burghs left the wife of the Government's patronage secretary, Charles Arbuthnot, with the impression that 'the manners & customs of Rob Roy's day prevail more in Scotland now than one had imagined'. The narrative had gained in Scott's telling: nevertheless the magistrate charged with convening the Elgin Burgh councillors to elect their delegate was forcibly abducted and then almost drowned as he was removed from the town in an open boat, while councillors had to be locked in the town gaol for their own safety.[130]

More significant than incidents of mob violence, perhaps, were instances of the sudden deepening of political entrenchment. At Reading, where the ministerial candidate beat a radical Whig by only four votes on a 93 per cent turn out, a resident recollected: 'never before or since [was] seen such an unfortunate display of party feeling; it caused boycotting in trade, engendered a feeling of aversion amongst those who were formerly friends … and also caused division in families.'[131] In County Durham a wide-ranging group of ministerial supporters including several clergymen, published an elaborate attack on Lord Lambton, for 'the vehemence of his hostility' to Liverpool's measures, which it described as 'of essential moment to the best interests of the country'. Another anti-Lambton squib referred to 'Radical Jack, the Friend of Thistlewood'.[132] North of the Tyne, Whigs appealed loudly to the principles of 1688 and attacked the Ministry's supporters for their 'love of Lordly Domination', 'slavish Submission to power', 'Approbation of the late Proceedings at Manchester' and 'Admiration of Gagging Bills'.[133]

However, it would be mistaken to conclude that electoral violence was exclusively, or even mainly, directed at supporters of the Ministry. The newly elected MP forced to flee Banbury so ignominiously happened to support the Liverpool Ministry; but the crowd was directing its wrath at the failure of his patron to dispense the beer and favours they were accustomed to receive during an election. This suggests that the elaborate treating of non–voters at elections may actually have helped cement social stability. The violence in Elgin had no party political basis but was part of a battle between factions loyal to the rival earldoms of Fife and Seafield. And at Coventry William Cobbett, at the risk of stating the obvious, was no supporter of Liverpool's Ministry. He blithely ignored broader other indicators that he was unpopular: for example the opposition he met on his journey to the city from London, including the refusal of some publicans to hire him a chaise or, even, to permit him to enter their premises.[134] Similarly, Henry Hunt's decisive defeat at Preston, a constituency he chose to contest because of its unusually inclusive electorate, shows that there was no natural disposition to support candidates who stood on democratic principles. Hunt had called for the repeal of the six acts, an inquiry into Peterloo, civil and religious liberty, tax reductions and Corn Law repeal, annual parliaments, the ballot and universal suffrage. Popular support for Hunt ebbed away after he had to leave Preston during the election for his trial on charges derived from Peterloo and he came bottom of the poll.[135]

Hunt's primary purpose, however, was to exploit the election to promote discussion that was otherwise stifled by the six acts. Electoral meetings provided the first legal, public opportunities to do this, a fact of which the Ministry was acutely aware. 'The question is now really not one between Man & Man', Arbuthnot observed to Sidmouth, 'it is a Struggle between the Friends of good order & the Reformers; & the chief outcry with the latter is against the late Bills which we have carried through Parliament'.[136] Frank O'Gorman has argued for a surge in electoral radicalism at the general elections of 1818 and 1820: 'most speeches reported in the newspapers at these two elections have a Victorian ring to them: they are veritably stuffed with issues'.[137] Yet, Whig candidates made little headway. 'Whether it tends from poverty, prudence, or apathy I cannot tell you', Tierney (Whig leader in the Commons) wrote to Grey. Tierney deplored the lack of good candidates with some money: 'the fact is there is little disposition stirring for parliamentary honours'.[138] Lord Holland, nephew of the great Whig leader Charles James Fox, similarly believed that what their interest lacked most were wealthy men, hungry for power: Lord John Russell 'will come in triumphantly for Huntingdonshire', he correctly predicted, '& had we nine Russells instead of three or four we could I think place them all in Parliament'.[139] Several commentators, however, shared Holland's perception (see Chapter 1) that the middling sorts were becoming detached from the ruling class and from the institutions of government. Lord Lansdowne, for example, thought polling during the first fortnight revealed 'the want of confidence of the middling orders in the institutions of the country'. Robert Peel thought he discerned 'a feeling, becoming daily more general and more confirmed … in favour of some undefined change in the mode of governing the country'. He also thought that revolutionary 'events in Spain diminish the probability' of such a change being long resisted.[140]

Figure 3   Liverpool's Cabinet dance round a maypole from which are suspended
severed heads of the executed Cato Street conspirators. © National Portrait
Gallery, London

William Huskisson noted with alarm how many of the Ministry's 'best and
steadiest props' decided to retire from the Commons. Given the volatile mood of
the country at large, Huskisson feared new MPs coming in would be more
susceptible to 'the impression they received at their election'.[141] Charles
Arbuthnot spoke of feeling 'very uneasy about our returns', pointing to sitting
supporters' last-minute desertions and over-optimistic accounts from constituencies. 'I know that in divisions it scarcely signifies a straw whether we get three or
four more or less at a general election; but in point of impression the evil is
great'.[142] Liverpool himself similarly thought retirements had done damage, but
also that 'public feeling' was more clearly on the administration's side than it had
been in 1818.[143] However, what Holland called 'the windfall of the Cato Street
conspiracy' worked hugely to the Ministry's advantage (see Figure 3). Many
ministerial candidates worked energetically to add Thistlewood to the traditional
Tory demonology, at the expense of their Whig opponents: 'Huzza! For Lord
Ebrington and his clients, the Pope and Thistlewood – Pillars of Ebrington's
cause', a squib put out by 'Church and King' candidates in Devon declared.[144]

The thrust of the Government's electoral claims was that Cato Street vindicated its decision to introduce the controversial six acts; this also embarrassed the
Whigs, who had opposed the measures. Painting the Whigs as careless of the
nation's security, or at least as guilty of poor judgment, added to the polarised
climate of contemporary politics. The private correspondence of leading Tories

suggests this was a not a cynical ploy. 'It appears clearer every day that there are but two national parties in the country: the church and king party, and the radicals. The latter, however, are become truly formidable', Liverpool told Canning.[145] In a letter to Arbuthnot he fretted, 'I feel the Radicals have gained ground in many parts of England, & still more in Scotland'.[146] The Paymaster General concurred: 'the country is fast dividing itself into the friends of the government and radicals.'[147] Huskisson discerned that 'the infection of Radicalism, which is prevalent in the town is gradually making its way into the Villages', while for Lord Egremont the election showed that 'Radicals and Revolutionaries are powerful and rising everywhere'. Like Peel, he thought events in Spain would soon tell on British politics.[148]

The opinions of reformers impatient with Whig cautiousness chimed in with this outlook, even if they were cheered rather than apprehensive at the prospect. John Cam Hobhouse, newly elected MP for Westminster, was the focal point of reformers' hopes. 'If you want to find a true blackguard, chimneysweep-seeking politician – a truly mean mobhunting master of the dirty art commend yourself to a Whig, but do not expect to find him amongst the Reformers', he told Byron after the contest.[149] Wellington privately expressed the view that J. C. Hobhouse was fully cognisant of the Cato Street conspiracy and prepared to take office had it succeeded, though the evidence was limited to a single spy's report and Hobhouse, though a correspondent of the prisoners after their arrest, kept a discrete distance.[150]

Ministerialist accusations that Hobhouse and the senior radical candidate for Westminster, Sir Francis Burdett, condoned Cato Street failed to stop either being elected. (Hunt also contested the two-member constituency.)[151] The Government could never expect, however, to win Westminster. It was one of a handful of borough constituencies whose electoral peculiarities meant it more nearly resembled a universal male franchise than was generally the case. The notable defeats for ministerial candidates occurred elsewhere. At York 'Whig principles … were unequivocally and repeatedly stated to be unfriendly to the English Constitution, and favourable to rebellion and anarchy'.[152] Despite this both the Ministry's candidates were defeated. In the boroughs of Berwick, Ipswich and Northampton, Whig candidates prevailed over sitting Tories. In Hampshire, Whigs and independent Tories rebuffed the Ministry's attempt to secure both the county seats and the second ministerialist candidate withdrew before the poll.[153] In Staffordshire, a seat that had not polled since 1742, the sitting member Lord Gower, son of the Marquess of Stafford, conceded defeat three days before polling to a candidate sponsored by the county's Freeholders' Association, established in 1810 partly to resist rent increases on the Stafford estates. The Staffordshire county contest also provides a good example of the pitfalls of uncritically following contemporary labels in analysing the politics of the period. Contemporaries spoke of seats falling into the hands of the Radicals and Staffordshire was one of these. The Postmaster General thought the result evidence that 'radicalism had spread in the Potteries … we have arrived at times when if the rich will not fight their battles we shall be overwhelmed by the rabble and their wild doctrines'. Lord Clare believed that 'the exchange of a nobleman for a radical is atrocious'. Some of the rhetoric of the opposition to Gower reinforced this interpretation, for example a banner paraded at the nomination ceremony inscribed 'gold cannot buy nor peers compel us'. Gower himself believed there was 'a radical dislike among the freeholders to being represented by a nobleman'. Yet the 'radical' elected in his place was Sir John Fenton Boughey, of Aqualate Hall: a baronet, coal owner and, although a Whig, an opponent of concessions to Roman Catholics.[154]

Conclusion

The royal petulance preceding the election served to make ministers especially conscious of opposition forces and, perhaps, to over-estimate the latter's strength. George IV's threat to dismiss them was nugatory when the parliamentary opposition was itself incapable of commanding a majority in the House of Commons. The Whig front bench exhibited little appetite for power in 1820, acutely conscious as it was that Whiggism's traditional espousal of the liberties of the subject was compromised at a time of acute popular political unrest. Thus for all the rhetorical heat generated during the general election, Liverpool's Ministry was barely dented by the result. The best estimate would be that the Whigs gained thirteen English seats.[155] John Hatsell, the long-standing clerk of the House of Commons, described the damage to the Ministry as 'very trifling, perhaps not exceeding ten'. Henry Bankes MP, a ministerial supporter, was more pessimistic: though he put Liverpool's losses at between seven and ten, he believed this 'will tell upon the back of 150', this being the notional maximum majority Liverpool's Ministry could have commanded before the election.[156] Given the volatility of the House of Commons and the fluid character of the 'parties' within it, his pessimism had some justification. Furthermore, although the deepening of the Whig-Tory divide in the country had little impact on the overall outcome of the general election, it did have longer-term significance, by helping fastidious Whigs overcome their reluctance about throwing in their lot with popular radical opposition to the Ministry, when the royal divorce shot to prominence later in the year.

For the moment, however, a combination of external factors held the drift within the electorate towards Whiggism in check. Cato Street seemed to vindicate the Ministry's stance during the preceding winter and its unfolding details constituted a powerful counterpoint to electioneering. Election issues jostled for column inches with revelations about Thistlewood's intentions. Furthermore, in pro-Ministry papers especially, other news items tended to reinforce the cumulative message of the constitution in danger. To give just one example, the *Courier* of 14 March, squarely in the middle of the election period,

printed only these news items: the Cato Street investigation; the funeral of the
Duke of Berry; the trial of Ribbonmen at the Roscommon Assize; a threatened
Ribbon assault upon the town of Birr and plot to kill the Earl of Rosse;
anti-clearance riots in Ross-shire; and Hunt's declaration that he would turn
his impending trial into that of 'the ------ butchers of Peterloo'. The sole incon-
sequential news story concerned a dispute between an English merchant and
the Norwegian customs. This emphasis is all the more significant given the
tendency of provincial papers to feed off material appearing in the London daily
papers. During the week before, news of revolution in Spain was also seeping
into the British and Irish press. It is scarcely exaggerating to say that the general
election of 1820 was almost a sideshow in comparison with other events in the
spring of 1820.

Notes

1 G. Dixon and B. J. D. Harrison, *Guisborough before 1900* (Leeds: Rigg, 1994), p. 133.
2 J. E. Crowther and P. A. Crowther (eds), *The Diary of Robert Sharp of South Cave: Life in a Yorkshire Village, 1812–37* (Oxford: Oxford University Press, 1997), pp. 6–7.
3 J. Palmer (ed.), *Truro in the Age of Reform, 1815–1837* (Truro: n.p., 1999), p. 42; TNA, HO/100/198/118 (4 February).
4 *Peeps into the Past, Being Passages from the Diary of Thomas Asline Ward* (London: Leng, 1909), p. 264; M. Goffin (ed.), *The Diaries of Absalom Watkin: A Manchester Man, 1787–1861* (Stroud: Sutton, 1993), p. 44.
5 A. Aspinall (ed.), *The Diary of Henry Hobhouse, 1820–1827* (London: Home & Van Thal, 1947), p. 3.
6 TNA, HO 40/11, fols 10-11 (Harwood Folliott to Sidmouth, 6 February).
7 *The Times*, 15 and 29 January, 16 and 23 February; *Courier*, 15 January and 23 February.
8 P. Harling, 'The law of libel and the limits of repression, 1790–1832', *Historical Journal*, 44:1 (2001), p. 126.
9 *Black Book* 16 (8 January), inside rear cover; 17–18 (22 January), inside front cover; 19–20 (15 February), rear covers and pp. 457–8.
10 TNA, HO 40/11 fol. 77 (Wilson to Sidmouth).
11 *Black Dwarf*, 5 and 12 January.
12 *PP* 1831–32 (679) SC Dramatic Literature, evidence of William Moore, p. 225, and Thomas Morton, p. 219.
13 *Ibid.*, pp. 85 and 76.
14 Playbill, 7 December 1819, quoted by D. Worrall, *Theatric Revolution: Drama, Censorship, and Romantic Period Subcultures 1773–1832* (Oxford: Oxford University Press, 2006), p. 202; J. Moody, *Illegitimate Theatre in London, 1770–1840* (Cambridge, Cambridge University Press, 2000), pp. 41, 119.
15 *British Stage and Literary Cabinet*, 4:39 (March 1820), 141.
16 Sybil Rosenfeld, *York Theatre* (London: Society for Theatre Research, 2001), p. 209.
17 *Hampshire Telegraph*, 24 January.
18 G. Cruikshank, 'Coriolanus Addressing the Plebeians', 29 February 1820, (British Museum, Department of Prints and Drawings, AN168079001); J. Bate, *Shakespearean Constitutions: Politics, Theatre, Criticism, 1730–1830* (Oxford: Oxford University Press, 1989), pp. 102–3.

19 William Duncombe, *Lucius Junius Brutus* (1735).
20 *British Stage and Literary Cabinet*, 3:26 (February 1819), pp. 40–3.
21 BL, Playbills 306, Drayton (24 May); see also 264, vol. 1, Stafford (3 December 1819).
22 *Quarterly Review,* 22:44 (1829), 404. See also 'Vindex', 'Mr Howard Payne and the Quarterly Reviewers', *Theatrical Inquisitor, and Monthly Mirror,* 16:93 (March), pp. 128–34 for an attack on the *Quarterly's* criticism of *Brutus*.
23 *Liverpool Mercury*, 30 June; York Minster Library, Playbills Collection, LT[A] 1820-08-YOR, 8 March.
24 *The Times*, 27 October 1795; Moody, *Illegitimate Theatre*, p. 48n1.
25 SC Dramatic Literature, evidence of Morton, p. 219.
26 G. Colman, *Observations on the Notice of a Motion to Rescind Certain Powers of His Majesty's Lord Chamberlain*, quoted in Worrall, *Theatric Revolution*, p. 293.
27 TNA, HO 44/4 fols 3, 9, 14, 16 (10, 28 and 29 January).
28 TNA, 44/5 fol. 7 et seq (examination of B); D. Johnson, *Regency Revolution: The Case of Arthur Thistlewood* (Salisbury, Compton Russell, 1974), p. 89.
29 TNA, HO 44/4 fol. 7 (27 January) and HO 44/5 fol 7 et seq (examination of B).
30 TNA, HO 44/5 fol. 32 (1 March).
31 TNA, HO 44/1 fol. 185 (13 February).
32 G. T. Wilkinson, *An Authentic History of the Cato Street Conspiracy, with the Trials at Large of the Conspirators*, 2nd edn (London: Kelly, 1820), pp. 150, 156.
33 *Ibid.*, pp. 150–1.
34 *Ibid.*, pp. 154–5; *Diary of Henry Hobhouse*, pp. 11–14; F. K. Donnelly, 'The general rising of 1820: a study of social conflict in the industrial revolution' (PhD thesis, University of Sheffield, 1975), p. 95.
35 M. Chase, 'Thomas Preston', in J. Bellamy and J. Saville (eds), *Dictionary of Labour Biography* (Basingstoke: Macmillan, 1987), vol. 8, pp. 192–8; M. Chase, 'John George', in J. Bellamy and J. Saville (eds), *Dictionary of Labour Biography* (Basingstoke: Macmillan, 2000), vol. 10, pp. 64-8.
36 *The Times*, 28 February.
37 M. Chase, *'The People's Farm': English Radical Agrarianism, 1775–1840* (Oxford: Oxford University Press, 1988), p. 119; I. Prothero, *Artisans and Politics in Early Nineteenth-Century London: John Gast and his Times* (Folkestone: Dawson, 1979), p. 127; TNA, HO 42/182 (5 November 1818); HO 42/188 (30 June 1819); HO 42/190 (21 June 1819); HO 44/4 fols 3 and 5 (10 and 25 January 1820); HO 44/4/300 (28 February).
38 TNA, HO 44/4/275 (27 February).
39 *Diary of Henry Hobhouse*, p. 13.
40 TNA, HO 44/6 fol. 127 [April?].
41 F. K. Donnelly, 'A Cato Street conspirator in North America', *Labour History Review* (forthcoming 2013).
42 J. Brown, *Sixty Years' Gleanings from Life's Harvest: A Genuine Autobiography* (Cambridge: Palmer, 1858), p. 278. See also N. Mansfield, 'John Brown: a shoemaker in Place's London', *History Workshop Journal*, 8 (Autumn 1979), p. 134.
43 P. Benton, *The History of Rochford Hundred* (Rochford: Harrington, 1867), p. 343.
44 'A master shoemaker', 'My life and adventures', *Boot and Shoemaker*, 14 June–9 August 1879.
45 TNA, HO 102/32/218 (1 March).
46 A. Richmond, *Narrative of the Condition of the Manufacturing Population* (London: Miller, 1824), p. 184.
47 TNA, HO102/32/222 (Monteith to Sidmouth, 2 March).
48 John Belchem, 'Republicanism, popular constitutionalism and the radical platform in

early nineteenth-century England', *Social History*, 6 (1981); John Belchem, *'Orator' Hunt: Henry Hunt and English Working-Class Radicalism* (Oxford: Oxford University Press, 1985), pp. 110–11, 130–1, 147–9, 151, 153–5, 256; see also G. Pentland, *The Spirit of the Union: Popular Politics in Scotland, 1815–20* (London: Pickering & Chatto, 2011), pp. 67, 90, 92, 107.

49 'Statement of Joseph Brayshaw relating to his political mission', *Republican*, 4 October 1822, p. 586; J. Brayshaw, *An Appeal to the People of England, on the Necessity of Parliamentary Reform, Pointing Out the Corruptions of the Present System, and some of the Evils Flowing Therefrom and the Means of Accomplishing a Parliamentary Reform, Recommended to the Serious Attention of Every Honest Man* (Newcastle upon Tyne: printed for the author by J. Marshall, 1819).

50 J. Christodoulou, 'The Glasgow Universalist Church and Scottish radicalism from the French revolution to Chartism: a theology of liberation', *Journal of Ecclesiastical History*, 43:4 (1992); Chase, *'The People's Farm'*, pp. 50, 52, 109–10, 150.

51 *Leeds Mercury*, 11 December 1819; *Caledonian Mercury*, 16 December.

52 'Statement of Joseph Brayshaw', *Republican*, 4 October 1822, pp. 584-90; *Caledonian Mercury*, 2 March 1820.

53 *Republican*, 4 October 1822, pp. 585, 587. Mann's mission was confirmed to the Home Office on 19 March: TNA, HO 44/1/218. He subsequently admitted having not checked the major Midland towns, and claimed that Cartwright warned him off meeting Thistlewood lest he be arrested see *Cobbett's Two-penny Trash*, April 1832, p. 211.

54 TNA, HO 40/11 fols 83–4 (Deposition of Palmer, 20 February).

55 TNA, HO 40/11 fol. 203 (Beckett to Sidmouth, 14 March); E. Baines, *History, Directory and Gazetteer of the County of York*, vol. 2 (Leeds: Baines, 1823), p. 217.

56 TNA, HO 40/13 fol. 7 (report by Alpha, 25 May, referring to conversations on the 5th).

57 TNA, HO 44/4/263 (27 February). Chippendale worked for the Home Office, 1801-21 and, according to Henry Hobhouse (Sidmouth's Under Secretary), 'obtained for the government far more useful information than any other individual': see John Foster, *Class Struggle and the Industrial Revolution* (London: Methuen, 1974), p. 288.

58 TNA, HO 40/11 fols 57 (29 February, Lyon to Byng) and 109–10 (Dunne to Byng).

59 TNA, HO 40/11 fol. 101 (deposition of Sarah Turner, 3 March).

60 TNA, HO 40/11 fols 48 (Cartledge to Allsopp, 28 February) and 50 (Haigh Allen to Hobhouse, 28 February), fol. 113 (Dukinfield to Sidmouth, 5 March).

61 WYAS (Leeds), WYL/250/6/2/B1/1/17 (Byng to Lascelles, 2 March); TNA, HO 40/11 fol. 66 (Mayor of Leeds to Lascelles, 29 February).

62 TNA, HO 40/11 fols 105 (Horton to Sidmouth), 170 (deposition of Abel Grove) and 164–6 (Lloyd to Hobhouse).

63 *The Private Letters of Princess Lieven to Prince Metternich, 1820–1826*, edited and with a biographical foreword by Peter Quennell (London: Murray, 1937), pp. 17–18, quoting letter to Metternich, 1 March.

64 DRO, 152M/C/1820/OH/43 (Sidmouth to Harrowby, 30 March).

65 DRO, 150M/C/1820/OH/2 and 18 (letters to Grant, 24 February and Bloomfield, 3 March).

66 TNA, HO 40/11 fol. 105v (draft reply to Horton).

67 TNA, HO 44/6 fol. 9 (4 April).

68 TNA, HO 40/11 fols 85–6 (3 March).

69 TNA, HO 44/1/208 (6 March) and HO 44/5/346 (Howell to Home Office, 13 March); DRO, 152M/C/1820/OZ (26 February) and 152M/C/1820/OF (1 March).

70 *Evans and Ruffy's Farmers' Journal*, 28 February; TNA, HO 102/32/413–21. J. Parkhill, *History of Paisley* (Paisley: Stewart, 1857), p. 60.

71 TNA, HO 40/14 fols 131 (information of Alpha, 21 June), 13–12 (copy of Wilson letter, 6 July), 135 (Toothill and Lang's address to France [copy] 11 July), 137 (Wilson, 20 July).

72 WYAS (Leeds), Harewood Mss, WYL250/6/2/B2/1/12 (Byng to Lascelles, 29 December 1819); TNA, HO 40/12, fols 53–6, 166–7 (4 and 13 April).

73 H. Martineau, *The History of England during the Thirty Years' Peace, 1816–46* (London: Knight, 1849), p. 243.

74 DRO, 152M/C/1820/OH/6 and 9 (26 and 27 February).

75 C. D. Yonge (compiler), *The Life and Administration of Robert Banks, Second Earl of Liverpool* (Macmillan, 1868), vol. 3, pp. 11–22.

76 BL, Add. Mss 38283 fol. 155, Eldon to Liverpool, '10 o'clock' [8] February 1820; see also *Letters of Princess Lieven*, p. 13 (letter to Metternich 16 February): Leach 'is always with the king and goes on telling him from morning to night that a Whig ministry would undertake the divorce, whereas the present Ministry evades the question'.

77 *Letters of Princess Lieven*, (9 February), p. 12.

78 For the minute see Yonge, *Life and Administration*, vol. 3, pp. 25–33 (quotations from pp. 29 and 31) and BL, Add. Mss 38283 fols 46–62. See also R. A. Melikan, *John Scott, Lord Eldon, 1751–1838: The Duty of Loyalty* (Cambridge: Cambridge University Press, 1999), pp. 279–81.

79 BL, Add. Mss 38282 fol. 341, undated document in which the Archbishop 'humbly submits to His Majesty' liturgical alterations; F. Fraser, *The Unruly Queen: The Life of Queen Caroline* (New York: Anchor, 2009), pp. 348–9.

80 Yonge, *Life and Administration*, vol. 3, pp. 34–8; N. Gash, *Lord Liverpool: The Life and Political Career of Robert Banks Jenkinson* (London: Weidenfeld, 1984); L. Strachey and R. Fulford (eds), *The Greville Memoirs, 1814–1860: Volume 1, January 1814–July 1830* (London: Macmillan, 1938), p. 89.

81 DRO, 152M/C/1820/OH/67 (13 February); TNA, HO40/15 fol. 6 (report of Shegoe).

82 See Yonge, *Life and Administration*, vol. 3, pp 38–44 for the text. *Diary of Henry Hobhouse*, p. 9.

83 Yonge, *Life and Administration*, vol. 3, pp. 44–5.

84 *The Times*, 31 January; letters to Lord Lonsdale, 2 and 4 February, reprinted in *The Letters of William and Dorothy Wordsworth … The Middle Years, Part II: 1812–1820*, arr. and ed. by E. de Selincourt, rev. and ed. by M. Moorman and A. G. Hill (Oxford: Oxford University Press, 1970), p. 581.

85 *HP*, vol. 1, pp. 218–19.

86 *The Poll for Members in Parliament to represent the City of York* (York: Sotheran, 1818), p. ix.

87 J. G. Lockhart (ed.), *Memoirs of the Life of Sir Walter Scott*, 2nd edn (Edinburgh: Cadell, 1839), vol. 6, p. 210.

88 TNA, HO 43/29/254–6 (Hobhouse to Pemberton, 6 March).

89 TNA, HO 33/2/135 (18 March).

90 'Pensioner Dick' squib, in NCL, 'Addresses, songs &c., connected with the 1820 Durham County Election'.

91 G. Peel (ed.), *The Private Letters of Sir Robert Peel* (London: Murray, 1920), p. 28;

Ashburnham quoted in J. McQuiston, 'Sussex aristocrats in 1820', *English Historical Review*, 88 (1973), p. 540.

92 DRO, 152M/C/1820 OZ (8, 12, and 17 March).

93 *HP*, vol. 2, p. 623.

94 *Storr's Impartial Narrative of the Proceedings for the Contested Election at Grantham* (Grantham: Storr, 1820), pp. 27–8 and appendix pp. 3–42.

95 1820 election broadside, reprinted in H. Barker and D.Vincent (eds), *Language, Print and Electoral Politics, 1790–1832: Newcastle-under-Lyme Broadsides* (Woodbridge: Boydell, 2002), pp. 231–2.

96 *Glasgow Herald*, 31 March.

97 DRO, 152M/C/1820/0Z (Sheffield to Sidmouth, 17 March).

98 *Freemen of Newcastle, Resident in Darlington and Neighbourhood*, in NCL, 'Addresses and squibs in the contested election' (Newcastle, 1820).

99 E. C. Curwen (ed.), *The Journal of Gideon Mantell, Surgeon and Geologist, Covering the Years 1818–52* (Oxford: Oxford University Press, 1940), p. 17.

100 Carmarthenshire CRO, Dynevor MSS, Carmarthenshire Parliamentary Elections (1820), quoted in F. O'Gorman, 'Campaign rituals and ceremonies: the social meaning of elections in England 1780–1860', *Past and Present*, 135 (1992), pp. 96–7.

101 *Letters of Princess Lieven* (20 March), p. 23. Pink was the election colour of the Whig magnates, the Cavendish family.

102 Private Collection, Correspondence respecting Brandling's Northumberland election campaign: Robert Thorp's election accounts, entries for 15 March.

103 NCL, 'Collection of papers, speeches, &c., &c., delivered at the Newcastle election of 1820'.

104 Private Collection, Correspondence respecting Brandling's Northumberland election campaign: Correspondence respecting 1820 Northumberland County Election: Fenwick to Clayton, schedule of bills paid, 20 March; general statement of election bills, 17 April; list of constables and special constables, March 1820.

105 *HP*, vol. 2, pp. 787–8.

106 *Ibid.*, pp. 777–8.

107 *Ibid.*, p. 335.

108 H. Maxwell (ed.), *The Creevey Papers: A Selection from the Correspondence and Diaries of the Late Thomas Creevey, MP*, 3rd edn (London: Murray, 1912), pp. 373–4.

109 P. Searby, 'Paternalism, disturbance and parliamentary reform: society and politics in Coventry, 1819–32', *International Review of Social History*, 22 (1977), p. 207.

110 Sheffield Archives, Wentworth Woodhouse Muniments F/49/57 (Graham to Fitzwilliam, 4 February).

111 Sheffield Archives, Wentworth Woodhouse Muniments F/48/157 (Hotham to Fitzwilliam, 2 November); E. A. Smith, *Whig Principles and Party Politics: Earl Fitzwilliam and the Whig party, 1748–1833* (Manchester: Manchester University Press, 1975), 362; see also *HP*, vol. 3, p. 289.

112 *HP*, vol 2, pp. 200, 154.

113 H.T. Dickinson, *Caricatures and the Constitution, 1760–1832* (Cambridge: Chadwyck-Healey, 1986), p. 275.

114 *HP*, vol. 3, p. 74; T. H. B. Oldfield, *A Key to the House of Commons. Being a History of the Last General Election in 1818* (London: Dolby, 1820), p. 37.

115 Quoted in *The Times*, 31 March.

116 I. d'Alton, *Protestant Society and Politics in Cork, 1812–44* (Cork: Cork University Press, 1980), p. 102.

117 *HP*, vol. 3, pp. 674, 662, 680, 842, 696, 764, 872 and 785.

118 F. O'Gorman, *Voters, Patrons and Parties: The Unreformed Electoral System of Hanoverian England 1734–1832* (Oxford: Oxford University Press, 1989), p. 256.

119 TNA, HO40/11 fols 151–2, 167–202 (12 and 14 March); *Jackson's Oxford Journal*, 18 March; G. Herbert, *Shoemaker's Window: Recollections of Banbury in Oxfordshire before the Railway Age* (Chichester: Phillimore, 1971), pp. 6, 84, 128.

120 DRO 152M/C/1820/OZ (Sidmouth to Sheffield, 19 March).

121 *Hampshire Telegraph*, 24 July; *Morning Post*, 28 July.

122 *Durham Chronicle*, 5 August; NCL, 'Proceedings of the Durham County Election, 1820'.

123 *HP*, vol. 3, p. 26.

124 *Liverpool Mercury*, 14 March 1820.

125 *HP*, vol. 3, p. 266.

126 *Morning Post*, 4 March.

127 *Morning Post*, 14 March; *Cobbett's Weekly Political Register*, 25 March, pp. 114–15; G. Spater, *William Cobbett: The Poor Man's Friend* (Cambridge: Cambridge University Press, 1982), vol. 2, pp. 393–7.

128 *HP*, vol. 1, p. 107.

129 *HP*, vol. 3, p. 568.

130 F. Bamford and G. W. Wellington (eds), *The Journal of Mrs Arbuthnot, 1820–32: vol. 1, February 1820 to December 1825* (London: Macmillan, 1950), p. 11; *HP*, vol. 3, pp. 604–5; M. Fry, *The Dundas Despotism* (Edinburgh: Edinburgh University Press, 1992), p. 346.

131 [W. S. Darter], *Reminiscences of Reading. By an Octogenarian* (Reading: Blagrave Street Steam Printing Works, 1889), pp. 133–4.

132 NCL, 'Addresses, songs &c., connected with the 1820 Durham County Election', fols 19 and 64.

133 *A Whig of 1688*, in NCL, 'Collection of papers, speeches, &c., delivered at the Northumberland election in 1820', fol. 20.

134 *The Times*, 6 March.

135 Belchem, *'Orator' Hunt*, p. 117; *HP*, vol. 3, pp. 604–5.

136 DRO, 152M/C/1820/OZ (8 March).

137 O'Gorman, *Voters, Patrons and Parties*, p. 308.

138 Letter, 27 February, Grey Mss, cit by D. R. Fisher, 'The Election of 1820', *HP*, vol. 1, p. 217.

139 BL, Add. Mss 51609, Letter to Sir Robert Adair, 8 March [1820].

140 Letter to Lord Murray, 20 March, cited by Fisher, 'Election of 1820', *HP*, vol. 1, p. 218; Peel to Croker, 23 March, reprinted L. J. Jennings (ed.), *The Croker Papers: The Correspondence and Diaries of the Late Right Honourable John Wilson Croker … 1809 to 1830* (London: Murray, 1884), p. 170.

141 BL, Add. Mss 38742 fol. 7, quoted by G. I. T. Machin, *The Catholic Question in English Politics, 1820 to 1830* (Oxford: Oxford University Press, 1964), p. 22.

142 BL, Add. Mss 38458 fol. 321, Fisher, 'Election of 1820', *HP*, vol. 1, p. 218.

143 Letter to Canning, 23 March 1820, Harewood Mss, Fisher, 'Election of 1820', *HP*, vol. 1, p. 218.

144 DRO, Fortescue Manuscripts, 1262M/Elections/19.

145 Letter to Canning, 23 March 1820, Harewood Mss, cit by Fisher, 'Election of 1820', p. 218.

146 Letter to Arbuthnot, 29 March 1820, A. Aspinall (ed.), *The Correspondence of Charles Arbuthnot*, Camden 3rd ser, vol. 65 (Royal Historical Society, 1941), p. 19.

147 Letter to Lonsdale, Cumbria RO, Lonsdale Mss, quoted by Fisher, 'Election of 1820', p. 218.

148 Huskisson to Arbuthnot, 24 Mar. 1820, Huskisson Papers, Brit. Mus., Add. Mss 38742 fol. 6; Letter to Ashburnham, 28 March 1820, quoted by McQuiston, 'Sussex aristocrats in 1820', p. 553.

149 Letter to Byron (31 March 1820) quoted in P. W. Graham, *Byron's Bulldog: The Letters of John Cam Hobhouse to Lord Byron* (Columbus: Ohio State University Press, 1984), p. 286.

150 Arbuthnot, *Journal*, p. 17 (8 May).

151 *HP*, vol. 2, p. 663.

152 *The Poll for Members in Parliament to represent the City of York* (York: Sotheran, 1820), p. ix.

153 R. Foster, *The Politics of County Power: Wellington and the Hampshire Gentlemen, 1820-52* (London: Harvester, 1990), pp. 107-8.

154 *HP*, vol. 3, p. 6.

155 *HP*, vol. 1, pp. 219–20.

156 *Diary and Correspondence of Charles Abbot, Lord Colchester, edited by his son Charles, Lord Colchester* (London: Murray, 1861), vol. 3, pp. 124–25 (6 and 10 April).

4 Easter risings

Introduction

'Accounts from Manchester, Leeds, Glasgow, etc., are unsatisfactory', Lord Sidmouth told the Duke of Wellington on 21 March: 'A Simultaneous Explosion appears to be meditated at an early Period. Much will depend on the result of the Trials at York, Lancaster, Leicester and Warwick.'[1] The Home Secretary was deeply preoccupied. He doubted that the Banbury election riots had been apolitical: they were evidence, he thought, of 'a most malignant Spirit [which] is incessantly at work, the prompt and effectual Controul of which can alone avert from this Country the Horrors of Anarchy'.[2] He was also smarting at the jury's verdict in the trial of the Leeds bookseller James Mann, the previous week, that though Mann was 'guilty of uttering' a seditious publication (an issue of *Sherwin's Political Register*) he had not done so with any seditious intention. Such a verdict was tantamount to an acquittal. It would be vain, Sidmouth told George IV's private secretary the previous day, to predict the outcome of Hunt's trial at York.[3] Hunt's route there had included a tumultuous torchlit welcome at Leeds. His journey, in the words of a Leeds paper, 'more resembled the triumphal march of a conqueror than the journey of a culprit advancing to trial'. However prosecution witnesses were waylaid and 'assailed with hisses, groans & imprecations'. Rather than risk the same, the judges had decided to take a circuitous route to the assize. 'I cannot say I feel secure of our Jury', George Maule, the Government's agent at the trial had told Sidmouth.[4] The other impending trials that concerned Sidmouth were less momentous but collectively they constituted a significant signal of the Government's determination to neutralise radicalism. Sir Francis Burdett was on trial at Leicester to answer sedition charges arising from his criticisms, in an address to his Westminster electorate, of how authority had handled Peterloo. Doubting that a London jury would find him guilty, the Government had initiated a risky prosecution at the Leicestershire Assize on the grounds that Burdett had initially written the address while staying in the county.

At Lancaster eight men were stranding trial for attending a political meeting at Burnley in November 1819, 'armed and arrayed in a warlike manner', and a ninth for the manufacture of pike heads. At Warwick five men, Major Cartwright and the *Black Dwarf*'s editor Thomas Wooler among them, were standing trial for conspiracy in the election of Sir Charles Wolseley as a 'legislatorial attorney' for Birmingham the previous July. Birmingham, population 102,000, had no MP of its own: it was proposed Wolseley would present himself to the House of Commons and insist upon taking a seat. He never did so, and in April he too was gaoled for sedition and conspiracy.[5]

However, what exercised the Home Secretary most was intelligence from several directions that the exposure of Cato Street had done nothing to neutralise plans for widespread insurgency. While it may be an exaggeration to claim that a general rising was planned for the spring of 1820, or that there was a 'Scottish insurrection' that Easter, the evidence for a co-ordinated campaign of insurgency across several regions (including perhaps Ireland) is compelling.[6]

Ireland

> Oh! fatal was the day,
> When the Union passed away,
> And our Parliament had crossed over the main,
> Dissension they did sow,
> Which caused our overthrow,
> And deprived us of our Chruskeen lawn.
> …
> Brave Irishmen so dear,
> The time is drawing near,
> When our Shamrock will appear in full green,
> So cheerful and so gay,
> Oh! come then happy day,
> When in friendship we will take our Chruskeen lawn.[7]

Insurgents in the west of Ireland continued to challenge the region's social and political elites. Attacks on gentry homes to seize arms met little resistance. 'The ribbon system has made an alarming progress in Galway & is rapidly diffusing itself', Under Secretary Grant told Sidmouth just before the Lord Lieutenant arrived back from his compassionate leave. Existing troops were not sufficient and although the Peelers were forming fast they were still not at full strength; Dublin Castle rescinded an order for the Irish Veteran Battalion to leave for Scotland and diverted it to Galway. In all 3,145 Irish army pensioners were mobilised by April.[8] However, both senior Irish civil servants and army officers scorned the Cabinet's request that 'at least Half of the Militia' in Ireland should be called out. Not only was there no provision in the Irish budget for 1820 to do so, ballots for the militia ('almost invariably … considered an obnoxious

measure') had not taken place for five or six years. There were fears for the consequences of placing a significant portion of the Irish population under arms; the
view of the army's commander in Ireland was that Irish militia regiments should
only serve if sent to do so in Britain, while his Adjutant General frankly doubted
the discipline even of the militia's commissioned officers.[9] However, uniquely in
the United Kingdom, Irish yeomanry regiments could be billeted beyond their
home county.[10] Deploying yeomanry from loyalist areas was therefore an attrac-
tive alternative to embodying the militia. Some 1,200 Ulster yeomen were
mobilised to release regular troops for service in Connacht.[11] Regular troops
stationed in Connacht numbered 2,542 in January 1820. By 16 March there
were 5,886 of them, more than 28 per cent of all regular troops in Ireland.[12]

Of these soldiers 3,696 were sent to Galway where initially many were
forced to sleep in the open for want of billets. The situation was similar in
County Mayo, where it was reported on 8 March: 'our posts are weakened by
illness of the men who at some of them have not taken off their clothes for 36
nights.' Local people 'were sworn not to provide the military with anything on
their arrival', one officer reported to his commander.[13] The Peace Proclamation
Force (1,142 men when finally at full strength) experienced similar difficulties.[14]
Communication between the force's dispersed and isolated attachments was
difficult and individual groups operated in a spirit of grim self-reliance. Some
detachments without billets forced their way into empty houses. Major John
Wills, commander of the Roscommon Peace Proclamation Force seized the
corpse of a Ribbonman killed in a skirmish. 'In an exalted situation, he was
exhibited to the gaze of the surrounding multitude, wearing at his breast a label,
on which was inscribed in large and conspicuous characters, the odious designa-
tion: "Ribbonman".'[15] At Ahascragh in east Galway, basic supplies were seized by
force from villagers. At Belmont in County Mayo an eleven-strong police
detachment, sent to arrest a Ribbon captain, disobeyed an order for only one of
them to shoot at a gathering crowd. All eleven opened fire and five Ribbonmen
fell, one killed outright. At Ballinlough, Roscommon, the police station was
stormed by a crowd demanding the release of Ribbonist prisoners: two demonstrators were shot dead.[16]

There were recurrent skirmishes as Ribbonmen attacked billets, or
ambushed troops or Peelers. Two Ribbonmen were killed when a crowd of 160
attacked police at Aghrane, Galway: at the funeral of one of them, mourners knelt
on the coffin vowing revenge.[17] On 26 February there were several simultaneous
(and highly symbolic) attacks on Peelers as they attended church parade – at
Ahascragh with fatalities on both sides. The following night the 78th Highlanders
fought a battle with insurgents on the road out of Moylough, while at Castlebar,
police were attacked on patrol then besieged for five hours inside their makeshift
barracks. Having taken hostages they thought they were safe, but ladders, straw
and torches were brought to burn them out. Then the owner of one of the
houses was dragged before the barracks and the police compelled to release their

prisoners to ensure his safety. In the melee that followed one of the prisoners was allegedly killed by Ribbonmen.[18]

Just before he returned to Ireland Talbot had told Sidmouth 'I cannot entertain any apprehension of their [the Ribbonmen] giving much serious trouble to government, as they have not, as far as I understand, any person of consequence among them'. His confidence betrayed a complete failure to comprehend the reality of politics beyond the Irish capital. So many of the Galway gentry had fled that all army officers of the rank of captain or above in the county had to be sworn in as magistrates.[19] Within a week of arriving in Dublin Talbot was writing of a resurgence of Ribbonism beyond Connacht, of Protestants forced to swear they would convert to Rome and of his horrified conviction 'beyond all doubt' that Thistlewood had recently visited Ireland. This at least Sidmouth could refute, but to Talbot's report that 'a general rising may be expected to take place on or about St Patrick's Day' he had no response.[20]

Such were the tensions in early 1820 that across Ireland any unexplained stranger was regarded with suspicion, though the evidence marshalled against them was generally circumstantial. In Chapter 2 we noted 'English pedlars' exhibiting printed handkerchiefs depicting the field of Peterloo. There were unsubstantiated rumours of English and Scottish visitors passing through Roscommon, disguised as pedlars and talking 'a good deal about distress'. Hawkers and singers of 'inflammatory' ballads were also suspected to be agitators, though of the songs that reached Dublin Castle only one was plausibly treasonable (two of its verses head this section).[21] In Ulster an unknown Englishman 'of the lowest order' spent a fortnight at Clondavaddog on the Donegal coast in March. He aroused particular distrust because, a local Church of Ireland parson claimed, Clondavaddog had supported the 1798 Rebellion and was 'where the Ribbon association is known to have originated'. 'The part in question of the County is the last to which a Stranger of that rank could have any good discoverable motive for resorting, & none at all for remaining in.'[22] No-less conjectural was anonymous information that British and Irish radicals communicated with each other through commercial travellers: this one might dismiss were it not perhaps for the date (16 February) and its clear conclusion that some momentous event was in preparation.[23]

Delegates were said to pass frequently to and from Ireland, 'stirring up a Rebellion', and considerable sums of money 'from persons in decent circumstances' had been taken across the Irish Sea. 'The famous Toole', a captain in the 1798 rebellion now living in Manchester, was a pivotal figure, claimed the informer Samuel Fleming. Delegates from Ireland were expected to visit Manchester during the second week of March to agree a time 'to rise together & at the same Moment', Toole told Fleming. Irish ex-patriots in Stockport spoke of lying in ambush to 'shoot all ye Men in power … as the Ribband Men did in Ireland'.[24] Tootall, whom we encountered in the previous chapter apropos of correspondence with France, stated in May 1820 that a delegate meeting at

Nottingham the previous November had chosen him 'to cross the Herring Pool' to investigate 'organization' in the 'Sister Nation'.[25] An alternative and more plausible version of the Thistlewood in Ireland rumour was that it was his son Julian who was there, sighted distributing copper tokens depicting a cap or tree of liberty, specifically at Sixmilebridge on the Limerick-Clare border. Coincidentally, or not, County Clare's chief stipendiary magistrate at the time believed that 'a more extended conspiracy' was spreading from Dublin through 'the ribbon system', information about which specifically derived from Sixmilebridge.[26]

A variety of other intelligence sources referred to written communications, though direct interception seems to have been beyond the authorities' means.[27] We have already seen (Chapter 2 above) that when police raided the home of the Spencean James Watson in late February, correspondence with an Irish radical 'desirous of promoting a connection' was discovered.[28] A soldier in the 84th Foot confessed to a senior officer that, while on leave near Manchester, he had learnt from 'disaffected persons' of correspondence with Ireland: 'a disturbance would be raised in that country for the purpose of drawing away the troops from England – whereby an opportunity would be afforded for renewing the commotions here, with better hopes of success.'[29] One report, upon which Sidmouth believed 'great reliance can be placed', offered precise information concerning contact between Britain and Ireland. It claimed that key correspondence was routed through Edward and James Tynan (or Dynan), respectively of Dublin and Edgeworthstown, County Longford; and through one Macready of Dundalk, Louth. One of the Tynans had recently been travelling in Ireland, checking 'the state of preparation for general rising', and assurances had been sent to England concerning 'the state of forwardness that the Irish preparations are in'. All concerned awaited 'some great national calamity, which they intimate cannot be very distant, or some striking political occurrence give the signal for a general rising'.[30]

Ribbonism was as close to folk-Catholic and Gaelic traditions as it was to English and Scottish radicalism.[31] So it is improbable that there was a complete sympathy and understanding between insurgent elements on both sides of the Irish Sea. Yet indications of correspondence between Ireland and Britain, though individually elusive, are sufficiently numerous to suggest that there was an element of collusion between insurrectionary elements in the United Kingdom, and perhaps some pattern to their activities, during early 1820. Galway's chief magistrate told Dublin Castle the situation in the county had worsened over the period 23 February to 3 March.[32] With the spring there was in any case some change in the nature of Ribbon protests. It was now that the movement's objective of reversing the drift to livestock farming in western Ireland became fully apparent. 'The nocturnal lawgivers' were giving pastoral farmers notice 'that the Cattle have had possession long enough of the rich pastures, and that it is time for Man to have his turn'. Livestock were being abandoned in the fields.

The Ribbonmen had forced 'the total neglect of the Spring Business', Talbot was told, 'not a plough or a spade are at work'.[33] Landowners in east Galway discovered their 'Stock driven home to their doors and delivered up to them ... their herds[men] as well as their tenants being sworn to give no assistance' as their pasture lands were seized for potato grounds.[34] In early March, an army billeting officer noticed just one plough at work, the length of a twenty-seven-mile ride across eastern Galway: 'the face of the County appeared desolate in the extreme'.[35] Over the border in County Clare, grasslands were destroyed in nocturnal protests. Placards, some signed 'Captain Ribbin Man from Cannaught', were even posted announcing which fields were to be 'turned-up' by spade-wielding protesters. This form of agrarian protest was especially prevalent in south Munster.[36] Herdsmen, shepherds and tenant farmers were intimidated. At Drum in south-east Roscommon a tenant was murdered after refusing to quit his land; others had the thatched roofs stripped from their homes.[37] Possibly the most shocking of this phase of Ribbon protests occurred at Rahara (Roscommon) where eight pregnant ewes were slaughtered, their lambs ripped from their carcasses. Animal maiming of this severity was extremely rare and may plausibly be interpreted as a form of symbolic murder. No meat was taken away: protest and intimidation, not sheer hunger politics, were at the root of the action.[38]

Perceptions of a crisis in Ireland increased during early March but the cause of this stemmed from events (or, more correctly, non-events) just beyond Connacht at Athlone on the Westmeath-Roscommon border and, twenty-five miles to the south, Birr (Parsonstown) in King's County. Athlone would, it was said, be the focal point for a general rising on either St Patrick's Day or 21 March, its annual fair. The town was hurriedly fortified and horse artillery sent from Dublin.[39] Nothing happened: whether the rumour was false, or the preparations sufficient to discourage an attack, was never clear. Mass military confrontation of this nature was not characteristic of Ribbonism at this time. Despite this, the greatest credibility was ascribed to reports of a plot to murder the Earl of Rosse at his seat at Birr Castle. With Birr's garrison empty because the 9th Royal Veterans had been sent west to Galway, all was 'anarchy and consternation'. The mooted assassination of Rosse, a prominent Irish peer increasingly noted for reactionary anti-Catholic views, would have been by far the biggest single incident of the 1820 Ribbon rising. It was communicated in an anonymous letter received by Mrs Legge, who ran a printers, reading room and circulating library with her husband in Birr; her brother-in-law was also the Earl's agent. Rosse determined to resist, fortified his castle and swore in as special constables all the town's male residents capable of bearing arms.[40] Army pensioners wheeled out ageing artillery pieces. The Castle was barricaded and selected buildings in and near the town turned into fire posts. The 44th infantry, on the march to Galway, were diverted and arrived in Birr on 8 March just in time for the anticipated assault.[41]

Again, nothing happened and the letter was exposed as a hoax. Indicative of anxiety within the political establishment about a coordinated British and Irish insurrection, the finger of suspicion immediately fell on a Scottish journeyman printer, employed by the Legges and known to have been in London at the end of 1819. When he was shown to be innocent, Mrs Legge herself was identified as the perpetrator, for motives that were never discovered.[42] Yet fears that Birr was to be stormed by a Ribbonist army of redressers, far from subsiding, simply shifted onto the anticipated reaction to the funerals on 25 March of two Ribbonmen killed by the authorities. Rosse maintained both town and castle on a war footing: all trade was suspended. By the 26th many Birr residents were reportedly 'ill in consequence of the cold and fatigue and anxiety … sitting up at night' to repel an onslaught of Ribbonmen that never came.[43] At the root of this extraordinary episode lay not Mrs Legge's hoax but a misperception about the nature and potentiality of the Ribbonist insurgency. It was not a re-enactment of the 1798 Irish Rebellion. Ribbonism, *if* it was centrally coordinated at all, mustered no armies but was a dynamic and shifting web of guerrilla activities.

Ultimately it was this that seems to have assured Dublin Castle that widespread calls for the Insurrection Act could be refused, even once the new Parliament had assembled following the general election. There was no shortage of such calls: the Grand Juries at both the Roscommon and Galway Assizes formally petitioned for the Act and Talbot was strongly inclined to accede to their requests.[44] However, by April the concentration of troops and Peace Proclamation constabulary in Connacht was taking its toll of the Ribbonmen. It did so not by defeating them militarily, but by making widespread arrests. Swiftly translated into judicial retribution these sapped the morale, though not the sense of resentment, of those who supported Ribbonism. Fortuitously the Assizes for both counties took place in early spring. At Roscommon the judge prolonged the Assize to accommodate the quantity of prosecutions: even so twenty-seven cases were postponed to the next Assize. However, nine Ribbonmen were sentenced to death, eight to transportation, and five to be whipped and imprisoned. The remorseless Major Wills urged that all the executions should be staged at the scene of the crime, and the corpses then retained for burial in the gaol rather than (as was the practice) returned to their families.[45] At Galway all forty-six prosecutions of Ribbonmen were successful: nineteen were found guilty of minor misdemeanours; nineteen more were sentenced to be publicly whipped and then imprisoned for more serious offences; five were transported for seven years and two for life; two were executed, including the supposed local Captain.[46] Beyond Connacht, five Roman Catholics were executed for sectarian murders at the County Down assize, and five for Ribbon offences at County Derry; in Antrim six Ribbonmen were whipped through the streets of Ballymena. In Tipperary an alleged insurgent from Galway was whipped through the village of Two Mile

Barns simply for wearing a green ribbon round his hat and 'exciting the people'.[47]

All these sentences were carried into effect within days, leaving no time in which to organise appeals, demonstrations or campaigns for clemency. And when the Assizes returned to the west of Ireland that summer the momentum was maintained: at Roscommon seventeen Ribbonmen were sentenced to death, and nine others to transportation.[48] In addition to the hangings, an indeterminable number had been killed in fighting with the police and military – at least forty-six in Galway, Mayo and Roscommon by the end of March.[49] Thoughtful observers, however, were far from triumphant. 'I wish I could tell you that the Evil has been destroyed', wrote the commander of troops in Connacht, but he detected 'little Effect on the minds of the people, and the System is secretly & silently working its way'. The *Dublin Evening Post* observed wearily that 'the sword is an instrument too clumsy to cut the gangrene from the Country'. By gangrene it meant the exploitation of the peasantry: 'there are no Peasantry, we say it with grief and shame, in Europe', it added, 'more miserable than that of Ireland'. Even Wills, who thought that tithe and rent grievances were merely a pretext to overturn 'Religion and Government and to establish the Popish Religion', argued that the expansion of livestock farming rendered the 'lower Class' of the west the worst-off in Ireland.[50]

From the last two weeks of March the west of Ireland gradually returned to something like a state of normality. The *Tuam Gazette* reported that 'the Spring Business, which seemed entirely neglected … totally forgotten or disregarded' was at last being resumed. Senior army officers reported 'tranquillity' in Clare and Mayo, the 'more orderly appearance' of Galway and 'no appearance of distur-bance' round Athlone.[51] On 24 March the Archbishop of Tuam, who over the previous weeks had ridden the breadth of his diocese at the head of a makeshift armed column, wrote to Dublin Castle:

> I think the County in General is become more tranquil – this can not be attributed to reformation or contrition; but in my opinion to the spread of the Military over the face of it, to the long days and short nights, or probably because their work for the present is done; almost the whole of the population is sworn and well armed.

Attention momentarily shifted to Ulster where Ribbon violence flared around traditional sectarian loyalties in late March.[53] But by the 30th the *Dublin Evening Post* could dare to comment that 'the Western part of Ireland is fast returning to tranquillity'. A few days later, in Easter week, it replaced its regular 'State of Ireland' column with a new one, titled 'State of Great Britain'.

The State of Great Britain

During late February labour militancy erupted into unrest in West Yorkshire. Woollen blanket weavers belonging to the region's clothiers' union systematically attacked 'Blacks' at Batley on the 21st and then rioted the next day at nearby Dewsbury.[54] 'Blacks' was an abusive term for weavers who worked at prices below those stipulated in the union's list. The enforcement of such a list had been the primary objective of the union for some months, and these actions were a desperate attempt to impose it on the area's two largest manufacturers. No arrests could be made in Batley; and at Dewsbury attempts to raise the *posse comitatus* foundered on the reluctance of the town's retailers to risk being boycotted by local weavers. A squadron of dragoons, sent from Leeds, was needed to clear the streets. Sixteen weavers were arrested and immediately sent for trial at the York Assize. There they pleaded guilty but, in a carefully stage-managed proceeding, the prosecution declined to move for them to be sentenced and the judge instead delivered a stern homily. Forcibly to seek a rise in wages, he told them, was 'an offence of very great magnitude, but it is also an act of the greatest folly and imprudence, to seek by rioting the redress of any imaginary or even real grievance … Go home and be good men.'[55] The blanket weavers' dispute was a specific and localised one; but in the close-knit communities of the West Riding woollen district the defeat of the clothiers' union reinforced a general determination to assert the rights of labour.

The trial of the Dewsbury weavers was overshadowed by that of Henry Hunt at the same Assize. Much rested on the outcome. Hunt had repeatedly claimed that it was not he but the magistrates of Manchester who were really to be tried at York. The Ministry might be able to face down the public clamour that would greet an acquittal, but the whole thrust of Government policy since 16 August would stand exposed to even more hostile criticism from the Whigs. 'God grant the Jury may not be contaminated with Fitzwilliam's leaven', a Lancashire magistrate wrote to Sidmouth. George Maule, a senior Government official, sent daily commentaries on the proceedings at York to the Home Secretary who seldom relished what he read; he was 'annoyed' by them, he told Lord Harrowby, 'more than all that has passed within the last Twelve months'.[56] Justice Bayley, 'really appears to have been intimidated by Hunt', wrote one ministerialist MP, behaving to the accused 'as he would to a leading counsel on the Circuit'. The Secretary to the Admiralty expressed 'great apprehensions of the acquittal of Hunt and his fellows'. 'Hunt's conviction is beyond my hope', Lord Grenville told the Marquess of Buckingham'.[57] 'I cannot say that I feel quite secure of our Jury', Maule confided, 'there are two or three bad ones among them and I fear a little leaven May affect the whole mass'; the defence 'was certainly much our superior in their knowledge of the witnesses' characters'; 'our opponents are not only too numerous but also too much of partisans to allow us to cope with them'. 'The Judge seems to have formed a decisive opinion in favour of the Orator', he continued on the seventh day of the trial, 'and seems to be impressed with the opinion that the assembly was not unlawful'. Finally on the penultimate day, 25 March, Maule wrote despondently to London, 'I consider the result of this trial as unfortunate indeed'.[58]

Yet the jury did indeed convict Hunt, albeit on only one of the seven counts, for 'an unlawful assembly for the purpose of exciting discontent & to bring the Government into hatred & contempt'. Hunt and the other organisers of the 16 August meeting had called many witnesses to testify to the peaceable nature of their intentions and the occasion in general. But from the very start, Justice Bayley had ruled all matters that related to the conduct of the Manchester authorities inadmissible and Hunt was denied the opportunity to arraign the magistrates and yeomanry that he had so publically pledged to do. He also, crucially, had no convincing answer to the prosecution's claim that had the meeting proceeded uninterrupted, he would as chairman have permitted the same resolutions to be presented as he had at Smithfield in July 1819: namely that the House of Commons was not fairly and freely chosen and that compliance with its laws and taxation should not be 'obligatory upon those who are unjustly excluded from giving their voice or voices in the selection of Representatives'.[59] Bayley's summing up was coolly calculated to circumvent the manifest weaknesses of the prosecution case. The mode of those attending was not unambiguously illegal; the meeting had been forcibly dispersed before a word was spoken from the platform; and it had not been proved that actual fear had been instilled in anyone prior to the dispersal. However, the 16 August demonstration was unlawful, the judge directed, because the words *intended* to have been spoken *would* have caused fear. This 'highly dubious' ruling, to quote a modern legal authority, 'rested not on actual fear, but on the likelihood of fear should the conspiracy be fulfilled'.[60] The ruling may well also have connected with jurors' own apprehensions of electoral disorder, since the hustings for the county of Yorkshire were held in the yard outside the court on the fourth day of the trial.

Much though the Government was relieved and confident that the outcome vindicated its support for the Manchester magistracy, the latter themselves were aggrieved that the trial had given them no platform from which to defend their actions: Bayley's ruling on what was, and was not, admissible, disappointed them every bit as much as it did Hunt. William Hulton, the only magistrate to have been called to give evidence at York, wrote in disgust to Sidmouth. All the magistrates, he argued, 'feel the necessity that their motives and conduct should be further vindicated … some of them would rejoice – as I should – in a Parliamentary Inquiry'. Some were prepared to bring private prosecutions to justify their actions. The Home Secretary's reply was emollient but scarcely concealed his alarm: he and Liverpool concurred in the view that the justices could not bring forward a case; they should rest assured in the knowledge that none of their adversaries would move either a civil case or criminal indictment against them; Hulton's call for a parliamentary inquiry Sidmouth studiously ignored.[61]

Northern England, 30 March–1 April

The week before the Peterloo trial, Robert Davis, of the Manchester Union Society, was heard to say that there would certainly be 'another Brawl' when Hunt's trial was over, whatever the outcome.[62] 'Committees of the Disaffected have met more frequently of late in several parts of the Kingdom', Sidmouth explained to the King on 9 March, 'and it is evident they are in close communication with each other, and that they are on the Watch for a favourable opportunity of exciting Disturbance, or of striking a Blow'.[63] Three days after the trial had begun, the Lord Provost of Glasgow reported about thirty delegates had left Glasgow for different parts of the country, while Thomas Sharp, Manchester's boroughreeve, sent the Home Office news that the activities of its radical committees were on the increase. 'A decided opinion prevails, that a crisis is near at hand', Sharp confided.[64] In short, there was scarcely any lull in conspiratorial politics following the exposure of Cato Street. And while it is perhaps just possible to dismiss the latter as primarily the work of a fanatical few, what followed in the spring of 1820 was an altogether broader and more deeply rooted phenomenon. It has to be understood in the multiple and overlapping contexts of post-war economic dislocation and its impact on the lives of many working people, of labour unrest, of the vivid demonstration at the general election of the fundamental apathy of Parliament towards arguments for reform, of the popular reaction to Peterloo, of the curtailment of what were generally seen as constitutional rights, and of awareness of dramatic political developments on the continent. So far this study has referred only to the assassination of the Duke of Berry in February, but there followed in early March a revolution in Spain, extensively covered in the British and Irish press and warmly approved by British radicals. The pivotal role of the Spanish army was applauded and held up as an exemplar that British troops should imitate. The revolution brought to power many reformers who had been imprisoned following the failure of the 1812 constitutional changes, and because of its revival of the constitution of 1812 the revolution could be portrayed as restorative rather than destructive.

The day before the jury reached its verdict at York, Glasgow's Lord Provost confidently predicted that wide-scale disturbances were intended for 1 April, the Saturday of Easter weekend.[65] However, the first overt insurrectionary activities occurred in the early hours of Good Friday with an ostensibly curious attempt to capture the West Riding town of Huddersfield. A messenger from Nottingham was thought to have called at the town during the previous week and on Thursday a bayonet had been noticed protruding from a heavy box awaiting collection at the Huddersfield mail office. On the same day 'women were seen passing about to each other's houses, many of them in tears' in the manufacturing villages around Huddersfield. That night perhaps as many as 2,000 armed men from these communities gathered at four vantage points above the town. Fire arms were discharged, sky rockets sent up and at one location late-night travellers who chanced on a contingent were seriously assaulted. On the signal of a beacon being lit on Castle Hill the plan was to march down into the town: two divisions were to secure the cavalry and infantry barracks, the others were to arrest the civil authorities (who had set up a temporary headquarters in the George Hotel) and put the principal residents under house arrest. The stoppage of mail coaches was then to signal to adjacent major towns that a general rising had begun.[66]

Shortly after 2.00am the beacon was lit but for reasons that have never been completely clear the planned attack on the town never occurred. No concerted attempt was made to stop any mail coach, though the Leeds mail was briefly waylaid by a group who told the horsemen and guard 'we will soon put the[e] down no Red Colours for us'.[67] This was presumably an act of bravado by men intent on demonstrating the capability to disrupt the mail if they wanted to. Like the other would-be insurgents, they had almost certainly concluded their rising had mustered insufficient numbers. Like them, they slipped back into the night. House-to-house searches the following day discovered some arms, and also that suspected leaders in the affair had absconded. In all there were thirty-five arrests, just over half of them textile workers. However, puzzling though it was (and remains), it is clear that the Huddersfield Good Friday 'rising' was not under-taken in isolation. Senior army officers noted that all round Bradford radicals had 'been very much <u>on the stir</u>' since Monday, when the York jury's verdict was expected. Bradford's radicals were planning to assemble on Ekelsey Moor, north of the town, prior to marching on Leeds.[68] Bodies of armed men had also assembled in various parts of Halifax and begun moving towards Huddersfield, returning when it became apparent that plans had been abandoned.[69]

For twenty-four hours the Huddersfield area was seized by apprehension and alarm. At Thornton, four miles out of Bradford, the usually scrupulous curate Patrick Brontë cancelled all Good Friday services; he then sat up all night, alarming a house guest with reminiscences of Ireland in 1798.[70] Further afield, army intelligence suggested arms had been distributed in Oldham. There was a general expectation of disturbance in Manchester where the Boroughreeve described radical delegates on 1 April as 'waiting in Town to ascertain the arrival or non-arrival of the North [i.e. Scottish] Mail; the latter circumstance being considered as a signal that operations have commenced in the North'.[71] At 1.00am on Saturday around sixty armed men had gathered outside Great Bolton, and thirty more at Little Bolton, apparently intending to march to Halshaw Moor (on the Manchester Road). An unexpected strike the previous day had seen Tootall leading demonstrators through Bolton. At about 7.00 p.m. a messenger from Carlisle called on Tootall and presented him with 'the compli-ments of the Reformers of the North, saying that in fourteen Hours, the Radicals there would all be in Arms'.[72] There was a nocturnal meeting on Aspull Moor, north of Wigan on Good Friday evening. A few arms were found when houses were searched in Wigan the following day. A Warrington contingent was involved in this gathering. It was reported that the meeting dispersed when it became apparent that only 300, not the promised 1,000, had assembled. 'The object of the meeting was said to be make prisoners of the Justices, the Constables, and the Soldiers, and to confine them in the Church till they had gained their ends.'[73]

Scotland, 1–9 April

The news from northern England was soon overtaken by events in Scotland. 'It seems possible that some Explosion will take place', Sidmouth told Dublin in Easter week, in the west of Scotland, the West Riding of Yorkshire and Lancashire, all of which he described as 'in a restless & agitated State'.[74] On 22 February twenty-seven delegates to the secretive central committee of the west Scotland union societies had been arrested in the act of fomenting 'the most wicked Conspiracy ever contrived in this Country', in the opinion of Kirkman Finlay, Glaswegian cotton manufacturer and ministerialist MP. His supposition was based on a widely shared suspicion that union societies' were less innocent than their public persona of engagement in reform politics and earnest self-improvement suggested.[75] Suspicions were compounded by the central committee's destruction of all its papers moments before the arrests. There was considerable popular sympathy for the prisoners, 'chiefly Weavers, and Cotton Spinners'. The riflemen charged with escorting them through the streets of Glasgow were insulted and pelted with mud and stones.[76] The confidence of the Sheriff of Lanarkshire, that 'the whole system of the Combination of the disaffected people here will be fully disclosed', proved to be misplaced.[77] A second secret committee emerged and rumours of covert arming escalated: Paisley reformers were even said to be equipping themselves with poisoned darts, known colloquially as 'Radical Clegs'.[78]

Among the papers destroyed on 22 February were possibly drafts of the *Address to the Inhabitants of Great Britain and Ireland*, placards bearing which appeared all over central western Scotland on 1 April, signed by 'the Committee of Organization for forming a PROVISIONAL GOVERNMENT' (see the appendix to this chapter). We saw in Chapter 3 how Joseph Brayshaw had toured the north in February, sent by the Leeds secret committee to ascertain radical preparedness for revolution. On his return he was thought to have moved back to Yorkshire in readiness for Hunt's trial. However, Scottish newspapers reported him back in Glasgow and Paisley at the very end of February, when he is supposed to have assisted writing the *Address*. A Glasgow magistrate specifically claimed the *Address* was compiled when Brayshaw was staying in Glasgow at the home of a Parkhead weaver named James Armstrong. In the coming weeks, 'a zealous disciple of Brayshaw' was sufficient to label an ultra-reformer and, it would seem, justify their arrest.[79]

Not all the stories concerning Brayshaw can have been true, but there are stylistic and ideological pointers to him making a significant English input to the document. Within days of its appearance the *Glasgow Herald* commented that, 'We should suppose it of English composition, from its dwelling much upon Magna Charta and the Bill of Rights, in which Scotland has no interest'.[80] However other evidence can be adduced if the *Address* is compared with Brayshaw's *Remarks upon the character and conduct of the men who met under the name of the British Parliament at the latter end of the year 1819*. Both refer to the encouraging precedent of continental European peoples throwing off the yoke of despotism: *Remarks* (which appeared earlier in the year) refers to the French Revolution and the Address more topically to Spain. The *Address* is emphatic that the reformers' case is rooted in the British constitution: *Remarks* refers to the constitution eighteen times in twenty pages.[81] The argument of the *Address* stresses the authority of public meetings, as does Brayshaw's *Remarks*, ten times in all. The *Address* 'distinguishes the FREEMAN from the SLAVE' on the basis that the latter is not 'giving consent to the laws by which he is to be governed'. 'The man who is compelled to submit to laws which he has no interest in forming', Brayshaw declared in his *Remarks*, 'is a slave'.[82]

Yet Brayshaw's input into the *Address* does not have to be proven in order to make the case that this document is suffused with an English (or more correctly British) radical perspective on popular discontent. The argument that the events of Easter 1820 in west Scotland constituted a proto-nationalist Scottish insurrection rests on a combination of wistful thinking and over-emphasis on incidentals such as the (admittedly plangent) inscription on the Strathaven Union Society's banner: 'Scotland Free or a Desert.'[83] The events of Easter 1820 were conceived as a British rising and are fully intelligibly only in that light: 'the extremity of our sufferings, and the contempt heaped upon our Petitions for redress' justified resorting to 'ARMS for the redress of our *Common Grievances*'; government disregards the constitution, 'Corruption has degraded us'. 'Join together and make it one CAUSE.' As a second address issued later in the month declared: 'Let it not be said by future Historians that in the years 1819 and 1820 Britons tamely submitted to become Slaves.'[84]

Gordon Pentland, in a masterful dissection of the events of 1820 in Scotland, has pointed out how the wide distribution of the *Address* was itself evidence for a 'considerable level of organization'. It was placarded all over Lanarkshire, Renfrewshire, Dumbartonshire and much of Ayrshire and Stirlingshire, posted on house walls, market crosses, church and meeting house doors, toll booths, shop windows and wells. In Glasgow crowds of around 200 people assembled 'at the cross and other places' to prevent the removal of copies.[85] But because it was a weekend, and moreover Easter, it took two days for the enormity of what was intended to become fully apparent. The Committee of Organisation's earnest 'request of all to desist from their Labour' was widely heeded. On Easter Monday (3 April) what would have been a normal working day saw the economy of Glasgow halted. 'In addition to the unemployed weavers, we have now Masons, joiners, Smiths, labourers &c., in consequence of a total stop of building', wrote Dugald Bannatyne, the Glasgow postmaster, adding the comment 'many will have been drawn into it from want and despair – for the people are in great distress'. 'In the mist of confusion in which we are constantly kept it is impossible to give a very active account', the Lord Provost told London on the Tuesday.[86] Bannatyne was more measured: this was the morning upon which the non-arrival of the English mail coach in Glasgow 'was to have been the signal for a general rising, shewing that the party in England had been successful & had stopped the ordinary intercourse'. However the coach arrived as normal at 5.30 a.m. 'The streets continue crowded with people, the whole working class being set loose, but there was no appearance of any hostile movement'.[87] Bannatyne thought that later that day some communication between English and Scottish reformers occurred, for after the arrival of the mail coach on the Wednesday a drift back to work began. 'Some feeble attempts were made to raise the People in the Suburbs; but the numbers they were able to bring together were so small that they immediately dispersed'.[88]

It was however beyond Glasgow's centre, where the military presence was decidedly thinner, that the most notable events of this Easter rising occurred. On Monday at Kilsyth, twelve miles to the north-east, a yeomanry troop was 'cut and stoned' after trying to intervene in a strike.[89] Near Paisley a demonstrator was shot dead in an attack on a cotton mill which was still working. In the evening, also at Paisley, a raiding party in search of arms was met by shots from a house just outside the town and a youth was killed.[90] On Wednesday groups of up to fifty men were drilling with impunity in broad daylight close to Glasgow.[91] One of these groups, armed with guns and pikes, marched off from Glasgow Green apparently to seize the Carron iron works, twenty-two miles away at Falkirk. Under their leader Andrew Hardie, a weaver, they gathered a few extra supporters, principally from the Dunbartonshire village of Condorrat, led by a Peninsular War veteran, John Baird. Four miles west of Falkirk, they rested on Bonnymuir, a stretch of scrubland south of a village called Bonnybridge. They had seen a number of people along their way, including Sergeant Thomas Cook of the 10th Hussars, riding alone to rejoin his troop at Kilsyth. Cook declined to hand over his arms but told them he was a former weaver and sympathetic to their aims. So they gave him a copy of the *Address* and let him continue on his way. Sergeant Cook was among the combined troop of hussars and yeomanry who arrived at Bonnymuir later that day to arrest Hardie and Baird. The radicals resisted (indeed, prosecution witnesses at the subsequent trial claimed they had charged the cavalry). An officer's horse was killed by a pike, and three cavalrymen injured along with eight of the rebels. In all eighteen were arrested and taken to Stirling Castle.[92]

Twenty-five miles to the south the mood in the small Lanarkshire town of Strathaven was one of 'considerable bustle and excitement', handloom weaver John Stevenson later recalled. Strathaven's delegate to the secret committee had returned from Glasgow with 200 copies of the *Address* which were posted all over the town on Easter Sunday. Early Wednesday evening word arrived from Glasgow that a twin-pronged attack on the city was to be made the following day. 'A profligate Court, a rapacious Ministry, and a debt of nearly ten millions, lay like a vampire upon industry; the patience of the industrious classes were nearly exhausted', Stevenson wrote in 1835 in an attempt to justify what happened next. 'We entered with devotion upon what we considered the service of our country.' Householders and shopkeepers were relieved of firearms and by midnight perhaps a hundred armed men had assembled. However the party that finally set out on the Glasgow road in torrential rain at dawn mustered only twenty-five. The weather, 'sagacious advice of friends, and a report that all was quiet in Glasgow' accounted for the desertions. The party expected to find 5,000 to 7,000 men on Cathkin Braes, a commanding ridge above the Clyde valley, about five miles south of Glasgow. They arrived to find it, Stevenson ruefully related, 'unoccupied; we gazed anxiously around, but could not perceive a living creature'. 'Scotland Free or a Desert' fluttered forelornly on the brow of the hill.[93] There was no battle on the braes as there had been at Bonnymuir. Furtive and demoralised, John Stevenson and his comrades made their way back to Strathaven.

Stevenson argued 'that the rebellion in 1820, was begun and carried on by spies and informers, paid out of secret service money, by Lords Liverpool and Sidmouth'. He also sought to establish that the men of the Strathaven Union Society had acted, however misguidedly, out of noble sentiments. The noblest of them all, but certainly not the leader of the enterprise, was sixty-three-year-old James Wilson. 'The name of liberty was not an empty sound to Wilson, but the object of his affections, ever dear and present, and twined round his heart, by all the tenderest ties of nature'.[94] A weaver, Wilson had been the local delegate to the conventions of the Friends of the People in the 1790s. He was the first of the Strathaven party to be arrested: his record as a radical activist was to tell against him.

The skirmish at Bonnymuir had already turned the Scottish radical war of 1820 into a rout. In Glasgow a nightly seven pm curfew was imposed, without any popular resistance.[95] 'I am satisfied that the radical gentlemen are completely frightened', Sir William Rae MP, the Lord Advocate (Scotland's senior legal officer) wrote to Sidmouth on Thursday. 'The unhappy wretches are flying in every direction – skulking in woods & coalpits, & sleeping in the fields', reported Bannatyne.[96] Two months later young weavers were reportedly still being 'hunted like Partridges on the mountains' in south-west Stirlingshire.[97] However, the attitude of the authorities quickly hardened into a determination to exploit the chance to demonstrate where real power resided in Scotland. William Rae had effectively taken direct charge of Glasgow's response to the rising; but he was soon to lament that its radicals were so cowed that there might be 'no opportunity of bestowing upon them that discipline of Chastisement which I came here in the wish of being inflicted'.[98] He was candid to Sidmouth that his purpose now was to spread alarm among the radicals of Scotland. Another loyalist MP, Alexander Boswell, writing to Sidmouth of the defeat of 'the Vipers' expressed the hope 'we shall soon intimidate these rebels'.[99] General searches for arms in the working-class communities of Anderton, Bridgton and Calton in Glasgow, and further afield in Airdrie, Hamilton, Kilsyth and Paisley, were one means of accomplishing this. Conspicuous military display was another. The quiescent state of the Scottish capital meant that its barracks were emptied to provide reinforcements for the west. The Midlothian Yeomanry mustered to take their place. Although 'Edinburgh was as quiet as the grave, or even as Peebles', the Whig lawyer Henry Cockburn jested, 'we were obliged to pass about a month as if an enemy had been drawing his lines round our very walls'.[100] No less-eloquent testimony was provided by the daughters of the novelist Walter Scott: such was the 'mass response of volunteers for service', they complained, 'not a feasible looking beau was to be had for love or money'.[101]

Since Peterloo local authorities had been wary of deploying the yeomanry. Of the 156 English and Welsh yeomanry regiments, only eleven were called on to assist the civil powers in 1820, mainly to keep order during the general election. (Hardly surprisingly yeomanry were used in neither Lancashire nor Cheshire.) Many English and Welsh corps had also fallen significantly beneath their agreed establishment. Forty-six operated at less than 90 per cent of their established strength in 1820. Some were considerably poorer than that, for example Cardiff stood at 65 per cent and Havering (Essex) 26 per cent. However, the picture in Scotland was utterly different. Fifteen of the twenty-five Scottish regiments saw duty in aid of the civil power in 1820, while only six stood below 90 per cent of their establishment. Furthermore of Britain's nine effective volunteer infantry regiments, no less than six were Scottish and all were deployed on civil duties in 1820. None of the three English regiments were.[102] Huddersfield and South Yorkshire accounted for two of the only three significant English yeomanry deployments in 1820 (Warwickshire was the third, policing the tumultuous Coventry election).[103]

The triumphalist character of the Scottish authorities' reaction to the rising met an unexpectedly tragic response in Greenock, twenty-two miles down river from Glasgow, the following weekend. In the bloodiest incident of the entire rising, eight townspeople were killed and at least twenty-six wounded by the Port Glasgow Volunteers. Greenock had hitherto been largely passive: even Glasgow's Lord Provost thought the Volunteers had inflamed local opinion by marching, 115-strong, into Greenock with drums beating and fifes playing when they arrived to deliver five radical prisoners to the town's gaol. Shots fired into the air outside the prison had no perceptible effect on a throng that jeered and pelted them with mud and stones. Then, as the Volunteers tried to march away, they were jostled by crowds on both sides to prevent them resuming a marching formation. Discipline crumpled and a number of the soldiers then fired indiscriminately and at close range into the crowd. Meanwhile nothing was done to prevent the crowd from forcing its way into the prison and liberating the prisoners.[104] That the incident was rooted in the reactions of an enraged community, rather than the premeditated plans of organised radicalism, was evident in the details of the killed and wounded. The youngest was just eight years old and most were mere lads (the median age of the eight dead and nine seriously wounded was 17½ years).[105] Greenock, understandably, was plunged into grief but Rae had to concede to Sidmouth that the incident had 'made no perceptible sensation' on the rest of Scotland.[106] The threat to stability was now arguably from loyalists who were members of yeomanry regiments or who had enlisted in the hastily formed volunteer corps. Greenock was probably on the Home Secretary's mind a few days later when he impressed on senior army officers that volunteers should only be used 'in case of actual necessity'.[107] Conceivably, the extent of loyalist enthusiasm in west Scotland was becoming part of the problem of maintaining public order, rather than part of the solution.

Yorkshire, 11–13 April

English radicals were galvanised by the news emerging from Scotland during Easter week. During the first few days of April nocturnal armed meetings were reported in villages just south of Blackburn.[108] The *Leeds Mercury* concluded that the capture of Huddersfield had been intended to signal general upheaval 'throughout all the manufacturing districts … even to Scotland'.[109] Huddersfield's yeomanry had been called out on Good Friday. It was soon joined by the 120-strong Huddersfield Independent Association, a hurriedly recruited and 'highly praiseworthy, though unorganised' volunteer infantry corps.[110] The initial expectation had been that both units would be needed for one week only. However, such were the continuing problems experienced in the region, they were finally stood down only on 20 April. On the Easter Tuesday market day 'Universal Shouting, Hooting & Hissing' greeted the Huddersfield Yeomanry wherever it appeared. Low-level demonstrations of this nature obscured a deeper belligerence. The commander of the army's northern district, Major General John Byng, predicted on 9 April that 'the least excitement' in the West Riding textiles district 'would cause an insurrection'; meanwhile Glasgow radicals had 'got it into their heads', said Rae, that there was to be a second English rising in a few days'.[111] Soon Huddersfield magistrates were predicting there would be a rising in Lancashire on Tuesday 11 April, with the Yorkshire town the target the following day of concerted marches from Dewsbury, Halifax, Bradford, Wakefield (the administrative centre of the West Riding) and the linen weaving centre of Barnsley.[112] Manchester's magistrates heard a different and perhaps more plausible scenario, 'from so many quarters and so corroborative': simultaneous Lancashire and Yorkshire commotions were planned, around Burnley, Blackburn and Huddersfield, on 12 April explicitly to draw troops from Manchester: 'if they can remain in any strength during the day' then this would be communicated 'to the Radicals of this town & Neighbourhood … & the blow is to be struck at Manchester' on Thursday. Simultaneously a demonstration by the unemployed would tie down troops in Leeds.[113]

This ambitious plan came to nothing. Manchester's stipendiary magistrate and the boroughreeve ascribed its deliverance to a combination of poor communication, effective preparation on the part of the military and civil power, and the corrosive impact on radical morale of events in Scotland.[114] Home Office correspondence is littered with information about intended disturbances, some well-meaning but much of it anonymous hoaxing. Examples of the latter in the fortnight after Easter included information about imminent attacks on Edinburgh and Stirling castles, an allegation that notices posted in Forfar warned that the stoppage of the London mail would be the signal for a march on London, 'to Kill King & Ministry at once and establish a Convention', and a spurious commission from London to a Paisley printer for a revised version of the 1 April *Address to Britons*.[115] However, corroboration that rumours of a rising on 12 April did have solid foundation was all-too apparent when a second disturbance in the vicinity of Huddersfield occurred on the night of Tuesday the 11th. This time the focus of activity was Grange Moor, high ground at the confluence of two major rivers, eight miles east of Huddersfield on the Wakefield road. This was to be the rendezvous of rebels from the industrial valleys of the Spen, Colne and Calder and from Barnsley ('a very bad place, & neighbourhood', in Byng's judgment).[116] Once rested the combined force was to march on Huddersfield. So confident were the members of the Barnsley contingent of success that they made no secret of their departure. 'A Great Drum which they beat as they went' served to summons further supporters on the twelve-mile march. Perhaps 500 strong, the marchers were relatively well equipped with ten-foot pikes, a variety of firearms, provisions, blankets and banners. 'Hunt, the intrepid champion of the Rights and Liberties of the People', said one, 'He that smiteth a Man so that he die, shall be surely put to death', another.[117] The centre of Huddersfield meanwhile presented an extraordinary sight. Each of the streets leading onto the market place was barricaded with carts and wagons; infantry arrived to reinforce the Independent Association. Cavalry and horse artillery were drafted in and General Byng established a temporary headquarters in the Strafford Arms.[118] All the garrisons under his command were placed on high alert. 'You cannot be too silent on this letter, & in all your preparations make no shew to create either suspicion or alarm,' Byng wrote to his Leeds Colonel.[119]

Only the Barnsley contingent, however, ever arrived on Grange Moor. It dispersed rapidly when a detachment of dragons and yeomanry was sighted cantering towards the moor from Huddersfield. Fifteen were arrested within minutes; Barnsley magistrates issued warrants for seventy-one more, though only twenty prisoners were finally committed for trial for high treason. Over the next two days 'meetings on the Mosses', outside Manchester and Salford, waited for news.[120] Key delegates loitered on Manchester's main streets, 'all in anxious expectation of news from Huddersfield ... enquiring of every coach, whither from Yorkshire or the North'. Finally an observer who had been sent to Huddersfield

> arrived and made known the melancholy result, viz: that 500 Radicals had run away at the very first approach of the Yeomanry, and thrown away their pikes. The members of the Committee <u>cursed and swore,</u> Lang declaring that no blow could ever be successfully struck without a thorough organization throughout the Kingdom. Johnson from Flixton, Whitworth from Staley[bridge], Wood from Stockport &c., all hastened to their respective places to communicate the unpleasant tidings.[121]

After Grange Moor the Home Office was able to assemble evidence of national delegate movements in the days preceding it. Representatives from Blackburn, Bolton (Tootall), Manchester, Stalybridge and Stockport had met on Saturday 8 April to digest the news that Nottingham 'refused to take any lead', and that Hull and Birmingham had never received details of what had been planned over Easter weekend. The Scottish delegates, feeling exposed and betrayed, had demanded further action by the English. Carlisle at least was apparently placarded over the weekend with notices from Glasgow, censuring 'the apathy of their brethren in the South', and arms drill and training took place on Coalfell Hill, seven miles north-east of the city.[122] And at Sheffield an intended attack on the barracks to seize arms was postponed only as 200 demonstrators approached its gates. At their head was John Blackwell, leader of a similar attack on a militia armoury in 1812, as well as a leading figure in Sheffield's demonstrations that coincided with the 1816 Spa Fields rally.[123]

On Wednesday 12 April a small crowd gathered on Beacon Hill near Halifax, beneath a flag and with musical accompaniment. Pistols were fired into the air, a sky rocket sent up and a bundle of straw was set ablaze − reckless defiance, perhaps, rather than a serious insurrectionary move.[124] However, in Lancashire low-level violence continued for several days. Rumours of a rising in Blackburn were revived on the 17th after a farmer near Accrington was roused in the early hours of the morning by twenty armed men who commandeered his grindstone to sharpen their pikes. Drilling was reported on Black Moss, eight miles from Blackburn, and two pikes were found when a house in Mellor, north of Blackburn was searched. On the same day a systematic search of homes in Ashton-under-Lyne discovered fifteen pikes at the home of one radical weaver and three at another. Simultaneously, attempts at fomenting a general strike were reported in Leeds, Manchester, Oldham and Stockport.[125] Then there was talk of another attempted rising on 23 April, and again on 7 May. But talk was all it was. The 1820 insurrection was over.

Conclusion

> We are so much discouraged at our Brethren not coming forward in a more tumul-
> tuous form that we are at a loss which way to pursue. It was useless for us to
> persevere unless England would have stepped forward with a helping hand … We are
> compelled to submit on account of the Military who seem to have an unlicensed
> authority to do anything they may think proper and 'til we hear from you and 'til
> something further is executed on your part we shall remain dormant … We remain
> yours in bonds of Union and Liberty. (Letter to Manchester from the Glasgow
> Central Committee, 18 April 1820: TNA, HO 40/13, fol. 1)

In his history of the French Revolution, Thomas Carlyle captured with typical
acuity the quandaries that threaten to consume any rising:

> Reader, fancy not, in thy languid way, that Insurrection is easy. Insurrection is
> difficult: each individual uncertain even of his next neighbour; totally uncertain of
> his distant neighbours, what strength is with him, what strength is against him;
> certain only that, in case of failure, his individual portion is the gallows![126]

Uncertainty of neighbours, both close and distant, was all too apparent in 1820.
The disturbances that spring were deeply rooted in their local communities.
Though the mindset of Britain's would-be insurgents was moulded by their
acquaintance with the political arguments of Cobbett, Hunt, the *Black Dwarf* and
the *Black Book*, it required a distinctive combination of local factors to catalyse
real commitment. Scarcity and want were not enough, nor anger at the exploita-
tive nature of wage labour. Had they been, then more men like Burnley weaver
William Varley would have taken up arms. On 7 April he wrote in his diary:

> The country is all on an uproar some say that Huddersfield castle is pul'd down, there
> is great disturbance in Scotland and Spain and well there may be because there is no
> trade to be had, the poor man may now go to dispare indeed for it appears very plain
> we must have no better days unless the be got by compulsion.[127]

An established radical tradition was one ingredient that helped mobilise communities. James Wilson seems to have been pivotal at Strathaven, even though his
role in the actual leadership was marginal. Three men who had taken a
prominent part in Luddism were among those who made their way to Grange
Moor, two of them (Craven Cookson and Stephen Kitchenman) were also
members of the Barnsley Union Society's 'secret committee'.[128] The first
historian of Yorkshire Luddism, Frank Peel, notable for his use of oral testimony,
located Grange Moor at the close of his final chapter, 'The last struggles of
Luddism'.[129] And it is conceivable that this was how some of the marchers
conceived it, especially those weavers who joined the Barnsley men as they
marched north.

Not just textile centres but specifically communities specialising in weaving are prominent in the narrative of events around Easter 1820: Barnsley, the satellite villages of Huddersfield, Paisley and Strathaven. Spinners of course participated (Glasgow shows that) but weaving had yet to be mechanised. It was a domestic industry whose workers had considerable discretion and control over the production process and a strong sense of a lost 'golden age' before the French wars. The mobility of weavers may also have helped generate a broader political awareness and certainly helped establish cross-regional networks: there were large numbers of Lancastrians in the weaving industry of West Yorkshire as well as Irish-born workers in both counties. Spinning, on the other hand, was mainly located in large mills where it was more difficult to generate the momentum for strike action – as the fatal incident near Paisley on 3 April showed.

If a predilection to civil disobedience was partly contingent on the economic make-up of a community (and as a corollary a tradition of confrontational mobilisation to defend what its inhabitants saw as the rights of labour), then we can easily discern some powerful reasons why the risings of 1820 were so regionally specific: Clydeside but not Midlothian, the West Riding but not the English midlands. A powerful part of the explanation for why the United Kingdom withstood the tempestuous circumstances of the spring of 1820 is quite simply regional differentiation. Furthermore, broader based urban economies – Halifax, Huddersfield, Leeds, Manchester, Nottingham – tended not to have high profiles as centres of insurrectionary action: even Glasgow, though solidly behind the general stoppage of labour in Easter week, generated fewer violent episodes than its hinterland. Of course the relative quiescence of Glasgow, central Huddersfield and Manchester was also a reflection of the greater ease with which they could be policed (in the broadest sense of the word). It is here that we can glean some insight into the forces of political stability and coercion that the Government had at its disposal.

It was in the interval between the Scottish and Grange Moor risings that the Cabinet decided to call out half of Britain's militia for training and exercise. This entailed placing a large number of civilians under military discipline and was intended to have both a direct practical and general psychological impact. As the Government struggled to manage the United Kingdom in the spring of 1820, it was forced to confront the uncomfortable realisation that British and Irish insurgents' strategy of tying down troops to diminish severely the capacity to deploy military resources elsewhere was close to working. Wellington argued the case thus:

> If the schemes stated to be in agitation, of which we have so many accounts that we cannot doubt their truth, should be put in execution what is to become of us if we have not some force in Reserve upon which we can rely? ... If anything serious happens any where in any part of the World the whole force is already so completely employed that the Cmdr-in-Chief has not a single Reg^t of either Cavalry or Infantry at his disposal ... without withdrawing it from Service on which it is at present employed.[130]

The Government was also forced to reduce the size of the military establishment, a recurrent economy it had achieved annually since 1815. The medium-term solution was to reverse these economies, which the Ministry did citing 'the urgent necessity of finding additional protection for the loyal and industrious part of the population of the country'. Not only was the army augmented but an additional 2,000 were recruited into the Royal Marines for garrison duties on shore.[131] Embodying the militia, however, was the only immediate solution to troop shortages. Earlier in this chapter we saw how, in the second week of April, Dublin Castle had rebuffed London's request to call out the Irish militia. Its mobilisation would have released regular troops for service in Britain. The timing of the decision to call out the militia was significant. Strictly speaking it was unconstitutional because it was made while Parliament was dissolved. When the Government was later forced to defend the move in the Commons, it argued the situation was 'so pressing as to require the assemblage of such a force', specifying that Cato Street and the Scottish and Yorkshire risings together constituted an emergency.[132] There was, as Dublin argued, considerable risk in increasing the quantity of arms circulating in Ireland: but it was a risk mitigated by the downturn in Ribbonism. That had been bought at the cost of considerable military intervention that had left England and Scotland exposed. In the days after Easter 1820 there could be no certainty this exposure might not have severe consequences.

    In the event the Irish militia was not embodied in 1820 but 11,000 British militia men were. The Government spent more on the militia in 1820 than it had at any time since the end of the Napoleonic wars, and it was a level of expenditure that would never be exceeded again.[133] Militia service was not popular and in peacetime militia regiments were meant to be embodied for exercise and training only. The Ministry's action was only just short of declaring a state of emergency. Raising the militia also had a psychological dimension. It evoked that spirit of loyalism that had been one of the hallmarks of Britain during the French Revolutionary and Napoleonic Wars. However, the failure of localities adequately to respond to security challenges was a frequent complaint among Government members and senior army officers. As we have seen, it applied with greatest frequency to Ireland; but the Cabinet believed that disturbances in Britain were also exacerbated by local lethargy. Sidmouth for example declined requests from local magistrates to send troops to Dewsbury and Batley, to maintain the peace after the February riots and attacks on 'blacks'. His argument was that 'the mischief of which you complain has been enhanced by the concession which the Masters in the first instance made to the illegal combinations of the Journeymen'.[134] Harriet Arbuthnot was possibly echoing Wellington and her husband when she speculated that it was 'rather a good thing people sh^d be frightened' since it would energise 'the respectable and quiet … to exert themselves to protect their lives & property & not trust everything to the soldiers'.[135] Yet in the late spring there was a string of embarrassing failures to launch new volunteer units and expand existing ones in the industrial north. The Earl of Harewood did raise an infantry corps in Leeds, but initiatives failed at Ashton-under-Lyne, Blackburn, Burnley, Bury, Halifax, Preston and Rochdale.[136] Even Huddersfield's volunteer infantry association failed to meet the target officially for its establishment, while in Scotland, a Kilmarnock volunteer association was established only after 'much and repeated exertion'.[137] Tranquillity cannot long prevail, Sidmouth wrote forcefully to a Scottish ministerialist, if civil authority is not 'constantly vigilant'.[138] General Byng hoped that the events of early April would 'infuse a little spirit and exertion where it is wanted' in the West Riding. 'Military means may for a time prevent or defeat insurrection – but local means & Exertions can alone restore peace.'[139] Robert Ward, effectively Wellington's deputy at the Board of Ordinance, predicted 'supineness and apathy as to public *exertion* ... would in the end ruin us'.[140]

Appendix

ADDRESS TO THE INHABITANTS OF GREAT BRITAIN AND IRELAND; FRIENDS AND COUNTRYMEN,

ROUSED from that torpid state in which WE have been sunk for so many years, We are at length compelled, from the extremity of our sufferings, and the contempt heaped upon our Petitions for redress, to assert our RIGHTS at the hazard of our lives, and proclaim to the world the real motives which, (if not misrepresented by designing men, would have United all ranks,) have reduced us to take up ARMS for the redress of our *Common Grievances*.

The numerous public meetings held throughout the Country, has demonstrated to you, that the interests of all Classes are the same. That the protection of the Life and Property of the *Rich Man*, is the interest of the *Poor Man*, and, in return, it is the interest of the Rich, to protect the poor from the iron grasp of DESPOTISM; for, when its victims are exhausted in the lower circles, there is no assurance but that its ravages will be continued in the upper, for, once set in motion, it will continue to move till a succession of Victims Fall.

Our principles are few, and founded on the basis of our CONSTITUTION, which were purchased with the DEAREST BLOOD of our ANCESTORS, and which we swear to transmit to posterity unsullied, or PERISH in the Attempt. Equality of Rights (not of Property) is the object for which we contend, and which we consider as the only security for our LIBERTIES and LIVES.

Let us show to the world that We are not that Lawless Sanguinary Rabble, which our Oppressors would persuade the higher circles we are, but a BRAVE and GENEROUS PEOPLE, determined to be FREE. LIBERTY or DEATH is our *Motto*, and We have sworn to return home in *triumph*, or return *no more*. SOLDIERS!

Shall YOU, Countrymen bound by the sacred obligation of an Oath, to defend your Country and your King from enemies, whether foreign or domestic, plunge your BAYONETS into the bosoms of Fathers and Brothers, and at once sacrifice, at the *Shrine of Military Despotism*, to the unrelenting Orders of a cruel faction, those feelings which you hold in common with the rest of mankind? SOLDIERS! Turn your eyes toward SPAIN, and there behold the happy effects resulting from the UNION of Soldiers and Citizens. Look to that quarter, and there behold the yoke of hated Despotism broke by the Unanimous wish of the people and the Soldiery, happily accomplished without Bloodshed. And, shall you, who taught those Soldiers to fight the battles of LIBERTY, refuse to fight those of your own Country? Forbid it, Heaven! Come, forward, then, at once, and Free your Country and your King, from the power of those that have held them *too, too long* in thraldom.

FRIENDS AND COUNTRYMEN. The eventful period has now arrived where the Services of all will be required for the forwarding of an object so universally wished, and so absolutely necessary. Come forward, then, and assist those who have begun in the completion of so arduous a task, and support the laudable efforts which we are about to make, to replace to BRITONS, those rights consecrated to them by MAGNA CHARTA and the BILL OF RIGHTS, and Sweep from our Shores that Corruption which has degraded us below the dignity of man.

Owing to the misrepresentations which have gone abroad with regard to our intentions, we think it indispensably necessary to DECLARE inviolable all Public and Private Property. And, We hereby call upon all JUSTICES of the PEACE, and all others, to suppress PILLAGE and PLUNDER, of every description; and to endeavour to secure those Guilty of such offences, that they may receive that Punishment, which such violation of justice demand.

In the present state of affairs, and during the continuation of so momentous a struggle, we earnestly request of all to desist from their Labour from and after this day, the FIRST OF APRIL; and attend wholly to the recovery of their Rights, and consider it as the duty of every man not to recommence until he is in possession of those Rights which distinguishes the FREEMAN from the SLAVE; viz: That of giving consent to the laws by which he is to be governed. We, therefore, recommend to the Proprietors of Public Works, and all others, to Stop the one, and Shut up the other, until order is restored, as we will be accountable for no damages which may be sustained; and which, after this Public Intimation, they can have no claim to.

AND We hereby give notice to all those who shall be found carrying arms against those who intend to regenerate their Country, and restore its INHABITANTS to their NATIVE DIGNITY, We shall consider them as TRAITORS to their Country, and ENEMIES to their King, and treat them as such.

By order of the Committee of Organization for forming a PROVISIONAL GOVERNMENT.

GLASGOW, 1st April, 1820

Britons. – God. – Justice. – The wishes of all good Men, are with us. – Join together, and make it one CAUSE, and the Nations of the Earth shall hail the day when the Standard of LIBERTY shall be raised on its *native soil.*

(The text of a printed copy in TNA, HO 102/32/296)

Notes

1 DRO, 152M/C/1820/OH/68 (21 March 1820).
2 DRO, 152M/C/1820/OZ (Sidmouth to Sheffield, 19 March).

3 *Leeds Mercury*, 18 March; DRO, 152M/C/1820/OH/28 (18 March) and 152M/C/1820/OZ (20 March).

4 *Leeds Mercury*, 18 March; TNA, HO 40/11 fols 207 and 212 (16 and 16 March).

5 *The Times*, 24 March; *Lancaster Gazette*, 18 March; *Morning Post*, 6 April.

6 F. K. Donnelly, 'The general rising of 1820: a study of social conflict in the industrial revolution' (PhD thesis, University of Sheffield, 1975); P. B. Ellis and S. Mac a' Ghobhainn, *The Scottish Insurrection of 1820* (London: Gollancz, 1970); M. Huggins, *Social Conflict in Pre-Famine Ireland: The Case of County Roscommon* (Dublin: Four Courts Press, 2007), pp. 93–7.

7 'Shamrock of green Erin', a printed ballad found at Castlebar, County Mayo, in March): copy in NAI, SOC/2175/58. 'Chruskeen Lawn' is an Anglicisation of the Irish *Cruscin Lán* (The Full Jug), also the title of a popular drinking song.

8 TNA, HO 100/198/144 (21 February).

9 TNA, HO 79/7 (Sidmouth to Talbot, 9 April); HO 100/198/338 (Gregory to Hobhouse, 12 April); HO 100/198/449–54 (Sorrell to Taylor, 3 June); HO 100/198/464 (Aylmer to Beckwith, 17 August 1818 [sic]); HO 100/198/470 (Aylmer to Gregory, 27 May).

10 During 1820 legislation permitting this was renewed (1 Geo. IV cap. 48). A. Blackstock, *An Ascendancy Army: The Irish Yeomanry, 1796–1834* (Dublin: Four Courts Press), pp. 232–68.

11 TNA, HO 100/198/216–9 (Talbot to Sidmouth, 7 March).

12 TNA, HO 100/198/248 (16 March) and 359–74 (Galway Summary, 25 April).

13 TNA, HO 100/198/220 and 223 (3 and 4 March); NAI, SOC 2175/57 (8 March).

14 NAI, SOC/2188/17 (list of proclaimed districts for 1820).

15 *Athlone Herald* quoted in *Dublin Evening Post,* 24 February.

16 NAI, SOC/2172/5 (3 March); SOC/2175/57 (8 March); SOC/2176/26 (13 March).

17 TNA, HO 100/198/220 (3 March).

18 NAI, SOC/2171/84 (26 and 28 February); *The Times*, 9 March.

19 TNA, HO 100/198/359–74 (Galway Summary, 25 April).

20 TNA, HO 100/198/216–19 and 241 (7 and 13 March).

21 *Dublin Evening Post*, 8 February; NAI, SOC/2176/49 (8 June); SOC/2175/58 (Castlebar, Mayo, 11 March), SOC/2184/7 (County Kerry, 11 March).

22 NAI, SOC/2187/9 (6 and 22 March).

23 NAI, CSO/LB/419 (16 February), p. 292.

24 TNA, HO40/11 fols 136–141 (9 March).

25 TNA, HO 40/13 fol. 3 verso (25 May; copy of Tootall to 'men of Nottingham', 17 May).

26 *PP* 1825 (20) SC State of Ireland, evidence of George Warburton, pp. 139, 135.

27 TNA, HO 44/4/263 (Chippendale to Sidmouth, 27 February); HO 100/198 fols 281–2 (information concerning the Gibby brothers of Manchester, 23 March, sent by Talbot to Sidmouth); HO 40/14 fol. 177 (Allsop to Home Office, 10 August).

28 TNA, HO 79/7 (Hobhouse to Grant, 28 February); NAI CSO/LB/419 (28 February).

29 TNA, HO40/11 fol. 230 (22 March).

30 TNA, HO 79/7 (Hobhouse to Grant, 2 March); NAI CSO/LB/419, pp. 290–1.

31 The same point is made with reference to Ribbonism and later Irish Fenianism in T. Garvin, 'Defenders, Ribbonmen and others: underground political networks in pre-Famine Ireland', in C. H. E. Philpin (ed.), *Nationalism and Popular Protest in Ireland* (Cambridge: Cambridge University Press, 1987), pp. 242–3.

32 NAI, SOC/2172/5 (5 March).

33 TNA, HO 100/198/134, 144 and 162 (14, 20, 21 February).

34 TNA, NAI, SOC 1/2171/80 (26 February).

35 HO 100/198/220 (Gray to Browne, 3 March).

36 *Dublin Evening Post*, 7 March; *Evans and Ruffy's Farmers' Journal*, 12 March; NAI, SOC 1/2182/9–10 (4–10 April).

37 NAI, SOC/2181/17 (3 June); SOC/2176/32–3 (11, 13 April). See also *Glasgow Herald*, 10 March, quoting *Athlone Herald*.

38 NAI, SOC 2176/29 (20 March). I have located only one other similar incident in 1820, the less sensational killing of three calves during a raid on a dairy in County Cork, see NAI, SOC/2182/11. This interpretation is indebted to J. E. Archer, 'Animal maiming: "a fiendish outrage"?', in his *'By a Flash and a Scare': Arson, Animal Maiming, and Poaching in East Anglia, 1815–70* (Oxford: Oxford University Press, 1990), pp. 198–221.

39 TNA, HO 100/198/241 (13 March); *Dublin Evening Post*, 7 March. See also NAI, SCO/2176/21 and 25 (4 and 13 March).

40 *The Times*, 9 March; *Morning Post*, 9 March.

41 *Morning Chronicle*, 16 March.

42 See the extensive correspondence and depositions in the State of the Country papers for King's County: NAI, SOC/2179/28–9, 34, 37, and 48; TNA, HO 100/198/246 (15 March); *Dublin Evening Post*, 16 March.

43 NAI, SOC/2179/37 (26 March). See also SOC/2179/35–6, 38, 40, 43.

44 NAI, SOC/2176/24 (7 March); TNA, HO100/198/291–93 (23 and 30 March) and 325–7 (8 April).

45 NAI, SOC/2176/14, 21, 25, and 27 (21 February, 4, 7 and 13 March).

46 NAI, SOC/2172/144 (28 March).

47 NAI, SOC/2187/34 (27 March); SOC/2187/42 (31 March); SOC/2187/3 (29 March); SOC/2186/10–12 (19 and 26 March).

48 NAI, SOC/2176/50 (21 July).

49 Based on definite fatalities as reported to Dublin Castle, Home Office and in Irish Papers, 25 January to 28 March.

50 DRO, 152M/C/1820/OI/26 (Brown to Taylor, 22 April); *Dublin Evening Post*, 7 March; NAI, SOC/2176/49 (8 June).

51 *Tuam Gazette* quoted in *Dublin Evening Post*, 18 March; TNA, HO 100/198/271 (21 March).

52 NAI, SOC/2172/39 (24 March).

53 TNA, HO100/198/283 (Antrim, 26 March); NAI, SOC/2187/2–4 (Antrim, 21 March–4 April), SOC/2187/34 (Down, 27 March), SOC/2187/49 (Monaghan, 29 March).

54 TNA, HO 40/11 fols 53–4 (28 February); *Leeds Mercury*, 26 February; *The Times*, 28 and 29 February.

55 WYAS, WYL250/6/2/B2/2 (Stocks to Lascelles, 25 February); *Leeds Mercury*, 18 March.

56 TNA, HO 40/11 fol. 136 (9 March); DRO, 152 M/C/1820/OH/43 (30 March).

57 *Diary and Correspondence of Charles Abbot, Lord Colchester*, edited by his son Charles, Lord Colchester (London: Murray, 1861), vol. 3, p. 126 (Wilbraham to Colchester, 11 April); L. J. Jennings (ed.), *The Croker Papers: The Correspondence and Diaries of the Late Right Honourable John Wilson Croker … 1809 to 1830* (London: Murray, 1884), vol. 1, p. 169; R. P. Grenville, *Memoirs of the Court of George IV, 1820–1830* (London: Hurst, 1859), vol. 1, p. 15.

58 TNA, HO 40/11 fols 212 to 274, passim (16 to 27 March).

59 J. MacDonell (ed.), *Reports of State Trials*, new series, (London: HMSO, 1858), vol. 1 pp. 476–7, 482; see also *Morning Chronicle*, 22 July 1819.

60 M. Lobban, 'From seditious libel to unlawful assembly: Peterloo and the changing face of political crime, c. 1770–1820', *Oxford Journal of Legal Studies*, 10:3 (1990), p. 345.

61 DRO, 152 M/C/1820/OH/44–5 6 and 11 April.

62 TNA, HO40/11 fol. 138 (deposition of Samuel Fleming, 8 March).

63 DRO, 152 M/C/1820/OH/23 (9 March).

64 TNA, HO 40/11 fol. 221 (19 March).

65 TNA, HO 102/32/275 (26 March).

66 This account is based on *Leeds Mercury*, 8 April, correspondence and depositions in HO 40/11 and 40/12 and examinations and depositions in TNA, TS 11/1013/4131.

67 TNA, HO 33/2/145 (Leeds postmaster to the General Post Office, London, 1 April).

68 TNA, HO 40/11 fols 280 (Haigh Allen to Byng, 30 March), 285 (Lyon to Byng, 30 March) and 287 (Campbell to Byng).

69 TNA, HO 40/12 fol. 19 (1 April).

70 J. Lock and W. T. Dixon, *A Man of Sorrow: The Life, Letters and Times of the Rev. Patrick Bronte* (Nelson, 1965), pp. 201–2.

71 TNA, HO 40/11 fol. 285 (Lyon to Byng, 30 March); HO 40/12 fol. 8 (Sharp to Sidmouth, 1 April).

72 TNA, HO 40/12 fols 53–8, quotation from fol. 55 (Fletcher to Sidmouth, 4 April).

73 TNA, HO 40/12 fol. 61 (Nicholson to Sidmouth, 5 April) and fol. 64 (deposition of John Smith).

74 TNA, HO 79/7 (Sidmouth to Talbot [?1] April).

75 DRO, 152M/C/1820/OH/4 (25 February); see also TNA, HO 102/32/186–92 and 233–6 (23 February and 9 March).

76 TNA, HO 102/32/186 fols 187–8, 192 (23 February).

77 TNA, HO 102/32/216 (1 March).

78 TNA, HO 102/32 fols 263 and 284 (30 and 31 March); *Manchester Observer*, 22 April; J. Parkhill, *History of Paisley* (Paisley: Stewart, 1857), pp. 49–50. A *cleg* is a horsefly.

79 *Caledonian Mercury*, 29 February, 2 March and 20 April; *Glasgow Herald*, 3 March; M. I. Thomis and P. Holt, *Threats of Revolution in Britain, 1789–1848* (London: Macmillan, 1977), p. 73.

80 *Glasgow Herald*, 3 April 1820.

81 [J. Brayshaw], *Remarks upon the Character and Conduct of the Men who Met under the Name of the British Parliament at the Latter End of the Year 1819: With an Account of the Manner in which they Obtained their Seats. To which is Added, a Letter to the Lord Advocate of Scotland, on the State of that Country* (Newcastle upon Tyne: Marshall, [1820]), pp. 4–23 (British constitution), p. 35 (France). This pamphlet was published shortly after the general election results were known.

82 *Remarks*, p. 18 (slaves), pp. 17, 26–8, 31 and 37 (public meetings).

83 See particularly Ellis and Mac a' Ghobhainn, *The Scottish Insurrection of 1820*.

84 TNA, HO 102/32/444–5 (18 April).

85 G. Pentland, *The Spirit of the Union: Popular Politics in Scotland, 1815–20* (London: Pickering & Chatto, 2011), p. 99; TNA, HO 33/2/148, 153 and 335.

86 TNA, HO 33/2/153 (3 April); HO 102/32/317 (4 April).

87 TNA, HO 102/32/328, report of Bannatyne, (4 April).

88 TNA, HO 33/2/157, Bannatyne to GPO London (7 April).

89 TNA, HO 102/32/326 (3 April).

90 TNA, HO 102/32/317 (Lord Provost to Sidmouth, 4 April); Parkhill, *History of Paisley*, pp. 61–2.

91 TNA, HO 102/32/345 (report of Bannatyne, 5 April).

92 *Trials for High Treason, in Scotland, Under a Special Commission, held at Stirling, Glasgow, Paisley, Dumbarton, and Ayr, in the Year 1820*, vol. 1 (Edinburgh: Manners & Miller, 1825), pp. 184–204; TNA, HO 102/32 fol. 351, (Lord Advocate to Sidmouth, 5 April). See also *Glasgow Herald*, 7 April.

93 J. Stevenson, *A True Narrative of the Radical Rising in Strathaven* (Glasgow: Miller, 1835), pp. 4–8.

94 Stevenson, *True Narrative*, pp. 5, 15.

95 TNA, HO 102/32/328 and 345 (4 and 5 April).

96 TNA, HO 102/32/373 (8 April).

97 TNA, HO 102/33/54–6 (Downie to Rae and petition from Balfron, 29 May).

98 TNA, HO 102/32/353 (6 April).

99 TNA, HO 102/32/367 (7 April); DRO 152 M/C/1820/OH/55 (11 April).

100 H. Cockburn, *Memorials of his Time* (Edinburgh: Black, 1856), pp. 363–4.

101 J. G. Lockhart (ed.), *Memoirs of the Life of Sir Walter Scott*, 2nd edn (Edinburgh: Cadell, 1839), vol. 6, p. 229.

102 *PP* 1821 (189) Army: yeomanry and volunteer corps. See also TNA, HO 102/32/429 (General Bradford to Sidmouth, 16 April).

103 *PP* 1821 (189) Army: yeomanry and volunteer corps. Significance is here defined as a reimbursement costs exceeding £200. There were twelve such deployments in Scotland.

104 Account reconstructed from depositions and reports in TNA, HO 102/32/431-4 and 481-583; HO 102/32/377 (Monteith to Sidmouth, 9 April). See also HO 102/32/384 (Rae to Sidmouth, 10 April) and *Caledonian Mercury*, 10 April.

105 TNA, HO 102/32/563 (Dr John Spiers, list of killed and wounded, 8 April).

106 TNA, HO 102/32/390 (11 April).

107 DRO, 152/M/C/1820/OH/53 (Sidmouth to Boswell, 13 April).

108 *Lancaster Gazette*, 22 April.

109 *Leeds Mercury*, 8 April.

110 TNA, HO 40/12 fol. 137 (Haigh and Haigh Allen to Byng, 12 April).

111 TNA, HO 40/12 fol. 109 (Byng to Sidmouth, 9 April); HO 102/32/313 (Rae to Sidmouth, 3 April).

112 TNA, HO 40/12 fols 121 and 131 (11 and 12 April).

113 TNA, HO 40/12, fols 140–1 (Sharp to Sidmouth, 11 April), 146–9 (Norris to Sidmouth, 12 April), 150–1 and 152–3 (Harewood, and Norris, to Sidmouth, 13 April).

114 TNA, HO 40/12, fols 140–1 and 153.

115 TNA, HO 102/32 fol. 361 (7 April); HO 102/32/442–4 (18 April).

116 WYAS (Leeds), WYL250/6/2/B2/1, Byng to Lascelles (28 November 1819).

117 TNA, HO 40/12 fols 128 and 136 (Beckett to Beckett, and Major Batho to Byng, 12 April); HO 40/16 fol. 146 (examination of Farrimond, 8 March).

118 TNA, HO 40/12 fols 128, 137, 163 (12–13 April); *Newcastle Courant*, 22 April.

119 WYAS (Leeds), Harewood Mss WYL250/6/2/B2/1/22 (Byng to Campbell, 11 April).

120 *Courier*, 17 April.

121 TNA, HO 40/12 fol. 322 (report from Fletcher, Bolton, 24 April).

122 TNA, HO 40/12 fols 166 (Fletcher to Sidmouth, 13 April) and 240 (Byng to Taylor, 16 April); *Manchester Observer*, 22 April; *Newcastle Courant*, 22 April.

123 *Lancaster Gazette*, 22 April; F. K. Donnelly and J. L. Baxter, 'Sheffield and the revolutionary tradition, 1791–1820', in S. Pollard and C. Holmes, *Essays in the Economic and*

Social History of South Yorkshire (Sheffield: South Yorkshire County Council, 1976), pp. 103-6, 108-9.

124 *Lancaster Gazette*, 22 April.

125 *Lancaster Gazette*, 22 April; TNA, HO 40/12 fols 245 (Campbell 17 April), 247 (Lloyd, 16 April) and 274 (Harrison, 18 April) all reporting to Byng.

126 T. Carlyle, *The French Revolution: A History* (London: Fraser, 1837), vol. 2, p. 400.

127 BCL, Memorandum Book of William Varley, pp. 4–5.

128 Donnelly, 'The general rising of 1820', pp. 239, 249, 301–2.

129 F. Peel, *The Risings of the Luddites*, first edn (Heckmondwike: Senior, 1880), pp. 158–61.

130 DRO, 152/M/C/1820/OM (letter to Sidmouth, 23 April).

131 Vansittart's budget speech – *HC Deb*, 19 June (vol. 1, col. 1162).

132 Speeches by Palmerston, *HC Deb*, 2 June (vol. 1, p. 838) and 14 June (vol. 1, col. 1080).

133 *PP* 1830 (427) Militia Return, p. 3.

134 TNA, HO 43/29/239 (26 February).

135 F. Bamford and G. W. Wellington (eds), *The Journal of Mrs Arbuthnot, 1820–32: vol. 1, February 1820 to December 1825* (London: Macmillan, 1950), p. 30 (5 August).

136 *London Gazette*, 25 July; HO 40/13 fols 116 and 245 (7 May and 5 June).

137 WYAS (Leeds), WYL250/6/2/B1/5/64 (Fenton to Harewood, 10 December); DRO 152M/C/1820/OH/61 (Boswell to Sidmouth, 8 November).

138 DRO, 152/M/C/1820/OH/56 (18 April).

139 TNA, HO 40/12 fols 154 and 240 (13, 15 April).

140 E. Phipps (ed.), *Memoirs of the Political and Literary Life of Robert Plumer Ward* (Murray: 1850), vol. 2, p. 44.

5 Late spring and early summer

Introduction

There was scant sense of the tide of unrest abating during the remainder of April. In a speech on 18 March, George Canning had asked his Liverpool constituents 'whether any country, in any two epochs, however distant, of its history, ever presented such a contrast with itself as this Country in November, 1819, and this country in February 1820?' 'What an unhappy commentary all these commotions offer on Mr CANNING'S speech', observed *The Times*. Cobbett expostulated: 'Will you still hold out? Will you still insist, that measures of defiance, of scorn, and of chastisement are the only ones to pursue?'[1] Events in Yorkshire and Scotland vied for newspaper space with the outcome of further high-profile trials. Sir Charles Wolseley, the Birmingham radicals' erstwhile 'legislatorial attorney', was convicted at Chester and subsequently gaoled for eighteen months. James Wroe, former editor of the *Manchester Observer*, was gaoled for a year and fined £100 for selling Carlile's *Republican*. (Proceedings were soon initiated against his successor as editor, Thomas J. Evans, for a libel against the army in the 29 April issue.) Joseph Harrison, a dissenting minister at Stockport, received an eighteen-month sentence for seditious speech from the Peterloo platform shortly before the yeomanry struck; London printer Thomas Davison, publisher of the journal *Medusa* (an early casualty of the six acts) was indicted for blasphemous libel. Jacob McGinnis – working man, alleged reformer and infidel – was sentenced to death for shooting a Stockport policeman with intent to kill.[2]

Even the loyalist sheet, the *Courier*, spoke in terms of rebellion in Scotland. It dutifully scoured around for news devoid of any connection to disturbances but was often hard pressed to find any. All it could offer its readers on 17 April, for example, was a story that George IV had recently ridden from Brighton Pavilion to the edge of the South Downs and back. Henry Lascelles, the Government's recent choice as the West Riding of Yorkshire's Lord Lieutenant (who had just succeeded his father as Earl of Harewood), used the Yorkshire disturbances to lobby the Prime Minister for greater protection of the West Riding woollen trade: the 'most pressing distress amongst the Manufacturing Labourers', had sadly made them receptive of 'sedition, and every sort of discontent'.[3] At one point it seemed possible Harewood would call a county meeting to draw up a remonstrance on the issue. However as Robert Chaloner, who managed Whig political interests in York, pointed out to Earl Fitzwilliam, the Tories would find it impossible to discuss current events without opening up scrutiny of their causes. The meeting never happened.[4] The Government regarded the York parliamentary constituency as a sensitive barometer of opinion in the county as a whole. It had failed at the general election to take either seat but now had hopes of capturing one as the Whig incumbent, Lawrence Dundas, was poised to succeed to the family peerage, his father being close to death. Sidmouth monitored Dundas senior's health closely, keeping the King's private secretary informed.[5] However when the expected by-election was held on 28 June, Fitzwilliam's nephew by marriage Chaloner was returned unopposed in Dundas's place. Though the depth of the Fitzwilliam purse was a powerful factor in the result, the absence of any ministerial challenge was an embarrassment to Yorkshire loyalists. It also gave Chaloner uninhibited rein in his acceptance speech to attack the six acts as unconstitutional, the 'baneful' situation in Ireland (for which his proposed solution was Catholic relief), and the persecution of Queen Caroline. He also called for the 'practical reform' of Parliament.[6]

The Ministry was also under pressure closer to Westminster. Having, or so it seemed, resolved its differences of opinion with George IV over his demand for a divorce, the Cabinet ran into a further storm in the fourth week of April when it refused the King's request to increase the Civil List. Technically George's request was not for an increase but for the annual sum hitherto voted to his father to be added to the portion he had received as Regent. However in the context of the imperative to enforce economy and opposition politics (both within and beyond the Commons) very much focussed on the issues of corruption and venality, the royal request was untenable. Liverpool had prepared early and thoroughly for this moment, recognising it 'will require much management'. Detailed breakdowns of the Regent's household accounts in the year ending October 1819 had been carefully assembled over several months. They revealed expenditure of astonishing proportions, such as £32,920 on food and wine, £11,793 on candles, oil and gaslight, and £5,000 on silverware. (In all George had purchased half-a-million ounces of gold and silver since 1812, at a total cost of £110,000.) Knowing that the unenviable task of defending the Civil List before a sceptical House of Commons could only be entrusted to Castlereagh, Liverpool delayed detailed discussion by the Cabinet until the Foreign Secretary could attend.[7]

Neither monarch nor first minister had a good opinion of each other (George 'hated' Liverpool according to one Cabinet minister).[8] Liverpool shrewdly deputed Sidmouth to talk the King round. Sidmouth's capital at Carlton House was high since the exposure of Cato Street: 'he is the Duke of Wellington on Home Service', George was known to say.[9] Yet when the draft speech from the throne at the forthcoming opening of Parliament was submitted for royal approval, it was returned with the sections concerning the Civil List struck through. Liverpool summoned his Cabinet, at just a day's notice, for 24 April: 'I have an answer from Windsor of the most unsatisfactory kind, and such as I think should lead to the dissolution of the Government.' According to Sidmouth's Under Secretary the Cabinet had to persuade Liverpool that talk of resignation was premature. Instead it reiterated the case for economy and bluntly threatened George that the only alternative would be 'to bring the whole subject now (at whatever disadvantage), under the investigation of Parliament.'[10]

The following day George conceded, confirming he was 'fully sensible of the importance of publick economy and is desirous to make every sacrifice on his part for that object'. Clearly these were the words – and the sentiments – not of the monarch but of his private secretary, Sir Benjamin Blomfield.[11] The following day a 'furious' King personally confronted some of his ministers. He had 'got into temper again', Lord Chancellor Eldon told his daughter and 'was pretty well disposed to part with us all'. He told Sidmouth 'it was time to determine whether the Ministers were the servts. of the King or the servants of Lord Liverpool'. This time the Home Secretary was more severe, according to Henry Hobhouse:

> Lord S. answered that the minute had been fully discussed and approved by the whole Cabinet, that they were not the servants of Lord L. but of the King; and, speaking for one, he could say that they would only continue so while they could enjoy his confidence. Upon this remark the King checked himself, and assured Lord S. of his high regard and so forth.[12]

There were also tensions within the Cabinet. Some of this focussed on the temperament of the Prime Minister. Wellesley-Pole 'as usual complained of the want of warmth in Ld Liverpool', a junior Government member noted on 4 May. 'He said he shut himself up with his clerks, was very honest and very able in his way, but was totally ignorant of the arts of party government.'[13] Harriet Arbuthnot, Wellington's confidante and wife of the Joint Secretary of the Treasury, lamented Liverpool's obsession with augmenting the Ministry in the Commons at the expense of a 'hold on the mind & opinion of the nation generally'. This was occasioned by a discussion between the Duke and her husband, after a bruising debate on 15 May in which a Whig motion of censure (for failing to reduce the Scottish judiciary in line with the recommendations of a select committee) saw the Government's majority in the Commons reduced to twelve.[14] 'A gross job of Lord Melville's', Harriet Arbuthnot called it – a reference to the Ministry's political manager in Scotland whom, she felt, was given too much discretion by Liverpool. Her opinion is resonant with Wellington's (and later the King's) that this was 'a Government of Departments' and Wellesley-Pole's that the Prime Minister left ministers 'to themselves or to chance'.[15]

Oh give me Death or Liberty

tho in Newgate Close Confined
No fears Alarm the Noble mind
tho death itself Apears in View
Daunts not the Soul Sincerely true

Let S------h And his Base Colleagues
Cajole And Plot their Dark intrigues
Still each Brittons Last words shall be
Oh give me Death or Liberty.[16]

The Home Secretary was also not immune to colleagues' criticism. There were rumours that the Cato Street arrest warrants were defective and that charges of treason, perhaps even of murder, would not stick. Wellington complained of 'gross mismanagement' at the Home Office, and of it being in 'inefficient hands'.[17] The cause of his outburst was that the name of one of the conspirators, the tailor Abel Hall, had been included in neither the indictment nor the list of witnesses that the prosecution was required to provide in advance of the trial. Yet Hall had now made such a full confession that his inclusion would have eliminated the need to rely on the tainted testimony of the spy George Edwards. Having secured two peripheral conspirators to turn King's evidence, Sidmouth and the Attorney General had actually decided to dispense with Edwards altogether. Roughly treated by London workers in the days after the trial and in fear of his life, Edwards was soon hiding out in Guernsey, and then fled to the Cape Colony under a new identity. This thwarted attempts by the City of London alderman Matthew Wood to initiate a parliamentary enquiry into his role in the conspiracy, and likewise a move led by Thistlewood's wife Susan to serve an indictment on Edwards for high treason.[18] That there were weaknesses in the Cato Street prosecution case Liverpool and Sidmouth were fully aware. They sought to eliminate them by taking unprecedented care to ensure that juries would be empanelled that would provide a guilty verdict upon each of the conspirators. The Middlesex County poll book for March's general election was scrutinised for how potential jurors had voted. Names were annotated: 'bad very', 'bad', 'middling', 'good', 'very good', 'warranted as good', 'likely to give true verdicts according to the evidence', 'a strong anti-radical'.[19] Both prosecution and defence had the right to challenge a considerable number of potential jurors without explanation, but Home Office diligence ensured that when the trials began on 17 April the prosecution was the better equipped to do so.

For two weeks a sense of unreality then hung over proceedings because the Chief Justice ruled against all press reporting until the separate trials of each of the defendants were all completed. Only those who each day thronged round the court learned what was going on, along with readers of the London *Observer* for Sunday 23 April, the editor having decided to flout the prohibition. It is a measure of public interest in the trials that he at least doubled his circulation. He later claimed he had met the £500 fine for the infringement and 'put, over and above, a very handsome sum into his own pocket'.[20] Finally, however, on Friday 28 April the trials were concluded. Arthur Thistlewood, John Brunt, James Ings, William Davidson and Richard Tidd were each found guilty of high treason and sentenced to be hanged, beheaded and quartered. Sentences of death on six further conspirators who had changed their plea to guilty were commuted to transportation for life. Robert Adams, who had become the Crown's principal witness, was released without trial, but almost immediately gaoled for debt. Six further prisoners who had been arrested on suspicion of high treason were discharged the following week after the Crown offered no evidence against them. The six included Thomas Preston, Robert George, Thomas Hazard and Abel Hall. The Home Office had taken a gamble in its handling of Hall: the tailor reciprocated with weekly secret reports on the activities of metropolitan radicals that continued into the mid-1830s.[21]

'With respect of the immorality of our project', Thistlewood told the court in his address before sentencing, 'I will just observe that the assassination of a tyrant has always been deemed a meritorious action. Brutus and Cassius were lauded to the very skies for slaying Caesar':

> Indeed, when any man, or any set of men, place themselves above the laws of their country, there is no other means of bringing them to justice than through the arm of a private individual. If the laws are not strong enough to prevent them from murdering the community, it becomes the duty of every member of that community to rid his country of its oppressors.
>
> High treason was committed against the people at Manchester, but justice was closed against the mutilated, the maimed, and the friends of those who were upon that occasion indiscriminately massacred. The Sovereign, by the advice of his Ministers, thanked the murderers, while yet reeking in the blood of their hapless victims! If one spark of honour – if one spark of patriotism – had still glimmered in the breasts of Englishmen, they would have risen to a man – for Insurrection then became a public duty – and the *Blood of the Slain* should have been the watchword to vengeance on their murderers. The banner of independence should have floated in the gale that brought the tidings of their wrongs and their sufferings to the metropolis! – Such, however, was not the case, and Albion is still in the chains of slavery – I quit it without regret – I shall soon be consigned to the grave – my body will be immured beneath the soil whereon I first drew breath. My only sorrow is, that the soil should be a theatre for slaves, for cowards, for despots.[22]

Thistlewood's body was not immured beneath the soil whereon he first drew breath, but under copious quantities of quicklime. The graves of all five conspirators, beneath a corridor inside Newgate, were then paved over with heavy flagstones.[23] Before that was accomplished, however, the considerable problems attendant upon a public execution had to be negotiated. Public hangings seldom had other than a carnivalesque character and were frequently attended by unrest and demonstrations in favour of the condemned. So sensational was the crime, however, that particular precautions were taken, mindful too that there was considerable sympathy for the five men. Those who unequivocally endorsed their actions were, at least publically, few in number; but the burden of their defence had been that Edwards at the very least should have been arraigned beside them and, indeed, bore the greatest responsibility for what was planned. Thistlewood's bravura speech from the dock had deliberately sought to locate his actions in the context of Peterloo, and the passage of eight months had done little to diminish popular revulsion at the actions of authority there.

As the sentences had been handed down on a Friday it was Monday, 1 May, before they could be carried out. Over the weekend a specially enlarged scaffold was built in front of the Old Bailey. Double rows of railings were erected to control access to the site. Some 150 infantry were stationed inside Newgate Prison or nearby; other detachments patrolled the neighbouring streets. Early on Mayday morning the infantry were reinforced by three troops of the Life Guards and six teams of horse artillery. Elsewhere, the City Light Horse (a yeomanry regiment) and the Twelfth Lancers waited in barracks, saddled up and under arms if required. They never were needed and if the spectacle on the scaffold had not been so shocking, the demeanour of the crowd (cheering the clowning and nonchalant bravado of the condemned and roundly abusing officials, but never riotous) might have been accounted the most remarkable feature of the morning.[24] Of the execution itself the best that could be said was that quartering the bodies was remitted. The decapitations, however, did take place and 'the crowd were actually more excited by the mutilation of the dead, than at the destruction of the living': 'exclamations of horror and of reproach', 'howlings and groans', 'hissings and hootings', 'yells and execrations', cries of 'Murder the villain' and 'Shoot that ------ murderer' [directed at the masked executioner], and 'Bring out Edwards'.[25] These were the first beheadings in the capital since Despard's in 1803. Speculation and mythology quickly adhered to the event: the dexterity with which the operations were conducted, with surgical knives rather than the axe that had been provided, encouraged the view that the masked perpetrator must have been a medical man. In the months that followed popular suspicions alighted on two men in particular: an attempt was made to castrate a St Thomas's Hospital medical student as he walked through Southwark one night; and the young Thomas Wakley, future radical MP and founder of the *Lancet*, was violently assaulted and left for dead in an arson attack on his home in August.[26]

'The Men died like heroes', the radical Whig and Middlesex MP John Cam Hobhouse wrote in his diary that night. Less sympathetic commentators – and they were in a clear majority – deplored their 'most hardened & brutal want of religion or any proper feeling'.[27] Abel Hall had alleged that Hobhouse had agreed to head a provisional government if the conspiracy succeeded (Wellington for one believed this). Letters taken from the conspirators after their arrest included one from Ings to Hobhouse, thanking him for 'the comforts I receive'; but how far the future Baron Broughton, Secretary of State for India, actually knew them, still more was complicit in their plans, is highly speculative (and he was in prison from mid-December until 29 February).[28] More significant was the persistence with which critics of Liverpool's Ministry promoted the idea that Thistlewood and his associates were essentially the dupes of government agents. 'Another plot manufactured by Ministers', said Carlile. 'Authorised spies assisted at the orgies of the desperadoes', John Wade claimed. The great unstamped newspaper *Poor Man's Guardian* would later write of Thistlewood that he was 'high-minded and unfortunate' and betrayed by 'Castlereagh's SPIES'. William Linton, poet, engraver and gentlest of Chartists, believed the five were 'Conspirators by contrivance of the government'. Thomas Frost (born 1821), Chartist, socialist and radical author, could remember only three books in his Croydon childhood home: the Bible, a volume of *Cobbett's Weekly Political Register* and the proceedings of the Cato Street trials.[29] The active complicity of the Government in the conspiracy became a necessary myth, used both to make sense of an extraordinary episode and to distance the English radical tradition from the taint of revolution.

Love, bitter wrong

Upper floor rooms of houses that overlooked the scaffold were let for the occasion for high fees. Harriet Arbuthnot's twenty-four-year-old brother Cecil Fane was among these select spectators: having 'never seen an execution … he had a great curiosity' he told his sister. However just as Thistlewood prepared to take his leave of the 'theatre for slaves' Fane, nauseated, turned away from the window and 'retired into a corner of the room & hid himself that he might not see the drop fall, which excited great contempt in the people who were in the room with him'. Public executions were a form of popular theatre but not for the faint-hearted.

Drama of a more refined variety was available throughout the season at the capital's theatres and as May drew to an end Harriet and Charles Arbuthnot joined an evening audience for a new tragedy, *Virginius, or the Fall of the Decemviri*, 'which I liked extremely', she wrote in her diary.[30] We saw in Chapter 3 how even carefully regulated 'legitimate' theatre often supplied critical commentary on the tone of politics and government in 1820. Of all the new plays that season, *Virginius* was the most daring in its depiction of 'love, bitter wrong, freedom, sad pity, and lust of power', to quote its epilogue.

Virginius was the work of James Sheridan Knowles. (His middle name honoured his father's cousin Richard Sheridan, dramatist and close associate of the Whig hero Charles James Fox.) Both the content of this play and the socio-political context within which it was first staged rendered it hugely controversial. Knowles depicted as corrupt and debauched the regime of the Decemviri, a commission of ten patricians who ruled Rome in 450–459 BC and, when its term of office expired, refused to stand down. Furthermore, unlike the heroes of the other Roman plays revived in response to the political climate of 1820, Virginius was a common citizen, a soldier serving away from Rome. The chief of the Decumvirate, Appius Claudius, lusts uninhibitedly after Virginia, the soldier's teenage daughter, and kidnaps her. Then, when she repels his advances, Appius devises rigged legal proceedings to have her declared the fatherless slave of one of his cronies. The play's climax comes when Virginius, returned from the war, contrives to kill his daughter rather than see her fall victim to Appius's lust. Thus abridged, *Virginius* has limited resonance with the events of 1820. However informed audiences would have known that the story had a solid factual basis; and that the case of Virginius and Virginia triggered a revolt against the Decumvirate and the restitution of constitutional rule.

Knowles's depiction of debauchery and despotism in the highest realm of the empire, melded to a tale of persecuted female innocence, was a potent drama to place on the British stage in 1820. Not only is Appius depicted as shamelessly dismissive of all legal propriety or conventional morality, the ordinary Roman people are thrust into the action of the play to an extent without parallel, even in an age that relished spectacular crowd scenes in its drama. One critic indeed complained about 'the frequent introduction of the populace on the stage'.[31] One of the functions of the crowd is to offer increasingly vocal dissent at the rigged trial, as Appius repeatedly claims, 'The law is just – most reasonable – I framed that law myself – I will maintain that law'.[32] Knowles wrote *Virginius* in great haste during the early months of 1820. Its premiere in Glasgow coincided with the Scottish rising. Presumably the Lord Chamberlain's office scrutinised *Virginius* very carefully, but not it would seem enough. According to William Macready, the actor who took the title role, on 16 May, the eve of its London premiere, the script was recalled by 'Carlton House' (i.e. George IV's London residence) and returned the following morning with several deletions indicated 'of some lines in the part of Appius Claudius, expiating on tyranny'.[33] Both London's *Morning Herald* and the *Glasgow Herald* reported rumours of a last-minute demand 'for inspection in a high quarter', while the publisher John Murray declined to bring out any edition of the text, as was usual following a successful London premiere of a major new play.[34] The circumstances of reception for *Virginius* in 1820 gave it an extraordinary political resonance that could never be retrieved in subsequent productions. The play was lost to the sight of twentieth-century audiences, but it was specifically Covent Garden's experience in producing it in 1820 that prompted William Hazlitt to ask, 'is the name of liberty to be struck out of the English language, and are we not to hate tyrants even in an old roman play?'[35]

The play's contemporary audiences did not need to identify the character of Virginia precisely with Queen Caroline to sense reverberations in Knowles's depiction of feminine innocence assailed by tyranny, for by the end of May the future of the Queen was becoming less a matter of hypothetical speculation and more the substance of a developing drama itself. During February, as was seen in Chapter 3, the Cabinet hammered out a compromise with the King whereby the financial support enjoyed by Caroline while Princess of Wales would be renewed for the duration of his reign, on condition that she remained abroad and renounced the formal entitlements of the rank and status of Queen. Were she to return to the United Kingdom then proceedings would be initiated to dissolve the royal marriage. The Cabinet's hope was that an annual payment of £50,000 would assuage whatever injuries to her dignity Caroline might feel from not being crowned or mentioned in the Anglican liturgy, or from the ambiguities foreign courts might perceive in her status. There was however a delay of over a month before arrangements were made to communicate these terms to her, indicative perhaps of a certainty complacency that while the Ministry needed to apply itself to retaining the King's approval, his queen would be biddable. The years she had spent in Europe since 1814 suggested that leisured recreation and luxury were what she valued most; furthermore her apparent lack of intellectual refinement was widely interpreted among unsympathetic male observers as indicating limited interest in matters of State or politics. Even Henry Brougham, her legal adviser, viewed Caroline as a largely pliant vehicle through which he could further his own legal career.

The Ministry seems not to have comprehended the full implications of its heavy reliance upon this disingenuous careerist as the medium through which it communicated with Caroline, or at least not to have done so until it was too late – probably in March when Brougham tried to finesse an appointment as a King's Counsel as the trade-off for his not accepting a position as one of the Queen's legal officers. Details of the terms that had been agreed with the King were shared with Brougham only in April, by which time Caroline – encouraged by Brougham – was setting out from Rome (where she had been living since her husband's accession) to travel north.[36] That there would be haggling over the terms of her settlement was clear and Liverpool appears to have accepted without qualms Brougham's statement that he was encouraging the Queen to make her way to Brussels or northern France so that he could more conveniently consult with her and represent her interests. Yet as early as 16 March Caroline had concluded a personal letter about her exclusion from the liturgy, with a demand 'before she arrives in London to receive satisfactory answer from Lord Liverpool'. To her closest political advisor Alderman Matthew Wood, a former Lord Mayor of the City of London and one of its MPs, she wrote of being at Calais by 30 April 'for certain', intercalating the letter with detailed instructions about silk gowns she wanted commissioned in London ready for her return. The Government was also aware of her fury that ministers of the Papal States, in the absence of clarification about her status from the Ministry, had declined to treat her according to the protocol demanded for a queen. Indeed, the whole country was aware of this after 1 April, when Vatican correspondence on the issue found its way into the Whig newspaper, the *Morning Chronicle*. For the avoidance of doubt, extensive references to her 16 March letter to Liverpool appeared in sympathetic papers within a week.[37]

In retrospect it is clear that the question was not *if* the Queen would return to Britain but *when*. But her progress across Europe was dilatory. All concerned were playing elaborate games of bluff: the Government seeking to convince Caroline that both her reputation and her finances would be ruined if she landed in Britain; Brougham hinting to her that there was a prospect of renegotiating terms; Brougham letting the Government form the impression that his influence over his client was greater than it actually was; and Caroline convincing everyone that she was aggrieved enough to become a real political nuisance while still behaving with enough ambiguity to hold out hopes of a satisfactory resolution. The former Speaker of the House of Commons, Lord Colchester, who was on holiday in Italy, noted in his diary each letter from home predicting the Queen's movements: ministers did not think Caroline would carry out her threat to come to Britain, Henry Bankes, a Tory MP told him on 6 April. Four days later John Hatsell, an experienced former Clerk of the House of Commons wrote strongly doubting Caroline would ever appear. The following day the MP for Dover confided it 'not unlikely' the Queen would stay where she was. 'I cannot yet believe that Her Majesty will venture to set her foot on this island', Heneage Legge, Tory MP for Banbury, declared on 8 May. 'I do not believe that she will land upon our coast', Bankes reiterated on 16 May.[38] 'She will not come, *unless she is insane*', the Lord Chancellor told his daughter in late May: gamblers in fashionable London were laying extravagant bets that Caroline would not, as well as would, appear.[39] 'It is inconceivable to me that they will not find some way of preventing her coming,' Princess Lievan, wife to the Russian Ambassador, told the Austrian Chancellor Metternich, though she conceded that at the Ascot races on 1 June there had been 'great alarm' she might. 'The only topic of conversation here is the arrival of the Queen', the Princess wrote on 5 June, 'but even so, I doubt if she will come'.[40] Caroline landed at Dover at 5.00 that afternoon.

Kent's welcome to Caroline bordered on the tumultuous. Thousands thronged Dover harbour walls and beach. In the words of one unsympathetic observer, the clerk to the local magistrates:

> The carriage was drawn by hand preceded by Banners with music … a more numerous and noisy assemblage was never I think witnessed in Dover. The shops were all closed, the Windows above were filled with Females waving their handkerchiefs.[41]

Caroline in turn played the crowd shrewdly. Met at her hotel by a military guard of honour she 'instantly dismissed [them] saying, "I am in a land of Freedom and want no soldiers now".' Some enterprising citizens of Dover tried to separate the redundant soldiers from their firearms and were prevented only 'with the greatest difficulty', their commanding officer confessed.[42] At 6.30 the Queen was on her way again in the first stage of an extraordinary progress across Kent. Canterbury was illuminated for her arrival. Here a crowd implausibly estimated at 'upwards of ten thousands' (the total population was less than 13,000) greeted her arrival which was followed by ceremonial addresses from the mayor and corporation. When she left the following morning officers from cavalry regiments garrisoned in Canterbury escorted Caroline as far as Sittingbourne where the horses, as they had been at Dover, were removed from her carriage and the vehicle pulled by hand through the streets. The same reception was declined in the Medway towns with the plea that the Queen had to arrive in London before nightfall, but it was repeated later in the day at Gravesend and Dartford. All along her route church bells peeled, local dignitaries delivered impromptu addresses, and women were conspicuous in the welcoming crowds.[43]

Queen Caroline made her triumphant entry into London over Westminster Bridge shortly after 7.00 on Tuesday evening. Her route to Alderman Wood's home in South Audley Street took her past Carlton House where, to the delight of anti-Government papers, the sentries saluted. The Woods themselves moved out to a nearby hotel. 'The Queen of England is at present every thing to every body', *The Times* editorialised. Joseph Farington noted in his diary the following day that Caroline's arrival 'is a universal subject of conversation', and so it proved. His maidservant walked over to South Audley Street and returned with a graphic account of how it was thronged by crowds 'crying out in favour of the Queen, and obliging every person whether in Carriages – on Horseback or on foot to pull off their hats when they passed Alderman Wood's'. On Friday the artist John Constable called by to share gossip about the Queen's rumoured eccentric behaviour while in the Mediterranean, wearing 'a Man's hat … a Coloured handkerchief round her neck … short petticoats and Hessian Boots. Her appearance was very masculine.' Within a few days the disturbances were spreading across Westminster. A near neighbour of Farington was said to have 'died of fright … in consequence of the mob who were calling out for illuminations for the Queen'. Farington noted with relief when troops began patrolling past his Charlotte Street home each night, but still householders flooded their windows with lamps and candles 'from the general apprehension of the Windows being otherwise broken by the Mob'. The crowds, claimed *The Times*, consisted mainly 'of the refuse of St Giles', a slum district near Covent Garden; but it also published a report of proceedings before local magistrates where it was revealed that those charged with public order offences included 'very decent young men'.[44] Order was maintained but only at the expense of flooding London's most fashionable streets with troops, some brought up to the capital for the purpose, an operation supervised by Wellington on the Cabinet's behalf.[45]

Don't be too sure of the Guards

The extensive deployment of troops itself carried risks. Barracks were still something of a novelty except in Ireland. The normal practice until the 1790s had been to billet soldiers in small parties wherever their regiment was stationed. To a considerable extent this persisted: it may even have increased for a while after 1815 due to budgetary constraints. We saw in Chapter 2 that securing barrack accommodation was a major preoccupation for senior military officers in Scotland in 1820, seeking to eliminate 'the risk of contamination' of billeted soldiers. Temporary barracks were seldom satisfactory: Paisley's was a disused fever hospital, rented from the burgh, and even with this addition a third of troops stationed in the town still had to be billeted.[46] The problem was especially acute in London. The Second Life Guards, for example, were dispersed in lodgings across Marylebone, their horses in numerous hired stables: directly provided accommodation was limited to that used by a guard and duty piquet.[47] Sir Herbert Taylor MP (a senior officer in the Coldstream Guards and Military Secretary at the War Office) sent Wellington a frank confidential appraisal:

> The manner in which the Guards are quartered in London renders the constant presence and attention of the officers impossible. The barracks do not afford room for officers, and the quarters are of the very worst description and do not afford the same facility of visit and inspection which attaches to country quarters. In these respects the Guards are worse off than any other corps, and while this evil cannot be remedied by the government it is in vain to hope for the removal of its effects.

Soldiers with complaints could not make representations to officers, Taylor continued, but 'in many late instances' resorted instead to 'complaint of injustice done, often tumultuously urged'.[48] 'The great evil in the Guards', he repeated to Wellington on another occasion, 'is the want of intercourse between the officer and the soldier, and the consequent want of knowledge on the part of the former of the soldier's character and habits'.[49] 'They loved Thistlewood as they did their lives & would Pawn their Shirts to support him', soldiers from the Tower garrison told a Customs official. 'We are all ripe and ready' they added, pointing to the Tower.[50] This may have been only drink talking, but one of the most significant – if least remembered – disturbances of 1820 concerned the Third Foot Guards in the week following Queen Caroline's arrival in the capital.

On Thursday 15 June nine soldiers of the regiment stationed at the King's Mews mutinied. On returning from duty at Carlton House, where the George IV was celebrating his birthday, they refused to give up their ammunition. Various explanations were offered. Lord Palmerston, the Secretary at War, told Parliament the incident derived only from an unfounded notion 'that the duty they were called upon to discharge was more severe than other battalions performed'.[51] An alternative explanation was that the men were dissatisfied with their accommodation. It is pertinent here that the King's Mews (the site of the present-day National Gallery) was exactly that – stabling for the royal horses. It had been fitted up as barrack accommodation only days before in response to the need to concentrate troops in Westminster to deal with the Caroline disturbances.[52] This became the official line, one for example that the authorised biography of Sidmouth repeated in 1847. A report was placed in the *Courier* of 16 June stressing that the incident was '*unconnected with any political feeling whatever*'.[53] The senior civil servant at the Home Office, however, ascribed the incident to a cluster of issues: dissatisfaction with the new barracks and extra duties 'arising out of the recent riots', plus 'very relaxed' discipline after the Duke of Gloucester, the commanding officer, attempted 'to dispense with corporal punishment'. Bootle Wilbraham MP, however, believed that Gloucester had exacerbated 'disaffection and discontent' by an ill-timed announcement that the regiment was to be sent on field exercises. In addition, guardsmen in billets were accustomed to leisure and opportunities for paid civilian work; now roll-call four-times daily was uncongenial.[54] Thomas Croker, Secretary to the Admiralty, sent a revealing account to Lord Melville:

> The truth is … that this regiment … has long been in an unsatisfactory state … they have been lately removed into temporary barracks in the Mews; this removal from quarters and a good deal of duty are supposed to have disgusted them; and the lower orders of the people knew on Wednesday and yesterday morning that the regiment intended to strike work, as the tradesmen would say.[55]

A highly particular explanation for the incident was suggested in an anonymous letter to Sidmouth: London prostitutes were withdrawing their services from guardsmen who did not support Caroline: 'You cannot conceive what Influence these whores have over the men one said at the Crown Dam your Eyes. If you present arms you shall not come to Bed with me I am for Caroline.'[56]

One may well discount the latter explanation, but clearly Thursday 15 June was about much more than nine guardsmen who refused to return their ammunition at the end of a duty. 'What a pretty bunch of B------ your 3d Regt are, not to stick to your Words,' a soldier from elsewhere in the Household Brigade was reported saying: 'we & the Coldstream should have been called out to have taken away your Arms, & then you know we should have join'd you'.[57] Prince Frederick, Duke of York, the Commander in Chief of the army, intervened immediately and ordered the regiment at six hours' notice to march to Portsmouth. The first wing marched out at four o'clock on Friday morning; the second, confined to barracks during the interim, marched at dawn on Saturday, after an inspection by the Duke of Wellington. Unamused at how he was forced to mark the anniversary of the eve of Waterloo, the Duke rounded on the battalion: 'they had disgraced themselves, and placed a stain on their colours.'[58]

During the night 'a formidable mob' had demonstrated outside the King's Mews in their support, calling on them to come and join it. A non-commissioned officer of the First Foot Guards in the crowd was heard to claim 'the soldiers had struck for wages', and that the mood of the Third had spread to the First Foot and to the Life Guards and was now becoming general. An appalled Sidmouth was among the first to witness the commotion as he returned for an evening stint in his office after dinner nearby. He diverted his coach to the War Office and ordered the Second Life Guards to intervene. Order was eventually restored but only after the Riot Act had been read and 'not without the application of considerable force'.[59] The following day a Sunday paper, the *Examiner*, apparently on the basis of conversations with guardsmen, stated that the Household Brigade was 'far from being destitute of political feeling as the *Courier* would represent, and that they entertain not very pliable sentiments on the subject of the Queen's treatment'. The paper was also one of several sources to report continuing insubordination among the Third Foot as they marched to Portsmouth, adding that they had been cheered on their way 'by a portion of the Coldstream Regiment'. Many of the Guards were drunk as they passed through Brentford, the Marquess of Worcester told Charles Greville, crying out, 'God save Queen Caroline'.[60] Vice-Admiral Sir Thomas Williams and Henry Grey Bennet MP heard something very similar. Bennet commented in his diary, 'as usual all this was denied by the government and the officers, but it is true'.[61] The *Examiner* subsequently alleged that the Third Foot Guards continued to be mutinous even when they had reached Portsmouth, refusing first to be ordered on foreign service and then to embark for the Isle of Wight on the grounds that this might be a trick to take them abroad. On the streets soldiers talked of marching to London rather than going to the island. The status of these claims was dubious and the Cabinet moved to prosecute the paper. However, the advice of Government law officers was to proceed only if the *Examiner's* claims were entirely unfounded: even then, they advised that members of the regiment, and not the Government, should initiate the prosecution. The matter was dropped.[62]

'In one of the most critical moments that ever occurred in this country, we and the public have reason to doubt in the fidelity of the troops', Wellington told Liverpool. 'The sergeants and corporals of the Guards are certainly excellent soldiers ... but it must be observed that they are taken from the ranks, and of the class of the people, and liable to be influenced by the views and sentiments of the people.' In the same memorandum, Wellington referred to the Duke of York expressing 'great uneasiness respecting the Coldstream Guards; while ... there are, as usual, reports without number in circulation respecting all the Guards, both cavalry and infantry, the greater number false, no doubt, but whether true or false no man can tell ... none of us could say he was surprised if ... there was a mutiny in more of these corps'.[63] Lord Liverpool himself told Charles

Arbuthnot 'that the aversion to the king was risen to the greatest possible height, that the Guards in London were all drinking the Queen's health & had the greatest possible contempt for the King from thinking him a coward & afraid of shewing himself amongst them'.[64] Even the level-headed Major General Byng, commander of the army in northern England, was so unnerved that he burnt the Home Office's communication to him about the problems in London as soon as he received it, rather than risk it being seen by others.[65] In conversation with Robert Plumer Ward on 6 July Wellington frankly stated, 'I do not disguise that in the whole constitution of Guard discipline there is something awkward'. Ward recorded another conversation the same day in which an unnamed Whig peer, the brother of a Guards officer, predicted that Caroline 'if we did not take care … might play the part of Catherine the second [of Russia] who, by means of the Guards, murdered her husband and usurped the throne'. The Whig lord hoped the Coronation (due to take place on 1 August) would be postponed, 'for he feared the mob would bring down the Queen during the ceremony … tumult would ensue, in which probably the Guards would not act. He said, "Don't be too sure of the Guards".'[66]

'A more wholesome state'

In the midst of domestic turmoil the business of normal government had to continue. Such was the incidence of disorder during 1820 that our view of the Liverpool Ministry is apt to become two-dimensional, accentuating the extent to which it was purely reactive in its domestic policies rather than proactive and seeking to direct policy. Its room for manoeuvre, however, was tightly restricted, given the challenge of both post-war economic dislocation and the financial and political imperative to cut Government expenditure. Of course demobilisation had eased public expenditure and some historians have hailed the demise of the fiscal-military State.[67] But this can be exaggerated and, of course, civil unrest in the first four months of the year had forced the Government to expand the armed forces. In 1820 the UK still maintained an armed establishment that exceeded in size that of every other European power except France and Russia. It did so for several reasons, including the need to maintain a sizeable Indian army and to maintain the peace in Ireland, the latter being (as should by now be clear) a garrisoned nation, the military establishment of which was double that of Britain relative to the size of the population.

The post-1815 peace dividend was also eroded by the extensive list of army and navy officers retired on half-pay. More than £1.8 million was set aside in the 1820 budget for half-pay.[68] To place that into perspective, the total pay bill for the officers and other ranks of the combined British cavalry regiments in 1820 was only £547,000.[69] Liverpool's Ministry therefore struggled to make the economies it needed. In 1816 it had failed to persuade Parliament to accept the continuation of income and property tax, with the result that an increased burden was thrown onto taxing consumables with predictable consequences in terms of popular resentment. Even though real reductions in the armed services were achieved, the Government was still forced to borrow heavily to make up a short-fall in its income from taxation, so much so that by January 1820 the Whig *Edinburgh Review* (admittedly not a dispassionate commentator) was claiming that, with interest on the national debt now exceeding £5.2 million, the Treasury would soon be insolvent. Government never succeeded in bringing the civil service back to earlier peacetime levels: on the contrary, the need to expand the Customs service to protect taxation revenues meant that by 1820 the non-military payroll stood at 24,000, 50 per cent larger than it had been in 1797, and costing 130 per cent more.

The true cost of revenue protection, moreover, was disguised by the Navy absorbing all the costs of 1,300 personnel manning a coastal blockade against smuggling to reinforce the Customs and Excise services in Kent and Sussex.[70] A continual war was waged upon smuggling, the post-war years being one of the peaks of its intensity. There were moments in 1820–21 when the authorities' grip, never total, appeared to be lost. All 300 men of the notorious Aldington gang (established in 1820) escaped with their contraband, after they were discovered by blockade men unloading a large vessel near Folkestone in November. Three sailors were injured on that occasion; then, on Christmas Day, an officer was killed during a shoot-out. The following February 250 gang members were involved in the 'Battle of Brookland' against the blockade, which left five dead and twenty-five injured, yet the gang's activities would continue unabated to 1830, even as the coastal blockade's strength was more than doubled.[71] The most audacious incidents in the smuggling industry's defiance of authority, however, were a series of escapes from coastal gaols in the spring of 1820: four from Rye, two from Lydd and then a mass break-out from Dover on 24 May. Shouting 'Liberty or Death – Down with the blue Jackets & all will be well', a large crowd attacked Dover gaol 'with crow-bars, pick-axes, hammers, saws, &c., &c.', tore of the roof and demolished part of a wall and released eleven smugglers captured earlier that day by an excise cutter. Just one of them was recaptured, only to be released when the chaise taking him to the county prison was ambushed.[72] There were further incidents in November when a mob released three smugglers from Rye gaol, and Folkestone magistrates refused custody of smugglers brought in by excise officers, who were then assaulted and chased out of town.[73]

Had the Dover prison breakout occurred in the manufacturing north, the *York Herald* commented acerbically, it would doubtless have been blamed on the seditious press.[74] Yet neither the scale nor the frequent complicity of local authority in smuggling unnerved the Government. Smuggling was contained: ideologically it was criminal and not political; geographically it was largely limited to the south-east coast of England. Industrial unrest and political foment, on the other hand, appeared to go hand-in-hand. More than once in 1820

Liverpool and his colleagues must have appreciated all too well the force of Robert Southey's remark, 'Governments who found their prosperity on manufactures sleep upon gunpowder'.[75] Although highly suspicious of the press and actively concerned to curtail its circulation in industrial districts, there is no reason to suppose the Ministry desired to restrict industry itself. It may appear inevitable that a government of landowners, answering to a Parliament of the landed, should have scant empathy with, or understanding of, industry, but this was not the case. This was no government of landed magnates. Only the Lord Privy Seal, the tenth Earl of Westmorland, was unequivocally of the old aristocracy. Canning's grandfather was a minor County Derry gentleman, his mother a provincial actress who had married a Plymouth draper. Lord Harrowby (President of the Council) was the grandson of a Cheapside linen draper. Castlereagh's family were Ulster Scots with mercantile roots (he had been baptised a Presbyterian). Liverpool's father, the son of an army officer, was a public servant before becoming a MP, assisted by a baronetcy inherited from a cousin. Sidmouth's father was an asylum owner and doctor in general practice. Lord Chancellor Eldon was the son of a Newcastle upon Tyne coal factor. With the traditional aid of a ladder, the young Eldon had had to elope with his bride to Scotland to marry, since her family disapproved of his low social standing. Outside the Cabinet, Arbuthnot's merchant father was a former bankrupt, Charles Grant's father had begun adult life as shipping clerk, and Liverpool's economic advisers William Huskisson and Robert Peel were the sons respectively of a Worcestershire gentleman (largely educated by his uncle, a Parisian doctor) and the owner of a calico printing mill.[76]

This did not mean that Liverpool's Ministry pursued the expansion of the industrial and commercial sectors at agriculture's expense. Its strong preference was to strive to let economic activity be 'natural' or unregulated.[77] 'Natural' in this context meant free of government interference and tariff protection, also recognising that wartime conditions were artificial. War's impact on the labour market, rapid stimulus to industrial production and inflationary effects were unnatural. The Government's policy was therefore to apply what it believed were appropriate correctives to encourage the economy back in the direction of a natural state. This was the rationale behind the Corn Law of 1815: encouraging agricultural self-sufficiency would protect farmers who had responded to wartime conditions by investing heavily in improving the quality of their land and extending the cultivated area itself; it would curtail dependency on foreign suppliers to feed the nation; and by stimulating agriculture it would negate the 'push' factors that encouraged rural workers to move into industry and urban communities. Concomitant to this economic policy was a foreign policy that forestalled the possibility of military involvement which would otherwise intrude on the natural operation of the economy as well as commit the Government to additional expenditure at a time when the parliamentary political imperative was for retrenchment.

However, as Boyd Hilton demonstrated in his masterful history of the economic policies of the 1815–30 Tory administrations, the five years after Waterloo were occasion for a profound movement in government perspective. By May 1820 Huskisson was saying that the United Kingdom 'should not be dependent to too great an extent on foreign countries for the necessaries of life'. Within limits, then, foreign imports were acceptable. The 1815 Corn Law was an adjustment to the 'artificial protection [that] had been afforded to agriculture' during wartime conditions. 'The general principle of a free trade', Huskisson argued, had also been set aside to stimulate Irish agriculture by affording it privileged access to the British market.[78] However protected agriculture had not proved adequate to feed the Kingdom in 1816–17, nor had it shielded farming from business failures. Protection accentuated the competitive advantage enjoyed by cultivators in areas of better soil and climate. The result was a distorted market in which regionally specific over-abundance depressed prices, jeopardising low-yield cultivators, especially where rents remained at wartime levels. (We have already seen how, in Ireland, political and economic orthodoxy combined to make interference in the rents charged by landed proprietors unthinkable.) Agriculture in 1820 was in anything but a natural state. The principal reason for agricultural distress, argued Liverpool, was a consequence 'which had arisen out of the high price of corn during the war', namely over-investment in extending the acreage under the plough.[79]

In the spring of 1820 the agricultural interest was pressing for even greater levels of protection than the 1815 Corn Law had established. George Webb Hall led a well-organised Central Agricultural Association in lobbying for the interests mainly of southern and eastern agriculturalists. Described by a former president of the Board of Agriculture as, 'by his zeal, industry and talents … a species of "Hunt" in Agriculture', Hall vitalised the hitherto gentlemanly farming lobby.[80] The epitome of a farmer who had enjoyed a good war (he was a Bristol lawyer who had taken up sheep farming in 1799), Hall had seen the fortunes of his large-scale merino sheep operations plummet in the post-war period. As cereal producers in the south and east struggled to adjust to post-war market conditions, Hall persuaded some fifty local farming associations to federate around a London-based central organisation in January 1819.[81] It quickly proved a tenacious advocate of its supporters' interests, imitating the 1813–14 campaign to defend statutory apprenticeship in its use both of petitioning and the newspaper press.[82] Some 280 petitions with around 100,000 signatures were presented to Parliament in the first six months of the year and *Evans and Ruffy's Farmers' Journal* effectively turned over to an organ for the Association. 'The press [is] a far more powerful engine than an army', Hall observed, and 'we must avail ourselves of its operation if we mean to succeed'.[83]

Resisting Webb Hall and the Central Agricultural Association was in itself something of a dynamic policy measure, given the dominance of the landed interest at Westminster. This was especially so when Hall became secretary of the

Board of Agriculture, following the death of the highly regarded Arthur Young in July 1820. The protectionist lobby had clearly touched a raw nerve in Government. The President of the Board of Trade rounded on the exaggerated exertions 'in the agricultural districts to excite a conviction that the existing law for the protection of agriculture was inoperative':

> In addition to this, it was deeply to be lamented that a kind of manifesto had been issued by an individual, whose name had been very conspicuous in these transactions, in which manifesto (for he could call it by no other title) the case of the agriculturists had been stated with a great degree of culpable exaggeration.[84]

But in a decisive move explicitly distancing the Ministry from ultra-protectionists, Liverpool himself put the Board on a year's notice of the discontinuation of its Government grant, while in the Commons his front bench successfully decoyed a Select Committee on the protectionist petitions (forced upon it by back-bench agricultural interests) into the technical minutiae of how to calculate grain prices more accurately. A dismayed *Farmers' Journal* reduced the committee's 124-page report to four columns, and pointedly declined to make any comment.[85]

An even clearer indication of the new direction of Government thinking was evident from the Prime Minister himself, again in May 1820, in response to Lord Stanhope, a maverick ultra-Tory.[86] Stanhope was one of many contemporary enthusiasts (Robert Owen the most indefatigable) for spade husbandry of waste and marginal land. Answering an encomium to agrarian fundamentalism and a jeremiad concerning machinery from Stanhope, the Prime Minister extolled 'manufactures' and their capacity to improve material happiness, conferring on Britain 'a degree of power and glory which it could never have obtained without them'. He lauded inventors (specifying Arkwright, Boulton and Watt), men to whom 'England was indebted for its present greatness – men who were as useful to their country, in their generation, as any of the legislators of old were in theirs'. It was a defence of mechanised manufacturing from the commonplace charge that it was the sole cause of distress. Manufacturing had been forced 'beyond its natural level' but this was a temporary condition and no basis from which to 'retrograde … one single step' the technology it employed.[87]

It was a speech calculated to flatter industrial and commercial interests at a time when they, too, were restive: much-publicised petitions for free trade had been presented by London and Glasgow merchants in May; and we have seen how Yorkshire manufacturers linked the Grange Moor incident to stagnation in the woollen trade. However, this was no flash of pure pragmatism. On 26 May, in one of the major speeches of his career, Liverpool elaborated a case for limiting protective tariffs. The economic might of the Kingdom had been achieved not because of protection but 'in spite of that system'. British farming 'would not be what it now is … had not agriculture been fostered by manufactures and commerce'. It would be destructive of the interests of the country as a whole to legislate in favour of any one sector at the expense of others. 'There is nothing which alarms me so much as a meddling disposition, on the part of the legislature, with reference to these subjects ... on all commercial subjects, the fewer the laws the better.' However, he entered an important caveat: 'it is utterly impossible, with our debt and taxation, even if they were but half their existing amount, that we can suddenly adopt the system of free trade.'[88] Nevertheless, this was an agenda for incremental change that looked towards the refinement of the Corn Laws the Ministry would introduce in 1822. It is significant that Liverpool (abetted by Huskisson) was articulating it against the background of the Easter risings.

Liverpool was unpersuadable that even Ireland constituted a special case for economic treatment. In the dying days of 1819, Charles Grant had written at length to the Prime Minister, making a case for government intervention in Ireland for 'the promotion of public interests'. While in Britain such a policy 'would be disapproved by our modern œconomists', Ireland's pre-industrial economy needed the spur of government-directed financial stimuli, Grant argued, just as England's had in the later seventeenth century. The Chief Secretary was clear that the Ministry could not 'create funds where a whole nation was in want', but judicious expenditure would promote economic momentum as well as offering short-term palliatives for social distress. From the Exchequer, Vansittart poured cold water on Grant's musings.[89]

Six months later, however, Liverpool's Ministry did intervene in the Irish economy, its hand forced by a banking crisis that crippled southern Ireland. In the absence of any manufacturing base, Irish banks beyond Ulster and Dublin city existed for little purpose other than oiling the wheels of commercial agriculture. The secular trend of post-war price deflation, to which midland and southern Ireland was especially vulnerable because of over-dependence on victualling during the French wars, bit in the early summer of 1820. Eighty per cent of the circulating medium in counties Cork and Kerry consisted of notes issued by Cork's two banks and on 25 May both failed, closely followed the next week by two Limerick banking houses, and then by three others in Killkenny, Waterford and Clonmel. Only half of southern Ireland's banking houses survived and all these were ailing (six would close later in the decade). With one exception, Ulster's four houses with their close links to the linen trade were unaffected.[90] However, in the south the consequences were devastating. When news that the Cork house of Roche had failed reached Molahiffe (Kerry), where a cattle fair was in progress, trade ceased instantly. Cork's principal inhabitants lobbied the Lord Lieutenant, complaining that 'all confidence, as well as trade, is suspended'. The collapse of Waterford's bank left many 'destitute'; its director (brother of the city's MP) committed suicide.[91] The Bank of Ireland acted to save Dublin's six banks and only one of them went under; but it never assisted those elsewhere. It is tempting to discern a sectarian bias in its policy: certainly prosperous Munster Roman Catholics 'had so much confidence in their Popish friends the Roches that many of them had the whole of their properties, or nearly so, either in their notes, or lodged with them'.[92]

Preferential loans totalling £500,000 were made available by the Ministry for the relief of Irish trade and manufactures (it had sought to restrict this to only £300,000 but the Commons voted the higher amount). However, few could raise the collateral security required by the Government's commissioners to qualify for a loan. By 28 September only £80,000 had been lent, while applications totalling £200,000 had been refused. Five weeks later the amount lent had crept up to £100,000, a significant portion of it channelled not to southern Ireland but to Dublin merchants (among them a glue boiler) and to the north.[93] Ultimately forty-seven loans, totalling £286,750, were made: three of the largest (totalling £133,000) went to failing southern banks, two of which were enabled to pay off their creditors before liquidating their assets to redeem the loan. To this extent the initiative fulfilled its purpose. However the third and largest beneficiary failed completely in 1826, leaving £50,000 of its £80,000 loan unpaid. Embarrassingly for Grant, the only other major defaulter was the Kilkenny woollen manufacturer Nowlan & Shaw, whose loan had only been approved after the Chief Secretary's personal intervention.[94]

The attempt to ameliorate the consequences of the Irish banking crisis was not an episode likely to reconcile the Government to a policy of economic intervention. Cautious incrementalism was the keynote of Liverpool's economic policy, nowhere more obvious than in its approach to currency reform – 'the return to cash payments' in contemporary parlance. In 1797 Pitt's Government, struggling to cope with economic crisis, had been forced to prohibit the convertibility of banknotes into gold and silver. (A similar prohibition from honouring the promise to bearers of banknotes was laid upon the Bank of Ireland.) In 1819, a Resumption of Cash Payments Act, framed by a committee chaired by Robert Peel, set out a four-stage schedule by which, from February 1820 to May 1823, sterling would return to the gold standard. It is arguable that the transition, which had a deflationary effect and exacerbated unemployment during the 1820s, was too rapid. But in 1820 itself the practical impact was nugatory. Politically, the real damage at this point was the widely held perception that the Bank of England (which had benefitted massively from the extent of government borrowing during the war) had impelled Liverpool's Government to adopt its cautious approach – thus stoking popular denunciation of State jobbery and collusion with city financiers. Even manufacturing interests failed at first to recognise the advantages of a stable currency in which sterling was competitively priced against the international medium of gold (for the midlands, mainly selling to the domestic market, the advantages were in any case few unlike the textile-dominated and export-oriented north). Parliament's appetite for currency reform mostly derived not from a careful appraisal of economic theory and policy options, but from a vague feeling that the change was natural and morally desirable. 'Restoring a more wholesome state of currency', Horace Twiss, a new recruit to the Tory benches in 1820, called it.[95]

Little of the consequences of this policy was apparent in 1820, nor yet were there developed the technical arguments for using gold as the standard for sterling that would sustain the policy up to the First World War. However the policy had satisfied one of Liverpool's main criteria for effective government, namely that it should be active – and seen to be active – in pursuit of the national interest. Before Parliament's approval for 'Peel's Bill' was secured, Liverpool had written to Eldon forcefully stating his conviction:

> If we cannot carry what has been proposed, it is far, far better for the country that we should cease to be the Government.
>
> After the defeats we have already experienced during this Session, our remaining in office is a *positive* evil. It confounds all ideas of government in the minds of men. It disgraces us *personally*, and renders us less capable every day of being of any real service to the country, either now or hereafter. If therefore things are to remain as they are, I am quite clear that there is no advantage, in any way, in our being the persons to carry on the public service.
>
> A strong and decisive effort can alone redeem our character and credit, and is as necessary for the country as it is for ourselves.[96]

Liverpool was alluding here to the Whigs' tacit acquiescence in his Ministry remaining in office even when they were capable of defeating it. Few of those opposed to the Government in Parliament had the appetite for power. 'The great advantage of our present situation', Earl Grey told Lord Holland just after the Easter disturbances, 'is that it relieves [us] from all responsibility for the measures, which the times require'.[97] Whigs recognised that whatever monetary policy was pursued, in the context of the post-war depression it would cause – or be integrally associated in the public mind with – social dislocation. As Grey had pointed out to Holland on an earlier occasion, it would be impossible 'to resume cash payments, without encountering a degree of distress, which no Administration can encounter'.[98]

This study has stressed at several points the limitations of the Government benches in the House of Commons. This was obviated, however, by inadequacies among its parliamentary opponents. The candid assessment of one Cabinet member was that 'our only strength was our antagonists' weakness'.[99] Aversions to risk and responsibility among the Whig leadership were just two of their limitations. Their formal alliance with the Grenvillites (with whom the Whigs had served in the 1806–07 'ministry of all the talents') had come to an end in 1817. The 'third party' in the Commons was increasingly inclined to the Ministry: 'they did nothing that was not abominable', Grenville himself declared of his erstwhile colleagues.[100] The Whigs were also perceived as wanting stamina and unity. 'Lord Grey is in feeble health,' the ministerialist MP Henry Bankes observed. 'Tierney is by no means stout; they would all object to Leach for Lord

Chancellor.' Since 1819 the leader of the Whig interest in the Commons, George Tierney ('one of the first *sleeping* Whigs *of the day*', quipped William Benbow) was ailing and increasingly unable to exert his authority over the opposition benches (he was to resign in March 1821).[101] A minority of Whig MPs (H. G. Bennet, Brougham, Robert Chaloner, J. C. Hobhouse, 'Radical Jack' Lambton, Sir Robert Wilson) identified enthusiastically with popular causes; but the Whigs as a whole were defined in policy terms by little more than their commitment to Roman Catholic Emancipation. Parliamentary reform was a shibboleth they were happy to pronounce but happier still not to act upon. It is scarcely surprising, therefore, that radical reformers so vehemently rounded upon the institution of Parliament and barely discriminated between the political complexions of those who sat there. 'I would much rather blunder on under an *Irish ministry*', wrote Benbow with an inverted compliment to Lord Castlereagh, 'than exchange them for the Whigs'.[102]

Henry Brougham, however, was a significant exception to the picture of Whig inertia. Able, articulate and ambitious, he was one of the few leading Whigs genuinely hungry for power. All the indications are that in 1820 he was manoeuvring to take it. We saw in Chapter 3 how, as counsel for a private prosecution of a friend of Sidmouth, Brougham had taken a conspicuous role in harrying County Durham Toryism after the election. In the twelve months June 1819 to May 1820 he spoke over a hundred times in the Commons, and made a further twenty-five speeches in June. His declaration in May 'that no one party in that House was at present sufficient to form an administration that could meet the situation of the country, and give confidence to the people', was excitedly construed by Sir Robert Wilson as a bid to place himself at or close to the head of a coalition government.[103] In the summer Brougham brought forward an education bill to establish free elementary schooling in every English and Welsh parish. He used this to position himself as both socially progressive and an ally of the established church. However, it is inconceivable that Brougham believed his bill would pass the Commons when it stipulated every teacher in the proposed schools must be practicing Anglicans, but also that there should be no specifically Anglican content to the religious instruction given, thus alienating potential Whig and Tory support alike. This looked much like grandstanding to enlist support for a broader cause.[104] So too did his use of an adjournment debate to attack the droits of the Crown ('a foul blot on the honour of the country … a vile relic of feudal barbarism'), knowing all the while that these customary dues fell outside of the Civil List and, therefore, Parliament's authority. Brougham, however, exploited the opportunity to attack the 'absurd, confused, Gothic mode of keeping accounts' and accuse the Chancellor of the Exchequer of following procedures that 'in private life could be considered little short of absolute drivelling'.[105]

'The Queen's arrival supersedes all other considerations'

With the Civil List itself dominating parliamentary time in May more than any other single issue, it was a taxing period for the Government. The King himself, infatuated with his new mistress the Marchioness of Conyngham, appeared not to notice.[106] However his Queen's arrival in the capital changed everything. On 6 June George sent a formal message to the Commons, assuring MPs that he 'felt the most anxious desire to avert the necessity of disclosures and discussions which must be as painful to his people as they can be to himself; but the step now taken by the queen leaves him no alternative'. Papers concerning Caroline's conduct during the years she had had spent on the continent were placed before the House in a sealed green bag (the traditional receptacle for confidential matter requiring Parliament scrutiny). The same message, and a green bag with identical contents, was laid before the House of Lords by the Prime Minister who also announced that a secret committee of the Lords would be considering the papers. From the moment Castlereagh sat down, having read the royal message, things started to unravel for the Government. Details of its proposals to the Queen had appeared in the Sunday papers. Henry Grey Bennet disingenuously told the House:

> I can never give credit to the statement that a British ministry, without the authority and consent of parliament, would have dared to call upon the queen of Great Britain to divest herself of that title which she holds by the same right as the king himself does his title, for a bribe of £50,000 a year – a bribe too, not to be paid by the king himself, but to be taken out of the pockets of the people of England, labouring under the severest distresses.[107]

Unknown to the Government, Brougham had behaved with sufficient duplicity to alienate, albeit momentarily, the respect of the Queen.[108] But the ranks of Caroline's defenders were soon established, led by Henry Brougham as the Queen's Attorney General and the Nottingham MP Thomas Denman as her Solicitor General; Sir Matthew Wood, her closest confidante and for the time being also her host in the capital; and the more radical Whigs such as Bennet and Sir Robert Wilson (who with Burdett had ridden out to Shooter's Hill on 5 June to escort the Queen into the capital). The leading figures of the Whig party, on the other hand, were conspicuously lukewarm. However, beyond the Houses of Parliament was a multitude no man could number, consisting not of the capital's exuberant crowds alone but very soon throngs from across all Britain.

Broadsides welcoming the Queen poured from the presses: 'She generously comes to share our sorrows; she scorns to go and live at ease while we are left in misery', declared a Norwich ballad.[109] *The Queen Shall Enjoy her Own Again* (issued by *Black Book*'s publisher John Fairburn) was pointedly based on 'When the King enjoys his own again', a Royalist ballad of 1643 predicting the defeat of the parliamentarians.[110] The tunes of patriotic songs – 'Rule Britannia', 'Hearts of Oak', 'The Battle of the Nile', 'God save the King' – were appropriated for Caroline balladry.[111] Printed slips bearing alternative verses of the National Anthem had appeared in Manchester's theatres as early as February: 'Let her tread British ground, / She'll hear from all around, / Throughout the air resound – / God save the Queen'.[112] Now theatres across Britain became places of contention. The National Anthem was wildly contested at the Theatre Royal, Bristol. At Brighton's Theatre Royal, just yards George IV's Royal Pavilion, the management decided to cease playing 'God Save the King' altogether rather than face nightly rioting.[113] Soon even on Barbados in the West Indies, feelings ran so high that 'in the Theatre in a Contest for singing "God save *the King*" or "*the Queen*" the parties came to blows but the *Loyalists* carried it'.[114]

For almost a month after the Queen's arrival in the capital, the Cabinet were involved in the frantic and fruitless pursuit of trying to persuade the Queen to accept the annual £50,000 allowance, and the conditions attached, while simultaneously resisting pressure from a monarch who was furious it was not acting fast enough. 'Nobody here talks about anybody but the Q.', Eldon wrote to his daughter, 'Cabinets are quite in fashion: daily, nightly, hourly Cabinets are in fashion'.[115] The initial reaction of the Whig leadership was to disdain exploiting the Government's discomfort. 'The Queen's arrival supersedes all other considerations in the closet, the Cabinet, Parliament, or the public', Holland wrote to Lord Lambton but, he concluded, 'for the life of me I can feel no interest and little curiosity about these royal squabbles, degrading no doubt to all concerned, and disgusting and tiresome I think to the bystanders'.[116] However George IV's reaction, when denied what he immediately wanted, was to look to another government to provide it instead. On 11 June, after Canning had publically avowed his esteem for the Queen, the King made clear to Liverpool his expectation Canning would be asked to resign. Liverpool 'did not hesitate to declare that his own resignation wod. follow'. On 12 June, using Vice Chancellor Leach and other intermediaries, the King sounded out prominent opposition members. Simultaneously, George tried to persuade Sidmouth 'to accept the Premiership'. Sidmouth firmly declined. Would Wellington accept it? the King enquired. The Home Secretary as firmly refused to express an opinion and spoke up for Liverpool. A week later Sidmouth stood before the King again, this time deputed by his senior colleagues to disabuse his majesty of any lingering delusion that he was personally popular:

> The Cabinet thought it highly necessary, in consequence of the feeling betrayed by the Guards, the known bias of the lower orders of the metropolis, particularly of the women, in favour of the Queen, and the cry of "No Queen, no King" which has been heard in the country as well as in London.[117]

The Government had leached out news to its supporters about the breakdown of negotiations with the Queen, letting it be known that the Ministry, if defeated on its plans to introduce a bill of pains and penalties, would resign. On 22 June the highest Commons attendance (520) of the 1820 parliamentary session gave weight to an address to the Queen, moved by William Wilberforce, praying for conciliation. Caroline responded with a peevish reminder that she was 'an accused and injured Queen', entitled to appeal to the 'principles of public justice'. To the Lords she stated 'her perfect readiness to meet every charge affecting her honour'.[118] Such was the extent to which the royal marriage now dominated the news that serious riots by Shropshire coal miners were barely noticed in the national papers.[119]

Simultaneously George IV was sounding out the Whigs. 'I am sure Grey may be [Prime] Minister if he chooses', the King's confidant the Earl of Donoughmore told Tierney, adding the assurance that the monarch 'was perfectly ready to forget all that had passed' between the Whigs and Carlton House which had cemented the Tories in power in the first place. With deep misgivings, Earl Grey left his Northumberland country seat for London in the expectation that he might be requested to form a government. Distrust of Brougham was one thing that preoccupied Grey. If Brougham proved the architect of a compromise between King, Queen and Government it would place him in an unassailable position in the next Whig government, whenever that might be. However, as the prospect of any compromise receded Grey began to warm to the task. In the House of Lords on 27 June, in what Greville described as 'a speech for office', Lord Grey rounded on Liverpool and his 'loose, disjointed, and feeble administration', accusing it of vacillation and of hiding behind parliamentary process instead of acting with decisiveness. 'At a season of great public distress and danger, at a moment of great peril to the peace and tranquillity of the country, they had shown themselves unfit for the emergency.'[120] Instead only now was the Government forcing on the country the protracted parliamentary process of a bill of pains and penalties against the Queen.

Henceforward the normal business of government was suspended and with it, seemingly, the ability of the country to focus upon any issues that did not pertain to the proceedings against Caroline in the House of Lords.

Notes

1 *Speech of the Right Hon. George Canning, to his Constituents at Liverpool, on Saturday, March 18th, 1820, at the Celebration of his Fourth Election* (London: Murray, 1820), p. 7; *The Times*, 15 April; *Cobbett's Weekly Political Register*, 15 April, col. 349.
2 *The Times*, 10, 13, 20, 24 April; *Liverpool Mercury*, 14 April; *Courier*, 17 April. TNA, TS 11/697/2210 (R. v. Evans); TS 11/155/465 (prosecution brief, R. v. McGinnis).
3 BL, Add. Mss 38284 fol. 147 (Harewood to Liverpool, 16 April).
4 Sheffield Archives, Wentworth Woodhouse Muniments F/48/153 (21 April).
5 E.g. DRO, Sidmouth Papers 152M/C/1820/0Z (Howden to Sidmouth, 11 March) and (Sidmouth to Sir Benjamin Bloomfield, private secretary to George IV, 20 March).
6 *York Herald*, 1 July.

7   A. Aspinall (ed.), *The Correspondence of Charles Arbuthnot*, Camden 3rd ser (London: Royal Historical Society, 1941), vol. 65, p. 18 (letter to Arbuthnot, 29 March); BL, Add. Mss 38369 fols 139–57, 'Private Memorandum' (fol. 144); TNA, LC 1/8 (21 March and 20 April).

8   E. Phipps (ed.) *Memoirs of the Political and Literary Life of Robert Plumer Ward* (Edinburgh: Murray: 1850), vol. 2, p. 53, quoting William Wellesley-Pole, the Master of the Mint.

9   DRO, 152/M/C/1820/OZ (Bloomfield to Sidmouth, 12 March).

10 Historical Manuscripts Commission, *Report on the Manuscripts of Earl Bathurst, Preserved at Cirencester Park* (London: HMSO, 1923), p. 483 (Liverpool to Bathurst, 23 April); A. Aspinall (ed.), *The Diary of Henry Hobhouse (1820–27)* (London: Home & Van Thal, 1947), p. 19. See also N. Gash, *Lord Liverpool: The Life and Political Career of Robert Banks Jenkinson* (London: Weidenfeld, 1984), pp. 155–6.

11 Letter to Liverpool, 25 April, reprinted in A. Aspinall (ed.), *The Letters of King George IV, 1812–30* (Cambridge: Cambridge University Press, 1938), vol. 2, p. 326.

12 F. Bamford and G. W. Wellington (eds), *The Journal of Mrs Arbuthnot, 1820–32: Volume 1, February 1820 to December 1825* (London: Macmillan, 1950), p. 15 (27 April); H. Twiss, *The Public Life and Private Life of Lord Chancellor Eldon, with Selections from his Correspondence* (London: Murray, 1844), vol. 2, pp. 362–3 (letter, 26 April); *Diary of Henry Hobhouse*, p. 20.

13 Ward, *Memoirs*, p. 53.

14 *Journal of Mrs Arbuthnot*, pp. 18–9 (13 [sic] May). Two junior ministers abstained and a third (William Bagwell, Master of Irish Ordinance) voted with the opposition. Castlereagh was reduced to pleading with ministerial MPs in the lobby as they queued for the division: see *HC Deb*, 15 May 1820 (vol. 1, col. 385).

15 Ward, *Memoirs*, p. 53; *Letters of King George IV*, vol. III, p. 39 (George IV to Liverpool, 6 November 1823).

16 BL, Add. Mss 38284 fol. 216, lines written in Newgate by John Brunt.

17 *Diary and Correspondence of Charles Abbot, Lord Colchester, edited by his son Charles, Lord Colchester* (London: Murray, 1861), vol. 3, pp. 120–1; *Journal of Mrs Arbuthnot*, p. 14 (13 April).

18 Correspondence between Edwards and the Home Office in TNA, HO 44/6 fols 206–7, 249–50, 257–8, 259–62, 287–8, 293–4, 311 and 319 (May–August 1820); HO 44/6 fols 243 and 276 (high treason indictment).

19 TNA, HO 44/6 fols 14, 16, 18, 25, 31–3, 35–7, 41, 64, 74–5 (April); TNA, TS/203/874; BL, Add. Mss 38369 fol. 176.

20 *Blackwood's Magazine*, 16 (August 1824), 233. See also G. T. Wilkinson, *An Authentic History of the Cato Street Conspiracy*, 2nd edn (London: Kelly, 1820), p. 113; *Morning Chronicle,* 29 April. A. Aspinall, *Politics and the Press, c. 1780–1850* (Home & Van Thal, 1949), p. 305, claims the fine was unpaid.

21 Wilkinson, *Authentic History*, pp. 345–51, 393; M. Chase, 'Cato Street conspirators (act. 1820)', *Oxford Dictionary of National Biography*, Oxford University Press, 2004; online edn, Jan 2008 [http://0-www.oxforddnb.com.wam.leeds.ac.uk/view/article/58584], accessed 29 Jan 2012.

22 Wilkinson, *Authentic History*, p. 338.

23 David Johnson, *Regency Revolution: The Case of Arthur Thistlewood* (Salisbury: Compton Russell, 1974), p.146.

24 Wilkinson, *Authentic History*, pp. 360–90.

25 *Morning Post and Times*, 2 May.

26 Johnson, *Regency Revolution*, p. 147; *Morning Post*, 28 August.

27 *Recollections of a Long Life, by Lord Broughton, with Additional Extracts from his Diaries,*
    edited by his daughter, Lady Dorchester (London: Murray, 1909), vol. 2, p. 126; *Journal of*
    Mrs Arbuthnot, p. 15 (3 May).

28 *Journal of Mrs Arbuthnot,* p. 17 (8 May); HO 44/1 fol. 190 (14 March).

29 *Republican,* 3 March 1820; J. Wade, *British History, Chronologically Arranged,* 3rd edn,
    (London: Wilson, 1844), p. 761; *Poor Man's Guardian,* 3 November 1832; W. J. Linton,
    James Watson: A Memoir (Manchester: Heywood, 1880), p. 7; T. Frost, *Forty Years*
    Recollections, Literary and Political (London: Low, 1880), p. 6.

30 *Journal of Mrs Arbuthnot,* pp. 16, 20.

31 *Mirror of Fashion,* 18 May.

32 'Virginius; a Tragedy', in J. S. Knowles, *Dramatic Works* (London: Routledge, [1856]),
    p. 86.

33 F. Pollock (ed.), *Macready's Reminiscences: And Selections from his Diaries and Letters*
    (London: Macmillan, 1876), p. 159.

34 *Glasgow Herald,* 22 May; *Morning Herald,* 19 May, quoted in L. W. Conolly, *The*
    Censorship of English Drama, 1737–1824 (San Marino, Ca: Huntington Library,
    1976), p. 109–10.

35 Quoted by Conolly, *Censorship,* p. 110.

36 Detailed accounts of the Queen's movements and intrigues surrounding them may
    be found in J. E. Cookson, *Lord Liverpool's Administration: The Crucial Years, 1815–1822*
    (Edinburgh: Scottish Academic Press, 1975); F. Fraser, *The Unruly Queen: The Life of*
    Queen Caroline (New York: Anchor, 2009), pp. 351–63; J. Robins, *Rebel Queen: How*
    the Trial of Queen Caroline Brought England to the Brink of Revolution (London: Schuster,
    2006), pp. 105–20; E. A. Smith, *A Queen on Trial: The Affair of Queen Caroline* (Stroud:
    Sutton, 1993).

37 Smith, *Queen on Trial,* p. 19; BL, Add. Mss 38284 fol. 141 (15 April); *Morning Chronicle,*
    1 and 13 April; *York Herald,* 23 March; *Bury & Norwich Post,* 29 March; *Trewman's*
    Exeter Flying Post, 30 March; *Caledonian Mercury,* 17 April.

38 Colchester, *Diary and Correspondence,* vol. 3, pp. 124–6, 133, 135.

39 Twiss, *Lord Chancellor Eldon,* vol. 2, p. 366.

40 P. Quennell (ed.), *The Private Letters of Princess Lieven to Prince Metternich, 1820–1826*
    (London: Murray, 1937), pp. 37–8.

41 TNA, HO 44/2/154A (Stow to Hobhouse, 5 June).

42 TNA, HO 44/2/153 and 155 (Stow, and Lockyer, to Hobhouse, 5 June).

43 R. Huish, *Memoirs of Her Late Majesty Caroline, Queen of Great Britain* (London: Kelly,
    1821), vol. 2, pp. 78–84.

44 *The Times,* 7, 10 June; K. Cave (ed.), *The Diary of Joseph Farington: Volume XVI, January*
    1820–December 1821 (London: Yale University Press, 1984), pp. 5517–20.

45 *Despatches, Correspondence, and Memoranda of Field Marshal Arthur, Duke of Wellington,*
    K.G., edited by his son (London: Murray, 1867), pp. 131–2; *Private Letters of Princess*
    Lieven, pp. 41-2.

46 TNA, HO 102/32/80–88, (Bradford's report on barracks in the Western District,
    January).

47 TNA, HO 44/1 fol. 38 (Cathcart to Sidmouth, 1 March).

48 Taylor to Wellington, 19 September, reprinted in Wellington, *Despatches,* pp. 144–5.

49 Taylor to Wellington, 26 September 1820, reprinted in Wellington, *Despatches,* p. 147.

50 TNA, HO 44/6/97 (25 April).

51 *HC Deb,* 20 June (vol. 1, col. 1188).

52 Hobhouse, *Diary,* p. 25 (19 June).

53 G. Pellew (ed.), *The Life and Correspondence of the Rt Hon. H. Addington, First Viscount*
    Sidmouth (London: Murray, 1847), vol. 3, pp. 330–1. Pellew was Sidmouth's son-in-

law; see E. M. G. Belfield, *Annals of the Addington Family* (Winchester: Warren, 1959) for the probability Sidmouth himself helped compile it; *Courier*, 16 June, *Morning Chronicle*, 17 June.

54 Colchester, *Diary*, p. 143.

55 Letter, 16 June, reprinted in L. J. Jennings, ed., *The Croker Papers: The Correspondence and diaries of the Late Right Honourable John Wilson Croker ... 1809 to 1830* (London: Murray, 1884), vol. 1, p. 175–6.

56 HO 44/2/156 (letter of 'J. A.', 17 June).

57 HO 44/2/181 (Thomas Sorrell to Sidmouth, 17 June).

58 *Caledonian Mercury*, June 22; *Courier*, 17 June.

59 HO 40/13 fol. 311 (16 June); Pellew, *Sidmouth*, pp. 330–1.

60 *Examiner*, 18 June; L. Strachey and R. Fulford (eds), *The Greville Memoirs, 1814–1860: volume 1, January 1814–July 1830* (London: Macmillan, 1938), p. 97.

61 P. H. Fitzgerald, *Life of George IVth* (London: Tinsley, 1881), vol. 2, p. 243.

62 *Examiner*, 5 November 1820; TS 11/156/509.

63 Memorandum to Liverpool, June 1820, reprinted in Wellington, *Despatches*, vol. 1, pp. 127–9.

64 *Journal of Mrs Arbuthnot*, p. 26 (28 June).

65 TNA, HO 40/14 fol. 82 (Byng to Hobhouse, 31 July).

66 Ward, *Memoirs*, vol. 2, p. 55.

67 P. Harling, *The Waning of 'Old Corruption': The Politics of Economical Reform in Britain, 1779–1846* (Oxford: Oxford University Press: 1996); Cookson, *Lord Liverpool's Administration*; P. Harling and P. Mandler, 'From "fiscal-military" state to laissez-faire state, 1760–1850', *Journal of British Studies*, 32:1 (1993).

68 See *PP* 1820 (49) Estimates of army services, pp. 41–2; *PP* 1820 (83) Estimates of the charge of the Office of Ordnance for Great Britain, p. 17; *PP* 1820 (57) Estimates of ordinary of the navy, p. 33.

69 *PP* 1820 (49) Estimates of army services, p. 7.

70 R. Philp, *The Coast Blockade: The Royal Navy's War on Smuggling in Kent and Sussex, 1817–31* (Horsham: Crompton, 1999), pp. 64–96; W. Webb, *Coastguard: An Official History of H. M. Coastguard* (London: HMSO, 1976), p. 21.

71 M. Waugh, *Smuggling in Kent and Sussex, 1700–1840* (Newbury: Countryside Books, 1985), pp. 32, 81; Philp, *Coast Blockade*, pp. 75-6.

72 BL, Add. Mss 38286 fol. 28 (Bedford to Liverpool, June); TNA, HO 40/13 fols 196, 202–5; *The Times*, 29 May.

73 TNA, HO 43/30/27 and 41 (17, 27–8 November).

74 *York Herald*, 3 June.

75 Quoted by W. A. Speck, *Robert Southey, Entire Man of Letters* (London: Yale University Press, 2006), p. 122.

76 Twiss, *Lord Chancellor Eldon*, vol. 1, p. 75; entries for each minister in the *Oxford Dictionary of National Biography* (Oxford: Oxford University Press, 2004). See also J. W. Derry, *Politics in the Age of Fox, Pitt and Liverpool: Continuity and Transformation* (Basingstoke: Macmillan, 1990), pp. 160–1.

77 The discussion that follows is indebted to B. Hilton, *Corn, Cash, Commerce: The Economic Policies of the Tory Governments, 1815–30* (Oxford: Oxford University Press, 1972), pp. 69–126. For briefer accounts of economic policy at the time see Hilton's *A Mad, Bad and Dangerous People? England, 1783–1846* (Oxford: Oxford University Press, 2006), pp. 259–74, and M. J. Turner, *The Age of Unease: Government and Reform in Britain, 1782–1832* (Gloucester: Sutton, 2000), pp. 144–50.

78 *HC Deb*, 30 May 1820 (vol. 1, cols 678–9); Hilton, *Corn, Cash, Commerce*, pp. 3–97.

79 *HL Deb*, 30 May (vol. 1, col. 419).

80 John Sinclair to Arthur Young, 20 October 1819, quoted in Rosalind Mitchison, 'The Old Board of Agriculture (1793–1822)', *English Historical Review*, 74:290 (1959), p. 64.

81 For Hall see D. Spring and T. L. Crosby, 'George Webb Hall and the agricultural association', *Journal of British Studies*, 2 (1962), T. L. Crosby, *English Farmers and the Politics of Protection* (Hassocks: Harvester, 1977), pp. 29–47, and Hilton, *Corn, Cash, Commerce*, pp. 98–109.

82 For the 1813–14 campaign see the introduction to the present work; also M. Chase, *Early Trade Unionism: Fraternity, Skill and the Politics of Labour* (Aldershot: Ashgate, 2000), pp. 85–100.

83 Hall's annual report to the Central Agricultural Association, in *Evans and Ruffy's Farmers' Journal*, 24 July; *ibid.*, 16 November 1818.

84 *HC Deb*, 30 May 1820 (vol. 1, col. 642).

85 *Evans and Ruffy's Farmers' Journal*, 7 August; *PP* 1820 (255), SC petitions complaining of agricultural distress; Mitchison, 'The Old Board of Agriculture', p. 64; Hilton, *Corn, Cash, Commerce*, p. 102.

86 For Stanhope see the entry on his son by H. C. G. Matthew, 'Stanhope, Philip Henry, fifth Earl Stanhope (1805–1875)', *Oxford Dictionary of National Biography* (Oxford: Oxford University Press, 2004); online edn [http://0-www.oxforddnb.com.wam.leeds.ac.uk/view/article/26256], accessed 29 Jan 2012.

87 *HL Deb*, 16 May (vol. 1, cols 418, 421–2).

88 *HL Deb*, 26 May (vol. 1 cols 567, 577, 593); see also R. B. Jenkinson, *The Speech of the Right Hon. The Earl of Liverpool, in the House of Lords, on Friday, the 26th, of May, 1820* (London: Hatchard, 1820).

89 BL, Add. Mss 38282 fols 43–8 (Grant to Liverpool, 28 December 1819), and fols 74–5 (Vansittart to Liverpool, 30 December); see also Hilton, *Corn, Cash, Commerce*, pp. 84–6.

90 The crisis awaits a detailed history, though see G. L. Barrow, *The Emergence of the Irish Banking System, 1820–45* (Dublin: Gill & Macmillan, 1975), pp. 17–23, 208–14.

91 *Ibid.*, p. 21; *The Times*, 13 June and 28 July; *HP*, vol. 3, p. 905.

92 Quaker banker John Lecky, 25 May, quoted by D. Dickson, *Old World Colony: Cork and South Munster, 1630–1830* (Cork: Cork University Press, 2005), p. 487.

93 TNA, HO 100/199/230 and HO 100/199/250 (Grant to Sidmouth, 28 September and 4 November); Barrow, *Irish Banking System*, p. 22.

94 *PP* 1837–38 (723) Loans, Ireland; PP 1823 (414) (Ireland) Commercial credit. Copy of a letter to William Gregory, Esquire, from the secretary to the commissioners for the assistance of trade and manufactures … respecting the loan to Messrs. Nowlan & Shaw, in 1821.

95 Twiss, *Lord Chancellor Eldon*, vol. 2, p. 328.

96 Letter to Eldon, 10 May, reprinted in *ibid.*, p. 329.

97 Grey to Holland, 23 April, quoted in Hilton, *Corn, Cash, Commerce*, pp. 73–4.

98 13 December 1818 quoted in Hilton, *Mad, Bad and Dangerous*, p. 260.

99 William Wellesley-Pole, quoted in Ward, *Memoir*, p. 53.

100 Quoted in *Report on the Manuscripts of Earl Bathurst*, p. 490 (Arbuthnot to Bathurst, 29 November).

101 Colchester, *Diary*, p. 117; William Benbow, *The Whigs Exposed; or, Truth by Day-Light. Addressed to the Reformers of Britain* (London: Benbow, 1820), pp. 16.

102 Benbow, *Whigs Exposed*, p. 13.

103 *HC Deb*, 12 May (vol. 1, col. 340); A. Aspinall, *Lord Brougham and the Whig Party* (Manchester: Manchester University Press, 1927), p. 112.

104 *HC Deb*, 28 April (vol. 1, col. 39), 28 June (vol. 2, cols 49–91) and 11 July 1820 (vol. 2, cols 365–7).
105 *HC Deb*, 5 May (vol. 1, cols 115–16, 127); BL, Add. Mss 30123 fol. 155 (Wilson to Grey, 13 May).
106 *Private Letters of Princess Lieven*, p. 32; *Greville Memoirs*, pp. 93–4.
107 *HC Deb*, 6 June (vol. 1 cols 871–2).
108 Fraser, *Unruly Queen*, pp. 370–4.
109 *Character of the Queen!* (Norwich: Lane [1820]), copy in HO 33/3/169 (4 September).
110 Copy in BL, 1871.f.16; R. Palmer, *The Sound of History: Songs and Social Comment* (Oxford: Oxford University Press, 1988), pp. 21, 38.
111 A. Bennett, 'Broadsides on the trial of Queen Caroline: a glimpse at popular song in 1820', *Proceedings of the Royal Musical Association*, 107 (1980–81), pp. 74–5.
112 *Manchester Observer*, 19 February.
113 K. Barker, *The Theatre Royal Bristol, 1766–1966* (Salisbury: Compton, 1974), p. 98; C. Hibbert, *George IV: Regent and King* (London: Allen Lane, 1973), p. 156.
114 *Diary of Joseph Farington*, p. 5704 (22 July 1821).
115 Letter, [7?] June, reprinted in Twiss, *Lord Chancellor Eldon*, vol. 2, p. 372.
116 Quoted in Aspinall, *Lord Brougham*, p. 111.
117 *Diary of Henry Hobhouse*, p. 28; Lord Holland, letter to Earl Grey, 12 June, reprinted in *Further Memoirs of the Whig Party, 1807–21, with some Miscellaneous Reminiscences, by Henry Richard Vassall, Third Lord Holland, edited by Lord Stavordale* (London: Murray, 1905), pp. 400–3.
118 C. D. Yonge (complier), *The Life and Administration of Robert Banks, Second Earl of Liverpool* (Macmillan, 1868), vol. 3, pp. 84, 86.
119 *The Times*, 19 June; *Courier*, 22 June.
120 E. A. Smith, *Lord Grey, 1764–1845* (Oxford: Oxford University Press, 1990), pp. 229–30; *Greville Memoirs*, p. 100; *HL Deb*, 27 June (vol. 2, col. 12).

6 Autumn

Introduction

When the Duke of Berry, heir to the French throne, was stabbed to death on the steps of the Paris Opera in February his assassin (saddler Louis Pierre Louvel) was arrested immediately. But Louvel was not executed until 7 June, against a background of increasingly violent protest. On the 9th, close to the great Porte Saint-Denis, a journeyman tanner was killed by cavalry, while other workers were cut down or trampled under the horses' feet. The military, a demonstrator noted in his diary, charged when they heard the crowd shouting 'vivent nos frères de Manchester!'[1] The year 1820 was one of European revolution. This is no retrospective construction: 1820 was widely perceived at the time as a year of revolution. 'Paine thought that he lived in the age of revolution', the leading republican journalist, Richard Carlile wrote in September 1820, 'but the present moment better deserves that epithet'.[2] While in France the consequences of the Duke of Berry's assassination were contained and controlled, there followed a revolution in Spain in early March. The Kingdom of the Two Sicilies succumbed to revolution in Naples in July, shortly followed by an uprising in Palermo. Revolution in Portugal followed in August. And if we look for a moment to the early months of 1821, there was an insurgency in Piedmont, insurrections against the Ottomans in Moldavia and Wallachia, as well as the dramatic and better-known development of an independence movement in Greece.

That cries of 'Long live our brothers from Manchester!' should have met tragic consequences in Paris ten months after Peterloo is indicative of a growing internationalism within reform opinion in these years. The repercussions in Britain of the 1789 French Revolution were of course massive, but historians tend to be unmindful of the traffic of popular political ideas from Britain to France, while little attention is paid to popular internationalism before the French Revolution of 1830.[3] The disaffected contemplated Berry's assassination with pleasure, a retired naval officer reported from Ayrshire.[4] Carlile dated several

publications using revolutionary years after the manner of the French revolutionary calendar but using Spain as his marker.[5] London ultra-radicals formed an
'Anglo-Carbonarian Union', its title taken from the Neapolitan revolutionary
movement. The Neapolitan revolutionaries in turn issued an address to the
British, praising 'the patriotic exertions of thy forefathers' and quoting
Shakespeare, Sydney, Locke and Robert Burns.[6] The Whig reformer Edward
Baines, editor of the *Leeds Mercury*, warmly welcomed the Spanish revolution as
'evidence of that growth of knowledge, that spread of liberal ideas, that increase
of manly independence … which seem destined to produce a moral and political
renovation throughout the earth'. Of the Neapolitan revolutionaries Baines
commented approvingly, 'they do not cry either for blood or a different ruler;
their sole object is a REPRESENTATIVE CONSTITUTION'.[7] Such rhetoric
sharply contrasted that of the Cabinet. 'They are dumbfounded by the news',
wrote Princess Lievan. 'Devil take me. Prince Metternich must march', declared
Wellington. 'He must crush this Italian revolution.' For ten days Wellington
allegedly talked of nothing except Naples, though the Cabinet's decision was to
observe strict neutrality, other than if necessary to assist in ensuring the personal
safety of the Neapolitan royal family.[8]

The situation in France was watched with avidity. A Revolution in France
'would decide the fate of the whole continent instantly', thought Carlile, in
particular it would 'prove an irresistible and universal contagion to the English
people'.[9] That a militant republican and acolyte of Paine should enthuse about
the prospect of European revolution is predictable. But Carlile was far from
alone: inverted testimony to the perceived potency of revolution in France for
British domestic politics can be found in Sidmouth's correspondence where, as
we saw in Chapter 3, links between Louis Pierre Louvel and British conspirators
were conjectured. However it was the Portuguese revolution that especially
grieved the British Government, for the United Kingdom provided all the senior
officers of the Portuguese army. They included the Commander in Chief,
William Beresford, who exercised considerable power as a member of the
Council of Regency since Portugal's monarchy resided in Brazil. To Wellington's
horror Beresford had sailed to Brazil in April: 'I almost went upon my knees to
Beresford to prevail upon him not to quit Portugal', the Duke told the
Arbuthnots. 'I have been more annoyed by the Portuguese concern than I can
express.'[10]

Because of Portugal's close association with the United Kingdom, events
there had a greater potential to impact upon British opinion than the other
European Revolutions of 1820. It was the subject of an entire morning's discussion at Cabinet on 12 September. 'We trust', Baines acidly observed, 'that the
British government will not be so lost to consistency and reason as to interfere
with this revolution'. 'This new Revolution in Portugal comes famously to our
aid', the octogenarian reformer John Cartwright told Sir Robert Wilson.[11] 'This
year will certainly form a new era', Carlile declared in October, 'it is the year for

the emancipation of the human race'.[12] That same month 500 London radicals and Whig reformers dined at the Crown & Anchor in the Strand (the venue of radical choice for such occasions) to celebrate the revolutions in the Iberian peninsular and Kingdom of Naples. The leading speakers were all 'Queen's men': Cartwright, Wilson, Joseph Hume, John Cam Hobhouse, Grey Bennet and Alderman Wood. Another prominent Caroline supporter, Sir Gerard Noel, proposed the toast congratulating Naples and Sicily on 'consolidating their freedom', attacking as he did so the 'disgraceful' domestic policies of the British Government. An Irish Roman Catholic priest, Richard Hayes, used the occasion to announce a new weekly, *Catholic Advocate of Civil and Religious Liberty*.[13] During its nine-month life, the *Advocate* would attract contributions from Sir Charles Wolseley and Henry Hunt (who praised it as 'written with great talent, and in the true Radical spirit of civil and religious liberty') and win plaudits from Carlile.[14] Revolutions in Catholic states, Carlile concluded, proved Roman Catholicism was not incompatible with liberty and reform. This argument he then used to castigate further the iniquities of the British political and religious establishment. 'Falsehood's minions dare, / My bleeding country's vitals tear', ran a poet contribution to *Black Dwarf*, but

> Where superstition long had dwelt,
> And man to haughty tyrants knelt;
> Spain rises, awful and sublime,
> O'er slavery, error, woe, and crime.[15]

The apparently decisive role of standing armies in the southern European revolutions also encouraged English radicals. *Black Dwarf* pointedly linked this issue to the mutinous mood in the Guards. In both Spain and the Neapolitan kingdoms, *Leeds Mercury* argued, 'contrary to all former experience, standing armies have been the means of overturning the despotism which they were meant to uphold'; two months later as the pattern was repeated in Portugal the *Mercury* added that 'France may now with justice tremble'.[16] Carlile issued many appeals to British troops to follow their European counterparts; 'there is nothing wanting in England but a good understanding between the soldiers and people'.[17] Anonymous bill posters put up notices, 'Revolution in Naples, Effected by the Soldiers', in the Leicestershire textiles town of Loughborough. 'Remember Spain and Naples! Love and respect the soldiers', declaimed a placard drawn up by the Spencean Samuel Waddington, and for which he was prosecuted – unsuccessfully – for seditious libel.[18]

The Government (not without some risk, for the extent of the standing army was a politically sensitive issue linking the constitution and demands for retrenchment) made perfectly clear that contemporary political unrest was a justification for the size of the army. This was not despotism Palmerston, the Secretary for War, told the Commons: 'self-called, but misled reformers' were demanding changes which, if acceded to, would lead inexorably to military despotism.[19] Fortunately, his speech in Parliament preceded by just one day the breakdown of discipline in the Guards, otherwise the Ministry might have faced stormier criticism. John Cam Hobhouse had used the occasion to lampoon Palmerston's claim that 'some thirteen or twenty men plotting in a hay-loft to upset the state' justified raising the militia, especially when the trials of those arrested over Easter in Scotland and Yorkshire had been, or were, proceeding entirely peaceably. 'The disaffection of which we have heard this night', declared Hobhouse, 'arises solely from systematic misgovernment'.[20]

However, it must be stressed that Liverpool's Ministry comfortably won (by fifty-seven votes in a three-quarters empty chamber) the debate that Hobhouse and other radicals had initiated in the Commons. Of the leading Whigs, only Lords Lambton and Milton (Fitzwilliam's son) attended and voted with Hobhouse, and neither spoke. Conspicuous absentees included Bennet, Wilson and Wood. Opposition to the Government was hobbled by Whig uneasiness at any possibility of becoming associated with political extremism, and by the Easter risings' serious departure from supposed norms of political protest. Only one speaker deplored, or indeed even mentioned, 'the necessity of a large military force to prevent insurrection and rebellion in Ireland'.[21] Even in the country at large, whatever the disposition to conspiratorial violence, Carlile was very much in a minority in publically arguing that nothing 'short of downright intimidation can bring our opponents to just measures'.[22] Many reformers still adhered to the proposition that the political establishment was sufficiently flexible to adapt to stress and disorder without irreparably impairing liberty. The *Leeds Mercury* editorial, already cited, on the Portuguese revolution appeared alongside another drawing attention to the special Assize at York, where the Crown had just offered clemency to the twenty-five Huddersfield and Grange Moor insurgents in return for them pleading guilty to all charges. The juxtaposition was almost certainly deliberate. 'We are not in the habit of complimenting the Government on the wisdom and moderation of its measures', but compliment it on this occasion the paper did.[23]

The *Mercury* spoke of the likelihood that those convicted would speedily return to their family and friends: the sentences subsequently handed down at York, which included immediate transportation for twelve of the prisoners, therefore disappointed the paper. On the other hand three of the prisoners were discharged and the remaining ten, although sent to the hulks, received a pardon four months later.[24] The Crown avoided making martyrs of the Yorkshire rebels, a mistake manifestly committed in Scotland where special commissions following the Easter risings imposed twenty-four capital convictions. Three of these were carried to execution: Andrew Hardie and John Baird, rebel leaders at the Battle of Bonnymuir where the only fatality was a horse, were executed for treason the week before the York special Assize. Even more controversially, James Wilson of Strathaven was executed for the same offence on 30 August. The only concession made by the Crown was to remit both the quartering of the three men and (unlike the Cato Street conspirators) their beheading.[25] The consequences of these executions reverberated for decades and, indeed, continue to do so.[26]

The continuation of unrest

It is possible that the Government extended clemency to the Yorkshire prisoners, safe in the knowledge that exemplary justice had been already been secured in Scotland, but also apprehensive that the volatile popular political mood that summer needed manipulation and management rather than outright repression. Its unease centred partly on increasing enthusiasm for Caroline's cause and partly on concern about morale in parts of the army. Evidence for the latter had been low-level but continuous since problems first occurred in the Guards, while ever since Peterloo both regulars and yeomanry were subjected to abuse and casual violence in northern towns. In York fighting had even broken out during the annual dinner of the city's King and Constitution club between a military band and the diners they had been hired to entertain. And in June the Yorkshire Hussars complained of 'daily and repeated insults' on the streets of the city, and of 'cries of "No bloody Manchester butchers"', with other opprobrious epithets, as well as hooting and hissing'.[27] When a man was convicted at the Preston summer Assize of a violent assault on two members of the Manchester Yeomanry, the regiment shrewdly and earnestly appealed for a lenient sentence, such was the need to rehabilitate the regiment's reputation.[28] At a parade to mark George IV's birthday in Oldham, crowds taunted soldiers that their new uniforms would be their last. The following day a serious fracas occurred when regulars at the Bull's Head, armed with chair and table legs, set about six troopers of the 7th Dragoons who had misguidedly gone into the pub for a drink. One trooper escaped to fetch help and fourteen dragoons then smashed their way into the pub to rescue their comrades. The mood on the streets of Oldham so perturbed their commanding officer that he ordered the entire squadron back to regimental headquarters in Preston before local magistrates could even take depositions from them. Only three men were ever arrested for the attack.[29]

The Oldham incident deeply disturbed the Government and military authorities because it was plausibly linked to a sustained campaign, led by the *Manchester Observer*, to stir up hostility against the army. 'My weekly plague', General Byng, commander of the Northern District called the paper, passing on his often extensively annotated copy to the Home Office. Both the *Manchester Observer* and *Cowdray's Manchester Gazette* were prosecuted for libels upon the army, the first for claiming drunken troops had fired at random onto streets in Oldham, the second for alleging a 'wanton attack' by dragoons on peaceable spectators of a street procession in Manchester. The *Observer* was also thought to be encouraging military defections: one item in the paper to which Byng especially objected was a comment on the loyalty of the Foot Guards to George

IV, comparing them to the army shortly before James II's overthrow in 1688.[30] So sensitive was he to morale issues that Byng travelled from his Yorkshire headquarters to Macclesfield and Manchester personally to investigate complaints by individual soldiers, fearing they might prove 'to be Persons set on, & advised by, Discontented characters'. Byng was satisfied, however, that the soldiers concerned were merely 'grumblers'. Yet less than a month later systemic indiscipline did became apparent among men of the 90th Foot, stationed at Macclesfield. Their colonel himself wrote of a 'mutinous disposition' in the regiment: as many as seventy soldiers were rumoured to be prepared to rescue a private sentenced to flogging by a court martial. Fearing he and other officers would be attacked if the punishment was inflicted, the colonel decided not to impose the sentence. His explanation, somewhat lamely, was that the soldiers had been swayed by the townspeople of Macclesfield.[31] Perhaps a rumour among backbench supporters of the Ministry that Sir John Byng was 'heartily tired and harassed by his command' had some foundation.[32]

There was some – but certainly not wide - evidence that other regiments shared the 3rd Foot Guards' partiality for the Queen. Men of the 10th (Prince of Wales's Own) Hussars openly toasted her in a pub near their quarters at Hampton Court. Dragoons ostentatiously drank her health in Ipswich. In a Brighton pub, sergeants of the 51st infantry brawled with another from a Guards regiment when the latter toasted the Queen at a Waterloo dinner.[33] At Weymouth a regimental band obliged Queenite hecklers at the town's theatre by playing the national anthem over a second time so 'God Save the Queen' could be sung. Rumours swirled that a regiment garrisoned at Worcester had declared for the Queen (there was no garrison at Worcester, Byng furiously pointed out). Possibly this rumour related to a volunteer or militia regiment. The Royal East India Volunteers (a regiment recruited from the East India Company's London employees) was thought to be tainted.[34] When soldiers of the Leicestershire Militia sent a loyal address to Caroline and the Duke of Rutland insisted it was a fake, 420 of them publicly disavowed his claim.[35] We shall see later that on several occasions pro-Caroline demonstrations were accompanied by the bands of militia regiments.

Concerns about the loyalty of the army was one factor that shaped the Government's *volte face* on the coronation. On 6 May a proclamation had been issued that George would be crowned on 1 August. But as the summer wore on the wisdom of holding the ceremony looked increasingly shaky. On 7 July the Cabinet agreed on an indefinite postponement, 'for divers weighty reasons' the official proclamation stated. 'They have been forced to give up the Coronation', John Cam Hobhouse wrote to Byron, 'indeed they could not have crowned him without cannon'.[36] Caroline 'has completely jostled the coronation', a Ministerialist MP wrote to Lord Colchester: 'I believe they have had no bed of roses to sleep on since the death of the late King, and that no Minister ever had so difficult a task to perform as theirs.'[37] Inevitably tensions grew during August as the anniversary of Peterloo drew near. Acting on rumours that another attempted rising would coincide with the date, Captain Chippendale at Oldham sent Sidmouth two clegs. These, he had discovered, were being manufactured in and around Oldham 'in great Numbers'.[38] On 14 August at the funeral of the Duchess of York, there was no military presence at all, even though her husband was the army's Commander in Chief as well as heir to the throne.

However the events of 16 August 1820 were marked by quiet dignity. In Oldham parish churchyard (where Chippendale anticipated a major incident) groups visited the grave of cotton spinner John Lees, one of the most controversial of the Peterloo dead; but there never were more than thirty or forty at the graveside at any one time, and an evening procession of some 8,000 people passed without incident. In Manchester itself, the crowd at St Peter's Fields was even smaller, its focus a procession from the Union Rooms, mostly of young people who sung a dirge, 'The song of the slaughter', composed for the occasion. At Royton, crowds gathered in the market place by torchlight to sing the same hymn followed by the 17th psalm. 'Keep me ... from the ungodly that trouble me: mine enemies compass me round about to take away my soul. They are enclosed in their own fat, and their mouth speaketh proud things.'[39]

Ireland similarly confounded gloomy prediction, though it should be stressed the quiescence of Ireland was relative to that which had pertained over the previous months: incidents continued to occur there that in Britain would have occasioned extensive and enduring public concern. For example in May soldiers, detailed to protect a revenue officer at a fair in Leitrim, were attacked for their arms and killed two of their assailants; and in a series of savage incidents in Westmeath, raiders cut off the ears of English and Scottish stewards employed by unpopular landlords. As early as July Galway's magistrates were pleading to the Lord Lieutenant to maintain troop numbers in preparation 'for the approaching Winter'.[40] However the Government did pull back troops from Ireland, more than a thousand of them from Connacht by late September, because 'Ireland was never so quiet', Charles Grant told Sidmouth. 'One can scarcely make this remark without trembling', added the Chief Secretary. None could predict what sudden disturbance might erupt, but the harvest was 'abundant beyond all precedent, and provisions of all kinds plentiful and cheap'.[41]

Though the background noise of unrest was almost ceaseless, serious agrarian disturbance in Ireland was geographically episodic and shaped both by the circumstances of different regions as well as the nature of government repression. Forced by the systemic weaknesses of local authority, Dublin Castle flung troops and paramilitaries at every disturbance. The uneasy peace achieved after each episode was soon followed by an eruption elsewhere. Thus the Connacht Ribbon rising explored in these pages had been preceded by the east Leinster carders' movement of 1813–16; and it was in turn followed by the Rockite rebellion of 1821–24 in Munster.[42] Ribbonism lent a powerful impetus to the anti-Protestant millenarianism that underpinned the Rockite movement. In

Galway, a correspondent told Dublin Castle in February 1820, 'it is prophesied all the world are to be of one religion in the year 1825 or 1826'. Enlisting Ireland's banking crisis as a further sign of the apocalypse to come, one early Rockite ballad predicted 'Notes will be of nothing in the year 25'.[43] But for the moment Ireland was free from fever, it was free from want and it was also free from excitement about Queen Caroline. Grant knew of only one demonstration, in Belfast, and 'a miserable effort' it was too.[44]

Queen, Queen Caroline

Few English demonstrations supporting Caroline could have been described as miserable efforts, though once she had settled in London they were largely confined to the capital during the initial unfolding of the confrontation between her and the Government. In time however, formally constituted (and therefore immune from prosecution under the six acts) public meetings to draw up addresses of condolence and loyalty were held across Britain, from Dingwall and Wick in the far north to the furthest parishes of Cornwall in the West. Some from Wales were composed in Welsh, a rare departure from customary practice.[45] Those that could do so brought their addresses to her Majesty in person: for example the metropolitan Kent parish of Greenwich sent seven carriages, each drawn by four horses, headed by the officers of the vestry and escorted by the parish beadles bearing ceremonial maces.[46]

There were fundamental fissures in opinions regarding the Queen. Most of cosmopolitan 'high' society held her in little regard. At the very least she was seen as transgressing the boundaries of good taste and decorum. In Chapter 5 we glimpsed Joseph Farington and John Constable gossiping that Caroline was masculine in her dress. Another conversation with Farington's fellow Royal Academicians concluded that her behaviour was 'disgustingly offensive to propriety & delicacy'.[47] That discussion included Sir Thomas Lawrence, who had painted a warm and empathic portrait of Caroline and was himself suspected of impropriety with her when she sat for him in 1801–02. The Dowager Lady Vernon thought her 'very <u>disagreeably dirty</u> in her person'. Lord Hutchinson called her 'undignified as a queen' and 'unamiable as a woman'. Sir Walter Scott thought her 'most abandoned and beastly'.[48] For the Whig grandee Earl Fitzwilliam it was Caroline's alleged 'disgusting intimacy *with a menial*', that was most disturbing.[49] Even some of her sympathisers thought her mentally unbalanced. The Earl of Guilford (who was to give evidence in her defence) told Huskisson her 'infamous character' could only be explained as '*a disease*'.[50] Lord Holland variously described her as 'if not mad … very worthless' and 'a half-crazy woman'.[51] A decidedly unsympathetic Lord Chancellor declared her insane; Castlereagh's brother pronounced her actions 'the offspring of a weak or insane mind'.[52] Some who might have been expected to sympathise held extreme views against her. Shelley dismissed her as a 'vulgar cook-maid', declaring he would not be surprised if Caroline had committed bestiality.[53] The Queen's champion Henry Brougham punned 'the Queen is pure innocence' (in no sense), observing on another occasion: 'I can believe any folly on the part of that woman.'[54] The position of many at this level of society was summed up in the exchange recorded by the diarist Henry Crabb Robinson, recalling a conversation on the street with Samuel Coleridge who said, 'Well, Robinson, you are a Queenite, I hope?' – 'Indeed I am not.' – 'How is that possible?' – 'I am only an anti-Kingite.' – 'That's just what I mean.'[55]

Yet even among the social elite, more principled disagreements might open up, sometimes within a single family. Visiting the Isle of Wight for a family holiday, Joseph Farington discovered that his brother and three female relatives (wives of a colonel, a major and a naval captain) were 'all for the Queen's innocence'. The painter David Wilkie was asked to declare for King or Queen on arrival at a Cambridgeshire mansion, and discovered that the entire household cleaved down the middle on the issue.[56] 'I never knew a subject on which there was more discordant opinion amongst those attached to Government than there is on the question respecting the Queen', an Ayrshire landowner told Sidmouth: 'To reason is in vain. She was an ill-used woman is the impression and that being their conviction, proof seems of no avail.'[57] Even the ultra-loyal Walter Scott thought it scarcely surprising Caroline sought revenge on the King.[58]

Outside the elite of British society there was very little discordant opinion. 'It is quite evident that the question of guilt or innocence enters for nothing into the general publick feeling', Canning observed to Huskisson.[59] 'If the king did not behave he should be told of it as well as another man', a Penzance bookseller reasoned to a local magistrate who had demanded he remove pro-Caroline literature from his window.[60] The Queen 'gains ground in the affections of the middle and lower classes', a backbench MP wrote to Lord Colchester and 'by the common people she is looked upon as an injured and unprotected female'.[61] 'The common people, and I fear the soldiers, are all in her favour', Emily Lamb told her brother, 'as for her virtue, I don't think they care much about it.[62] 'It was the only question I have ever known', wrote William Hazlitt, 'that excited a thorough popular feeling. It struck its roots into the heart of the nation; it took possession of every house or cottage in the kingdom.'[63] The unanimity of contemporary opinion on this point at least is striking. The leading publishers John Murray even postponed the publication of several key books for the duration of the trial.[64] The 'Caroline fever' was the 'universal subject of conversation', 'the first subject, perhaps almost the only one about which the English world talks and thinks'; 'the queen of England is at present every thing with every body'; 'for several months the people of England have thought, talked, and dreamt of no other subject than the Queen'. 'The infatuation for the Queen prevails equally in the most secluded valleys of our moors as at Hampstead and Highgate.'[65] Caroline's sins, the bluestocking evangelical Hannah More confessed to William Wilberforce, 'occupy my thoughts more than my own'.[66]

'It is in the streets that the Queen's party is chiefly to be found', a junior minister noted,[67] and when the first reading of the bill of pains and penalties took place on 5 July the mood on London's streets swung even more decisively in her favour. Addresses professing loyalty to the Queen began pouring in from all over Britain, each of which received a formal reply exuding elegance and restrained indignation. William Cobbett was widely believed to be the real author of these responses, though it seems likely a large proportion were written by her secretary Robert Fellowes, or by Samuel Parr, the so-called 'Whig Dr Johnson' whom she had appointed as her chaplain.[68] But campaigning for Caroline certainly revived Cobbett's failing fortunes and he turned his *Political Register* over to her cause.[69] The 21 October issue alone printed twenty-three responses to loyal addresses, four of them adopted at public meetings of women in Halifax, Leeds, St Ives (Huntingdonshire) and Truro. 'It is not only my destruction that has been the object of my enemies', the Queen replied to the females of Truro, 'it is the destruction of everything that ought to be most dear to Britons; my fall was designed to prepare the way for their humiliation'. Such large claims could not be substantiated but few were bothered by this. The Queen's cause was seamlessly merging into the concerns of an aggrieved population that felt – variously – rebellious, indignant, chivalrous, patriotic, republican, socially and politically marginalised, or perhaps simply bored and frustrated at the unvarying daily round of making ends meet in a post-war recession. At other times the Queen's responses to loyal addresses struck a homely note: 'A deserted Queen be only a deserted woman', she confided to the females of Bristol; to the incorporated trades of Perth, 'the Nation has been insulted in the person of the Queen'; to the weavers of Edinburgh, 'injustice and oppression … raise me to a height of popular regard where, if I were ambitious, I might be giddy with the view'.[70]

Homely too were many of the gestures made to the Queen by those who came to her defence. Loughborough lacemakers made her a dress and Coventry silk weavers specially woven monogrammed ribbons; Mrs Morris and Miss Dryden of Goswell Street, London, sent Caroline a straw hat and bonnet made by themselves ('exactly her Majesty's favourite pattern', responded her lady-in-waiting); five elderly women, 'very humble individuals' from Sandwich in Kent, presented 'a very fine fat pig'; Sheffield workers sent her Sheffield plate; Kidderminster carpet weavers a rug; the shoemakers of Woodstock a pair of white satin shoes.[71] Meanwhile followers of fashion could purchase 'the Caroline turban' ('the favourite half-dress for the heads of matronly ladies; it is of white satin in light folds, interspersed with net or gauze').[72] Working people also acquired Caroline memorabilia for their own homes: engraved portraits, printed cotton handkerchiefs, and a profusion of plates, wall-plaques, jugs, cups and saucers. Most of this was cheap earthenware, suggesting high-volume sales to a working-class market, with inscriptions to match:

Would you wish to know a Bright Star of the Morn
That cheers a whole nation, all lost and forlorn
'Tis that Feminine Planet; O long may she shine
And Heaven protect her; Our QUEEN CAROLINE.[73]

In the absence of any *catalogue raisonné* it is difficult to assess this output in detail: but at least forty different lines were produced, a figure that places Caroline on a par of popularity with Nelson and far above Wellington or any British royalty before Queen Victoria. [74]

One of the most remarkable (and certainly colourful) material survivals from 1820 is a six-metre-square bed quilt, at its centre a printed cotton panel depicting Caroline and inscribed 'HER MOST GRACIOUS MAJESTY, CAROLINE QUEEN of ENGLAND', made by an unknown Welsh woman, probably in Brecon.[75] The participation of women in the campaign to defend her was its most unprecedented feature. Although women were no strangers to voluntary action and the public sphere, hitherto their energies had been channelled largely into charities, religious causes or the anti-slavery movement; and overwhelmingly the women involved were those of the more comfortably situated social strata. In the decades either side of 1800, however, women from working families were increasingly prominent and autonomous participants both in crowd actions protesting against food prices, turnpikes and machinery, and also in communal pageantry – Peterloo is a salient indicator of both.[76] The Queen's cause drew together both 'polite' female society with its tradition of voluntary organisation, and working-class women and the tradition of popular mobilisation in which they increasingly featured. The *Liverpool Mercury* prefaced its report of the usually loyalist town's greatest Caroline demonstration with the observation that:

> The milliner's [*sic*] shops were adorned with white ribbons, rosettes, mottoes, and devices, of every suitable description, for sale, which were bought up by an eager public with great avidity. In short, all classes provided themselves with ornaments of more or less value, according to their means: and the richness of gold and satin decorations were intermixed with the simple white rose, and unadorned inscription of 'God Save the Queen'.[77]

Women both mobilised to present her loyal addresses of their own and participated in the 800 or so general declarations of loyalty sent to her in 1820–21. Where details of the signatories survive, these indicate roughly equal gender participation as well as overwhelming popular support. Some 9,000 women and 10,000 men signed a loyal address sent from Exeter (the city's population in 1821 was 23,000). The Suffolk market town of Framlingham, a parish of around 2,300 souls, mustered 1,084 female and 1,105 male signatories.[78] Making every allowance for addresses drawing support from a community's wider hinterland, and even for the calculations being inflated, these are still remarkable figures. Women also took to the streets, a phenomenon many contemporary observers

noted as a novelty and by which several were astonished. In London, every time
the Queen appeared in public, the appalled wife of a diplomat noted,

> she is greeted with respect and enthusiasm, not by the mob – make no mistake about
> that – but by the solid middle classes who have won England her reputation for
> virtue and morality. You have to see for yourself what the Queen's escort is like to
> get an accurate notion of the cheering and the people who cheer. The streets are full
> of well-dressed men and respectable women, all waving their hats and handker-
> chiefs'.[79]

During the passage of the bill of pains and penalties, the sheer scale of popular
support for the Queen required unprecedented preparations to maintain the
peace. A naval vessel was moored in the Thames off the Houses of Parliament,
and nearly 750 infantry (plus officers and non-commissioned officers) were
based there for the duration of the trial. The Tower of London garrison was
increased to a full battalion and – an innovation reflecting earlier problems in the
Guards – all its officers ordered to reside there. Even the guard on the British
Museum was doubled. Three-hundred cavalry stood by at five locations within
two miles of Parliament: sixty of them (plus thirty infantry) protected the King
at Carlton House.[80] Provincial garrisons were moved up into barracks nearer the
capital, a move that entailed cutting by a fifth the troops hitherto stationed in
northern England.[81] Even these arrangements could not completely secure the
streets. 'All the walls in town are scrawled over with nice things of this kind', the
Russian ambassador's wife recorded: 'the Queen for ever, the King in the river.'

There were particular concerns about the foreign witnesses, brought to
London by the Government to give evidence concerning the Queen's behaviour
abroad. To avoid the ugly convergence of xenophobia and Caroline fever, these
witnesses were housed under guard in Cotton Garden, within the precincts of
the Palace of Westminster, so they could enter the House of Lords unseen from
the streets or public yards. On one occasion a mob almost succeeded in
unhorsing Wellington. More worrying was a rumoured plot to assassinate the
King. Sidmouth forcibly instructed the royal household that he was no longer to
reside at the Windsor cottage. For the rest of the year threats to kill or injure
various authority figures became almost commonplace.[82]

Though he was predictably lampooned for it, for much of the hearings
George IV retreated to the safety of the Solent aboard his yacht the *Royal George*.
Deputations from coastal towns rowed out to present loyal addresses as the
monarch only ventured ashore at Cowes, Isle of Wight. One of the hundreds of
visual satires produced during the episode depicted the 'poor old man',
staggering ashore beneath the weight of a green bag as bulky as himself (see
Figure 4). His 'gilded yacht has born him to your shore', the legend ran. 'Oh! give
three cheers, if you can give no more.'[83] This print was one of the kinder depic-
tions of the monarch at the time. Invariably depicted as obese and overwhelmed
by vanity, George was also variously portrayed as a dunghill cock, assorted

IN PITY GIVE THREE CHEERS!
A PARODY ON THE BEGGAR'S PETITION.

PITY the sorrows of a poor old man,
  Whose gilded yacht has borne him to your share:
Let not his wife chastise him with her fan;
Oh! give three cheers, if you can give no more.

These well-made clothes my wish to please bespeak,
  These curling locks disguise my lengthen'd years,
And the bluff whiskers on each ample cheek,
  Might strike an Indian warrior with fears.

The house which once I fondly thought my own—
  Scene of my triumphs—now has ceas'd to shine;
For Justice there shall fix her golden throne,
  And truth, and law, and liberty combine.

Hard is the fate of the infirm and weak!
  Here, as I crav'd them to disgrace my wife,
They said another bride I must not seek,
  And saucy Denman bade me mend my life.
        . . . .
Had fate reduc'd me, I should not repine;
  My friends have brought me to the state you see,
And your condition will be soon like mine—
  They'll bring you, too, to want and misery.

A huge Green Bag, delighted they display—
  Gay as a lark I view'd the vaunted prize:
But, oh, its treasures melt in dirt away,
  Beneath the flash of Brougham's inquiring eyes.

My sprightly Canning, soother of my cares,
  Keen as a Rat, the coming storm to see,
Departed, when I tamper'd with the pray'rs
  And left the Bag to Gifford and to me.

Pity the sorrows of a poor old man,
  Whose gilded yacht has borne him to your shore
Let not his wife chastise him with her fan;
  Oh! give three cheers, if you can give no more.

The above Stanzas were lately picked up on the shore near Cowes. The lines that are left out were illegible, apparently from the Manuscript, which was torn, having been used in keeping a pair of refractory whiskers in good order.

Figure 4   Street literature: 'In pity give three cheers', an anonymous satire on George IV's self-imposed exile on the Solent

bloated oriental despots including Kouli Khan (a bisexual libertine) and Runjumdildopunt (a lewd pantomime character), and more prosaically as the kettle calling the pot (i.e. Caroline) black.[84] And in the enduring Cruickshank-Hone parody *The Political House that Jack Built* (December 1819; see Figure 1), George was

> THE MAN—all shaven and shorn,
> All cover'd with Orders—and all forlorn;
> THE DANDY OF SIXTY,
>   who bows with a grace,
> And has *taste* in wigs, collars,
>   cuirasses and lace;
> Who, to tricksters, and fools,
>   leaves the State and its treasure,
> And, when Britain's in tears,
>   sails about at his pleasure,
> Who spurn'd from his presence,
>   the Friends of his youth,
> And now has not one
>   who will tell him the truth;

Who took to his counsels,
   in evil hour,
The Friends to the Reasons
   of lawless Power;
That back the Public Informer,
   who
Would put down the *Thing*,
   that, in spite of new Acts,
And attempts to restrain it,
   by Soldiers or Tax,
Will *poison* the Vermin,
That plunder the Wealth,
That lay in the House,
That Jack built.[85]

The verse may be execrable but it underlines how closely Queenite propaganda connected with popular culture, and how her cause was woven into a broader canvas of radical grievances: the Civil List, George's political interference as Regent to the detriment of the Whigs, the Government's employment of spies and informers, corruption, the six acts, a standing army, taxation, and the venal State.

Queenite literature arguably constituted the greatest publishing phenomenon of the early nineteenth century. Least-tangible in terms of their survival were true ephemera: alternative wording for the National Anthem surreptitiously introduced into theatres, or songs urging the Guards to support Caroline casually dropped in the streets. Ballad sheets rolled off presses, metropolitan and provincial, extolling Caroline and her cause. They were said to have made fortunes of several thousand pounds for each for the leading London publishers of street balladry.[86] 'All the exertion possible is made here to work up and inflame the minds of the lower class of people', wrote the Norwich postmaster who sent the Home Office a wad of locally printed ballads, and reported 'shabby looking men' hawking them round the city on market day.[87] Some of this material, rooted as much in oral as in print culture, was strikingly enduring. Variants of a children's rhyme (Queen, Queen Caroline / Dipped her hair in turpentine …) were found in Edinburgh in the 1880s, rural Oxfordshire in the early 1900s, and in the Midlands as late as 1959.[88]

Similarly enduring but more celebrated were pamphlets of satirical verse, generally illustrated with woodcuts. At least fifty-two editions of *The Political House that Jack Built* had been published by the end of 1820 (see Figure 1), along with other exuberant fruits of the Cruikshank-Hone collaboration, for example *The Queen's Matrimonial Ladder* (see Figure 5), plus a shoal of imitations.[89] Then there were the cartoons, as they would now be called. This sub-genre benefitted from considerable licence because of the legal difficulty in prosecuting graphic work. Three-quarters of 1820's record annual output of more than 600 graphic

So let him stand • • • • • •
• • • • • • • • • • • •   *Byron.*

DEGRADATION.

To this have they brought thee, at last!

Figure 5   George IV at the height of the divorce crisis, as seen by Cruikshank

satires referred to the divorce case.[90] Overwhelmingly this deluge of print favoured the Queen. However, there were exceptions. Theodore Lane's *Grand Entrance to Bamboozl'em* (see Figure 6) conjured up Caroline's triumphal entry into London as the Ministry and its supporters doubtless viewed it. Among those waiting to greet her are depicted 'Sir Frank Demagogue' [Burdett], 'William Tompaine Weathercock Cobt' [Cobbett], 'Jack Cam [Hobhouse] Westminster's Darling', Henry Hunt, 'Little Waddy' [the Spencean Samuel Waddington] and Sir Robert Wilson. Banners declaim 'Innocence', 'Hoax', 'Radical Reform', 'Rights & Privileges', 'Disaffection', 'Revolution' and 'Anarchy'. The Queen is depicted as Mother Redcap (Jacobin *bonets rouges* appear on poles in the crowd) and seated with her retinue on donkeys. The latter was a portmanteau allusion, encompassing stupidity, ugliness, the donkey's role in the popular burlesquing of cuckoldry, and a painting commissioned by Caroline, 'The Queen's Entry into Jerusalem', exhibited in Pall Mall in August 1820.[91]

Figure 6   Anti-radical satire, depicting Caroline's *Grand Entrance to Bamboozl'em* (i.e. London) © British Museum, London

Even her fiercest critics sometimes caught Caroline fever. For example the Duke of Wellington, accompanied by the Treasury Secretary's wife, Harriet Arbuthnot, joined the throng to view 'The Queen's Entry into Jerusalem'.[92] By then Caroline's residence at Alderman Wood's was no longer suitable, given the press of visitors and delegations that flocked to see her. She provocatively moved to St James Square, into the house close to Castlereagh's: he removed his valuables, boarded up the windows, and moved a bed into the Foreign Office. Then rumour that the Queen was to move again, this time next door to the Lord Chancellor, prompted the latter to threaten to resign.[93] The crisis was averted when Caroline chose instead to move up-river to Brandenburgh House, Hammersmith. From here on 6 September Caroline and her supporters mounted one of the major demonstrations of her visit to the capital. On the eve of the conclusion of the prosecution case in the House of Lords, she sailed down river on the state barge (which had apparently been seized by the Thames watermen for the purpose). 'There was not a single vessel in the river that did not hoist their colours and man their yards for her', one witness related.[94] The Chartist and republican William Linton's earliest political memory was of walking, aged eight, through London 'and seeing daily the processions of the city companies (the old-time guilds) passing through the streets with banners and bands of music on their way westward to Hammersmith to present their loyal addresses to Queen Caroline'.[95] The processions were not quite daily, Wednesday each week usually being assigned to the delivery and reception of addresses and well-wishers, but the scenes were certainly memorable both in the capital and in the vicinity of her home (see Figure 7). Earl Fitzwilliam counted '140 Gentlemen's coaches, besides Hacks &c., &c.' in the procession of the females of Marylebone alone. Another on 18 October saw 3,000 carpenters and sawyers 'with music, banners, and favours', and at least ninety horse-drawn carriages make their way from central London to Hammersmith. During the course of that day alone day Caroline also received addresses from the Roman Catholics of the capital, two trade societies, three Welsh and five Scottish towns, nine London parishes and twenty-two English towns and villages.[96]

The Queenite cause was a colourful, invigorating and dramatic experience for those who joined it. It also seeped into legitimate theatre, not only via heckling the national anthem or forceful renditions of a radical alternative, but in the disruption of performances and, more subtly, the continuing presentation of plays that were heavy with contemporary political resonance. As we saw in the previous chapter, Sheridan Knowles' *Virginius* was the most conspicuous of these, but it was by no means alone. The 1820 Covent Garden production of Shakespeare's *Cymbeline* is a case in point. This drama of a chaste, British princess (Imogen), the victim of a vengeful husband, turns upon the perjured evidence of an Italian – Iachimo – that he had 'tasted her in bed'. At the play's dénouement, Imogen contrives to force Iachimo to admit his duplicity. What the audience has known all along, that the purity of the princess is unassailable, is revealed to her husband and the whole royal court. In October 1820, while the House of Lords investigation into Caroline was at its height, Covent Garden presented *Cymbeline* with William Macready, fresh from his success in Virginius, playing Iachimo. The play's reception in the London press suggests Macready acted up *Cymbeline*'s contemporary parallels. 'Iachimo has all the disbelief in principle that belongs to real vice', thought the *Examiner*, and 'the audience do not fail to apply the prominent passages about the calumniated princess and "false Italians"'. *The Times* reported that when a minor character suggested to Imogen's husband that the supposed evidence of her unfaithfulness had either been accidentally dropped by her or stolen, the actor was rewarded by two or three minutes of 'the most vehement applause'. The *Morning Post* called for Covent Garden's management to cancel after the first performance, referring to 'the manner in which certain passages of *Cymbeline* were taken up last night by the Radical part of the audience'. The paper warned 'that in times of public agitation, the source of our amusements should be poisoned, and that profit should be sought at the risk of public discord'.[97]

Cymbeline was not the only Shakespearian play to catch the imaginations of audiences simultaneously absorbed by the drama of Caroline. Productions of the Shakespeare/Fletcher history play *Henry VIII* gave particular prominence to the trial of Queen Katherine. *Henry VIII, Or, the Fall of Cardinal Wolsey* (its preferred title in 1820) had always been noted for its sympathetic portrayal of a dignified and wrongly accused Queen Katherine. Its unsympathetic treatment of her

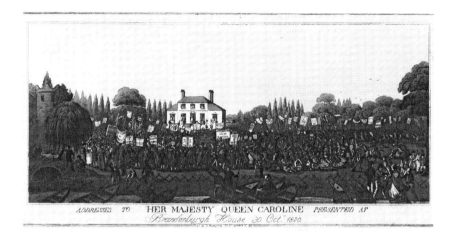

Figure 7   'Addresses to Her Majesty Queen Caroline, presented at Brandenburg
House 30 October 1820' (London: Humphrey, 1821)

husband was tempered by the implication that his advisor Cardinal Wolsey was
ultimately to blame for the persecution of the Queen. Frequent recourse was had
to the trope of a monarch misled by his ministers in political commentary in
1820; but the play also benefitted from 'The Trial of Queen Katherine' being one
of its central scenes, eminently suited for presentation as one of the set-piece
spectacles beloved by early nineteenth-century audiences, and flagged on posters
as one of the chief attractions of the production.[98]

The trial

Simultaneously an even-more absorbing drama was being played out in the
House of Lords, Queen Caroline's 'Trial, for such it virtually is', newspapers
pointed out, 'though it is not in exact conformity with the every-day forms of
the law'.[99] More than any other incident in the history of English, it was these
proceedings that cemented the word *intercourse* (hitherto a legalistic euphemism)
into the language as an explicit descriptor of the sexual act. And the adjectives
applied to it by ministerial prosecutors were deliberately intended to scandalise
and appal. The Queen was accused not merely of 'adulterous' intercourse but
'most improper ... most scandalous, most degrading, most licentious',
'disgusting', 'gross' and 'criminal' intercourse.[100] During the period (17 August to
9 November) that its second and third readings took place, the Bill of Pains and
Penalties paralysed Westminster. The House of Commons assembled only twice
between 18 September and the end of the year. Meanwhile in the Lords, the
proceedings grew increasingly bizarre, as the peers and bishops were asked to
consider – among many other things – the topography of sleeping arrangements
on a Mediterranean cruising vessel,[101] the evidence of chambermaids about

soiled bed linen,[102] and the proposition put by Thomas Denman, the Queen's Solicitor-General (albeit phrased in the decent obscurity of classical Greek) that the Queen's vagina was more pure than the King's mouth.[103] With the normal business of Parliament suspended, trial reportage dominated the press, titillating and enraging in equal measure. 'Such a scene of profligacy and vice as were never detailed in any novel', a senior House of Commons clerk wrote. 'Horrible', noted a Cotswold parson, 'a narrative of profligate amours … imputed adulteries and gross indecencies'. The loyalist *Morning Post* took to referring to the Queen as 'unsunned snow', an ironic quotation describing Princess Imogen in *Cymbeline*.[104] Sidmouth prohibited his daughters from reading newspapers during the length of the trial and was not alone in so doing. 'There were members present', York's Whig MP Robert Chaloner told the city's Whig Club, 'who, having females in their families, had taken pains to hide the public papers from their view'.[105]

Yet the longer the trial dragged on, and the more lurid the evidence became, so the Queen (whom protocol saved from giving evidence) seemed to grow in popular regard. It was not simply the '*hypocritical cant*' (to quote Chaloner again) of what was being done in the name of a morally deeply compromised monarch; Brougham and Denman also shredded the credibility of many of the continental witnesses, few of whom spoke adequate English. 'Je ne me rappelle pas', Louise Demont, Caroline's maid, repeatedly muttered.[106] She was not the only witness who had trouble remembering. Especially humiliating for the Government was the testimony of the first and most keenly anticipated prosecution witness, Teodoro Majocchi. A former member of the Queen's household and associate of her alleged lover, Bartolomeo Pergami, Majocchi spoke no English. 'Non mi ricordo' – I do not remember – Majocchi replied to question after question put by counsel and by members of the House of Lords. 'Non mi ricordo', indeed, was Majocchi's response more than a hundred times.[107] 'Non mi ricordo' became the catchphrase of the year, adopted for song, satire, a mock patent ('the Majocchi Mouthpiece or Non Mi Ricordo Whistle'), 'a favorite waltz, for the harp or piano forte', and for yet another Cruikshank-Hone collaboration, at its head a quotation from *Cymbeline*: 'This will witness outwardly, as strongly as the conscience does within.'[108]

The fate of Liverpool's Ministry seemingly hung in the balance. Robert Plumer Ward, a doggedly loyal ministerialist, confided in his diary that the Cabinet 'seemed like victims'. 'In the whole course of my life', Liverpool told Canning on 12 September, 'I do not recollect to have undergone such continued fatigue as during the three weeks of the proceedings in the House of Lords'. Lord Eldon, required as Lord Chancellor to preside over the whole trial proceedings 'was tired, and desired nothing so much as to retire'.[109] Wellington told colleagues of gossip 'from many quarters that the King abused us most furiously' and was conspiring to eject them. George IV's latest mistress, Lady Conyngham, was said to be communicating with Earl Grey. The Cabinet was also divided on itself.

George Canning had made clear his 'unaltered regard and affection' for the Queen, in a speech in the Commons which had enraged the King and compromised his Cabinet colleagues, and then retreated to Paris for the duration of the Bill's progress through Parliament.[110] On 20 October Wellington and Eldon voted against the Prime Minister on a technical point during the second reading of the bill. Wellington, seemingly incapable of a nuanced opinion,

> Considered it a question of the utmost importance & as likely to be most fatal in its consequences … He said Lord Liverpool was so fretful & so ill tempered it was impossible to say anything to him; that he, for his part, never did; that Lord Liverpool never consulted with or spoke to any of them, never w[d] listen to any argument or remonstrance & took the most important steps without consulting with them.[111]

To the Cassandra of the Cabinet, William Wellesley-Pole, the entire moral fabric of the kingdom was in the balance. 'Everything', he told Ward, was 'very bad – Ministers, Opposition, King, Queen, country, and what was more, no prospect of getting right – all ties were loosened. Insolence and insubordination out of doors, weakness and wickedness within'.[112]

However we should note that Wellesley-Pole was not so pessimistic that he thought the innocence of the Queen had been established. Despite the farcical nature of much of the testimony against her, a sufficient catalogue of indiscretions was accumulating to make an adultery verdict likely. However, Whig political opportunism ('we don't give a fig about her guilt', quipped Hobhouse) and a broader disposition to censure the conduct of the King and his Government, combined to suggest a Lords' majority would never be secured for a royal divorce.[113] By the end of October the Cabinet was meeting nightly and its discussions were increasingly fraught. Liverpool threatened to resign if the bill was defeated. On 6 November the second reading of the bill was carried by a majority of only twenty-eight. It was an ill omen for how it would be treated in the Commons, of which the Government's management was far less assured. On the 8th a ministerial compromise, whereby the divorce clause would be dropped to clear the way for a simple verdict of guilt against the Queen, was defeated by a majority of sixty-nine. On the 9th, debate in the Cabinet reached its nadir. 'There was a terrible scene', Charles Arbuthnot told his wife

> Three fourths of them were for getting rid of the Bill; but L[d] L[iverpool] was in a phrenzy, & his rage got so high that for a time it stopped all deliberation. He abused the Chancellor. He complained of the ill usage he had received from several in the room, without particularising them, & ended by crying.[114]

Liverpool handed Eldon a note of apology the next day, saying 'sorry if what I said last night gave you pain'.[115]

But Friday 10 November was notable for much more than this display of prime ministerial contrition. The House of Lords voted on the third reading of the bill, intact as the Ministry had originally intended but now no longer wanted. The majority was so small (just nine votes) that Liverpool immediately announced its effective abandonment. The Lords *had* reached a verdict that Caroline had committed adultery while Princess of Wales, but few regarded it as anything other than a triumph for the Queen and most of the country saw it as an acquittal. Inside Westminster the next stage was unclear. Earl Grey lingered in the capital in the expectation he would be summoned to form a ministry. The King talked of leaving Britain for his other kingdom, Hannover. He had vacillated between insisting the bill should progress and entertaining the notion that he himself would graciously withdraw it, thus clawing back some popularity. Either way, he wanted the House of Commons to reassemble immediately and vote his Queen sufficient money to persuade her to leave the country. Thwarted in this by a first minister who yet again threatened to resign if Parliament was not immediately prorogued, George's 'language & manner were those of a Bedlamite'; on 16 November he drafted but never sent a letter informing Liverpool his administration was at an end.[116] The following week he summoned Lord Grenville, apparently with a view to persuading him to head a new government. Predictably news of this 'put Lord L in a fever'; but Grenville expressed deep distaste for the Whigs (on whom he would have had to rely to form a ministry), telling the King they 'were so mixed up with Radicalism that they did nothing that was not abominable'.[117] George then began overtures to leading Whigs, a move hampered by Grey having set out for his Northumberland seat around 22 November. But then, in one of its more adroit parliamentary manoeuvres, the Ministry assembled the Commons on 23 November, for only its second sitting since 18 September. Just as Denman rose to read to the House a message from the Queen, Black Rod arrived from the Lords to announce Parliament was prorogued. Amidst calls for Denman and cries of 'Shame! Shame!' the Speaker left the Commons. Above the chorus of derision Grey Bennet could be heard shouting 'this is scandalous!' Thomas Creevey, diarist and Whig MP, was adamant that 'such a scene has never occurred in the H. of Commons since Charles the 1st's time'.[118]

Caroline fever

Lord Liverpool was gambling that MPs and their constituencies would alike begin to tire of Queen Caroline. If the term 'Caroline fever' had been hyperbole before 10 November it was singularly apt after it. That the bill of pains and penalties had been approved by the House of Lords was totally ignored. Instead, its abandonment by the Government was taken as signalling the victory of an 'innocent and persecuted' or 'illustrious' Queen. When the news reached Burnley, weaver William Varley noted in his diary, 'Our Queen has got her trial'.[119] 'Queen Caroline won her trial in the House of Lords', declared a County Durham journeyman printer, 'nothing has ever occurred to show that the Queen was guilty of the infamous charges brought against her'.[120] Across Britain 'the joy which spread through the country with the news of the abandonment of the Bill was beyond the scope of record', according to the usually dispassionate Harriet Martineau.[121] Such was their extent it is easier to précis where demonstrations did *not* occur than where they did. Responses in Ireland were muted. In Ulster there were illuminations in Belfast, Carrickfergus and County Down, in County Cork at Bantry, and 'a splendid and very general illumination', led by Daniel O'Connell in Dublin, where ships also illuminated along the river.[122] The paucity of the response in Ireland is even more apparent when compared with the extent of illumination in even the most remote communities in Britain, for example the villages on the north-eastern rim of the Yorkshire Moors, the west Cornwall fishing villages of Newlyn and Mousehole, and Dingwall in the far north of Scotland.[123]

The commonest form of demonstration was illumination – the placing of candles and lamps in their windows by householders, with those able to do so adding 'laurel, and white bows, and gold paper' or a transparency (typically a handkerchief printed with the Queen's portrait).[124] At Dingwall, Gaelic mottoes 'excited much attention'.[125] Some of these illuminations assumed epic proportions and were advertised by public proclamation, often a week in advance, to allow householders time for elaborate preparation. Reading's was so lavish and protracted that crowds travelled in from its hinterland to view the spectacle. In York glass painters prepared elaborate transparencies bearing texts (e.g. 'Take away the evil Counsellors from before the King, and the Throne shall be established as righteousness') or depicting figures from the trial (e.g. Majocchi in a pillory). A triumphal arch was erected over the main road into the city from the East Riding. Salisbury 'presented one scene of light – of life – and joy!' In Crediton, Devon, '*Transparencies, Motto's, Triumphal Arches, Coloured lamps, Crowns, "Carolines", "C . R."s* and the *Imperial Star of Brunswick*, shone everywhere conspicuous'. At Lewes transparencies included a Minister offering Caroline £50,000 and an all-seeing eye mounted above a green bag inscribed 'perjury, poisoned bowl and horse-leech' (a reference to George IV's advisor Sir John Leech).[126]

With illumination went carnival, sometimes spontaneous but often carefully prepared and choreographed. The ritual procession and burning of green bags was especially popular. At Guisborough, then the most northerly town in Yorkshire, the offending article was marched round the town on the end of a pole borne by a Waterloo veteran, accompanied by the band of the 3rd North Yorkshire Militia, whose captain Robert Chaloner MP lived in the town. Seven miles away, up on the moors in the tiny village of Castleton, the green bag was preceded by 'a young girl – the appropriate emblem of innocence' born aloft on a chair. At Middleton in south-east Lancashire the green bag procession was led by a man in a cap of liberty. At Stroud in Gloucestershire it was tied to the tail of an ox. The animal, decorated with ribbons and laurels, was then led around the town while the bag became predictably filthy. In Stockton-on-Tees it was hung from the neck of an effigy of the Devil and paraded with a band. After a mock trial a formal proclamation was issued that the Devil had been found guilty of conspiracy against the Queen and was sentenced 'to be committed to his own realm at 8 o'clock this evening'. At Carmarthen the bag was ceremonially placed on a bonfire outside the Guildhall, to music by the band of the local militia. Invariably and symbolically these green bags were filled with soot, floor sweepings, 'filth' and loyalist newspapers.[127]

Burning effigies of the European witnesses was also commonplace. At Chipping Ongar, Essex, three were drawn through the streets on a hurdle (a precursor to executing a traitor), then hung from a gallows under which a bonfire was lit. At Lostwithiel, Cornwall, they were mounted on donkeys to be paraded through the town en route to their ceremonial burning, preceded by a Union Flag inscribed 'innocence protected' and 'faith and justice triumphant, as a band played 'the rogue's march'. Darlington's effigy, a green bag hanging from its neck, was similarly paraded on a donkey. In neighbouring Stockton the green bag and devil, mentioned above, joined the devil's, 'particular friends', effigies of three perjured witnesses plus 'a non-descript' (half bishop, half courier − a visual pun on the title of the ultra-loyalist newspaper). All five effigies were then hung from a gibbet in the market place where a bonfire was lit beneath them.[128] In the north Derbyshire village of Hadfield, Majocchi's effigy was ritually executed and then burnt on the precise spot where, twenty years before, an effigy of Thomas Paine had suffered similarly at the hands of loyalists. In Abergavenny, an effigy of Majocchi was 'paraded on horseback through the streets', accompanied 'by all the respectable inhabitants, male and female' prior to being hung from a gallows and burnt. Effigies of local hate-figures were frequently incorporated into these nocturnal carnivals. A dummy representing the curate of Aston Tirrold (Berkshire) was burnt outside his door after he had failed to prevent a jubilant crowd from entering the church tower to ring the bells. 'I had the honor (for so I esteem it)', a Maidstone magistrate told Sidmouth, 'of being burnt in effigy, in several parts of the county'.[129] However, the incineration of effigies representing ministers or the King was almost unheard of. The King may have been consigned to the flames at Kentish Town, north London; a teenage farmer's son, visiting York, claimed in later life to have 'found the people in much tumult and disorder, being engaged in burning an effigy of the reigning king', but there is no corroborative evidence for this.[130] The ubiquitous green bag stood in both for the monarch and his ministers. Indeed it had come to symbolise and embody the very political system itself.

In many communities the celebrations were also an occasion to pay off old scores and a smoke screen for civil disobedience in the face of local authority. At its most basic this took the form of breaking the windows of houses that refused to illuminate. At Poole (Dorset) windows were broken at the home of the port's comptroller of customs. At Burwash (Sussex) several hundred paraded the village in the company of musicians. Homes of the 'respectable inhabitants' who refused to illuminate were attacked – over ninety panes were broken in the Rectory. This demonstration may well have gained in ferocity because of the repressive attitude taken to poor relief by Burwash's recently formed select vestry (see Chapter 1). The Rectory was also extensively damaged at Ewelme (Oxfordshire), whose incumbent was the Tory pluralist William Van Mildert, (Dean of St Pauls and Bishop of Llandaff). As he made one of his rare appearances in the village, parishioners availed themselves of the opportunity to stone Van Mildert himself. Other clerical targets included a Peterborough magistrate who tried to commit a boy to the town gaol for wearing a hat inscribed 'Long live Queen Caroline'.[131] In Maidstone the office of the Tory *Maidstone Journal* was stoned along with the shops of known Tory tradesmen. The offices of the pro-Government *Yorkshire Gazette* were also attacked and a sweep's sootbag containing copies of the paper burnt outside. In Merthyr Tydfil copies of the *Courier* were publicly burned after a public meeting condemned it as 'an Enemy to every thing bordering on truth'. At Watford the 7th Earl of Bridgewater, a local landowner who had voted against Caroline, was pelted with animal entrails from local slaughter houses as he passed through the town. Abbatoir waste and mud were the missiles of choice for Aylesbury Queenites against the leading Grenvillite peer, the Marquess of Buckingham, as he returned to his seat from the London after the trial. At Newcastle on Tyne a lucky Duke of Northumberland was assailed by mud alone.[132]

Inevitably many of these demonstrations drew down the wrath of the local political establishment. Most attempts to suppress illuminations failed totally, except in Brighton (but curiously not Windsor), and after just one night Oxford, where in September there had been a serious attack on the office of the local Tory newspaper.[133] Special constables were sworn in in large numbers, for example in Canterbury, Grantham, Portsmouth and Totnes; in Newcastle-under-Lyme both specials and the local yeomanry were used.[134] In England serious violence was limited to Cambridge, though troops were deployed in Canterbury and Maidstone.[135] It was in Scotland, where memories of the Easter rising were still raw, that violence most spiralled out of hand. Largely peaceable illuminations were organised in some eighty Scottish locations.[136] However, in Edinburgh attempts by the council to suppress celebrations provoked a riot in which the Lord Provost's home was attacked.[137] Controversially, volunteer cavalry were deployed. The volunteers were also deployed elsewhere in Scotland, though their effectiveness was compromised by conflicting loyalties within their own ranks.[138] Police were stoned and firearms discharged at random in Paisley. At Ayr furious demonstrators built a giant bonfire at the main junction in the town from tar barrels stolen from quayside after the town council prohibited an illumination to honour the Queen. The situation was worst in Glasgow. Neither troops nor a curfew could prevent two nights of disorder in which the homes of those who did not illuminate were attacked and flaming tar barrels recklessly rolled through the streets.[139]

Some demonstrations were followed by retribution. The Duke of Dorset evicted his Northamptonshire tenantry after they organised 'a dinner to celebrate the *Queen's triumph*', but this act of extraordinary vindictiveness was unique. A Bungay (Suffolk) schoolmaster was dismissed for encouraging the townspeople to celebrate and loyalists threatened to withdraw their custom from tradesmen and shopkeepers who had illuminated. Similar threats were made by some Cambridge colleges. However, at Ayr the three ringleaders of the bonfire just mentioned were each fined ten shillings, 'to be paid when they were able (which they never were)'.[140] As much as anything the Caroline celebrations were occasions for paternalist and charitable gestures that acted as a social cement, momentarily diminishing the distance between the political establishment and the politically excluded. At Horbury, in the heart of the West Riding textiles district and very close to Grange Moor, a public subscription permitted 420 of the local poor to dine off four fat sheep washed down with a pint of ale each (the women were given tea). To the north at Heckmondwike, 'the principal manufacturers regaled their workmen in the most liberal manner'. Twenty miles north-west, the Earl of Thanet distributed 'ale, money, & a large quantity of wood and other combustibles' for the celebrations at Skipton. The Earl of Darlington celebrated Caroline's victory by 'causing the great guns at Raby Castle, to fire a royal salute; and ordered a quantity of strong ale to be distributed in Staindrop, Auckland, Barnard-Castle, Stockton and Darlington'. William Crawshay, the great Merthyr Tydfil ironmaster 'set his cannons roaring' to lead the town's celebrations. In Somerset at Honiton, 'the whole of the labouring classes assembled in the open streets' to share hogsheads of cider and strong beer, bread, cheese, pipes and tobacco, while an appalled resident of Wellington related to Lord Liverpool that a clergyman, a magistrate and an excise collector had taken the lead in organising celebrations. In the Devon town of Tiverton the cost of free cider was met by a subscription among the more prosperous residents of the town. In the then rural Middlesex parish of Stanmore, a local brewer distributed two barrels of ale to lubricate proceedings. In Stroud (Gloucestershire) an ox and four sheep were roasted for distribution to the poor of the parish along with four hogsheads of strong beer.[141]

The form and content of communal celebration was also a form of social bonding, the opportunity for a collective statement about what constituted the local community. The port of Liverpool staged one of the most lavish events, a procession on 20 November that wound round the principal streets and comprised trumpeters, Scotch pipers, three bands and four drum and fife bands, fifteen carriages, over 130 riders and representatives of thirty-two trades, ranging from brushmakers to watchmen, and from the Free & Hopeful Tobacconists to the Friendly Society of Revenue Officers. There were also thirty-three non-trade specific friendly societies, a diverse assembly that included at least four women-only organisations, the Amicable Society of St Patrick, and the Church of England, Benevolent Hibernian, Hibernian Mechanics', Cambrian and North Britons' societies. Friendly societies and the organised trades were staple features of many Queenite demonstrations, as well as being organisers of large numbers of addresses and petitions on the Queen's behalf. Their participation was a signifier of corporate strength on the part of working people, just as the often virulent sentiments inscribed on banners, transparencies and other devices signified a collective opposition to the ways and means of aristocratic government. This was the real reason why the once scandalous behaviour of the former Princess of Wales so little troubled her supporters. 'I rise to defend the cause of an injured, persecuted, desolate, and most innocent woman', a speaker told a Hull meeting on 25 November, convened to adopt a petition in her support. 'Our interests and hers are united; we must sink or swim together. If we support her, she will support us; if we desert her cause, ours will perish with it.'[142]

The micro-politics of these events were complex and seldom reducible to a one-way transaction. Around the bonfires at the heart of many communities' celebrations was a reassertion of popular control over the customary festivities of early November. Since the late-eighteenth century attempts to prohibit bonfires on Guy Fawkes' Night had been increasing, while the customary doleing days of late autumn, of which 5 November was just one, were also increasingly opposed by local establishments. Parish churches were also contested territories. Crowds demanded, tricked or forced their way into belfries to ring celebratory peels (sometimes lasting for days), but their intention was not only to vindicate the Queen but also to assert communal 'ownership' of the State Church.[143] Clearly, many clergy opened belfries only under duress, just as many 'Kingites' illuminated only to protect their windows. But reluctant supporters were also yielding to momentary misrule as a means of strengthening the status quo in the longer term. Describing festivities in Plymouth, local landowner and banker Sir William Elford wrote perceptively:

> In general little mischief was done ... I informed the Mayor that for my own part I was very glad to see the great fermentation of the public mind evaporating in noise and smoke – that it was a very good exit for it, and that I would join in no attempt to <u>prevent</u> illumination.[144]

Reciprocity was also important. We have seen how ministerialists and Grenvillites were waylaid by the Queen's supporters and made the targets of their jeering, or worse. Whigs and independents were also stopped, but demonstrators then removed the horses from their carriages and pulled in them triumph to the centres of impromptu local celebrations. Thus Lord Dundas, returning to his North Riding seat, found himself addressing the residents of the small market town of Stokesley. 'The very spirit which would have tyrannized the Queen today', Dundas declared, 'would have been ready to have done the same thing to our-selves tomorrow'.[145]

What exactly did Dundas mean by *our-selves*? For all their personal distaste for the conduct of the Queen, the Whigs ultimately were able to exploit the affair for their political advantage. They had seen their parliamentary opponents humiliated and the monarch (who, as Regent, had humiliatingly ignored their claims to form a government) exposed to public censure. But Whiggism had a second set of opponents, mostly outwith Parliament, in the form of political radicalism. In Chapter 1 we saw that Lord Holland defined the Whigs' difficulties in March 1820 thus:

> The truth is that, very short of positive Radicalism or Universal Suffrage, there is a spirit grown up & growing every day throughout the country, against the nature & practice of our Government, & tending I fear to the separation of the Upper & middling classes of Society.[146]

John Cam Hobhouse saw it from a different perspective: 'the Whigs are such liars and have so bedevilled themselves ... that it requires much opportunity as well as honesty to see the truth as it really stands between them & the people'. The Caroline affair was an unparalleled chance for Whiggism to seek to heal the rift identified by Holland and Hobhouse. According to his close friend the poet Thomas Moore, Lord Russell was confident 'that the Queen's business has done a great deal of good in renewing the old and natural alliance between the Whigs and the people, and weakening the influence of the Radicals with the latter'.[147] But this popularity was bought at the price of unfeasibly high popular hopes being invested in Whiggism. If we are seeking to understand the dynamics of the 1831–32 Reform Crisis and the alleged duplicity of the Whigs' that rapidly followed it, then much of the explanation lies in a brittle marriage of convenience in 1820. This was the marriage of Whig opportunism and the hopes of the politically excluded, riskily sustained by a rhetoric of opposition to public corruption. The marriage was perhaps more solid in Scotland, where loyalist reaction to the year's events forced Whiggism and mass politics into a closer convergence. Yet even here, as Pentland argues, 'the natural rights precepts of popular radicals' (anathema to the Whigs) 'helped to crystallize radicalism as an ideology into the 1820s'.[148] Radicalism's challenge to aristocratic government was stayed but not suppressed.

However, in the short term the Liverpool Ministry was the beneficiary, both of the political opportunism of the Whigs and their disinclination to exploit the advantages they had accrued. The Whigs had little appetite for forming a government, in having to deal with a petulant and obsessively self-absorbed monarch, in commanding a House of Lords where they had no natural majority, or managing a Commons wherein their talents were weak (except for Brougham, whom none of them trusted). Ironically as we have seen, Liverpool's Cabinet felt exactly the same about the lower house. As the initial euphoria concerning

Caroline gave way to rounds of petitioning and counter-petitioning from loyalists and Queenites, the Government gave every appearance of not knowing what it should do next. 'I wish only to be thoroughly & honourably released', Liverpool confided to Arbuthnot the week after Caroline's 'acquittal'.[149] Shortly before Christmas, Canning predicted to Huskisson that the Ministry would 'break down, or be broken down before Easter', while Sidmouth informed Charles Bathurst that the Prime Minister was 'in a very weary State of Mind, & Spirits'. Following the storms of November, Cabinet government had virtually ceased. 'It appears to me to be very doubtful', said Sidmouth (referring to Liverpool's Whitehall home, Fife House), 'from the Irritability at one great House, & the Restlessness &c &c at a greater, whether the Government will hold together'. In conclusion, Sidmouth added that he too was 'sick, & tired'.[150]

Notes

1   R. Gossez (ed.), *Un Ouvrier en 1820. Manuscrit inédit de Jacques-Etienne Bédé* (Paris: Presses Universitaires de France, 1984), p. 12. (My thanks to Fabrice Bensimon for this reference.)

2   *Republican*, 15 September, p. 79.

3   Though see H. Weisser, *British Working-Class Movements and Europe. 1815–48* (Manchester: Manchester University Press, 1975), pp. 7–31.

4   TNA, HO 40/11 fol. 109 (2 March).

5   E.g. *A New Year's Address to the Reformers of Great Britain* (London: Carlile, [1821]), p. 16 – 'Jan. 1st, Second Year of the Spanish Revolution from Despotism to Liberty'; Carlile's subsequent periodical *To the Reformers of Great Britain* was similarly dated.

6   TNA, HO 44/7 fol. 66 (9 March 1821); *Courier*, 16 September. For the anglophile leanings of Neapolitan revolutionaries around this time see illuminated in M. Isabella, *Risorgimento in Exile: Italian Emigrés and the Liberal International in the Post-Napoleonic Era* (Oxford: Oxford University Press, 2009), esp. 137–46.

7   *Leeds Mercury*, 8 April and 5 August.

8   P. Quennell (ed.), *The Private Letters of Princess Lieven to Prince Metternich, 1820–1826* (London: Murray, 1937), pp. 53 and 56; BL, Add. Mss 38387 fol. 212 (Castlereagh to the Admiralty, 13 September).

9   *Republican*, 15 September, 10 March.

10   Letter, 14 September, quoted in *Wellington and his Friends: Letters of the First Duke of Wellington … selected and edited by the seventh Duke of Wellington* (London: Macmillan, 1965), p. 9.

11   F. Bamford and G. W. Wellington (eds), *The Journal of Mrs Arbuthnot, 1820–32: vol. 1, February 1820 to December 1825* (London: Macmillan, 1950), p. 37; *Leeds Mercury*, 16 September BL, Add. Mss 30109, fol. 125 (14 September); see also fol. 124 (12 September).

12   *Republican*, 13 October.

13   *Morning Chronicle*, 3 October; *Black Dwarf*, 4 October. *Republican*, 6 October.

14   *To the Radical Reformers, Male and Female, of England, Ireland, and Scotland*, 10 Feb 1821; *Republican*, 8 December 1820.

15   N., 'Ode to the genius of revolutions', *Black Dwarf*, 2 August.

16   *Black Dwarf*, 21 June; *Leeds Mercury*, 29 July, 16 September.

17   *Republican*, 20 October. See also 18 February and 9 June. Carlile returned to the same

theme early the following year with his *The Character of a Soldier; by Philanthropos* (London: Carlile, 1821).

18 HO 40/14 fols. 200–02 (21 August); *The Times*, 22 September; I. McCalman, *Radical Underworld: Prophets, Revolutionaries and Pornographers in London, 1795–1840* (Cambridge: Cambridge University Press, 1988), pp. 173–4.
19 *HC Deb*, 14 June (vol. 1, col. 1081).
20 *Ibid.* (cols 1086, 1092).
21 *Ibid.* (col. 1094).
22 *Republican*, 21 April 1820.
23 *Leeds Mercury*, 16 September.
24 F. K. Donnelly, 'John Vallance', in J. Bellamy and J. Saville (eds), *Dictionary of Labour Biography* (Basingstoke: Macmillan, 1993), vol. 9, p. 282.
25 G. Pentland, *The Spirit of the Union: Popular Politics in Scotland, 1815–20* (London: Pickering & Chatto, 2011), pp. 110–11.
26 G. Pentland, '"Betrayed by infamous spies"? The commemoration of Scotland's "Radical War" of 1820', *Past & Present*, 201 (2008); Pentland, *Spirit of the Union*, pp. 131–44.
27 *York Herald*, 29 January; *Yorkshire Gazette*, 3 June.
28 *York Chronicle*, 27 July.
29 *The Times*, 9 May, 1 August; *York Herald*, 13 May; HO 40/13 fols 57–9 (30 April), 79–110 (May). For later 'insults to the military' in Preston see HO 40/13 fol. 310 (proclamation, 16 June).
30 HO 40/14 fols 82 (Byng to Hobhouse, 31 July), 117, 126, 152 (July–August); *Manchester Observer*, 12 July.
31 HO 40/14 fols 59 (Byng to Hobhouse, 14 and 25 July); fol. 165 (Maj.Genl Lyons to Sidmouth, 19 August).
32 *Diary and Correspondence of Charles Abbot, Lord Colchester, edited by his son Charles, Lord Colchester* (London: Murray, 1861), vol. 3, p. 127 (Wilbraham to Colchester, 11 April).
33 P. H. Fitzgerald, *Life of George IVth* (London: Tinsley, 1881), vol. 2, p. 243; *Ipswich Journal*, 18 November; E. Phipps (ed.), *Memoirs of the Political and Literary Life of Robert Plumer Ward* (London: Murray: 1850), vol. 2, p. 55.
34 HO 44/3/164 (6 December).
35 *York Herald*, 11 November; *The Times*, 14 August, 20, 25 September; HO 40/14 fol. 105 (12 August).
36 *The Journal of Mrs Arbuthnot*, vol. 1, p. 27; *London Gazette*, 15 July; Hobhouse to Byron, 14 July, quoted in C. P. W. Graham (ed.), *Byron's Bulldog: The Letters of John Cam Hobhouse to Lord Byron* (Columbus: Ohio State University Press, 1984), p. 295.
37 Colchester, *Diary and Correspondence*, p. 146 (letter from Legge, 10 July).
38 HO 40/14 fol. 87 (3 August).
39 *The Times*, 15 August; HO 40/14 fols 87, 145–8; *Manchester Observer*, 19 August.
40 HO 100/198/449–54 (Colonel Sorrel, 3 June); NAI, SOC/2181/17 (3 June); SOC/2173/40 (24 July).
41 HO 100/199/230 (28 September), see also 100/199/161 (1 September).
42 K. T. Hoppen argues this phasing typified the period 1806–32, see his *Ireland since 1800: Conflict and Conformity* (Harlow: Longman, 1999), p. 50.
43 J. S. Donnelly, Jr, *Captain Rock: The Irish Agrarian Rebellion of 1821–24* (Cork: Collins, 2009), pp. 124–5; NAI, SOCP/1/2171/4 (23 February); *A New Cathaleen Thrial* (Limerick, 1821), quoted in G-D. Zimmermann, *Songs of Irish Rebellion: Political Street Ballads and Rebel Songs, 1780–1900* (Dublin: Figgis, 1967), p. 30.
44 HO 100/199/230 (Grant to Sidmouth, 28 September).
45 E.g. from Llangyfelach and Llandeilo-Talybont (Glamorganshire), *HP*, vol. 3, p. 416.

46   *The Times*, 17 August.

47   K. Cave (ed.), *The Diary of Joseph Farington: Volume XVI, January 1820–December 1821* (London: Yale University Press, 1984), p. 5533 (conversation with Lawrence, Smirke and Dance, 3 July).

48   H. G. Mundy (ed.), *The Journal of Mary Frampton* (London: Sampson Law, 1885) p. 317 (2 October); BL, Add. Mss 38285 fol 172 (Hutchinson to Liverpool, 3 June); J. G. Lockhart (ed.), *Memoirs of the Life of Sir Walter Scott*, 2nd edn (Edinburgh: Cadell, 1839), vol. 6, p. 229.

49   E. A. Smith, *Lord Grey, 1764–1845* (Oxford: Oxford University Press, 1990), p. 229 (present author's emphasis). See also Fitzwilliam's correspondence with his son, and a notebook kept, during the trial: Sheffield Archives, Wentworth Woodhouse Muniments G/14/1–39, and F/64/100.

50   A. Temple Patterson, *Radical Leicester: A History of Leicester, 1780–1850* (Leicester University Press, 1975), p. 129; *The Journal of Mrs Arbuthnot*, p. 40.

51   H. E. Vassall (ed.), *Memoirs of the Whig Party During My Time by Henry Richard Lord Holland* (London: Longmans, 1854), vol. 2, p. 121; *Further Memoirs of the Whig Party, 1807–21, with some Miscellaneous Reminiscences, by Henry Richard Vassall, Third Lord Holland, edited by Lord Stavordale* (London: Murray, 1905), p. 285.

52   Horace Twiss, *The Public and Private Life of Lord Chancellor Eldon, with Selections from his Correspondence* (London: Murray, 1844), vol. 2, p. 366; Charles Stewart to Castlereagh, quoted in J. Bew, *Castlereagh: Enlightenment, War and Tyranny* (London: Quercus, 2011), p. 470.

53   *The Letters of Percy Bysshe Shelley, Volume 2: Shelley in Italy*, edited by Frederick L. Jones (Oxford: Oxford University Press, 1964), pp. 207 (letter to John and Maria Gisborne, 30 June) and 220 (to Thomas Medwin, 20 July).

54   *Private Letters of Princess Lieven*, pp. 87 (31 October) and 70 (6 September).

55   T. Sadler (ed.) *Diary, Reminiscences, and Correspondence of Henry Crabb Robinson* (London: Macmillan, 1872), vol. 1, p. 196.

56   *Diary of Joseph Farington*, vol. XVI, pp. 5553, 5546 (28 August and 3 September); A. Cunningham, *The Life of Sir David Wilkie* (London: Murray, 1843), vol. 2, p. 46 (Wilkie to his sister, 25 October).

57   DRO, 152M/C/1820/OH/61 (Boswell to Sidmouth, 8 November).

58   Lockhart, *Sir Walter Scott*, p. 229.

59   BL, Add. Mss 38742 fol. 31 (1 October).

60   TNA, HO 40/14 fol. 84 (3 August).

61   Colchester, *Diary and Correspondence*, p. 146 (letter from Wilbraham, 20 June), p. 141.

62   T. Lever (ed.), *The Letters of Lady Palmerston, Selected and Edited from the Originals at Broadlands and Elsewhere* (London: Murray, 1957), p. 36 (26 June).

63   *The Complete Works of William Hazlitt*, ed. P. P. Howe (London: Dent, 1934), vol. 20, p. 136.

64   E. M. Seymour (ed.), *The 'Pope' of Holland House: Selections from the Correspondence of John Whishaw and his Friends* (London: Fisher Unwin, 1901), p. 227 (Whishaw to Charles Romilly, 11 November).

65   *Yorkshire Gazette*, 19 August; Farington, *Diary*, p. 5517; *Diary and Correspondence of … Lord Colchester*, pp. 141, 161; *The Times*, 7 June; the Earl of Carlisle, quoted in C. W. New, *The Life of Henry Brougham to 1830* (Oxford: Oxford University Press, 1961), p. 252.

66   A. Stott, *Hannah More: The First Victorian* (Oxford: Oxford University Press, 2003), p. 317.

67   Ward, *Memoirs*, p. 94.

68 A. Gordon, 'Fellowes, Robert (1770–1847)', rev. Mark Clement, *Oxford Dictionary of National Biography* (Oxford: Oxford University Press, 2004), online edn [http://0-www.oxforddnb.com.wam.leeds.ac.uk/view/article/9266]; L. W. Cowie, 'Parr, Samuel (1747–1825)', *Oxford Dictionary of National Biography* (Oxford: Oxford University Press, 2004), online edn [http://0-www.oxforddnb.com.wam.leeds.ac.uk/view/article/21402], both accessed 22 Aug 2011.

69 G. Spater, *William Cobbett: The Poor Man's Friend* (Cambridge: Cambridge University Press, 1982), vol. 2, p. 398.

70 *Cobbett's Weekly Political Register*, 7 October, 9 December, 18 November.

71 *The Times*, 12 September, 12 and 24 October; T. W. Whitley, *Parliamentary Representation of Coventry* (Coventry: Curtis, 1894) p. 264; Thomas W. Laqueur, 'The Queen Caroline affair: politics as art in the reign of George IV', *Journal of Modern History*, 54:3 (1982), pp. 427–8; *Morning Chronicle*, 20 November; *HP*, vol. 2, p. 834.

72 *Observer*, 2 October.

73 Inscription on lusterware jug, illustrated in D. Drakard, *Printed English Pottery: History and Humour in the Reign of George III, 1760–1820* (London: Horne, 1992), p. 258.

74 Figure based on personal observation in addition to listings in the following: [Blewitt, James] Bethnal Green Museum of Childhood, *Jubilation: Royal Commemorative Pottery from the Collection of James Blewitt* (London: HMSO, 1977), pp. 9–11; Drakard, *Printed English Pottery*, pp. 257–60; D. H. Flynn and A. H. Bolton, *British Royalty: Commemoratives* (Atlglen, PA: Schiffer, 1999), p. 179; John and Griselda Lewis, *Pratt Ware: English and Scottish Relief Decorated and Underglaze Coloured Earthenware, 1780–1840*, 2nd edn (Woodbridge: Antique Collectors' Club, 2006), pp. 128–31.

75 Sue Prichard, *Quilts, 1700–2010: Hidden Histories, Untold Stories* (London: V&A, 2010), pp. 80, 186. Brecon was a noted centre of Queenite activity, see: *Selections from the Queen's Answers to Various Addresses Presented to Her* (London: Hatchard, 1821), p. 48; *Cambrian*, 4 November; *Bristol Mercury*, November 27; *The Times*, 27 December; *HP*, vol, 3, pp. 340.

76 P. A. Custer, 'Refiguring Jemima: gender, work and politics in Lancashire 1770–1820', *Past and Present*, 195 (2007). See also A. Randall, *Riotous Assemblies* (Oxford: Oxford University Press, 2006), pp. 100–13, 176, 212, 224, 232, 241–3, 312–13, 319; N. Rogers, *Crowds, Culture and Politics in Georgian Britain* (Oxford: Oxford University Press, 1998), pp. 214–47.

77 *Liverpool Mercury*, 24 November.

78 *HP*, vol. 2, p. 270; A. F. J. Brown, *Chartism in Essex and Suffolk* (Chelmsford: Essex RO, 1982), p. 16. See also K. Gleadle, *Borderline Citizens: Women, Gender, and Political Culture in Britain, 1815–67* (Oxford: Oxford University Press, 2009), pp. 42–3, 67.

79 *Private Letters of Princess Lieven*, p. 66 (27 August).

80 BL, Add. Mss 38287 fol. 44–5 (16 August); *Letters of Lady Palmerston*, p. 39 (17 August); H. Maxwell (ed.), *The Creevey Papers: A Selection from the Correspondence and Diaries of the Late Thomas Creevey, MP*, 3rd edn (London: Murray, 1912), p. 318.

81 Calculation based on Stanley Palmer, *Police and Protest in England and Wales, 1780–1850* (Cambridge: Cambridge University Press, 1988), Table 5.1, p. 190.

82 *Private Letters of Princess Lieven*, pp. 69 and 77 (28 August and 3 October); DRO, 152M/C/1820/OR/44 (Liverpool to Sidmouth, 20 July), 152M/C/1820/OH/82 (Sidmouth to Bloomfield, 19 September). For death threats see especially TNA, HO 44/3/166–193 (October to November) and BL, Add. Mss 38288 fols 171 and 259 (22 November and 9 December).

83 TNA, HO 44/3/18 (28 September).

84 *The Old Black Cock and the Dunghill Advisers in Jeopardy; or, the Place that Jack Built*

(London: Wilson, 1820); *Sultan Sham and his Seven Wives* (London: Benbow, 1820); *Kouli Khan; or, the Progress of Error* (London: Benbow, 1820); *The Queen and the Mogul: A Play in Two Acts* (London: Benbow, 1820); *Lucretia and Runjumdildopunt; or, John Bull in Search of the Pathetic. A serious musical farce, in Three Acts* (London: Benbow, 1820); *The Kettle Abusing the Pot. A Satirical Poem by the Black Dwarf* (London: Johnston, 1820).

85 *The Political House that Jack Built* (London: Hone, 1819), fols 5–6.

86 TNA, HO 44/1/108 (19 February); HO 44/2/158 (18 June); L. Shepard, *John Pitts, Ballad Printer of Seven Dials, London, 1765–1844* (London: Private Libraries Association, 1969), p. 60. See John Gardner, *Poetry and Popular Protest: Peterloo, Cato Street and the Queen Caroline Controversy* (Basingstoke: Palgrave, 2011), pp. 157–214, for an insightful reading of the Queenite literature, extending the frame of reference to Byron and Shelley.

87 HO 33/2/166–172 (4 September).

88 H. C. Bolton, *Counting-out Rhymes of Children: Their Antiquity, Origin, and Wide Distribution. A Study in Folk-Lore* (London: Elliot Stock, 1888), p. 116; Flora Thompson, *Lark Rise* (Oxford: Oxford University Press, 1939), p. 167; I. and P. Opie, *Lore and Language of Schoolchildren* (Oxford: Oxford University Press, 1959), p. 20.

89 E. Rickword, *Radical Squibs and Loyal Ripostes* (London: Adams & Dart, 1971).

90 Vic Gatrell, *City of Laughter: Sex and Satire in Eighteenth-Century London* (New York: Walker, 2006), p. 232.

91 For other readings of this print see McCalman, *Radical Underworld*, pp. 173–5 and Gatrell, *City of Laughter*, p. 202.

92 *The Journal of Mrs Arbuthnot*, vol. 1, p. 33. The picture is described in detail in the *Examiner*, 6 August.

93 Hobhouse, *Diary*, p. 34; *Private Letters of Princess Lieven*, p. 62 (19 August); BL, Add. Mss 38287, fol. 168 (Lord Henry Bathurst to Liverpool, 3 September).

94 *Creevey Papers*, p. 318.

95 W. J. Linton, *Memories* (London: Lawrence & Bullen, 1895), p. 2.

96 Sheffield Archives, Wentworth Woodhouse Muniments G/14/1/17 (3 September); *Morning Chronicle*, 19 October; *Examiner*, 22 October; Ward, *Memoirs*, p. 69.

97 *Examiner*, 22 October; *The Times*, 19 October; *Morning Post*, 19 and 20 October.

98 University of York, Borthwick Institute, Raymond Burton Collection 29/20, Theatre Royal Hull, 15 December; Leeds Central Library, Local Studies Library, playbills collection, Leeds Theatre 13 June 1821.

99 *Yorkshire Gazette*, 19 August.

100 *The Important and Eventful Trial of Queen Caroline, Consort of George IV for Adulterous Intercourse with Bartolomo Bergami* (London: Smeeton, 1820), pp. 37, 40–1, 43, 45, 47–8, 393–4, 396, 403–4.

101 *The Trial of Her Majesty, Queen Caroline, Consort of George IV for an Alleged Adulterous Intercourse* (London: Kaygill, 1820), pp. 202–3, 342, 391–5, 592, 598, 637, 642, 658, 668–9, 681–2.

102 *Important and Eventful Trial*, pp. 174–5; *The Trial at Large of Her Majesty Caroline Amelia Elizabeth, Queen of Great Britain, in the House of Lords* (London: Kelly, 1821), vol. 1, p. 366.

103 *Trial at Large of Her Majesty*, vol. 2, 461. The quotation was from Tacitus (*Annals*, book 14, ch. 60), concerning Nero's attempt to divorce his empress Octavia.

104 *Morning Post*, 24 August – 26 December, around fifty times in all. The phrase also appears elsewhere, e.g. *Courier*, 14 November.

105 Colchester, *Diary*, p. 162; D.Verey (ed.), *The Diary of a Cotswold Parson: Reverend F. E. Witts, 1783–1854* (Stroud: Sutton, 1978), pp. 22–3; *York Herald*, 30 September.

106 *Important and Eventful Trial*, pp. 287–89.

107 *Ibid.*, pp. 72–145 passim.

108 *The Cock of Cotton Walk and Maid of all Work, alias "Non mi Ricordo"* (London: Pritchard, 1820); *Doll Tear-Sheet alias the Countess "Je ne me rappelle pas" a match for "Non mi ricordo"* (London: Fairburn, 1820); *New Inventions! The Conyngham Trap ... Demont's Machine ... The Majocchi Mouthpiece; or, Non Mi Ricordo Whistle* (London, 1820); Non Mi Ricordo (London: Pitts, 1820); *Non Mi Ricordo, &c. &c. &c.* (London: Hone, 1820, at least thirty-one editions in 1820); *Non mi Ricordo, a Favorite waltz, for the Harp or Piano Forte, etc* (London: Bates, n.d.).

109 Ward, *Memoirs*, pp. 63 and 71 (19 and 30 October); C. D.Yonge (compiler), *The Life and Administration of Robert Banks, Second Earl of Liverpool* (London: Macmillan, 1868), p. 106.

110 *The Journal of Mrs Arbuthnot*, pp. 41–2; *HC Deb*, 7 June 1820 (vol. 1 col. 967).

111 *Ibid.*, p. 45.

112 Ward, *Memoirs*, p. 70 (2 November).

113 Letter to Byron, 14 July, reprinted in Graham, *Byron's Bulldog*, p. 296.

114 Letter, received 10 November, quoted in *The Journal of Mrs Arbuthnot*, p. 52.

115 Twiss, *Lord Chancellor Eldon*, vol. 2, p. 399.

116 *The Journal of Mrs Arbuthnot*, p. 53, 57; *Wellington and His Friends*, p. 12; copy of the dismissal notice in A. Aspinall (ed.), *The Letters of King George IV, Volume 2, January 1815–January 1823* (Cambridge: Cambridge University Press, 1938), p. 380.

117 Aspinall, *Letters of George IV*, pp. 386–7; Historical Manuscripts Commission, *Report on the Manuscripts of Earl Bathurst, Preserved at Cirencester Park* (London: HMSO, 1923), p. 490 (Arbuthnot to Bathurst, 29 November). See also N. Gash, *Lord Liverpool: The Life and Political Career of Robert Banks Jenkinson* (London: Weidenfeld, 1984), p. 166.

118 Aspinall, *Letters of George IV*, vol. 2, pp. 388–9, 391–3; *The Times*, 24 November; *Creevey Papers*, p. 342.

119 *Durham Chronicle*, 25 November; *York Herald*, 25 November; BCL, Memorandum Book of William Varley (13 November).

120 H. Heavisides, *Centennial Edition of the Works of Henry Heavisides* (London: Simpson, 1895), pp. 393–4.

121 H. Martineau, *The History of England during the Thirty Years' Peace, 1816–46* (London: Knight, 1849), p. 258.

122 *HP*, vol. 3, pp. 663, 667, 731; *Dublin Evening Post*, 21 November; *Leinster Journal*, 25 November, 6 December; *The Times*, 25 November.

123 *York Herald*, Saturday 25 November 1820; *The Times*, 18 November; *Inverness Courier*, 7 December, cited in *HP*, vol. 3, p. 650.

124 M. R. Mitford, *Our Village: Sketches of Rural Character and Scenery*, 3rd edn (London: Whitaker, 1825), p. 3 (describing Three Mile Cross, south of Reading).

125 *Inverness Courier*, 7 December, cited in *HP*, vol. 3, p. 650.

126 *Durham Chronicle*, 18 and 25 November; *York Herald*, 25 November; *Morning Chronicle*, 18 November; *Trewman's Exeter Flying Post*, 23 November; *The Times*, 18, 21 November.

127 *York Herald*, 25 November; *Yorkshire Gazette*, 2 December; *Manchester Observer*, 2 December; *Morning Chronicle*, 22 November; *Durham Chronicle*, 18 November; *HP*, vol. 3, p. 372; *The Times*, 21 November.

128 *The Times*, 24 November; *West Briton*, 8 December, quoted in *HP*, vol. 2, p. 171; Heavisides, *Centennial Edition*, p. 393–4; *Durham Chronicle*, 18 November.

129 BL, Add. Mss 38288 fol. 186; TNA, HO 44/7/5 (4 January 1821).

130 Rogers, *Crowds, Culture and Politics*, pp. 254, 265–6; *The Times*, 22 November; W. B. Lighton, *Narrative of the Life and Sufferings of William B. Lighton* (Concordia, NY: the author, 1838), p. 49.
131 *HP*, vol. 2, p. 331; R. A. E. Wells and J. Rule, *Crime, Protest and Popular Politics in Southern England, 1740–1850* (Hambledon, 1997), p. 179; *Bury and Norwich Post*, 22 November; *Jackson's Oxford Journal*, 18 November; *The Times*, 20 November; *HP*, vol. 2, p.762.
132 *The Times*, 16, 21, 20, 23 November; *York Herald*, 18 November; *Dublin Evening Post*, 8 December.
133 Lever, *Letters of Lady Palmerston*, p. 60; *Jackson's Oxford Journal*, 18 November.
134 *The Times*, 20 November; *HP*, vol. 2, pp. 301, 532, vol 3, p. 15; *Hampshire Telegraph*, 20 November; Rogers, *Crowds, Culture and Politics*, p. 262.
135 C. H. Cooper, *Annals of Cambridge* (Cambridge: Warwick, 1842), vol. 4, p. 529; *The Times*, 17–18, 23 November; *HP*, vol. 2, p. 532.
136 C. M. M. Macdonald, 'Abandoned and beastly? The Queen Caroline affair in Scotland', in Y. G. Brown and R. Ferguson (eds), *Twisted Sisters: Women, Crime and Deviance in Scotland since 1400* (East Linton: Tuckwell, 2004), p. 103.
137 *Caledonian Mercury*, 18 December.
138 Pentland, *Spirit of the Union*, p. 118.
139 J. Strawhorn, *The History of Ayr: Royal Burgh and County Town* (Edinburgh, Donald, 1989), p. 155: *Glasgow Herald*, 17, 20 November.
140 *The Journal of Mrs Arbuthnot*, p. 58 (7 December); Strawhorn, *Ayr*, p. 155; *The Times*, 21 November.
141 *York Herald*, 25 November; *Leeds Mercury*, 9, 18 Nov 1820; *The Times*, 16, 23 November; WYAS (Leeds), Harewood Mss WYL/250/6/2/B1/5/56 (Chippendale to Harewood, 14 November); *HP*, vol. 2, pp. 277, 297; *Morning Chronicle*, 22 November; BL, Add. Mss 38288 fol. 231 (1 December).
142 *A Report of the Proceedings at a Meeting of the Town of Kingston-upon-Hull, for the Purposes of Considering the Measures that have been Adopted to Degrade, Dethrone & Divorce Her Majesty Queen Caroline* (Hull: Ross, 1820), p. 9.
143 For tensions round 5 November, doleing days and church ringers see B. Bushaway, *By Rite: Custom, Ceremony and Community in England, 1700–1880* (London: Junction, 1982), pp. 48–74, 180–90, 257–8, and E. Griffin, *England's Revelry: A History of Popular Sports and Pastimes, 1660–1830* (Oxford: Oxford University Press, 2005), pp. 110–12.
144 DRO, 152M/C/1820/OR/23 (11 December).
145 *York Herald*, 25 November.
146 BL, Add. Mss 51609, letter to Sir Robert Adair, 8 March).
147 Hobhouse to Byron, 31 March, reprinted in Graham (ed.), *Byron's Bulldog*, p. 287; Russell, conversation with Thomas Moore, 24 November 1820, quoted in *Memoirs, Journal, and Correspondence of Thomas Moore*, edited by the Right Honourable Lord John Russell, M.P. (London: Longmans, 1853), vol. 3, p. 172.
148 Pentland, *Spirit of the Union*, p. 125.
149 Liverpool to Arbuthnot, 13 November, reprinted in A. Aspinall, *The Correspondence of Charles Arbuthnot*, Camden 3rd ser (Royal Historical Society, 1941), vol. 65, p. 21. See Gash, *Liverpool* (London: Weidenfeld, 1984), p. 165 for Liverpool's own family afflictions at this time.
150 BL, Add. Mss 38742 fol. 156 (17 December); DRO, 152M/C/1820/OZ (15 December).

7 Conclusions

November's illuminations seen by winter's cold light

As 1820 drew to its close, there was little sense of achievement, still less triumphalism, within the Government. While staying at Wellington's country home a few days before Christmas, the Prime Minister relaxed enough to play charades, 'at which Lord Liverpool was very expert'. He drew the line, though, at blind man's buff ('such amusements w^d not sound well just now', Harriet Arbuthnot observed).[1] Cabinet members were preoccupied by a cluster of thorny issues. None could confidently predict how the pro-Caroline mood that had swept the country would play out. Some radicals were seized by an almost millenarian fervour: 'One year, such as the one we are now passing and approaching its close', declared Richard Carlile, 'is worth a life of twenty ordinary years'.[2] Viscount Exmouth (father-in-law of one of Sidmouth's daughters) was also in apocalyptic mood, but for very different reasons from Carlile: 'The people are mad, and the world is mad; and where it will end, the Lord only knows', he wrote to a brother admiral, 'but as sure as we live, the days of trouble are very fast approaching, when there will be much contention, and much bloodshed, and changes out of all measure and human calculation'.[3]

Writing to Exmouth on New Year's Eve, the Home Secretary was more optimistic: 'Reports from our Friends are extremely satisfactory. In fact, The Queen has destroy'd Herself.'[4] Yet the Christmas recess was suffused with anxious uncertainty. The abdication of the King could not be completely ruled out, still less his threat to dismiss Liverpool and invite the Whigs to form a government. And unexpectedly, the need for subterfuge had arisen concerning the resignation of George Canning as chairman of the Board of Control for India. As had been long anticipated, on 13 December Canning had resigned in protest at the treatment of Caroline; but Liverpool's failure to find any acceptable substitute threatened to expose the Ministry as incapable of effective government. Robert Peel had declined to rejoin the Cabinet even before Caroline's trial. Over

Christmas, with growing desperation, Liverpool and Sidmouth sought to persuade an unreceptive Charles Bathurst to take on India in addition to his Cabinet responsibilities as Chancellor of the Duchy of Lancaster. After considerable vacillation, which left his senior colleagues 'perplex'd in the extreme', Bathurst finally capitulated in January.[5]

It was fortunate for the Government that this small drama was played out during the parliamentary recess. Yet, even from the narrow perspective of party advantage, there were developments to lift Liverpool's spirits. During his overtures to the Whigs in the days following the collapse of the Caroline 'trial', it had been impressed on George IV that the restoration of the Queen to the Anglican liturgy was likely to be a Whig condition of office.[6] This was scarcely palatable; but the King had other reasons to ponder the desirability of a change of government, as he set out in a private memorandum headed 'THE EVILS ATTENDANT UPON A CHANGE OF GOVERNMENT':

> The known principles of the present Opposition may be designated under the term Libéraux; how are they to be met, for example, if they should propose the liberation of Bonaparté? How are they to be met, should they propose to change the system and spirit of my foreign policy – a policy, the successful application of which, has brought back everything to the country, and established a power and friendship with the Sovereigns and Govts of Europe, that England never before possessed? ... How are they to be met if they propose the emancipation of the Catholicks, a measure entirely opposite to my own conscientious feelings ... How are they to be met should they propose their two favorite objects, retrenchment, and at this moment, a reduction of the army; this latter measure would certainly place the country out of the pale of safety.[7]

Even in contemplating these evils, George IV could not resist complaining that Liverpool's ministers 'might have consulted my feelings more, and have added to my happiness, nay', he added, 'they have sacrificed both ... whatever of estimation I may have lost among my subjects ... I may justly date to them'. Yet he also conceded 'they have been a good Govt for the country'. The King's reservations were sufficiently clear to the Whigs to render them even less-enthusiastic about forming a ministry than they had been earlier in the year. By Christmas Earl Grey was able to conclude, not without some relief, that the King would 'have recourse to the devil himself rather than to the whig'.[8]

With benefit of hindsight, we can see that the year 1821 began, therefore, with the Government secure. The King could not stomach the Whigs, who in turn had no appetite for office; meanwhile the only alternative focus for a new ministry, the Grenvillites, declined to sup with the Whigs on account of their being (as we saw in Chapter 6) 'mixed up with Radicalism'. Their distaste for Whiggism was sufficient for the Grenvillites to join Liverpool's Ministry in 1822. Reconfiguring his administration that year, Liverpool also overcame Peel's reluctance to join the Cabinet with the offer of the Home Secretaryship; and both

Ireland's Lord Lieutenant and Chief Secretary, as unequal to the task of facing down the Rockites as they had been the Ribbonmen before them, were replaced. 'Among the measures taken by the government to restore tranquillity in Ireland was the recall of Lord Talbot and Mr Grant', the *Annual Register* commented.[9] Simultaneously the rigidly anti-papist Attorney General for Ireland was replaced by an energetic pro-Catholic.[10]

As the previous chapter showed, the Ribbonist rising in Connacht and adjoining districts was not sustained beyond the summer of 1820. The non-convergence of Irish and British disturbances beyond Easter powerfully contributed to the survival chances of Liverpool's Ministry. So too did the quietening of Scotland. We should also note in this context continuing calm (support for the Queen aside) of South Wales, the one British industrial region untouched by unrest in 1820. Scotland had constituted a major challenge to political stability in the spring of 1820, but all Wales offered was limited and polite debate around the future of its legal system, accompanied by little more than a flicker of nationalist sentiment. The absence of rural unrest in 1820 (a sharp contrast, for example, to England in 1822 and 1830, or Wales in 1843) similarly assisted the authorities. In Wales serious incidents were limited to isolated anti-enclosure riots at Maenchlochog Common (Pembrokeshire), and Mynydd Bach (Cardiganshire).[11] Nor did rural Scotland offer any parallel to the mood of the west-central industrial region, despite attempts by Clydeside radicals to capitalise on the sole Highland disturbance on the Culrain estate in Ross-shire. As Sidmouth noted with undisguised relief, 'no Political Feelings had any place in exciting or protracting them'.[12] And in rural England, reported unrest was limited to occasional arson attacks in East Anglia, at nineteen over double the previous year's total, but nevertheless spatially dispersed except for a cluster east of Ipswich.[13] Such incidents also abated in 1821.

In the country too, at least as far as the political nation was concerned, the Tory party might have faired worse. After the initial furore surrounding the 'acquittal' of Queen Caroline had subsided, attention turned to the issue of her exclusion from the liturgy. This was not an issue that could be progressed through the medium of demonstrations, however vibrant or solidly supported. It also opened up more scope for division than the general issue of the treatment of the Queen. Deploring that treatment was not incompatible with a belief that her past conduct had been unseemly or even adulterous. The liturgy question was more nuanced. Not all the population were attached to one of the established churches and therefore likely to hold strong views on the matter. In an age that took religion very seriously, liturgical matters would never be mere niceties; but this one did not necessarily embody substantial principles, particularly for those who felt that Caroline's behaviour fell short of what was expected of a princess, queen, wife or mother, however provocative her husband's behaviour. And tacti-cally it was far from clear whether the cause of the Queen (or her supporters at Westminster) would be advanced by associating the liturgy issues with broader topics such as the conduct of the Ministry or the case for political reform. Both Holland and Brougham believed that the liturgy alone should be the focal point for a nationwide campaign of petitioning and addresses. With the six acts still in force, meetings to adopt these had to be properly constituted according to the law. A plethora of resolutions were passed by public meetings but local cussedness would out. In some instances loyalists prevailed and an approving address to the King was sent. In others radical reformers sought to link the liturgical dispute to the broader issue of parliamentary reform.

Much emphasis was placed on county meetings. However, the Whigs' capacity to manage these proved very uneven. Some Whig grandees flatly declined to take the Queen's part; others thought the strategy might alienate support for the party. In Yorkshire two distinct lines of thought emerged, just as they had in the run-up to the October 1819 Yorkshire meeting. On that occasion, as we saw in Chapter 1, the county's leading Whigs had reluctantly acquiesced in their cautious draft resolutions concerning Peterloo being considerably widened, an act upon which Earl Fitzwilliam doubtless reflected darkly once dismissed as Lord Lieutenant for attending the meeting. This time caution got the better of the Fitzwilliam interest and plans for a meeting were abandoned. Brougham was similarly despairing in Cumberland; Oxfordshire Whigs carried the county meeting but could not obtain the Sheriff's signature, without which the adopted address had no legal status; and at the Shropshire meeting the Queenites led by Grey Bennet lost out to loyalists by a show of hands.[14]

Nonetheless, more pro-Caroline than loyalist addresses were sent up to London; and many loyal addresses came from closed corporations or had been adopted by subterfuge. The Whigs in general could bask in the lustre of their new-found status as friends of the Queen and her people but they failed utterly to translate this into political momentum inside Parliament, to the deep frustration of the radicals. 'What w^d they do if they failed?' Charles Arbuthnot asked Sir Robert Wilson. 'Oh! if we fail, our game is gone!', came the reply.[15] The House of Commons, to which Liverpool had dared not send the Bill of Pains and Penalties in November, voted down by thumping majorities in late January and February two motions to restore the Queen to the liturgy, and one criticising the policy of the Ministry as derogatory to the honour of the Crown.[16] It was a watershed in the Ministry's history and it reflected the unevenness of Whig claims to voice the views of country at large. As far as the country members were concerned, the situation was aptly summarised by James Stuart-Wortley. An independent and moderate Tory MP for Yorkshire, he was not unsympathetic to the Queen, having closely assisted Wilberforce in securing the conciliatory address adopted by the Commons the previous June. Now, referring to the first (and in retrospect most decisive) of the liturgy votes, Stuart-Wortley told the Commons:

He knew well in what manner the feeling of the country had been excited on the question; but if he were to be asked what was the wish of the country upon it, he would say, that it was, that the matter should be put entirely at rest, without any further persecution of her majesty, but with a strict care, at the same time, that her majesty should not triumph over any other party. In the vote which had been given on a former night, gentlemen had not looked so much at the justice or injustice of the particular question then before them, as to the point to which it was directed; and it was impossible to deny, that those who had voted for it had wished to use it as a means for turning out the present ministers and putting others into their places. Now, he was sure, the country had not sufficient confidence in any other set of public men to put them in the places of the present ministers.[17]

It seemed that the Queen, too, was now inclining towards putting things to rest. On 2 March she accepted the Government's offer of an annuity of £50,000. Although this still left a cluster of issues about her status and residence unresolved – not least her role, if any, in the long-postponed coronation – it fatally compromised the perception of Caroline as an innocent victim of governmental malice.[18] It is conceivable, too, that as memories of the glow of November's illuminations and bonfires receded in the cold light of winter, the Queen's personal reputation began to fall into perspective. Charles Arbuthnot's optimistic assessment of the events of November 1820 began to look realistic: 'She is blasted, & that is sufficient.'[19] 'The prospect is rather improving', an unusually sunny Sidmouth wrote to an old school friend on 14 February, 'the Weather has moderated, the Wind is not so loud and violent, and our good old Sea-boat is likely to ride out the Storm without damage'.[20]

Settling into a state of peace?

It is relatively easy to account for how Liverpool's Government rode out the parliamentary storm of 1820. It is more difficult to account for the moderation in the mood of those whom it governed. Throughout this study, weight has been placed upon the nature and extent of social unrest and on the forces that throughout almost all of 1820 tended to the destabilisation of normal order. However, histories of resistance risk descending into revolutionary antiquarianism. Resisters and resistance cannot be understood in isolation from the social and political forces that acted to hold them in check. There were many points in 1820 when those forces seemed close to rupture, and yet they held. How?

Any explanation needs to note first the quiet constitutional revolution identified in Chapter 1. The framework of local politics was easing to accommodate more of the middling sort, who had hitherto been marginalised or excluded. Despite appearances to the contrary during 1820, in England especially ongoing changes in the form and nature of local government were acting to strengthen social cohesion. Significantly this process was conspicuously absent in

Ireland. We saw in the first chapter how, since the early eighteenth century, innumerable local parliamentary acts had unevenly but steadily enhanced standards of public life. 'The rise of the parish as a dynamic politico-governmental forum', was one of the most notable features of the political landscape of the preceding decades.[21] Then, on the eve of 1820, there occurred through the select vestries acts a rapid evolution in the purpose and personnel of local government. Contemporaries saw in vestry reform a process through which local politics could be reinvigorated as well as a powerful instrument for controlling poor relief expenditure and the poor themselves. Improvement commissions and select vestries consolidated a sense of involvement in, and ownership of, local government among more substantial ratepayers who, however, fell below the threshold for service as magistrates and, typically, also the parliamentary franchise. Such bodies therefore had a powerful symbolic as well as practical value, especially during a period of heightened social tension. Sturges Bourne, the architect of the select vestry reforms, was disarmingly honest about their purpose. Referring to the tendency of open vestries 'to excite a violent democratic spirit', he told a Northumberland clergyman that his legislation 'was intended to counteract that spirit, which had driven men of property from the Vestry'.[22]

It is a commonplace of British history to portray the decades after 1832 as the age of reform, and to depict 1832 specifically as the point at which the middle classes were incorporated into the body politic. That, however, was a drawing out of processes that had been established earlier and it is not exaggerating to claim that the years around 1820 were ones of reforms, if not Reform. Historians, rightly impressed by the broad social cohesion evident among supporters of Queen Caroline, have overlooked the deeper and more enduring processes that the episode masked. In a similar way, the quiet renewal and reform of the ecclesiastical establishment (also touched on in the first chapter) is easily obscured beneath the dazzling irreverence and blasphemy, evident in so much of the popular literature of the period. Legislation of 1818 (Liverpool's 'Million Act') was beginning to bear fruit in a government-supported programme of church building and the division of the most populous parishes. It is important not to exaggerate the practical impact of this act, but psychologically it served to bolster the confidence of a hitherto sagging Established Church. The self-assurance of the Glasgow divine Thomas Chalmers, that revival within the establishment would 'bring us back again to a sound and wholesome state of the body politic' was ultimately misplaced.[23] Yet in Scotland as in England, the ecclesiastical establishment was not so inert that it contributed nothing to the maintenance of social order. We should note too that the main Protestant sects likewise tended to quieten rather than excite politics. 1820 stood in the midst of a prodigious increase in dissenting organisation in Wales, for example, with meeting houses opening in Cardiganshire at the rate of one every six weeks during the years 1816–20. Even this has been described as 'a fairly modest growth' compared with other Welsh counties, where the frequency was sometimes one every fortnight during the early nineteenth century.[24]

Another central factor in explaining social stability is almost prosaic, but demands serious attention nonetheless. The rhythm of restiveness was to a considerable extent dictated by forces beyond human control. In 1820 Ireland was recovering from a fever epidemic of a severity unparalleled in living memory. The Irish, like the British, were living with the consequences of 1819's poor harvest and, as a report from north-west England grimly observed, 'the harvest was scarcely finished when the winter set in'.[25] The effects of winter endured far into the summer. As a labourer told a Sheffield diarist in July, 'he was not so strong as he had been for last winter's starving had pulled him down'.[26] In both Britain and Ireland, however, the harvest of 1820 surpassed both hope and expectation. Food prices dropped sharply and remained there until 1825.[27] The significance of a good harvest was never far from the minds of those in government. 'The Weather is delightful; & though the Crops in the Neighbourhood of London have been very much laid by the late Rains, I still trust we shall have an abundant Harvest', Liverpool wrote to Sidmouth in July. 'The price of subsistence is very moderate, and still declining', Sidmouth reported to the King in September, adding 'the price of labour is gradually rising, the consequence of an increasing demand for it'.[28] Chief Secretary Grant similarly wrote from Dublin Castle to Westminster: though wages remained very low, the crops were good and the country 'thank God, is uninterestingly quiet'. Four weeks later he repeated the observation ('one can scarcely make this remark without trembling'), but overall the picture was even more satisfactory: 'the harvest is abundant beyond all precedent; and provisions of all kinds plentiful and cheap'.[29] William Huskisson (the intellectual force behind Government economic policy, though he would wait until 1823 for a Cabinet place) sent Lord Liverpool reports on wheat yields. The Prime Minister reciprocated with details from east Kent, where he was staying in late September: 'the Crops of every description have been greater than has been known for many years. I mention this as of considerable importance in its bearing upon the whole question ... Our internal situation is improving in all respects.'[30]

Liverpool's observations were not confined to the harvest. Robert Peel's 1819 Resumption of Cash Payments Act (see Chapter 5) meant that 'the Circulation is settled on a fixed foundation'. Notwithstanding the extent of military expenditure to assist in domestic peace-keeping, Government borrowing was more nearly under control ('annual Loans are beginning to be no longer wanted'). 'The Country appears, for the first time, to be settling itself into a state of Peace', the Prime Minister concluded.[31] The later history of the ultra-protectionist Central Agricultural Association (the initial progress of which was touched on in Chapter 5) offers further evidence of the blend of pragmatism, decisiveness and good fortune that carried the Liverpool Ministry into the calmer waters of 1821. The harvest was a major factor in stabilising domestic unrest. Abundance meant low prices, and low prices 'enable the Labourer and workman to subsist upon lower wages', Liverpool cheerfully observed.[32] These factors in turn fed recovery in the industrial sector; and overall economic improvement drew some of the force from opposition criticism of the Government. Visiting Manchester in October, the Whig Sidney Smith told a correspondent that the region's manufactures were 'materially mended, and are mending. I would not mention this to you, if you were not a good Whig', Smith added sardonically. 'The secret, I much fear, will get out ... There seems to be a fatality that which pursues us. When, oh when, shall we be really ruined?'[33]

The fall in agricultural prices might have translated into increasing restiveness among the landed interest. Yet it did not, even though *Evans and Ruffy's Farmers' Journal*, in a Christmas address to its readers, urged them on to greater effort, as so far 'all our anticipations of remedy (of just and necessary remedy) for our sufferings, have failed in fulfilment'.[34] Though obliged to consider a far broader range of complaints than its predecessor of 1820, the 1821 parliamentary committee on agricultural depression humiliated the Central Agricultural Association and its secretary, George Webb Hall. Its report (largely the work of Huskisson) firmly refuted all calls for increased protection in a document that has been read as envisioning 'an ever-open and progressively freer corn trade'.[35] The Government was helped by divisions in the agriculturalists' own ranks. A policy to maintain grain (and therefore feed) prices at an artificially inflated level would never be popular with livestock specialists, while the Association never marshalled significant support from landowners. The *Farmers' Journal* was most eloquent in the defence of tenant interests (even to the extent of defending protestors against the Ross-shire clearances). Webb Hall's parvenu status cannot have helped.

As we saw, Webb Hall had been dubbed 'a species of "Hunt" in Agriculture';[36] but this was a double-edged compliment. Rhetorical heat was no substitute for informed analysis and Hall exhibited too much of the former, and too little of the latter, before the 1821 committee. Ironically for a man who served for a quarter of a century as Clerk to the Corporation of Bristol, and also as agent to the city's dock company, Hall was a maladroit parliamentary witness. His elevation to the secretaryship of the Board of Agriculture also exposed his deficiencies as an administrator. The Board was a shadow of its former self; but it was still sufficiently close to the establishment for the real Henry Hunt to make political hay, claiming Webb Hall's appointment was a 'SOP' to keep him 'quiet and snug'. The chances of any extra-parliamentary alignment as a consequence of Hall's extension of the pressure group tactics of radicalism and anti-slavery into protection were nugatory. And his appointment, of course, was no sop at all. The cessation of the Association's government grant by Liverpool's diktat was a deathblow from which it never recovered. By July 1822 the Board of Agriculture was no more.[37]

Clearly, the Government benefitted from divisions within the landed and farming interest. Ultimately, however, the Ministry believed that its good fortune rested upon decisive action directed lower down the social scale. Reporting to the King in late September 1820, Sidmouth shamelessly advertised that 'the far greater Number of those who had been most active, & successful in perverting and inflaming the minds of the Labouring Classes are either imprisoned, transported, or fled from the country'.[38] It is the repressive policy of the Liverpool Ministry at this time that has most consistently caught the attention of posterity. All the key figures of the English radical leadership were gaoled for at least part of 1820 or living in the shadow of prison: Sir Francis Burdett, guilty of seditious libel, serving three months and fined £2000; Richard Carlile, guilty of seditious libel and sentenced in November 1819 to six years in Dorchester Gaol; William Cobbett, bankrupt and living under the rules of King's Bench prison between April and October; John Cam Hobhouse, gaoled from December 1819 until 29 February; Henry Hunt, convicted of sedition in March and gaoled for two and a half years; Robert Wedderburn, arrested in January, refused bail and sentenced in May to two years' imprisonment; Sir Charles Wolseley, found guilty of sedition and conspiracy in April, and sentenced to eighteen months; and *Black Dwarf's* editor Thomas Wooler, sentenced to fifteen months.

Those at liberty in 1820, but precariously so, included William Benbow, arrested in May 1821 and imprisoned for eight months without trial, largely on the personal initiative of the King;[39] Major Cartwright, convicted of sedition in August at the age of eighty and finally brought up for sentencing nine months later (when he was fined £100); and Thomas J. Evans, editor of the *Manchester Observer*, charged with libelling the army in its 29 April issue and gaoled twelve months later for a year. Then there is a penumbra of pressmen who may or may not have been aware that the Government's law officers were actively considering prosecuting them: Edward Baines of the *Leeds Mercury* (for the tone of his Peterloo reporting); John Wade (three separate cases relating to numbers of the *Black Book*); the editor of *The Times* (for remarks about George IV), and of the *Examiner* (for its reporting of the Guards' mutiny).[40]

Of lesser figures the list is almost endless: Samuel Bamford, weaver of Middleton, and John Knight, bookseller of Oldham, tried alongside Hunt and each gaoled for a year; Joseph Harrison, dissenting minister and schoolmaster of Stockport, tried alongside Wolseley for sedition and conspiracy and gaoled for eighteen months; Spencean James Watson, gaoled for debt in January; James Wroe, gaoled for a year and fined £100 for selling Carlile's *Republican*; two Birmingham men found guilty of selling *Black Book* number 12; vendors of radical papers in Exeter, London, Manchester and Southampton; twenty Yorkshire textile workers imprisoned or transported for high treason after Grange Moor.

Not all of these sentences were the result of central direction: local discretion was generally reliable in bringing minor offenders to court, while Cobbett and Watson were fortuitously subjects of civil prosecution. However even a brief perusal of the Treasury Solicitor's papers for the period reveals the extent to which the prosecution of alleged political offences was a central preoccupation of Government. As far as its containment of radical opposition was concerned, the success of Liverpool's administration rested less on the sentences handed down to the Cato Street conspirators, who were at best ambiguous martyrs. Rather success derived from the steady attritional consequences of prosecuting lesser political offenders. Almost the only radical figures of note at liberty throughout 1820 were William Hone and George Cruikshank, but their case raises interesting issues that further illustrate the efforts of the establishment to contain, and in certain circumstances even suppress, freedom of speech. As we saw in the last chapter, it was difficult to convict artists, engravers or publishers of graphic material, though this did not deter the Treasury Solicitor from accumulating ninety-one prints issued by thirteen different publishers, apparently with a view to prosecution. The usual (albeit haphazard) medium to regulate the trade was to buy off the perpetrators. William Benbow, for example, was paid £100 by the Crown to suppress cartoons he had published that depicted the King and Lady Conygnham, the latest royal mistress, in June 1820; he and his engraver received a further £45 in November for withdrawing a further print on the same subject, plus £50 for suppressing the verses he printed beneath. Benbow felt no obligation to act on these payments and this explains the eight months he spent in custody the following year, prior to a trial for publishing the prints at which – predictably – he was acquitted.[41] Benbow was not the only graphic publisher bought off in 1820, as Vic Gatrell's vivid and meticulous recreation of this shadowy world makes clear: 'The royal archives at Windsor reveal that between 1819 and 1822 George spent some £2,600 to achieve these silencings. The scale of this pay-off was substantial. That sum total equals about £100,000 in modern values.' Among the recipients of this regal hush money was George Cruikshank, who received £100 in June, 'in consideration of a pledge not to caricature his majesty in any immoral situation'.[42] Cruikshank was a spendthrift and an alcoholic. He needed the money; but unlike Benbow he kept his promise. His woodcuts continued to appear in further editions of his celebrated collaborations with Hone, but his output of full-scale political prints dwindled. Cruikshank had in any case always sold his talents to whoever was prepared to pay him, and his 1820 output included scarifying treatments of radicalism alongside the anti-loyalist material for which is more usually remembered (see Figure 8).

The silencing of Cruikshank and attempts to buy off others were not the only actions that helped shore-up the tottering reputation of authority. Arguably they were not even the most important. December 1820 saw a concerted attempt to reverse the progress of radical sentiment, first through 'the Constitutional Association for Opposing the Progress of Seditious and Disloyal Principles', and second *John Bull*. With cheerful abandon, this new Sunday

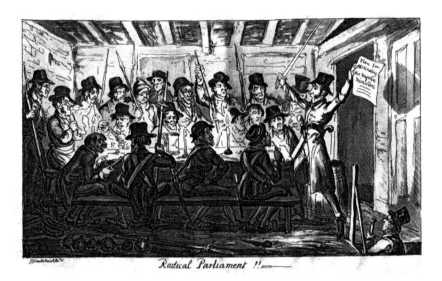

Radical Parliament !!

Figure 8 'Radical Parliament': the Cato Street conspirators plan the Cabinet's assassination

newspaper sought every opportunity to repay those who impugned the morality of the monarch in their own coin.

The founders of the Constitutional Association believed that 'a comparatively small number of individuals', via 'the medium of a licentious press … inundates the nation with an unexampled profusion of slanderous, seditious, and blasphemous publications', with the aim of fomenting revolution. Its strategy was to coordinate the efforts of local loyalist associations (which had declined since 1815), act as a prosecuting society, and actively encourage publications that refuted the 'wicked and designing'. Its objects 'must be deemed of prime importance by every reflecting mind', declared Wordsworth, an early supporter. Working closely with Government law officers, the Association was responsible for a number of high-profile prosecutions, including Benbow's, a burden it shouldered rather than expose the Government to the humiliation of failure in a highly speculative case.[43] The Government itself also redoubled its efforts to cultivate the mainstream press. It had long discretely subsidised the *New Times*, whose editor John Stoddart was one of the prime movers behind the Constitutional Association. By late November, copies of *New Times* and the *Courier* (the other main ministerial paper) were being sent by the Government to sympathetic Tory news offices in the provinces, their columns marked up to draw attention to items that might usefully be reprinted. On Castlereagh's instructions, his secretary also 'gave the tone' to the *Courier*'s coverage of domestic politics.[44]

John Bull may have originated in a discussion in late November between Liverpool and a senior official at the Treasury, about applying secret service money to give 'proper direction to the public mind' concerning Caroline.[45] The earliest biographer of its main contributor hinted that George IV discretely provided finance.[46] Certainly its proprietor, William Shackell, hitherto a printer of loyalist squibs, switched to newspaper production with surprising speed.[47] Since early 1820 the figure of John Bull had been located at the heart of popular loyalist literature. Bull, 'whose TASTE, in literary matters, is not very fastidious', to quote a Shackell pamphlet, 'will never be laughed out of his loyalty, and common sense … being rather prejudiced in favor of such old fashioned things, as kingly governments and the Bible'.[48] The 'John Bull' trope was a calculated move to reinstate masculinity at the heart of popular politics, which the Caroline cult had decentred. *John Bull* was on launched 17 December with an opening editorial salvo against 'this sickening woman'. Its rhetoric and ideology was emphatically anti-feminine, even misogynistic. Predictably it picked over the evidence from the Bill of Pains and Penalties to recycle every sensational or salacious detail that told against the Queen. It also made a particular point of embarrassing any woman who associated with her. Ladies in society, regardless of their status, who were presented to Caroline could now expect to be vilified for it, with the additional implication that a willingness to meet the Queen indicated approval of (even perhaps a shared taste for) sexual promiscuity. And where it could, *John Bull* went further. Brougham's wife was said to have conceived the couple's first child out of wedlock. The sculptor Anne Seymour Damer, a prominent figure in Whig circles, was branded a lesbian. The Countess of Tankerville was said to have been coerced into visiting the Queen by a husband who had threatened to expose her daughter's 'criminal intrigue with her menial servant', and the Duchess of Bedford by 'the base tyranny' of the Duke (a hint perhaps she was a victim of domestic violence).[49]

By the end of its first month *John Bull* was selling 10,000 copies every Sunday. A mystery donor met the costs of a special Monday edition, distributed free to coaching inns, as a means of extending its influence into the provinces.[50] Harriet Arbuthnot praised it as 'most ably written' and for having 'done more towards putting down the Queen than any thing', though she added 'it has certainly been wrong in attacking the characters of women'.[51] That, however, was a considerable factor in its success. Nor was *John Bull* the most extreme assault upon female support for the Queen's cause. That dubious accolade belonged to the anonymous *Gynecocracy*, published in Plymouth and London in March 1821. At its heart was a reaction to the mass mobilisation of female energies that had been one of the most striking aspects of the Queenite campaign:

> Women seem really to have been seized with a brain fever. They appear to be altogether a new race of beings; and are puffed up with a conceit, which ought to rather to suffuse their cheeks with blushes, than to thus elevate them in their own vain importance.[52]

But *Gynecocracy*'s obsessive focus was the Queen, 'advanced in grossness', 'guilty of such libidinous orgies … as to welter with as little shame in open lechery, as swine do in the common mire'. A nymphomaniac harridan had duped the women of Britain to invert the properly constituted relationships of gender, as well as 'the physical force of the country' into sounding 'the tocsin of revolt'. By its withdrawal of the Bill of Pains and Penalties, the Government had shrewdly arrested this unnatural reversal of the established order, secure in the knowledge 'that His Majesty would freely submit to personal mortification, for the general safety of his misguided people'.[53]

It is important not to exaggerate the influence of works like *John Bull* or *Gynecocracy*. Not everyone read them and the cumulative weight of loyalist publishing never matched the radicals' output. However, this phase of loyalist literature both reflected changes in the popular mood and accelerated them further. Simultaneously graphic satire increasingly targeted the Queen. Vic Gatrell sees in Cruikshank's silencing (followed as it was by the artist's immersion in the calmer waters of commercial book illustration and teetotalism) a metaphor for a wider shift in the popular mood from late 1820.[54] Contemporaries commented on the change palpably wrought during the early months of 1821. 'Had I not seen it, I could not have believed so great a contrast', a senior Austrian diplomat noted in February 1821: 'the duke of Wellington, who in 1814 and 1815 was regarded as a god, was hissed and insulted during the Queen's trial, now Parliament has given its verdict and the people submit to it.'[55] As Stuart-Wortley argued, a sense of popular fatigue hung over the Caroline affair, a feeling 'that the matter should be put entirely at rest'. There was also a sense of collective embarrassment about the effusive and uncritical reaction to the Queen's position during the previous autumn. Sometimes this embarrassment was tacit, but William Hazlitt thought largely not. Such was the loyalist backlash, he declared, that 'the general obloquy was so great that everyone was willing to escape from it in the crowd, or to curry favour with the victors by denouncing the excesses or picking holes in the conduct of his neighbours'.[56]

It would be unwise to repose too much confidence in the loyalist backlash in framing explanations for the general restoration of order in 1821. As we have seen, economic recovery consequent upon the 1820 harvest and the cumulative impact of legal containment are two important factors. So too was the nature of the November Caroline demonstrations themselves. Chapter 6's analysis of the complex micro-politics of these events noted that they were in part occasions through which popular control was reasserted over customary communal festivities and the 'ownership' of contested public space. They were also a form of social bonding, a collective statement about what constituted the local community, or signifier of corporate strength among working people. Their importance lay as much in these consequences as in the ephemeral occasion of their causation. The frequency with which the Caroline demonstrations appear in later reminiscences and parish histories suggests they were incorporated into the collective memory as moments that affirmed the distinctiveness of local culture. This may seem ironic, given the widespread uniformity evident in November's celebrations, but each demonstration was the product of local initiative, negotiation and often considerable advance preparation.

The Caroline demonstrations were also, as we saw, occasions for spontaneous charity and paternalism, the effect of which was to diminish the perceived distance between local political establishments and the politically and socially excluded. Some of the most serious cases of disorder in 1820 arose when patterns of paternalism broke down, while rural Ireland provided a woeful exemplar of a society where paternalism was perfunctory or totally absent. During the general election the worst violence occurred at Banbury, following the refusal to distribute customary favours to the non-electors. In the confidential murmurings of the establishment, mutinous currents in the Brigade of Guards were also ascribed to the erosion of regimental understandings of *noblesse oblige*. Wellington's belief was that the distractions of peacetime London had led to officers becoming too remote from the other ranks, and that therefore too much responsibility had devolved onto the sergeants and corporals. 'The duty of the officers of the Guards should, as far as possible, be assimilated to that of officers in the line', he advised the Prime Minister.[57] 'There never was any period when the utmost care and vigilance of the commanding officer was more required,' Sir Herbert Taylor, Military Secretary at the War Office and a colonel in the Coldstream Guards, commented to Wellington.[58]

The Caroline demonstrations may therefore have actually *diminished* social tension in the medium and longer term. They provided pretexts for a mobilisation of paternalism in countless localities. They also conjured up the illusion of a great radical triumph, a screen of November bonfire smoke, behind which the Government and moderate Whigs fell back into old habits of tacit collusion. Cobbett hailed it 'a glorious day for the people, who have, at last, begun to lay the axe to the root of Corruption'.[59] The chairman of Bolton's rally to mark Caroline's 'acquittal' proclaimed it, 'one Grand Complete victory over the Boroughmongering Faction … Had England ever such an instance of "A Nation to Be free only needs to will it?"'. Yet even as he concluded (with a call to 'be speedy as he wanted to go and enjoy himself with plenty of Good Company and Spirits') dissent was stirring, with a deeply pessimistic analysis of the episode's consequences offered by an old Jacobin. These, he said, would turn upon,

> … a Union of Whigs and Tories whereas the late proceedings caused a Union of Radicals and Whigs. But now Radicals would be brought into Contempt By Both of them … now Cobbett would be crying out Justice and the Constitution for ever, Government would extole the Ministers to the pinnacle of popularity and we should hear nothing but praise Bestowed upon the peers who have only Abandoned a point they could not – yea perhaps I may say durst not – go through with. No thanks to them for this, its a Blind and it will blindfold thousands that otherwise would have coincided with all that we anticipate.[60]

It took only a little hindsight to see that the 'Union of Radicals and Whigs' had actually drawn much of the heat from the reformers' challenge to the political establishment. Though *John Bull* fulminated against the new 'Whig-radicals', this back-handed compliment reflected how, as a consequence of the Queen Caroline affair, many reformers could and did look to the Whigs in the expectation of political change.[61] Furthermore, although the *Black Book* and its imitators seldom differentiated between Whigs and Tories, another shift in the balance of radical ideology also benefitted Tory government. This was the move away from the directly confrontational territory of parliamentary exclusion and towards a rhetoric of anti-corruption that could be legally sustained within a constitutionalist framework. The Caroline affair further facilitated this shift, focussed as it was on the failings of constitutional authority (the King's authority morally and personally, and the Government's politically).

There is no easy formula to explain the persistence of stability during 1820. Ultimately it was an untidy conjuncture of policy, policing, reform, repression, chance and contingency. The dynamic inertia of the Whig party also lies at the heart of the explanation. Nowhere would this be more apparent than on the day when George IV was finally crowned monarch of the United Kingdom.

Epilogue: Thursday 19 July 1821

Joseph Farington rose at 8.15 on Thursday 19 July 1821, noting 'a fine summer morning', the wind in the east and a temperature of 23 degrees. He had been woken at dawn by the sound of guns firing a royal salute, for this was Coronation Day. Farington shared in the general sense of foreboding. 'Much apprehension of riot at the coronation is now entertained', he had written two days before, 'in consequence Seats to view the procession are but in little request'. It was widely assumed that Queen Caroline would seek to force her way into Westminster Abbey. Meanwhile, the temporary staging and seating outside the Abbey had been threatened with arson.[62] Sarah, Farington's housekeeper, ventured out and brought back a report 'that 2 or 3 men had been killed contending her admission'.[63]

'This report happily proved erroneous', added Farington. The Queen's attempt to attend her husband's Coronation had been characterised by bathos, not tragedy. 'She looked like a blousy landlady', a friend told him. 'Her reception was very unfavourable. "Shame, shame" and "Off, Off" was the general cry though a few cried "Queen".'[64] As she approached the main door of Westminster Abbey the Lord Chamberlain called for it to be closed. Six of Regency England's most celebrated prize-fighters blocked her way. Caroline, suddenly an isolated and lonely figure, attended only by her chamberlain, now moved round to the south side of the Abbey. Here a secluded door permitted entry to the Abbey cloisters from the canons' residences. On its step stood an Essex landowner, Whig MP and baronet, Thomas Barrett Lennard, seeking relief from the heat inside the

Abbey. 'I have seen you at Southend; know me now as the Queen of England', exclaimed Caroline, 'I command you to afford me ingress to the church'. Barrett Lennard refused. 'Turning to the entrance, he exclaimed – "Keep the door fast, and let none enter unless I tell you to do so"'.[65]

Seven months earlier, flanked by images of Caroline and of the British lion trampling the bill of pains and penalties underfoot, Sir Thomas had told a Colchester meeting how the Liverpool Ministry had almost 'destroyed' the constitution through 'a system of infringement' that culminated in its assault upon Caroline.[66] Yet now, confronted by his injured Queen, he was deaf to her increasingly tearful pleading. Barrett Lennard was an undistinguished backbencher and the Coronation his chance to make a mark upon history. In common with the rest of the Whig party, Sir Thomas made his mark only by withdrawing all pretence to support her cause.

Notes

1 F. Bamford and G. W. Wellington (eds), *The Journal of Mrs Arbuthnot, 1820–32: Volume 1, February 1820 to December 1825* (London: Macmillan, 1950), pp. 59–60.

2 Richard Carlile, *Republican*, 17 November p. 414.

3 Edward Osler (ed.), *The Life of Admiral Viscount Exmouth* (London: Smith Elder, 1835), pp. 350–1 (letter to his brother, 29 Nov.).

4 DRO, 152M/C/1820/OZ (Sidmouth to Exmouth, 31 December).

5 *Ibid.* (Sidmouth to Bathurst, 9, 15, 25, 26, and 27 December; Bathurst to Sidmouth, 22 December).

6 A. Mitchell, *The Whigs in Opposition, 1815–1830* (Oxford: Oxford University Press, 1967), p. 148.

7 Undated memorandum of late November, reprinted in A. Aspinall (ed.), *The Letters of King George IV, 1812–30* (Cambridge: Cambridge University Press, 1938), vol. 2, pp. 390–1.

8 Letter to Wilson, 24 December, quoted in Mitchell, *Whigs in Opposition*, p. 169.

9 B. Hilton, *A Mad, Bad and Dangerous People? England, 1783–1846* (Oxford: Oxford University Press, 2006), p. 281; Annual Register for 1821, quoted by G. Broeker, *Rural Disorder and Police Reform in Ireland, 1812–36* (London: Routledge, 1970), p. 127.

10 S. J. Connolly, 'Union government, 1812–23', in W. E. Vaughan (ed.), *A New History of Ireland, Volume V: Ireland Under the Union, I (1801–70)* (Oxford: Oxford University Press, 1989), pp. 66–69.

11 TNA, HO 40/13 fols 137–8 and 221–4 (12 May and 3 June); HO 40/14 fols 50–53 (15 July); Richard Phillips, 'Ychwaneg am "Ryfel y Sais bach" 1820–29', *Ceredigion*, 6:3 (1970); D.J.V. Jones, *Before Rebecca: Popular Protests in Wales, 1793–1835* (London: Allen Lane, 1973), pp. 48–50.

12 E. Richards, 'Patterns of Highland discontent, 1790–1860', in R. Quinault and J. Stevenson (eds), *Popular Protest and Public Order: Six Studies in British History, 1790–1920* (London: Allen & Unwin, 1974), pp. 88–92; TNA, HO102/32/232 and 284 (6 and 31 March); DRO, 152/M/C/1820/OH (11 March).

13 J. E. Archer, *'By a Flash and a Scare': Arson, Animal Maiming, and Poaching in East Anglia, 1815–70* (Oxford: Oxford University Press, 1990), pp. 78–9.

14 Mitchell, *Whigs in Opposition*, pp. 151–3; *The Journal of Mrs Arbuthnot*, p. 68.

15 *The Journal of Mrs Arbuthnot*, pp. 67–8.

16 *HC Deb*, 26 January 1821 (vol. 4, cols 139–219); *HC Deb*, 5 February 1821 (vol. 4, cols 361–421) and 6 February 1821 (cols 429–507); *HC Deb*, 13 February 1821 (vol. 4, cols 620–65).

17 *HC Deb*, 31 January 1821 (vol. 4, cols 225–6).

18 F. Fraser, *The Unruly Queen: The Life of Queen Caroline* (New York: Anchor, 2009), pp. 452–6, provides a useful narrative of her pursuit of the unresolved remaining issues.

19 Letter to Harriet, 6 November, reproduced in A. Aspinall (ed.), *The Correspondence of Charles Arbuthnot*, Camden 3rd ser (Royal Historical Society, 1941), vol. 65, p. 20.

20 DRO, 152M/C/1821/OZ (letter to Nathaniel Bond, 14 February 1821).

21 J. Innes, 'Central government "interference": changing conceptions, practices, and concerns, c. 1700–11850', in J. Harris (ed.), *Civil Society in British History: Ideas, Identities, and Institutions* (Oxford: Oxford University Press, 2003), p. 47.

22 Sturges Bourne to Frederick Ekins, 25 June 1819, reprinted in R. Hawkins, *The Life of Robert Blakey, 1795–1878* (Morpeth: Morpathia Press, 2010), p. 101.

23 Letter to Wilberforce, 18 April, quoted in W. Hanna, *Memoirs of the Life and Writings of Thomas Chalmers* (Edinburgh: Sutherland & Knox, 1850), vol. 2, p. 263.

24 G. H. Jenkins and I. Gwynedd Jones (eds), *Cardiganshire County History, Volume 3: Cardiganshire in Modern Times* (Cardiff: University of Wales Press, 1998), p. 492.

25 Cumberland report for December, *Evans and Ruffy's Farmers' Journal,* 10 January.

26 T. A. Ward, *Peeps into the Past, being Passages from the Diary of Thomas Asline Ward* (London: Leng, 1909), p. 266.

27 B. R. Mitchell and P. Deane, *Abstract of British Historical Statistics* (Cambridge: Cambridge University Press, 1962), pp. 469–71.

28 DRO, 152M/C/1820/OR (20 July); 152M/C/1820/OH (25 September).

29 TNA, HO 100/199/161 (Grant to Sidmouth, 1 September); HO 100/199/230 (Grant to Sidmouth, 28 September).

30 BL, Add. Mss 38742 fol. 26 (29 September).

31 *Ibid.*

32 BL, Add. Mss 38288 fols 329–30 (letter to Calthorpe, 20 December).

33 Letter to Lady Mary Bennett, reprinted in *A Memoir of the Reverend Sydney Smith, by his daughter Lady Holland* (London: Longman, 1855), vol. 2, pp. 201–2.

34 'To the readers of the *Farmer's Journal*', [annual address prefacing the collected issues for vol. 13, 25 December], p. 1.

35 B. Hilton, *Corn, Cash and Commerce: The Economic Policies of the Tory Governments, 1815–30* (Oxford: Oxford University Press, 1972), p. 107.

36 *Evans's and Ruffy's Farmers' Journal*, 3 and 24 April 1820; John Sinclair to Arthur Young, 20 October 1819, quoted in R. Mitchison, 'The Old Board of Agriculture (1793–1822)', *English Historical Review*, 74:290 (1959), p. 64.

37 Hunt, in *To the Radical Reformers, Male and Female, of England, Ireland, and Scotland*, '25th day, 3rd month, 2nd year, of the MANCHESTER MASSACRE without enquiry' [10 December 1820], pp. 10–11; *Gentleman's Magazine*, vol. 94 (May 1824), pp. 464–5; Mitchison, 'The Old Board', pp. 64–5.

38 DRO, 152M/C/1820/OH (25 September).

39 See V. Gatrell, *City of Laughter: Sex and Satire in Eighteenth-Century London* (New York: Walker, 2006), pp. 531–5.

40 TNA, TS 11/155/468 and 471, TS 25/2035/581 (*Leeds Mercury*); TS 11/156 (*Black Book; The Times*); TS 11/156/209 (*Examiner*); TS 11/156/500 and 501, TS 24/7/21–23 and TS 25/2035/561–3 (*Black Book*).

41 The prints survive in TNA, TS 11/115; Gatrell, *City of Laughter*, pp. 534–5.

42 Gatrell, *City of Laughter*, pp. 537–8.

43 *Morning Post*, 8 January 1821; Wordsworth to Lonsdale, 18 December, reprinted in *The Letters of William and Dorothy Wordsworth … The Middle Years, Part II: 1812–1820*, arr. and ed. by E. de Selincourt, rev. and ed. by M. Moorman and A. G. Hill (Oxford: Oxford University Press, 1970), p. 657. See also Gatrell, *City of Laughter*, p. 536 and A. Aspinall, *Politics and the Press, c. 1780–1850* (Home & Van Thal, 1949), pp. 64–5.

44 Historical Manuscripts Commission, *Report on the Manuscripts of Earl Bathurst, Preserved at Cirencester Park* (London: HMSO, 1923), p. 489 (Arbuthnot to Bathurst, 29 November 1820); Aspinall, *Politics and the Press*, p. 200, citing a letter from Castlereagh to his brother (17 December).

45 BL, Add. Mss 38288 fol. 221 (Harrison to Liverpool, 30 November); see also Aspinall, *Politics and the Press*, pp. 99–100.

46 R. H. D. Barham, *The Life and Remains of Theodore Edward Hook* (London: Bentley, 1850), p. 198.

47 E.g. *The Loyal Man in the Moon* (London: Chapple, 1820) and *The New Pilgrim's Progress; or a Journey to Jerusalem* (London: Wright, 1820) – both printed by W. Shackell of Johnson's Court, Fleet Street; copy of sworn affidavit by William Shackell, proprietor, in *John Bull*, 28 January 1821. Ellerton & Henderson, also of Johnson's Court, published the Constitutional Association's 1821 launch *Address* in its broadside form. For the deliberately hazy circumstances of *John Bull's* production see also Jonathan Fulcher, 'The loyalist response to the Queen Caroline agitations', *Journal of British Studies*, 34:4 (1995).

48 *Loyal Man in the Moon*, p. 3.

49 *John Bull*, 17 December and 14 January 1821.

50 *John Bull*, 28 January 1821. Sales averaged 9000 copies a week across 1821, see *PP* 1822 (272) Stamps issued for newspapers.

51 *The Journal of Mrs Arbuthnot*, p. 89 (25 April).

52 *Gynecocracy; with an Essay on Fornication, Adultery, and Incest* (London: Stockdale; Plymouth: Haviland, 1821), p. 183.

53 *Ibid.*, pp. 285, 585, 589.

54 T. L. Hunt, 'Morality and Monarchy in the Queen Caroline Affair', *Albion*, 23:4 (1991), pp. 717–21; Gatrell, *City of Laughter*, pp. 538–40.

55 E. B. Chancellor (ed.), *The Diary of Philipp von Neumann, 1819–1850* (London: Allan, 1928), vol. 1, p. 54.

56 W. Hazlitt, *The Plain Speaker: Opinions on Books, Men, and Things* (London: Colbourn: 1826), vol. 2, p. 430.

57 Memorandum to Liverpool, June 1820, reprinted in *Despatches, correspondence, and memoranda of Field Marshal Arthur, Duke of Wellington, K.G., edited by his son* (London: Murray, 1867), vol. 1, pp. 127–9.

58 Taylor to Wellington, 19 September 1820, reprinted in Wellington, *Despatches*, pp. 144–5. See also p. 146 for a Brigade Order on the same issue, 31 July; also TNA, HO 40/14 fol. 82 (31 July) where General Byng makes the case that the Guards' officers were to blame.

59 *Cobbett's Weekly Political Register*, 11 November.

60 TNA, HO 40/15/110–11 (Fletcher to Sidmouth, 15 November); Nicholas Rogers, *Crowds, Culture and Politics in Georgian Britain* (Oxford: Oxford University Press, 1998), p. 272.

61 *John Bull*, 30 September 1821.

62 TNA, HO44/8/434 (6 July).

63 K. Cave (ed.), *The Diary of Joseph Farington: Volume XVI, January 1820–December 1821* (London: Yale University Press, 1984), pp. 5701–2.
64 Farington, *Diary*, p. 5703.
65 G. F. Berkeley, *My Life and Recollections* (London: Hurst & Blackett, 1866), vol. 4, p. 174.
66 *The Times*, 21 December.

Bibliography

Contemporary material

Archival sources

British Library (Department of Manuscripts), London
    Liverpool Papers: Add. Mss 38282-88; 38369
    Huskisson Papers: Add. Mss 38741-2
    Wilson Papers: Add. Mss 30109
    Holland Papers: Add. Mss 51609

British Library (Department of Printed Books), London
    Playbills Collection, volumes 264 and 306

Burnley Central Library, Community History Department
    William Varley's Memorandum Book (transcript of original by Linda Croft)
    William Varley's Accounts (transcript of original by Walter Bennett)

Devon Records Office, Exeter
    Fortescue Manuscripts: 1262M
    Sidmouth Papers: 152M/C/1819; 152M/C/1820; 152M/C/1821

Exeter Central Library, Westcountry Studies Library
    Playbills Collection

Leeds Central Library
    Playbills Collection

The National Archives, Kew
    Home Office Papers:
        HO 33/2 (Post Office Correspondence, 1817–22)
        HO 40/7 – HO 40/15 (Disturbances Correspondence, 1819–20)
        HO 42/136, HO 42/158, HO 42/165, HO 42/170, HO42/191–2, HO
            42/197, HO 42/200 (Domestic Correspondence, 1813–19)
        HO 43/29, HO 43/30 (Domestic Entry Books, 1819–1821)
        HO 44/1 – HO 44/8 (Domestic Correspondence, 1820–21)
        HO 79/7 (Private and Secret Entry Books, 1806–22)

HO 100/198, HO 100/199 (Ireland: Correspondence and Papers, 1820)
HO 102/32, HO 102/33 (Scotland: Correspondence and Papers, 1820)
HO 122/12, HO122/13 (Ireland: General Letters Books, 1816–27)
HO 126/3 (Caroline, Princess of Wales, 1804–20)

Lord Chamberlain and the Royal Household
LC 1/8 out letters (Correspondence, 1819–22)

Treasury Solicitor
TS 11/45/167 (R v. Wedderburn)
TS 11/115 (Prints and Cartoons Supporting the Queen)
TS 11/155/465-512 (Cases for Opinion, 1819–20)
TS 11/156 (Cases for Opinion, 1820)
TS 11/197 (Cato Street)
TS 11/202 – TS 11/208 (Cato Street)
TS 11/697/2210 (R v. Thomas J. Evans)
TS 24/7/21 (Case for Opinion v. Black Book)
TS 25/2035/561-3 (Case for Opinion v. Black Book)
TS 25/2035/580 (Case for Opinion v. Republican)
TS 25/2035/581 (Case for Opinion v. Leeds Mercury)

National Archives of Ireland, Dublin
Chief Secretary's Office, Private and Official Correspondence
CSO LB 419

State of the Country Papers, Series One: 1796–1820
SOC 2171-3 Galway
SOC 2174 Leitrim
SOC 2175 County Mayo
SOC 2176 Roscommon
SOC 2177 County Dublin
SOC 2178 Kildare
SOC 2179 King's County
SOC 2181 Westmeath
SOC 2182 County Cork
SOC 2183 Clare
SOC 2184 Kerry
SOC 2185 County Limerick
SOC 2186 Tipperary
SOC 2187 Ulster
SOC 2188 General

Newcastle Central Library, Local Studies Section
L324/D962: 'Addresses and squibs in the contested election (Newcastle, 1820)';
Addresses, songs &c., connected with the 1820 Durham county election';
'Proceedings of the Durham county election, 1820'
L324/N536: 'Collection of papers, speeches, &c., &c., delivered at the Newcastle
election of 1820'
L324/N878: 'Collection of papers, speeches, &c., delivered at the Northumberland
election in 1820'

Private collection
    Correspondence respecting the 1820 Northumberland county election

Sheffield Archives: Wentworth Woodhouse Muniments
    F/48/152-74; F/49/57; F/52/58; F/60/100; F/84/1-5; F/107/110; F/127/144/
    1-2; F/134/1-9; G/14/1-39

West Yorkshire Archives Service (Leeds)
    Harewood (Henry Lascelles) Manuscripts, WYL/250/6/2/B1/5/53-6;
    WYL/250/6/2/B2/1-4
    Stapleton Papers, WYL/887/2/1-21

University of York, Raymond Burton Humanities Research Library
    Play Bills, Hull

York Minster Library
    Playbills Collection

Parliamentary Papers

1820 (49) Estimates of army services, for the year 1820
1820 (57) Estimates of ordinary of the navy; and building and repair of ships; for the year
    1820
1820 (83) Estimates of the charge of the Office of Ordnance for Great Britain, for the
    year 1820
1820 (255) Report from the Select Committee on petitions complaining of agricultural
    distress
1820 (273) Report from the Select Committee on Administration of Justice in Wales
1821 (189) Army: yeomanry and volunteer corps. A return of the number of troops or
    corps of effective yeomanry, and of regiments or corps of volunteers ... in 1820
1822 (272) Stamps issued for newspapers. --1.-- An account of the number of stamps
    issued for newspapers, for the year 1801 ... for the year 1821
1822 (556) Report from the Select Committee on Poor Rate Returns
1823 (570) Report from the Select Committee on Poor Rate Returns
1823 (414) (Ireland.) Commercial credit. Copy of a letter to William Gregory, Esquire,
    from the secretary to the commissioners for the assistance of trade and manufactures,
    established in Dublin, by 1 Geo. IV. c. 39. dated 31st July 1822; respecting the loan
    to Messrs. Nowlan & Shaw, in 1821
1825 (20) State of Ireland. Minutes of evidence taken before the Select Committee
    appointed to inquire into the disturbances in Ireland, in the last session of Parliament;
    13th May--18th June, 1824
1825 (129) Report from the Select Committee on the state of Ireland: 1825
1825 (181) Minutes of evidence taken before the Select Committee of the House of
    Lords, appointed to inquire into the state of Ireland, more particularly with reference
    to the circumstances which may have led to disturbances in that part of the United
    Kingdom
1830 (215) Report from the Select Committee appointed to inquire into ... select and
    other vestries
1830 (427) Militia. Return relating to the militia of the United Kingdom, 1816-1829
1830-31 (92) Public offices employment. Returns of the number of persons employed,
    and of the pay or salaries granted to such persons, in all public offices or departments

1831–32 (679) Report from the Select Committee on Dramatic Literature
1837–38 (723) Loans, Ireland. Return of the sums advanced for the relief of commercial credit in Ireland, under the 1st Geo. 4, c. 39, &c

Newspapers and periodicals

Black Book, Hitherto Mis-named 'The Red Book'
Black Dwarf
Blackwood's Magazine
Bristol Mercury
British Stage and Literary Cabinet
Bury & Norwich Post
Caledonian Mercury
Cambrian
Cambro-Briton, and General Celtic Repository
Chute's Western Herald, or Kerry Advertizer
Cobbett's Two-penny Trash
Cobbett's Weekly Political Register
Courier
Derby Mercury
Dublin Evening Post
Durham Chronicle or General Northern Advertizer
Edinburgh Review
Evans and Ruffy's Farmers' Journal
Examiner
Freeman's Journal [Dublin]
Gentleman's Magazine
Glasgow Herald
Hampshire Telegraph and Sussex Chronicle
Hull Packet
Ipswich Journal
Jackson's Oxford Journal
John Bull
Kaleidoscope [Liverpool]
Lancaster Gazette and General Advertiser
Leeds Mercury
Leinster Journal
Liverpool Mercury
Manchester Observer
Mirror of Fashion
Morning Chronicle
Morning Post
Newcastle Courant
Poor Man's Guardian
Quarterly Review
Republican
Sheffield Independent
Sheffield Mercury
Theatrical Inquisitor, and Monthly Mirror
The Times
To the Radical Reformers, Male and Female, of England, Ireland, and Scotland

To the Reformers of Great Britain
Trewman's Exeter Flying Post
York Chronicle & General Advertizer
York Herald & General Advertiser
Yorkshire Gazette

Diaries, memoirs and other autobiographical material

ARBUTHNOT (CHARLES): A. Aspinall (ed.), *The Correspondence of Charles Arbuthnot*, Camden 3rd ser, vol. 65 (Royal Historical Society, 1941)

ARBUTHNOT, (HARRIET): F. Bamford and G. W. Wellington (eds), *The Journal of Mrs Arbuthnot, 1820–32: Volume 1, February 1820 to December 1825* (London: Macmillan, 1950)

BAKER: J. Bowen, *A Brief Memoir of the Life and Character of William Baker* (Taunton: May, 1854)

BATHURST: Historical Manuscripts Commission, *Report on the Manuscripts of Earl Bathurst, Preserved at Cirencester Park* (London: HMSO, 1923)

BEDE: R. Gossez (ed.), *Un Ouvrier en 1820: Manuscrit inédit de Jacques-Etienne Bédé* (Paris: Presses Universitaires de France, 1984)

BERKELEY: G. F. Berkeley, *My Life and Recollections* (London: Hurst & Blackett, 1866)

BROADBELT: *Memoirs of Ann Broadbelt, of Killinghall, Yorkshire* (London: Thompson, 1820)

BRONTE: J. Lock and W. T. Dixon (eds), *A Man of Sorrow: The Life, Letters and Times of the Rev. Patrick Bronte* (Nelson, 1965)

BROUGHAM: *Life and Times of Lord Brougham, Written by Himself* (Edinburgh: Blackwood, 1871)

BROWN: J. Brown, *Sixty Years' Gleanings from Life's Harvest: A Genuine Autobiography* (Cambridge: Palmer, 1858)

CAROLINE: R. Huish, *Memoirs of Her Late Majesty Caroline, Queen of Great Britain* (London: Kelly, 1821)

CHALMERS: W. Hanna, *Memoirs of the Life and Writings of Thomas Chalmers* (Edinburgh: Sutherland & Knox, 1850)

CLINTON: C. J. F. Clinton (ed.), *Literary Remains of Henry Fynes Clinton* (London: Longman, 1854)

COCKBURN: H. Cockburn, *Memorials of His Time* (Edinburgh: Black, 1856)

COLCHESTER: *Diary and Correspondence of Charles Abbot, Lord Colchester, edited by his son Charles, Lord Colchester* (London: Murray, 1861)

CREEVEY: H. Maxwell (ed.), *The Creevey Papers: A Selection from the Correspondence and Diaries of the Late Thomas Creevey*, 3rd edn (London: Murray, 1912)

CROKER: L. J. Jennings (ed.), *The Croker Papers: The Correspondence and Diaries of the Late Right Honourable John Wilson Croker … 1809 to 1830* (London: Murray, 1884)

DARTER: [W. S. Darter], *Reminiscences of Reading. By an Octogenarian* (Reading: Blagrave Street Steam Printing Works, 1889)

ELDON: H. Twiss (ed.), *The Public and Private Life of Lord Chancellor Eldon, with Selections from his Correspondence* (London: Murray, 1844)

EXMOUTH: E. Osler, *The Life of Admiral Viscount Exmouth* (London: Smith Elder, 1835)

FARINGTON: K. Cave (ed.), *The Diary of Joseph Farington: Volume XVI, January 1820–December 1821* (London: Yale University Press, 1984)

FRAMPTON: H. G. Mundy (ed.), *The Journal of Mary Frampton* (London: Sampson Law, 1885)

FROST: T. Frost, *Forty Years Recollections, Literary and Political* (London: Low, 1880)

GEORGE IV: A. Aspinall (ed.), *The Letters of King George IV, 1812–30* (Cambridge: Cambridge University Press, 1938)

GISBORNE: *A Brief Memoir of the Life of John Gisborne* (London, Whitaker, 1852)

GREVILLE: L. Strachey and R. Fulford (eds), *The Greville Memoirs, 1814–1860: Volume 1, January 1814–July 1830* (London: Macmillan, 1938)

HAWKER: *The Diary of Colonel Peter Hawker* (London: Longmans, 1893)

HERBERT: G. H. Herbert, *Shoemaker's Window: Recollections of Banbury in Oxfordshire before the Railway Age* (Chichester: Phillimore, 1971)

HOBHOUSE (HENRY): A. Aspinall (ed.), *The Diary of Henry Hobhouse, 1820–27* (London: Home & Van Thal, 1947)

HOBHOUSE (JOHN CAM): *Recollections of a Long Life, by Lord Broughton, with Additional Extracts from his Diaries, edited by his daughter, Lady Dorchester* (London: Murray, 1909)

—— C. P. W. Graham (ed.), *Byron's Bulldog: The Letters of John Cam Hobhouse to Lord Byron* (Columbus: Ohio State University Press, 1984)

HOLLAND: H. E. Vassall (ed.), *Memoirs of the Whig Party During My Time by Henry Richard Lord Holland* (London: Longmans, 1854)

—— *Further Memoirs of the Whig Party, 1807–21, with some Miscellaneous Reminiscences, by Henry Richard Vassall, Third Lord Holland, edited by Lord Stavordale* (London: Murray, 1905)

LAMB: T. Lever (ed.), *The Letters of Lady Palmerston, Selected and Edited from the Originals at Broadlands and Elsewhere* (London: Murray, 1957)

LIEVEN: L. G. Robinson (ed.), *Letters of Dorothea, Princess Lieven: During her Residence in London, 1812–1834* (London: Longmans, 1902)

—— P. Quennell (ed.), *The Private Letters of Princess Lieven to Prince Metternich, 1820–1826* (London: Murray, 1937)

LIGHTON: W. B. Lighton, *Narrative of the Life and Sufferings of William B. Lighton* (Concordia, NY: the author, 1838)

LINTON: W. J. Linton, *James Watson: A Memoir* (Manchester: Heywood, 1880)

—— W. J. Linton, *Memories* (London: Lawrence & Bullen, 1895)

LIVERPOOL: C. D. Yonge (compiler), *The Life and Administration of Robert Banks, Second Earl of Liverpool* (London: Macmillan, 1868)

LUCAS: G. E. Bryant and G. P. Baker (eds), *A Quaker Journal, being the Diary and Reminiscences of William Lucas of Hitchin* (London: Hutchinson, 1934)

MACREADY: F. Pollock (ed.), *Macready's Reminiscences and Selections from his Diaries and Letters* (London: Macmillan, 1876)

MANTELL: E. C. Curwen (ed.), *The Journal of Gideon Mantell, Surgeon and Geologist, Covering the Years 1818–52* (Oxford: Oxford University Press, 1940)

'MASTER SHOEMAKER': 'A master shoemaker', 'My life and adventures', *Boot and Shoemaker*, 14 June–16 Sept, 1879

MAYETT: A. Kussmaul (ed.), *The Autobiography of Joseph Mayett of Quainton* (Aylesbury: Buckinghamshire Record Society, 1986)

MITFORD: M. R. Mitford, *Our Village: Sketches of Rural Character and Scenery* (London: Whitaker, 1825)

MOORE: *Memoirs, Journal, and Correspondence of Thomas Moore, edited by the Right Honourable Lord John Russell, MP* (London: Longmans, 1853)

NEUMANN: E. B. Chancellor (ed.), *The Diary of Philipp von Neumann, 1819–1850* (London: Allan, 1928)

PEEL: C. S. Parker (ed.), *Sir Robert Peel from his Private Correspondence* (London: Murray, 1891)

—— G. Peel (ed.), *The Private Letters of Sir Robert Peel* (Murray, 1920)

ROBINSON: T. Sadler (ed.) *Diary, Reminiscences, and Correspondence of Henry Crabb Robinson* (London: Macmillan, 1872)

RUSSELL: R. Russell (ed.), *Early Correspondence of Lord John Russell, 1805–40* (London: Unwin, 1913)

SCOTT: J. G. Lockhart (ed.), *Memoirs of the Life of Sir Walter Scott*, 2nd edn (Edinburgh: Cadell, 1839)

—— H. J. C. Grierson (ed.), *The Letters of Sir Walter Scott* (Edinburgh: Constable, 1932–37)

SHARP: J. E. Crowther and P. A. Crowther (eds), *The Diary of Robert Sharp of South Cave: Life in a Yorkshire Village, 1812–37* (Oxford: Oxford University Press, 1997)

SHELLEY: F. L. Jones (ed.), *The Letters of Percy Bysshe Shelley, Volume 2: Shelley in Italy* (Oxford: Oxford University Press, 1964)

SIDMOUTH: G. Pellew, *The Life and Correspondence of the Rt Hon H. Addington, First Viscount Sidmouth* (London: Murray, 1847)

SMITH: *A Memoir of the Reverend Sydney Smith, by his daughter Lady Holland* (London: Longman, 1855)

TOWNSEND: *Memoirs of the Rev. John Townsend* (London: Courthope, 1827)

TUKE: *Memoirs of Samuel Tuke, Volume 1* (London: n.p., 1860)

WARD (ROBERT PLUMER): E. Phipps (ed.), *Memoirs of the Political and Literary Life of Robert Plumer Ward* (Edinburgh: Murray: 1850)

WARD (THOMAS ASLINE): *Peeps into the past, being passages from the diary of Thomas Asline Ward* (London: Leng, 1909)

WATKIN: M. Goffin (ed.), *The Diaries of Absalom Watkin: A Manchester Man, 1787–1861* (Stroud: Sutton, 1993)

WELLINGTON: *Despatches, Correspondence, and Memoranda of Field Marshal Arthur, Duke of Wellington, K.G., edited by his son* (London: Murray, 1867)

—— *Wellington and his friends: letters of the First Duke of Wellington to the Rt. Hon. Charles and Mrs. Arbuthnot, the Earl and Countess of Wilton, Princess Lieven, and Miss Burdett-Coutts, selected and edited by the seventh Duke of Wellington* (London: Macmillan, 1965)

WHISHAW: E. M. Seymour (ed.), *The 'Pope' of Holland House: Selections from the Correspondence of John Whishaw and his Friends* (London: Fisher Unwin, 1901)

WILKIE: A. Cunningham, *The Life of Sir David Wilkie* (London: Murray, 1843)

WITTS: D. Verey (ed.), *The Diary of a Cotswold Parson: Reverend F. E. Witts, 1783–1854* (Stroud: Sutton, 1978)

WORDSWORTH: *The Letters of William and Dorothy Wordsworth … The Middle Years, Part II: 1812–1820*, arr. and ed. by E. de Selincourt, rev. and ed. by M. Moorman and A. G. Hill (Oxford: Oxford University Press, 1970)

Other contemporary printed material

A Letter Addressed to the Hon. John Frederick Campbell, M.P. on the Poor Laws and the Practical Effect to be Produced by the Act of 59 Geo. III. c. 12. Commonly Called the Select Vestry Act. By a magistrate of the County of Pembroke (London: Longman, 1821)

[Atkinson, W.], *The Retort Courteous; or, the Descent of Mr Baines, from the Pinnacle of the Pickle-Pot. By the Old Enquirer* (Bradford: Inkersley, 1820)

—— *Letters to Lord Viscount Milton; to which is added a Sermon to Electors and Men in Office* (Bradford: Inkersley, 1821)

Baines, E., *History, Directory and Gazetteer of the County of York* (Leeds: Baines, 1822)

Barham, R. H. D., *The Life and Remains of Theodore Edward Hook* (London: Bentley, 1850)

Barker, F., and J. Cheyne, *An Account of the Rise, Progress, and Decline of the Fever Lately Epidemical in Ireland: Together with Communications from Physicians in the Provinces, and Various Official Documents* (London: Baldwin, 1821)

Benbow, W., *The Whigs Exposed; or, Truth by Day-light. Addressed to the Reformers of Britain* (London: Benbow, 1820)

The Blind Guide; or, Thomas Paine Ignorant of the Bible (London: Christian Knowledge Society, [1820])

Brayshaw, J., *An Appeal to the People of England, on the Necessity of Parliamentary Reform, Pointing Out the Corruptions of the Present System, and some of the Evils Flowing Therefrom and the Means of Accomplishing a Parliamentary Reform, Recommended to the Serious Attention of Every Honest Man* (Newcastle upon Tyne: Marshall, 1819)

—— *Remarks upon the Character and Conduct of the Men who Met under the Name of the British Parliament at the Latter End of the Year 1819: With an Account of the Manner in which they Obtained their Seats. To which is Added, a Letter to the Lord Advocate of Scotland, on the State of that Country* (Newcastle upon Tyne: Marshall [1820])

Brewster, J., *Parochial History and Antiquities of Stockton-upon-Tees*, 2nd edn (Stockton: Jennett, 1829)

Broughton, T., *The Age of Christian Reason: Being a Refutation of the Theological and Political Principles of Thomas Paine, M. Volney, and the Whole Class of Political Naturalists* (London: Rivington, 1820)

Canning, G., *Speech of the Right Hon. George Canning, to his Constituents at Liverpool, on Saturday, March 18th, 1820, at the Celebration of his Fourth Election* (London: Murray, 1820)

[Carlile, R.], *A New Year's Address to the Reformers of Great Britain* (London: Carlile, [1821])

—— *The Character of a Soldier; by Philanthropos* (London: Carlile, 1821)

Character of the Queen! (Norwich: Lane [1820])

'A clergyman, late of Oxford', *Radicals and True Patriots Compared; or, Living Evidence, from New York, of Paine's Character and Last Hours Contrasted with those of the Patriotic Duke of Kent and the Late Great and Good King George the Third* (London: Hatchard, 1820)

The Cock of Cotton Walk and Maid of all Work, alias 'Non mi Ricordo' (London: Pritchard, 1820)

A Collection of the Public General Statutes, Passed in the First Year of the Reign of His Majesty King George IV (London: Eyre & Straton, 1820)

The Committee Appointed to Manage a Subscription Raised for the Purpose of Affording Nightly Shelter for the Houseless (London: Crew, 1820)

Croker, T. C., *Researches in the South of Ireland* (London: Murray, 1824)

Doll Tear-Sheet alias the Countess 'Je ne me rappelle pas' a match for 'Non mi ricordo' (London: Fairburn, 1820)

Duncombe, W., *Junius Brutus: A Tragedy. As it is Acted at the Theatre Royal in Drury-Lane, by His Majesty's Servants*, 2nd edn (Watts: 1747)

The Electors' Remembrancer, or, Guide to the Votes of Each Member of the House of Commons (London: Sherwood, 1822)

[Elsley, H.], *A Discourse on the Demise of his Late Most Excellent Majesty, King George III* (Ripon: Lodge, 1820)

The Extraordinary Red Book, Containing a List of All Places, Pensions, and Sinecures … the Expenditure of the Civil List up to 1818 (London: Johnston, 1819)

Faussett, G., *The Claims of the Established Church to Exclusive Attachment and Support, and the Dangers which Menace her from Schism and Indifference, Considered* (Oxford: Oxford University Press, 1820)

Gardner, J., *Poetry and Popular Protest: Peterloo, Cato Street and the Queen Caroline Controversy* (Basingstoke: Palgrave, 2011)

Grenville, R. P., *Memoirs of the Court of George IV, 1820–1830* (London: Hurst, 1859)

A Groan from the Throne (London: Fairburn, 1820)

Gynecocracy; with an Essay on Fornication, Adultery, and Incest (London: Stockdale; Plymouth: Haviland, 1821)

Hazlitt, W., *The Plain Speaker: Opinions on Books, Men, and Things* (London: Colbourn: 1826)

—— *The Complete Works of William Hazlitt*, ed. P. P. Howe (London: Dent, 1934)

Hobhouse, J. C., *A Trifling Mistake in Lord Erskine's Recent Preface* (London: Stodart, 1819)

Horne, M., *The Moral and Political Crisis of England: Most Respectfully Inscribed to the Higher and Middle Classes* (London: Hatchard, 1820)

The Important and Eventful Trial of Queen Caroline, Consort of George IV for Adulterous Intercourse with Bartolomo Bergami (London: Smeeton, 1820)

Jack and the Queen Killers (London: Dolby and Fairburn, 1820)

Jenkinson, R. B., *The Speech of the Right Hon. The Earl of Liverpool, in the House of Lords, on Friday, the 26th, of May, 1820* (London: Hatchard, 1820)

Jones, W., *An Inquiry into the Legal Means of Suppressing Riots, with a Constitutional Plan of Future Defence* (London: Fairburn, [1819])

Kearney, R., *A Plan for the Payment of the National Debt, and for the Immediate Reduction of Taxation* (Dublin: Charles, 1816)

The Kettle Abusing the Pot. A Satirical Poem by the Black Dwarf (London: Johnston, 1820)

Kouli Khan; or, the Progress of Error (London: Benbow, 1820)

Knowles, J. S., *Virginius: A Tragedy in Five Acts* (London: Ridgway, 1820)

—— *Dramatic Works* (London: Routledge, [1856])

Le Mesurier, T., *Two Sermons Preached in the Parish Church of Haughton-le-Skerne ... on Occasion of the Death of our Late Beloved Sovereign George the Third* (Durham: Humble, 1820)

The Loyal Man in the Moon (London: Chapple, 1820)

Lucretia and Runjumdildopunt; or, John Bull in Search of the Pathetic. A serious musical farce, in Three Acts (London: Benbow, 1820)

MacDonell, J. (ed.), *Reports of State Trials*, new series, vol. 1 (London: HMSO, 1858)

Mackay, A., *A History of Kilmarnock, from an Early Period to the Present Time; Including Biographical Notices* (Kilmarnock: Wilson, 1848)

Martineau, H., *The History of England during the Thirty Years' Peace, 1816–46* (London: Knight, 1849)

New Inventions! The Conyngham Trap ... Demont's Machine ... The Majocchi Mouthpiece; or, Non Mi Ricordo Whistle (n. p., [1820])

The New Pilgrim's Progress; or a Journey to Jerusalem (London: Wright, 1820)

Non Mi Ricordo (London: Pitts, 1820)

Non Mi Ricordo, &c. &c. &c. (London: Hone, 1820)

Non mi Ricordo, A Favorite Waltz, for the Harp or Piano Forte, etc (London: Bates, n.d.)

The Old Black Cock and the Dunghill Advisers in Jeopardy; or, the Place that Jack Built (London: Effingham Wilson, 1820)

Oldfield, T. H. B., *A Key to the House of Commons. Being a history of the Last General Election in 1818* (London: Dolby, 1820)

The Palace of John Bull Contrasted with the Poor 'House that Jack Built' (London: Greenland, 1820)

Parkhill, J., *History of Paisley* (Paisley: Stewart, 1857)

The Political House that Jack Built (London: Hone, 1819)

The Poll for Members in Parliament to represent the City of York (York: Sotheran, 1818)

The Poll for Members in Parliament to represent the City of York (York: Sotheran, 1820)

The Queen and the Mogul: A Play in Two Acts (London: Benbow, 1820)

The Radicals Unmasked and Outwitted: Or, The Thistle Uprooted in Cato Field (London: Greenland, 1820)

Report of the Committee Appointed at Public Meeting of the Inhabitants of Sheffield, for the Purpose of Obtaining a Proper and Specific Settlement of the Town Trust (Sheffield: Iris Office, 1820)

A Report of the Proceedings at a Meeting of the Town of Kingston-upon-Hull, for the Purposes of Considering the Measures that have been Adopted to Degrade, Dethrone & Divorce Her Majesty Queen Caroline (Hull: Ross, 1820)

Rice, T., *An Inquiry into the Effect of Irish Grand Jury Laws* (London: Murray, 1815)

Richmond, A., *Narrative of the Condition of the Manufacturing Population* (London: Miller, 1824)

The Rights of the People; Containing the Principles and a Demonstration of the Practicality of Universal Suffrage, Without Ballot, Without Oaths, Bribery, Corruption, Vice, Riot, Tumult, Inconvenience, or Expence Whatsoever (London: Benbow, 1820)

Roberson, H., *The Select Vestry or Parish Committee* (London: Hatchard, 1818)

Selections from the Queen's Answers to Various Addresses Presented to Her (London: Hatchard, 1821)

Stevenson, J., *A True Narrative of the Radical Rising in Strathaven* (Glasgow: Miller, 1835)

Storr's Impartial Narrative of the Proceedings for the Contested Election at Grantham (Grantham: Storr, 1820)

Sultan Sham and his Seven Wives (London: Benbow, 1820)

The Trial at Large of Her Majesty Caroline Amelia Elizabeth, Queen of Great Britain, in the House of Lords (London: Kelly, 1821)

The Trial of Her Majesty, Queen Caroline, Consort of George IV for an Alleged Adulterous Intercourse (London: Kaygill, 1820)

Trials for High Treason, in Scotland, Under a Special Commission, held at Stirling, Glasgow, Paisley, Dumbarton, and Ayr, in the Year 1820 (Edinburgh: Manners & Miller, 1825)

Wade, J., *The Black Book, or, Corruption Unmasked!!!* (London: Fairburn, 1820)

—— *British History, Chronologically Arranged*, 3rd edn (London: Bohn, 1844)

Wilkinson, G. T., *An Authentic History of the Cato Street Conspiracy*, 2nd edn, (London: Kelly, 1820)

Wrangham, F., *An Apology for the Bible, Abridged from Bishop Watson's Answer to Second Part of Paine's Age of Reason* (n.p., 1820)

Young, G., *Parallel Between King David and King George: A Sermon Preached in Cliff Lane Chapel, Whitby, February 16, 1820* (Whitby: Clerk, 1820)

Secondary works

Albinson, A. C., P. Funnell and L. Peltz, *Thomas Lawrence: Regency Power and Brilliance* (London: Yale University Press, 2010)

Archer, J. E., *'By a Flash and a Scare': Arson, Animal Maiming, and Poaching in East Anglia, 1815–70* (Oxford: Oxford University Press, 1990)

Arnold, D. (ed), *'Squanderous and Lavish Profusion': George IV, his Image and Patronage of the Arts* (London: Georgian Group, 1995)

Aspinall, A., *Lord Brougham and the Whig Party* (Manchester: Manchester University Press, 1927)

—— (ed.), *The Letters of King George IV, Volume II: January 1815–January 1823* (Cambridge: Cambridge University Press, 1938)

—— (ed.), *The Diary of Henry Hobhouse, 1820–1827* (Home & Van Thal, 1947)

—— *Politics and the Press, c. 1780–1850* (Home & Van Thal, 1949)

Aspinall, A. and E. A. Smith (eds), *English Historical Documents, Volume XI: 1783–1832* (London: Eyre & Spottiswode, 1959)

Barber, B., 'William Wrightson, the Yorkshire Whigs and the York "Peterloo" protest meeting of 1819', *Yorkshire Archaeological Journal*, 83 (2011)

Barker, K., *The Theatre Royal Bristol, 1766–1966* (Salisbury: Compton, 1974)

Barker H. and D.Vincent (eds), *Language, Print and Electoral Politics, 1790–1832: Newcastle-under-Lyme Broadsides* (Woodbridge: Boydell, 2002)

Barrow, G. L., *The Emergence of the Irish Banking System, 1820–45* (Dublin: Gill & Macmillan, 1975)

Bate, J. *Shakespearean Constitutions: Politics, Theatre, Criticism, 1730–1830* (Oxford: Oxford University Press, 1989)

Beames, M. R., 'The Ribbon societies: lower-class nationalism in pre-Famine Ireland', in C. H. E. Philpin (ed.), *Nationalism and Popular Protest in Ireland* (Cambridge: Cambridge University Press, 1987)

Belchem, J., 'Republicanism, popular constitutionalism and the radical platform in early nineteenth-century England', *Social History*, 6 (1981)

—— *'Orator' Hunt: Henry Hunt and English Working-Class Radicalism* (Oxford: Oxford University Press, 1985)

Belfield, E. M. G., *Annals of the Addington Family* (Winchester: Warren, 1959)

Bellamy, J. and J. Saville (eds), *Dictionary of Labour Biography*, Volume 8 (Basingstoke: Macmillan, 1987)

—— *Dictionary of Labour Biography*, Volume 9 (Basingstoke: Macmillan, 1993)

—— *Dictionary of Labour Biography*, Volume 10 (Basingstoke: Macmillan, 2000)

Bennett, A., 'Broadsides on the trial of Queen Caroline: a glimpse at popular song in 1820', *Proceedings of the Royal Musical Association*, 107 (1980–81)

Bennett, W., *History of Burnley, 1650–1850* (Burnley: Burnley Corporation, 1948)

Bensimon, F., 'British workers in France, 1815–1848', *Past & Present*, 213 (2011)

Benton, P., *The History of Rochford Hundred* (Rochford: Harrington, 1867)

Bethnal Green Museum of Childhood, *Jubilation: Royal Commemorative Pottery from the Collection of James Blewitt* (London: HMSO, 1977)

Bew, J., *Castlereagh: Enlightenment, War and Tyranny* (London: Quercus, 2011)

Binfield, K., *The Writings of the Luddites* (Baltimore: Johns Hopkins University Press, 2004)

Blackstock, A., *An Ascendancy Army: The Irish Yeomanry, 1796–1834* (Dublin: Four Courts Press)

Bolton, H. C., *Counting-out Rhymes of Children: Their Antiquity, Origin, and Wide Distribution. A Study in Folk-Lore* (London: Elliot Stock, 1888)

Brockliss L. and D. Eastwood (eds), *A Union of Multiple Identities: The British Isles, c. 1750–c. 1850* (Manchester: University Press, 1997)

Brock W. R., *Lord Liverpool and Liberal Toryism: 1820 to 1827* (1939; 2nd edn, London: Cass, 1967)

Broeker, G., 'Robert Peel and the Peace Preservation Force', *Journal of Modern History*, 33:4 (1961)

—— *Rural Disorder and Police Reform in Ireland, 1812–36* (London: Routledge, 1970)

Brown, A. F. J., *Chartism in Essex and Suffolk* (Chelmsford: Essex Record Office, 1982)

Brown, C. G., *Religion and Society in Scotland since 1707* (Edinburgh: Edinburgh University Press, 1997)

Brown, S. J., *Thomas Chalmers and the Godly Commonwealth in Scotland* (Oxford: Oxford University Press, 1982)

Bush, M., *The Casualties of Peterloo* (Lancaster: Carnegie, 2005)

Bushaway, B., *By Rite: Custom, Ceremony and Community in England, 1700–1880* (London: Junction, 1982)

Carlyle, T., *The French Revolution: A History* (London: Fraser, 1837)

Carter, L., 'British masculinities on trial in the Queen Caroline affair of 1820', *Gender & History*, 20:2 (2008)

Chandler, J., *England in 1819: The Politics of Literary Culture and the Case of Romantic Historicism* (Chicago: University of Chicago Press, 1998)

Chase, M., *'The People's Farm': English Radical Agrarianism, 1775–1840* (Oxford: Oxford University Press, 1988)

—— *Early Trade Unionism: Fraternity, Skill and the Politics of Labour* (Aldershot: Ashgate, 2000)

Chittick, K., *The Language of Whiggism: Liberty and Patriotism, 1802–30* (London: Pickering & Chatto, 2010)

Christodoulou, J., 'The Glasgow Universalist Church and Scottish radicalism from the French revolution to Chartism: a theology of liberation', *Journal of Ecclesiastical History*, 43:4 (1992)

Clark, A., *Scandal: The Sexual Politics of the British Constitution* (Princeton: Princeton University Press, 2004)

—— 'Queen Caroline and the sexual politics of popular culture in London, 1820', *Representations*, 31 (1990)

Clark P. (ed.), *The Cambridge Urban History of Britain: Volume II, 1540–1840* (Cambridge: Cambridge University Press, 2000)

Colley, L., 'The apotheosis of George III: loyalty, royalty and the British nation 1760–1820', *Past and Present*, 102 (1984)

—— *Britons: Forging the Nation, 1707–1837* (1992)

Collet, D. C., *History of the Taxes on Knowledge: Their Origin and Repeal* (London: Unwin, 1899)

Connolly, S. J., *Priests and People in Pre-Famine Ireland, 1780–1845* (Dublin: Gill, 1982)

Connolly, S. J., R. A. Houston and R. J. Morris (eds), *Conflict, Identity and Development: Ireland and Scotland, 1600–1939* (Preston: Carnegie, 1995)

Conolly, L. W., *The Censorship of English Drama, 1737–1824* (San Marino, Ca: Huntington Library, 1976)

Cook, H., *The Long Sexual Revolution: English Women, Sex, and Contraception, 1800–1975* (Oxford: Oxford University Press, 2004)

Cookson, J. E., *Lord Liverpool's Administration: The Crucial Years, 1815–1822* (Edinburgh: Scottish Academic Press, 1975)

—— *The British Armed Nation, 1793–1815* (Oxford: Oxford University Press, 1997)

Cooper, C. H., *Annals of Cambridge* (Cambridge: Warwick, 1842)

Cragoe, M., 'Welsh electioneering and the purpose of parliament: "From Radicalism to Nationalism" Reconsidered', in D. Dean and C. Jones (eds), *Parliament and Locality, 1660–1939* (Edinburgh: Edinburgh University Press, 1998)

Crosby, T. L., *English Farmers and the Politics of Protection* (Hassocks: Harvester, 1977)

Crossman, V., 'Peculation and partiality: local government in nineteenth-century Ireland', in R. Swift and C. Kinealy (eds), *Politics and Power in Victorian Ireland* (Dublin: Four Courts Press, 2006)

Curtis, R. H., *The History of the Royal Irish Constabulary* (Dublin: McGlashen, 1871)

Custer, P. A., 'Refiguring Jemima: gender, work and politics in Lancashire 1770–1820', *Past and Present*, 195 (2007)

D'Alton, I., *Protestant Society and Politics in Cork, 1812–44* (Cork: Cork University Press, 1980)

Daunton, M. J., *Progress and Poverty: An Economic and Social History of Britain, 1700–1850* (Oxford: Oxford University Press, 1995)

Davidoff, L. and C. Hall, *Family Fortunes: Men and Women of the English Middle Class. 1780–1850*, revised edn (London: Routledge, 2002)

Davis, T. W., 'Introduction', *Committees for Repeal of the Test and Corporation Acts: Minutes 1786–90 and 1827–8* (London: London Record Society, 1978)

Derry, J. W., *Politics in the Age of Fox, Pitt and Liverpool: Continuity and Transformation* (Basingstoke: Macmillan, 1990)

Devine, T. M., *The Scottish Nation, 1700–2000* (London: Allen Lane, 1999)

Devine T.M. and G. Jackson (eds), *Glasgow. Volume 1: Beginnings to 1830* (Manchester: Manchester University Press, 1995)

Dickinson, H. T., *Caricatures and the Constitution, 1760–1832* (Cambridge: Chadwyck-Healey, 1986)

Dickson, D., *Old World Colony: Cork and South Munster, 1630–1830* (Cork: Cork University Press, 2005)

Dixon G. and B. J. D. Harrison, *Guisborough before 1900* (Leeds: Rigg, 1994)

Donovan J. et al (eds), *The Poems of Shelley: Volume 3, 1819–20* (Harlow: Longman, 2011)

Donnelly, F. K., and J. L. Baxter, 'Sheffield and the revolutionary tradition, 1791–1820', in S. Pollard and C. Holmes, *Essays in the Economic and Social History of South Yorkshire* (Sheffield: South Yorkshire County Council, 1976)

Donnelly, J. S., *The Land and the People of Nineteenth-Century Cork: The Rural Economy and the Land Question* (London: Routledge, 1975)

——— 'Pastorini and Captain Rock: millenarianism and sectarianism in the Rockite movement of 1821–4', in S. Clark and J. S. Donnelly, Jr, *Irish Peasants, Violence and Political Unrest, 1780–1914* (Manchester: Manchester University Press, 1983)

——— *Captain Rock: The Irish Agrarian Rebellion of 1821–24* (Cork: Collins, 2009)

Drakard, D., *Printed English Pottery: History and Humour in the Reign of George III, 1760–1820* (London: Horne, 1992)

Eastwood, D., *Governing Rural England: Tradition and Transformation in Local Government, 1780–1840* (Oxford: Oxford University Press, 1994)

——— *Government and Community in the English Provinces, 1700–1870* (Basingstoke: Macmillan, 1997)

Ellis, P. B. and S. Mac a' Ghobhainn, *The Scottish Insurrection of 1820* (London: Gollancz, 1970)

Feinstein, C., 'Pessimism perpetuated: real wages and the standard of living in Britain during and after the industrial revolution', *Journal of Economic History*, 58: 3 (1998)

Fisher, D. R. (ed.), *The History of Parliament: The House of Commons, 1820–1832* (Cambridge: Cambridge University Press, 2009)

Fitzgerald, P. H., *Life of George IVth* (London: Tinsley, 1881)

Flynn D. H. and A. H. Bolton, *British Royalty: Commemoratives* (Atlglen, PA: 1999)

Foster, J., *Class Struggle and the Industrial Revolution* (London: Methuen, 1974)

Foster, R., *The Politics of County Power: Wellington and the Hampshire Gentlemen, 1820–52* (London: Harvester, 1990)

D. Fraser (ed.), *A History of Modern Leeds* (Manchester: Manchester University Press, 1980)

Fraser, F., *The Unruly Queen: The Life of Queen Caroline* (New York: Anchor, 2009)

Fry, M., *The Dundas Despotism* (Edinburgh: Edinburgh University Press, 1992)

Fulcher, J., 'The loyalist response to the Queen Caroline agitations', *Journal of British Studies*, 34:4 (1995)

Gambles, A., *Protection and Politics: Conservative Economic Discourse, 1815–1852* (Woodbridge: Boydell & Brewer, 1999)

Garvin, T., 'Defenders, Ribbonmen and others: underground political networks in pre-Famine Ireland', in C. H. E. Philpin (ed.), *Nationalism and Popular Protest in Ireland* (Cambridge: Cambridge University Press, 1987)

Gash, N., *Mr Secretary Peel: The Life of Sir Robert Peel to 1830* (London: Longmans, 1961)

—— *Lord Liverpool: The Life and Political Career of Robert Banks Jenkinson* (London: Weidenfeld, 1984)

Gatrell, V., *City of Laughter: Sex and Satire in Eighteenth-Century London* (New York: Walker, 2006)

Gilmartin, K., *Print and Politics: The Press and Radical Opposition in Early Nineteenth-Century England* (Cambridge: Cambridge University Press, 1996)

Gleadle, K., *Borderline Citizens: Women, Gender and Political Culture in Britain, 1815–67* (Oxford: Oxford University Press, 2009)

Gray, P., *The Making of the Irish Poor Law, 1815–43* (Manchester: Manchester University Press, 2009)

Griffin, E., *England's Revelry: A History of Popular Sports and Pastimes, 1660–1830* (Oxford: Oxford University Press, 2005)

Harling, P., *The Waning of Old Corruption: The Politics of Economical Reform in Britain, 1779–1846* (Oxford: Oxford University Press, 1996)

—— 'The law of libel and the limits of repression, 1790–1832', *Historical Journal*, 44:1 (2001)

Harling, P. P. Mandler, 'From "fiscal-military" state to laissez-faire state, 1760–1850', *Journal of British Studies*, 32:1 (1993)

Hart, G., *A History of Cheltenham* (Leicester: Leicester University Press, 1965)

Harvey, A. D., 'Parish politics: London vestries, 1780–1830 (part 2)', *Local Historian*, 40:1 (February 2010)

Hawkins, R., *The Life of Robert Blakey, 1795–1878* (Morpeth: Morpathia Press, 2010)

Heavisides, H., *Centennial Edition of the Works of Henry Heavisides* (London: Simpson, 1895)

Hibbert, C., *George IV: Regent and King* (London: Allen Lane, 1973)

Hilton, B., *Corn, Cash and Commerce: The Economic Policies of the Tory Governments, 1815–30* (Oxford: Oxford University Press, 1972)

—— 'The political arts of Lord Liverpool', *Transactions of the Royal Historical Society*, 5th series, 38 (1988)

—— *A Mad, Bad and Dangerous People? England, 1783–1846* (Oxford: Oxford University Press, 2006)

Hone, J. A., *For the Cause of Truth: Radicalism in London, 1796–1821* (Oxford: Oxford University Press, 1980)

Hoppen, K. T., 'Nationalist mobilisation and governmental attitudes: geography, politics and nineteenth-century Ireland', in L. Brockliss and D. Eastwood (eds), *A Union of Multiple Identities: The British Isles, c. 1750–c. 1850* (Manchester: Manchester University Press, 1997)

—— *Ireland since 1800: Conflict and Conformity* (Harlow: Longman, 1999)

—— 'An incorporating Union? British politicians and Ireland 1800–1830', *English Historical Review*, 123 (2008)

Huggins, M., *Social Conflict in Pre-Famine Ireland: The Case of County Roscommon* (Dublin: Four Courts Press, 2007)

Hunt, N. C., *Two Early Political Associations* (Oxford: Oxford University Press, 1961)

Hunt, T. L., 'Morality and monarchy in the Queen Caroline affair', *Albion*, 23:4 (1991)

Innes, J., 'The local acts of a national parliament: parliament's role in sanctioning local action in eighteenth-century Britain', *Parliamentary History*, 17:1 (1990)

—— 'Central government "interference": changing conceptions, practices, and concerns, c. 1700–1850', in J. Harris (ed.), *Civil Society in British History: Ideas, Identities, and Institutions* (Oxford: Oxford University Press, 2003)

Isabella, M., *Risorgimento in Exile: Italian Emigrés and the Liberal International in the Post-Napoleonic Era* (Oxford: Oxford University Press, 2009)

Jenkins, G. H. and I. Gwynedd Jones (eds), *Cardiganshire County History, Volume 3: Cardiganshire in Modern Times* (Cardiff: University of Wales Press, 1998)

Johnson, D., *Regency Revolution: The Case of Arthur Thistlewood* (Salisbury, Compton Russell, 1974)

Jones, D. J. V., *Before Rebecca: Popular Protests in Wales, 1793–1835* (London: Allen Lane, 1973)

Jones, P. D., 'Swing, Speenhamland and rural social relations: the moral economy of the English crowd in the nineteenth century', *Social History*, 32:3 (2007)

—— 'I cannot keep my place without being deascent': pauper letters, parish clothing and pragmatism in the south of England, 1750–1830', *Rural History*, 20:1 (2009)

Jupp, P., *British Politics on the Eve of Reform* (Basingstoke: Macmillan, 1998)

—— 'Government, parliament and politics in Ireland, 1801–41', in J. Hoppitt (ed.), *Parliaments, Nations and Identities in Britain and Ireland, 1660–1850* (Manchester University Press, 2003)

—— *The Governing of Britain, 1688–1848: The Executive, Parliament, and the People* (London: Routledge, 2006)

Keith-Lucas, B., *The Unreformed Local Government System* (London: Croom Helm, 1980)

Knott, J. W., 'Land, kinship and identity: the cultural roots of agrarian agitation in eighteenth- and nineteenth-century Ireland, *Journal of Peasant Studies*, 12:1 (1984)

Larkin, E., 'Church and state in Ireland in the nineteenth century', *Church History*, 31:3 (1962)

Laqueur, T. W., 'The Queen Caroline affair: politics as art in the reign of George IV', *Journal of Modern History*, 54:3 (1982)

Lewis, J. and G. Lewis, *Pratt Ware: English and Scottish Relief Decorated and Underglaze Coloured Earthenware, 1780–1840*, 2nd edn (Woodbridge: Antique Collectors' Club, 2006)

Lobban, M., 'From seditious libel to unlawful assembly: Peterloo and the changing face of political crime, c1770–1820', *Oxford Journal of Legal Studies*, 10:3 (1990)

McCalman, I., *Radical Underworld: Prophets, Revolutionaries and Pornographers in London, 1795–1840* (Cambridge: Cambridge University Press)

Macdonald, C. M. M., 'Abandoned and beastly? The Queen Caroline affair in Scotland', in Y. G. Brown and R. Ferguson (eds), *Twisted Sisters: Women, Crime and Deviance in Scotland since 1400* (East Linton: Tuckwell, 2004)

Machin, G.I.T., *The Catholic Question in English Politics, 1820 to 1830* (Oxford: Oxford University Press, 1964)

McQuiston, J., 'Sussex aristocrats in 1820', *English Historical Review*, 88 (1973)

Malcolmson, R. and S. Mastoris, *The English Pig: A History* (London: Hambledon, 2001)

Mansfield, N., 'John Brown: a shoemaker in Place's London', *History Workshop Journal*, 8 (1979)

Matthew H. C. G. and B. Harrison (eds), *Oxford Dictionary of National Biography* (Oxford: Oxford University Press, 2004); online edition, ed. L. Goldman (Oxford: Oxford University Press, 2005–11)

Melikan, R. A., *John Scott, Lord Eldon, 1751–1838: The Duty of Loyalty* (Cambridge: Cambridge University Press, 1999)

Miller, K. A., *Emigrants and Exiles: Ireland and the Irish Exodus to North America* (Oxford: Oxford University Press, 1985)

Mitchell, A., *The Whigs in Opposition, 1815–1830* (Oxford: Oxford University Press, 1967)

Mitchell, B. R., *British Historical Statistics* (Cambridge: Cambridge University Press, 1998)

Mitchell B. R. and P. Deane, *Abstract of British Historical Statistics* (Cambridge: Cambridge University Press, 1962)

Mitchison, R., 'The Old Board of Agriculture (1793–1822)', *English Historical Review*, 74:290 (1959)

—— 'Permissive poor laws: the Irish and Scottish systems considered together', in S. J. Connolly, R. A. Houston and R. J. Morris (eds), *Conflict, Identity and Development: Ireland and Scotland, 1600–1939* (Preston: Carnegie, 1995)

Moody, J., *Illegitimate Theatre in London, 1770–1840* (Cambridge: Cambridge University Press, 2000)

Murray, N., *The Scottish Hand Loom Weavers, 1790–1850: A Social History* (Edinburgh: John Donald, 1978)

Navickas, K., '"That sash will hang you": political clothing and adornment in England, 1780–1840', *Journal of British Studies*, 49 (2010)

Neale, R. S., *Bath: A Social History, 1680–1850* (Routledge, 1981)

New, C. W., *The Life of Henry Brougham to 1830* (Oxford: Oxford University Press, 1961)

Ó Corráin, D. and T. O'Riordan, *Ireland, 1815–1870: Emancipation, Famine and Religion* (Dublin: Four Courts, 2011)

O'Ferrall, F., *Catholic Emancipation: Daniel O'Connell and the Birth of Irish Democracy 1820–1830* (Dublin: Gill and Macmillan, 1985)

O'Gorman, F., *Voters, Patrons and Parties: The Unreformed Electoral System of Hanoverian England 1734–1832* (1989)

—— 'Campaign rituals and ceremonies: the social meaning of elections in England 1780–1860', *Past and Present*, 135 (1992)

Ó Gráda, C., *Ireland Before and After the Famine: Explorations in Economic History, 1800–1925* (Manchester: Manchester University Press, second edn 1993)

—— *Ireland: A New Economic History 1780–1939* (Oxford: Oxford University Press, 1994)

Opie, I. and P. Opie, *Lore and Language of Schoolchildren* (Oxford: Oxford University Press, 1959)

Palmer, J. (ed.), *Truro in the Age of Reform, 1815–1837* (Truro: n.p., 1999)

Palmer, R., *The Sound of History: Songs and Social Comment* (Oxford: Oxford University Press, 1988)

Palmer, S., *Police and Protest in England and Wales, 1780–1850* (Cambridge: Cambridge University Press, 1988)

Parker, D. E., T. P. Legg and C. K. Folland, 'A new daily central England temperature series, 1772–1991', *International Journal of Climatology*, 12 (1992)

Patterson, A. T., *Radical Leicester: A History of Leicester, 1780–1850* (Leicester University Press, 1975)

Paulin, T., *The Secret Life of Poems: A Poetry Primer* (London: Faber, 2008)

Peel, F., *The Risings of the Luddites*, first edn (Heckmondwike: Senior, 1880)

Pentland, G., *Radicalism, Reform and National Identity in Scotland, 1820–1833* (London: Royal Historical Society, 2008)

—— '"Betrayed by infamous spies"? The commemoration of Scotland's "Radical War" of 1820', *Past & Present*, 201 (2008)

—— *The Spirit of the Union: Popular Politics in Scotland, 1815–20* (London: Pickering & Chatto, 2011)

Pentland, G. '"Now the great Man in the Parliament House is dead, we shall have a big Loaf!" Responses to the assassination of Spencer Perceval', *Journal of British Studies*, 51: 2 (April 2012)

Phillips, R., 'Ychwaneg am 'Ryfel y Sais bach' 1820–29', *Ceredigion*, 6:3 (1970)

Philp, R., *The Coast Blockade: The Royal Navy's War on Smuggling in Kent and Sussex, 1817–31* (Horsham: Crompton, 1999)

Pickering, P. A., 'A "grand ossification": William Cobbett and the commemoration of Tom

Paine', in P. A. Pickering and A. Tyrell, *Contested Sites: Commemoration and Popular Politics in Nineteenth-century Britain* (Aldershot: Ashgate, 2004)

Prichard, S., *Quilts, 1700–2010: Hidden Histories, Untold Stories* (London: V&A Publishing, 2010)

Prothero, I., *Artisans and Politics in Early Nineteenth-Century London: John Gast and his Times* (Folkestone: Dawson, 1979)

Pryde, G. S., *Central and Local Government in Scotland since 1707* (London: Historical Association, 1960)

Randall, A., *Riotous Assemblies* (Oxford: Oxford University Press, 2006)

Redford, A., *The History of Local Government in Manchester. Volume 1: Manor and Township* (London: Longman, 1939)

Richards, E., 'Patterns of Highland discontent, 1790–1860', in R. Quinault and J. Stevenson (eds), *Popular Protest and Public Order: Six Studies in British History, 1790–1920* (London: Allen & Unwin, 1974)

Rickword, E., *Radical Squibs and Loyal Ripostes* (London: Adams & Dart, 1971)

Robins, J., *Rebel Queen: How the Trial of Queen Caroline Brought England to the Brink of Revolution* (London: Schuster, 2006)

Rogers, N., *Crowds, Culture and Politics in Georgian Britain* (Oxford: Oxford University Press, 1998)

Rosenfeld, S., *The Georgian Theatre of Richmond, Yorkshire, and its Circuit* (London: Society for Theatre Research, 1984)

—— *The York Theatre* (London: Society for Theatre Research, 2001)

Sack, J. L., *The Grenvillites, 1801–29: Party Politics and Factionalism in the Age of Pitt and Liverpool* (Cambridge: Cambridge University Press, 1979)

—— *From Jacobite to Conservative: Reaction and Orthodoxy in Britain, c.1760–1832* (Cambridge: Cambridge University Press, 1993)

Searby, P., 'Paternalism, disturbance and parliamentary reform: society and politics in Coventry, 1819–32', *International Review of Social History*, 22 (1977)

—— *A History of the University of Cambridge, Volume III: 1750–1850* (Cambridge: Cambridge University Press, 1997)

Shepard, L., *John Pitts, Ballad Printer of Seven Dials, London, 1765–1844* (London: Private Libraries Association, 1969)

Simon, S. D., *A Century of City Government: Manchester, 1838–1938* (London: Allen & Unwin)

Smith, E. A., *Whig Principles and Party Politics: Earl Fitzwilliam and the Whig Party, 1748–1833* (Manchester: Manchester University Press 1975)

—— *Lord Grey, 1764–1845* (Oxford: Oxford University Press, 1990)

—— *A Queen on Trial: The Affair of Queen Caroline* (Stroud: Sutton, 1993)

Spater, G., *William Cobbett: The Poor Man's Friend* (Cambridge: Cambridge University Press, 1982)

Speck, W. A., *Robert Southey, Entire Man of Letters* (London: Yale University Press, 2006)

Spencer, F. H., *Municipal Origins: An Account of English Private Bill Legislation Relating to Local Government, 1740–1835* (London: Constable, 1911)

Spring, D., and T. L. Crosby, 'George Webb Hall and the agricultural association', *Journal of British Studies*, 2 (1962)

Stott, A., *Hannah More: The First Victorian* (Oxford: Oxford University Press, 2003)

Strawhorn, J., *The History of Ayr: Royal Burgh and County Town* (Edinburgh: Donald, 1989)

Sweet, R., *The English Town: 1680–1840: Government, Society and Culture* (Harlow: Pearson, 1999)

—— 'Local identities and a national parliament, c. 1688–1835', in J. Hoppitt (ed.),

Parliaments, Nations and Identities in Britain and Ireland, 1660–1850 (Manchester: Manchester University Press, 2003)

Temperley, H. W. V., *Life of Canning* (London: Finch, 1905)

Thomis, M. I. and P. Holt, *Threats of Revolution in Britain, 1789–1848* (London: Macmillan, 1977)

Thompson, E. P., *The Making of the English Working Class*, 2nd edn (Harmondsworth: Penguin, 1968)

Thompson, F., *Lark Rise* (Oxford: Oxford University Press, 1939)

Turner, M. J., *The Age of Unease: Government and Reform in Britain, 1782–1832* (Gloucester: Sutton, 2000)

Vaughan, W. E. (ed.), *A New History of Ireland, Volume V: Ireland Under the Union, I (1801–70)* (Oxford: Oxford University Press, 1989)

Wahrman, D., '"Middle-class" domesticity goes public: gender, class, and politics from Queen Caroline to Queen Victoria', *Journal of British Studies*, 32:4 (1993)

—— 'Public opinion, violence and the links of constitutional politics', in J. Vernon (ed.), *Re-reading the Constitution: New Narratives in the Political History of England's Long Nineteenth Century* (Cambridge: Cambridge University Press, 1996)

Walsh, J., C. Haydon and S. Taylor (eds), *The Church of England, c. 1689–c. 1833: From Toleration to Tractarianism* (Cambridge: Cambridge University Press, 1993)

Wardell, J., *The Municipal History of the Borough of Leeds, in the County of York: From the Earliest Period to the Election of the First Mayor under the Provisions of the Municipal Corporation Act* (London: Longman, 1846)

Waugh, M., *Smuggling in Kent and Sussex, 1700–1840* (Newbury: Countryside Books, 1985)

Webb, S. and B. Webb, *The Parish and the County (English Local Government from the Revolution to the Municipal Corporations Act, Volume 1)* (London: Longman, 1906)

—— *The Manor and the Borough (English Local Government from the Revolution to the Municipal Corporations Act, Volume 2)* (London: Longman, 1908)

—— *Statutory Authorities for Special Purposes (English Local Government from the Revolution to the Municipal Corporations Act, Volume 4)* (London: Longman, 1922)

Webb, W., *Coastguard: An Official History of H. M. Coastguard* (London: HMSO, 1976)

Weisser, H., *British Working-class Movements and Europe. 1815–48* (Manchester: Manchester University Press, 1975)

Wells, R. A. E., 'Social conflict and protest in the English countryside in the early nineteenth century: a rejoinder', *Journal of Peasant Studies*, 8:4 (1981)

—— 'Historical trajectories: English social welfare systems, rural riots, popular politics, agrarian trade unions, and allotment provision, 1793–1896', *Southern History*, 25 (2003)

—— 'Crime and protest in a country parish', in R. A. E. Wells and J. Rule, *Crime, Protest and Popular Politics in Southern England, 1740–1850* (London: Hambledon, 1997)

—— 'Poor law reform in the rural south-east: the impact of the Sturges Bourne Acts, 1815–35', *Southern History*, 23 (2001)

Whatley, C. A., *Scottish Society, 1707–1830: Beyond Jacobitism, Towards Industrialisation* (Manchester University Press, 2000)

Whetstone, A. E., *Scottish County Government in the Eighteenth and Nineteenth Centuries* (Edinburgh, Donald, 1981)

Whitley, T. W., *Parliamentary Representation of Coventry* (Coventry: Curtis, 1894)

Williams, W. R. *The History of the Great Sessions in Wales, 1542–1830* (Brecknock: the author, 1899)

Winch, D. and P. O'Brien (eds), *The Political Economy of British Historical Experience, 1688–1914* (Oxford: British Academy, 2002)

Worrall, D., *Theatric Revolution – Drama, Censorship, and Romantic Period Subcultures 1773–1832* (Oxford: Oxford University Press, 2006)

Wrigley E. A. and R. S. Schofield, *The Population History of England, 1541–1871* (Cambridge: Cambridge University Press, 1989)

Ziegler, P., *Addington: A Life of Henry Addington, First Viscount Sidmouth* (London: Collins, 1965)

Zimmermann, G., *Songs of Irish Rebellion: Political Street Ballads and Rebel Songs, 1780–1900* (Dublin: Figgis, 1967)

Unpublished

Donnelly, F. K., 'The general rising of 1820: a study of social conflict in the industrial revolution' (PhD thesis, University of Sheffield, 1975)

Index

Lightning Source UK Ltd.
Milton Keynes UK
UKOW03f1824170516

274431UK00004B/344/P